# Neuromorphic Computing for Brain Computer Interfaces

# Neuromorphic Computing for Brain Computer Interfaces

## Enhanced Synergies in Mind and Machine


*Edited by*

**Seifedine Kadry**
Department of Computer Science and Mathematics, Lebanese American University, Beirut, Lebanon; Department of Applied Data Science, Noroff University College, Kristiansand, Norway

**Rajesh Kumar Dhanaraj**
Symbiosis International (Deemed University), Pune, India

**Lalitha Krishnasamy**
Nandha Engineering College, India

**Michael Moses Thiruthuvanathan**
CHRIST University, India



ELSEVIER

ACADEMIC PRESS
An imprint of Elsevier

Academic Press is an imprint of Elsevier
125 London Wall, London EC2Y 5AS, United Kingdom
50 Hampshire Street, 5th Floor, Cambridge, MA 02139, United States



ISBN: 978-0-443-41594-4

For information on all Academic Press publications visit our website at https://www.elsevier.com/books-and-journals

*Publisher:* Megan Ball
*Acquisitions Editor:* Megan McManus
*Editorial Project Manager:* Swadha Puri
*Production Project Manager:* Sathyavani Deiva Sigamani
*Cover Designer:* Mark Rogers



Typeset by TNQ Tech

# Dedication

*To the researchers, engineers, and clinicians working at the intersection of brain–computer interfaces and neuromorphic computing.*

**This book is for the international community of researchers, engineers, and clinicians developing the research in brain–computer interfacing and neuromorphic computing. It is also for the students and young researchers who will take this field in the future.**

# Contents

## 5. EEG-based biomarkers for early detection and monitoring of Alzheimer's disease

*Venkat Ghodke and Suhas Gajre*



## 6. Enhanced decision-making through Neuromorphic Computing and BCI

*N. Naveena, P. Nisha Priya, A. Sugitha and K. Madhu Suganya*

## 8. Revolutionizing human–device interaction: Advancements and applications in brain–computer interfaces

*P. Nisha Priya, V. Priya, V. Divya and N. Naveena*

## 9. Optimizing logistics for smart cities: Intelligent fleet and delivery management

*Arpan Seth, Arijit Konar, Upasana Ghosh, Sumana Kundu and Anandaprova Majumder*



## 10. A biomimetic neuromorphic processor for enhanced brain–computer interface applications in neural rehabilitation

*T. Rajkumar, V. Karthi, M. Elayaraja, G. Brinda, S.D. Vijayakumar and M. Anitha*

## 15. Mapping the research landscape of neuromorphic computing: A bibliometric analysis of trends, collaboration, and research hotspots

*S. James Robert*



## 16. Neuro-driven smart homes: The future of adaptive and sustainable living

*S.D. Vijayakumar, G. Brinda, S. Shantha Kumar, R. Nagadeepa, V. Kumar and N. Saravanan*

# Contributors


**T. Abirami**, Department of Information Technology, Kongu Engineering College, Erode, Tamil Nadu, India

**M. Anitha**, Department of Electronics and Communication Engineering, M.P.Nachimuthu M.Jaganathan Engineering College, Erode, Tamil Nadu, India

**G. Brinda**, Department of Electronics and Communication Engineering, M.P.Nachimuthu M.Jaganathan Engineering College, Erode, Tamil Nadu, India

**V. Divya**, CSI College of Engineering, Department of Computer Science & Engineering, Ketti, Tamil Nadu, India

**M. Elayaraja**, Department of ECE, Fathima Michael College of Engineering and Technology, Madurai, Tamil Nadu, India

**Suhas Gajre**, Department of Electronics and Telecommunication Engineering, SGGS Institute of Engineering and Technology, S.R.T.M. University, Nanded, Maharashtra, India

**Venkat Ghodke**, Department of Electronics and Telecommunication Engineering, AISSMS'S Institute of Information Technology, S.P. Pune University, Pune, Maharashtra, India; Department of Electronics and Telecommunication Engineering, SGGS Institute of Engineering and Technology, S.R.T.M. University, Nanded, Maharashtra, India

**Upasana Ghosh**, Department of Computer Science & Engineering, Dr. B. C. Roy Engineering College, Durgapur, West Bengal, India

**S. Gokula Brindha**, Department of Electrical and Electronics Engineering, Velalar College of Engineering and Technology, Erode, Tamil Nadu, India

**S. James Robert**, Christ University, Bengaluru, Karnataka, India

**P. Jayadharshini**, Department of Artificial Intelligence and Data Science, Kongu Engineering College, Erode, Tamil Nadu, India

**V. Karthi**, Department of EEE, Kangeyam Institute of Technology, Nathakadaiyur, Tamil Nadu, India

**M. Karthick**, Department of EEE, Vimal Jyothi Engineering College, Kannur, Kerala, India

**R. Karunamoorthi**, Department of CSE, Sri Krishna College of Engineering and Technology, Coimbatore, Tamil Nadu, India

**Arijit Konar**, Department of Computer Science & Engineering, Dr. B. C. Roy Engineering College, Durgapur, West Bengal, India

**Lalitha Krishnasamy**, Department of Artificial Intelligence and Data Science, Nandha Engineering College, Erode, Tamil Nadu, India

**Kukatlapalli Pradeep Kumar**, Department of AI and Data Science Engineering, School of Engineering Technology, CHRIST University, Kengeri Campus, Bengaluru, Karnataka, India

**V. Kumar**, Department of Electronics and Communication Engineering, Hindusthan College of Engineering, Erode, Tamil Nadu, India

**Sumana Kundu**, Department of Computer Science & Engineering, MCKV Institute of Engineering, Howrah, West Bengal, India

**P. Loganath**, Department of ECE, SSM College of Engineering, Namakkal, Tamil Nadu, India

**K. Madhu Suganya**, Nandha College of Technology, Erode, Tamil Nadu, India

**Anandaprova Majumder**, Department of Computer Science & Engineering, Dr. B. C. Roy Engineering College, Durgapur, West Bengal, India

**Shruthi M G**, RV Institute of Technology and Management, Department of MCA, Bengaluru, Karnataka, India

**Sellappan Mohana Saranya**, Department of CSE, Kongu Engineering College, Erode, Tamil Nadu, India

**R. Mohemmed Yousuf**, Department of IT, Bannari Amman Institute of Technology, Sathyamangalam, Tamil Nadu, India

**Shibadri Mukherjee**, Department of Computer Science Engineering, School of Engineering and Technology, CHRIST University, Kengeri Campus, Bengaluru, Karnataka, India

**R. Nagadeepa**, Department of ECE, Fathima Michael College of Engineering and Technology, Madurai, Tamil Nadu, India

**N. Naveena**, Sri Krishna College of Engineering and Technology, Coimbatore, Tamil Nadu, India

**S. Parthiban**, Department of ECE, Nandha College of Technology, Erode, Tamil Nadu, India

**R. Prabavathi**, Department of Information Technology, Sri Sai Ram Institute of Technology, Chennai, Tamil Nadu, India

**R. Pradeep**, Department of Electrical and Electronics Engineering, Velalar College of Engineering and Technology, Erode, Tamil Nadu, India

**M.R. Prasanndh Raaju**, Department of CSE, Kongu Engineering College, Erode, Tamil Nadu, India

**R. Praveenkumar**, Department of ECE, Nandha Engineering College, Erode, Tamil Nadu, India

**P. Nisha Priya**, CSI College of Engineering, Department of Computer Science & Engineering, Ketti, Tamil Nadu, India

**V. Priya**, CSI College of Engineering, Department of Computer Science & Engineering, Ketti, Tamil Nadu, India

**S. Palanivel Rajan**, Department of Electronics and Communication Engineering, Rathinam Technical Campus, Coimbatore, Tamil Nadu, India

**M.G. Rajendrakumar**, Department of Electronics Engineering (VLSI Design and Technology), Velammal College of Engineering and Technology, Madurai, Tamil Nadu, India

**T. Rajkumar**, Department of ECE, Nandha College of Technology, Erode, Tamil Nadu, India

**B.S. Sabitha Rani**, School of Computer Science and Engineering, Digital University Kerala (DUK), Trivandrum, Kerala, India

**S. Santhiya**, Department of Artificial Intelligence and Machine Learning, Kongu Engineering College, Erode, Tamil Nadu, India

**N. Saravanan**, Department of Mechanical Engineering, Erode Sengunthar Engineering College, Erode, Tamil Nadu, India

**Arpan Seth**, Department of Computer Science & Engineering, Dr. B. C. Roy Engineering College, Durgapur, West Bengal, India

**M. Shanmugham**, Department of Electronics and Communication Engineering, Nandha Engineering College, Erode, Tamil Nadu, India

**S. Shantha Kumar**, Department of CSE, Nandha College of Technology, Erode, Tamil Nadu, India

**Elizabeth Sherly**, School of Computer Science and Engineering, Digital University Kerala (DUK), Trivandrum, Kerala, India

**T. Suganya**, Department of AI&DS, KGiSL Institute of Technology, Department of Computer Science and Engineering MCKV Institute of Engineering, CSE, Coimbatore, Tamil Nadu, India

**A. Sugitha**, Sri Krishna College of Engineering and Technology, Coimbatore, Tamil Nadu, India

**Ajantha Devi Vairamani**, AP3 Solutions, Chennai, Tamil Nadu, India

**T. Velmurugan**, Department of Computer Science and Design, Kongu Engineering College, Erode, Tamil Nadu, India

**S. Venkatesh Kumar**, Department of EEE, Dr. N.G.P Institute of Technology, Coimbatore, Tamil Nadu, India

**S.D. Vijayakumar**, Department of Artificial Intelligence and Data Science, Nandha Engineering College, Erode, Tamil Nadu, India

**G. Vijayakumari**, Department of ECE, Kangeyam Institute of Technology, Nathakadaiyur, Tamil Nadu, India

# Preface

The use of brain–computer interface (BCI) technology is expanding from experiments performed under controlled laboratory conditions into practical uses within the realms of medicine, assistive technology, and consumer products. However, this transition means that there will be increased pressure on the computational technologies that can be used to process neural signals and which are not capable of working at the speed, efficiency, and adaptability required due to the limitations inherent in the conventional von Neumann architecture. The solution might lie in neuromorphic computing.

*Neuromorphic Computing for Brain Computer Interfaces: Enhanced Synergies in Mind and Machine* is made up of 16 chapters looking at the intersection of the two from three different perspectives, which include the theoretical framework of the neuromorphic BCI system, the applications of neuromorphic BCIs in the diagnostics of neurodegenerative diseases, classification using EEG, clinical decision-making, neural rehabilitation, and medical image processing, as well as other applications, such as smart cities, smart homes, logistics, environment monitoring, computer vision, and social/behavioral data analysis.

This book is meant to be of use to researchers, graduate students, engineers in bioengineering or computer engineering fields, clinicians, and professionals in the industry who would like an up-to-date resource on neuromorphic computing and brain–computer interface systems.

The editors would like to thank the authors and reviewers who contributed to this book.

**Dr. Michael Moses T**
CHRIST University, Bengaluru, India

**Dr. Lalitha Krishnasamy**
Nandha Engineering College, Erode, Tamil Nadu, India

**Dr. Rajesh Kumar Dhanaraj**
Symbiosis International (Deemed University), Pune, India

**Dr. Seifedine Kadry**
Noroff University College, Kristiansand, Norway

# Introduction

Brain–computer interface (BCI) technologies allow for communication between the brain and the outside world. They have been widely used in diagnostics, rehabilitation, and assistive applications. Processing the information from these neural systems requires significant computing capacity from the classical architectures. Neuromorphic computing, inspired by the neural processes in the biological brain, allows for performing this task with lower energy consumption and lower latency. This book includes 16 chapters devoted to this convergence and presented in the following by topics.

## Foundations of neuromorphic computing and BCI systems

Chapters 1 through 3 provide the foundation necessary to understand the rest of the book. In Chapter 1, *Introduction to Brain–Computer Interfaces and Neuromorphic Computing: Foundations and Relevance to Neurodegenerative Disease Diagnosis*, concepts related to BCI and neuromorphic computing are introduced and their significance in neurodegenerative disease diagnosis is highlighted. Building on that knowledge, Chapter 2, *BCI Intelligence: Neuromorphic Computing and Brain–Computer Interfaces Characteristics and Challenges*, explores the characteristics of neuromorphic BCIs and the challenges that restrict their implementation. Chapter 3, *Neuromorphic Algorithms*, provides an overview of the algorithms that make these systems possible, namely, spiking neural networks and learning the rules inspired by the brain.

## EEG-based diagnosis, monitoring, and decision support

Chapters 4–7 explore the applications of EEG- and image-based signals in diagnostic and decision-making processes. Chapter 4, *EEG-Based Imagined Speech Classification—A Systematic Review by Exploring the Effective Hierarchical Deep Learning Approaches*, presents a systematic review of the hierarchical deep learning approaches used to classify EEG signals related to imagined speech. Chapter 5, *EEG-Based Biomarkers for Early Detection and Monitoring of Alzheimer's Disease*, continues the exploration of the potential of signals from an EEG in the context of early detection and monitoring of a specific condition, namely, Alzheimer's disease. Chapter 6, *Enhanced Decision-Making Through Neuromorphic Computing and Brain–Computer Interfaces*, adds another perspective to those mentioned previously by exploring the potential of neuromorphic computing in the context of decision-making in BCI applications. Finally, Chapter 7, *AI-Augmented Chest Radiography Pneumonia Detection: Balancing Sensitivity and Clinical Monitoring*, closes the group by exploring an example of the application of signals from medical images in the process of medical diagnostics.

## Human–device interaction and neural rehabilitation

Chapters 8, 10, and 13 focus on the interactions and rehabilitation after diagnosis. Chapter 8, *Revolutionizing Human–Device Interaction: Advancements and Applications in Brain–Computer Interfaces*, explores the advances in human–device interaction through brain–computer interface–enabled technology in assistive and consumer applications. Chapter 10, *A Biomimetic Neuromorphic Processor for Enhanced Brain–Computer Interface Applications in Neural Rehabilitation*, is a complementing chapter that discusses a biomimetic neuromorphic processor which can aid in improving the response of BCIs in neural rehabilitation. Lastly, Chapter 13, *Case Study on Neuromorphic Vision System: BCI-Infused Technologies for Advanced Image Processing*, further develops the theme through the discussion of the neuromorphic vision system using BCI technologies for image processing.

## Smart infrastructure and applied systems

Chapters 9, 11, 16, and 12 increase the scale from clinic to architecture and environment. Chapter 9 is entitled *Optimizing Logistics for Smart Cities: Intelligent Fleet and Delivery Management*. It investigates intelligent fleet and delivery management in the context of smart city logistics. Chapter 11, *Neuromorphic Solutions for Sustainable Smart Cities: A Brain–Computer Interface Perspective*, adds to that with the perspective of neuromorphic and BCI technologies in terms of their application in sustainable smart city solutions. Chapter 16, *Neuro-Driven Smart Homes: The Future of Adaptive and Sustainable Living*, narrows the scope of interest from cities to homes and introduces the concept of adaptive and sustainable neuro-driven smart homes as another practical use case of brain-inspired computing. Finally, Chapter 12, *An Artificial Intelligence–Based Real-Time Monitoring System to Study the Effect of Electrical Signals Between Ocimum Tenuiflorum and Coleus Amboinicus*, goes beyond architecture to discuss an AI-based real-time monitoring system in the natural environment to monitor bioelectrical signals between plants.

## Societal perspectives and the research landscape

Chapters 14 and 15 bring closure to the volume by looking beyond device engineering. Chapter 14, *Cross-Generational Data Analysis on the Mental Health Effect of Social Media*, examines the impact of social media on mental health among different generations and brings out the social aspect of networking technology. Chapter 15, *Mapping the Research Landscape of Neuromorphic Computing: A Bibliometric Analysis of Trends, Collaboration, and Research Hotspots*, complements Chapter 14 by bringing out a bibliometric study of the trends, collaborations, and research hotspots in neuromorphic computing. Both Chapters 14 and 15 place the technical chapters of the volume in a broader social and scholarly perspective.

Chapter 1

# Introduction to brain-computer interfaces and neuromorphic computing: Foundations and relevance to neurodegenerative disease diagnosis

Ajantha Devi Vairamani
*AP3 Solutions, Chennai, Tamil Nadu, India*

## 1. Introduction to brain-computer interfaces (BCIs) and neuromorphic computing

This section is a heartfelt exploration of the role of artificial intelligence (AI), neuroscience, and healthcare in curing neurodegenerative diseases. At the intersection of all these fields lies the potential of brain-computer interfaces (BCIs) and neuromorphic computing. They are technological phenomena already consigned to history books—but at a time when the research is still alive, they reveal how such protocols will revolutionize diagnosis, treatment, and management for people with neurodegenerative diseases.

How AI, the latest venture in programmatic, intersects with neuroscience, an evolution of human intellect. Comparing both medical sciences and these new technologies has yet to produce a winner.

- **Artificial intelligence (AI):** AI provides computational power and sophisticated algorithms that can sift through and make sense of mountains of complex data. It helps identify patterns as well as test predictions. To take two examples from the spheres of neuroscience and healthcare, AI will enable systems that can read the language spoken by neurons and model brain activity. Equally important, if a little more futuristically, is that fast

**Neuromorphic Computing for Brain Computer Interfaces. https://doi.org/10.1016/B978-0-443-41594-4.00005-8**

computers together with new computational techniques are beginning to simulate cognitive processes as well (Hassabis et al., 2017).

- **Neuroscience**: Neuroscience yields profound understandings about how the human brain is built and functions. By learning how neurons communicate, what networks of neurons are constructed like in their organization over space within living animal tissue, and the operation of brains—scientists can create technologies which interact with these processes or reproduce them (Kandel et al., 2013).
- **Healthcare**: And healthcare awaits the practical applications of these technologies. It takes science's discoveries and turns them into treatments or tools that benefit people. Already, the marriage of AI and neuroscience with medical practice has yielded advances in diagnostics, personalized medicine (being able to tailor drugs based on genetic information so they work better for an individual patient), and therapeutic interventions (Topol, 2019).

Consequently, together these areas give birth to such new systems as BCIs, as shown in Fig. 1.1 or neuromorphic computing devices, so that they can decipher a man's brain processes and then replicate them. This intersection is particularly crucial when trying to solve neurodegenerative diseases, where conventional treatments often fail.

## 1.1 Overview of neurodegenerative diseases and their impact

Neurodegenerative diseases, such as amyotrophic lateral sclerosis (ALS) and Parkinson's disease, characterize Through the progressive degeneration of neurons, they induce distressing symptoms Such losses of mobility, cognitive power and language use pose a major impact on patients with these diseases

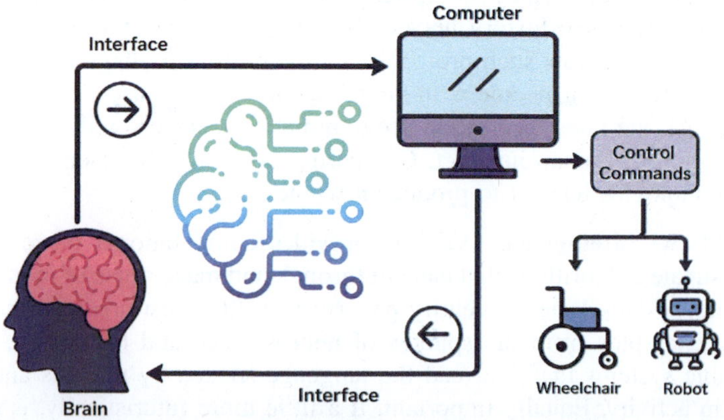


**FIGURE 1.1** A brain-computer interface (BCI) system.

their standard of living as well the phrase "these conditions" refers to Parkinson's disease, Alzheimer's disease (Feigin et al., 2019). Fig. 1.2 Shows the Anatomical regions affected in neurodegenerative diseases—Alzheimer's Disease (hippocampus and cerebral cortex), Parkinson's Disease (midbrain, nigrostriatal pathway, and substantia nigra), and Amyotrophic Lateral Sclerosis (motor cortex and lateral corticospinal tract).

- **Amyotrophic lateral sclerosis (ALS):** ALS is a fatal neurodegenerative disease that attacks motor neurons, resulting in muscle weakness, paralysis, and ultimately death by asphyxiation. People with ALS often lose the ability to speak, move, or breathe independently. This makes communication and existence extremely difficult for them (Brown and Al-Chalabi, 2017).
- **Alzheimer's disease:** Alzheimer's is the most common form of dementia, characterized by memory loss, cognitive decline, and behavioral changes. Worldwide, the number afflicted rises into millions, a figure that puts considerable strain on health care systems(Alzheimer's Association, 2021).
- **Parkinson's disease:** Parkinson's disease is hallmark marked by motor symptoms like tremors, rigidity, and bradykinesia. The disease also brings various nonmotor symptoms, such as sleep disorders and cognitive impairment (Poewe et al., 2017)

Although advances in medical science have been achieved, there are still many neurodegenerative diseases that cannot be cured. This highlights the urgent need for innovative solutions. However, up to now, treatment has often concentrated mainly on managing symptoms and taken little or no account of their cause. This brings home how important new technology, such as BCIs and neuromorphic computing, will be in the future.

## 1.2 BCIs and neuromorphic computing in revolutionizing health care

BCIs and neuromorphic computing are emerging as powerful tools to take on the key issues posed by neurodegenerative diseases by

**Brain-computer interfaces (BCIs):** BCIs allow direct interaction between the brain and external devices. This offer Figuring Out new methods for recovering wild functions, such as activities of daily living, movement, in patients with diseases such as ALS. For example, BC can allow paralyzed patients to control robotic limbs or use thought alone to communicate. Now, noninvasive BCIs, such as EEG-based systems, are advancing rapidly. And BCIs based on them, are likely to become one of the main forms of.

**Neuromorphic Computing:** Modeled after the brain, neuromorphic computers are elegant, adaptive systems for real-time processing of complex neural data. Like neural circuits that mimic the brain's capacity to learn and adapt, these devices are particularly suited to real-time analysis of neural

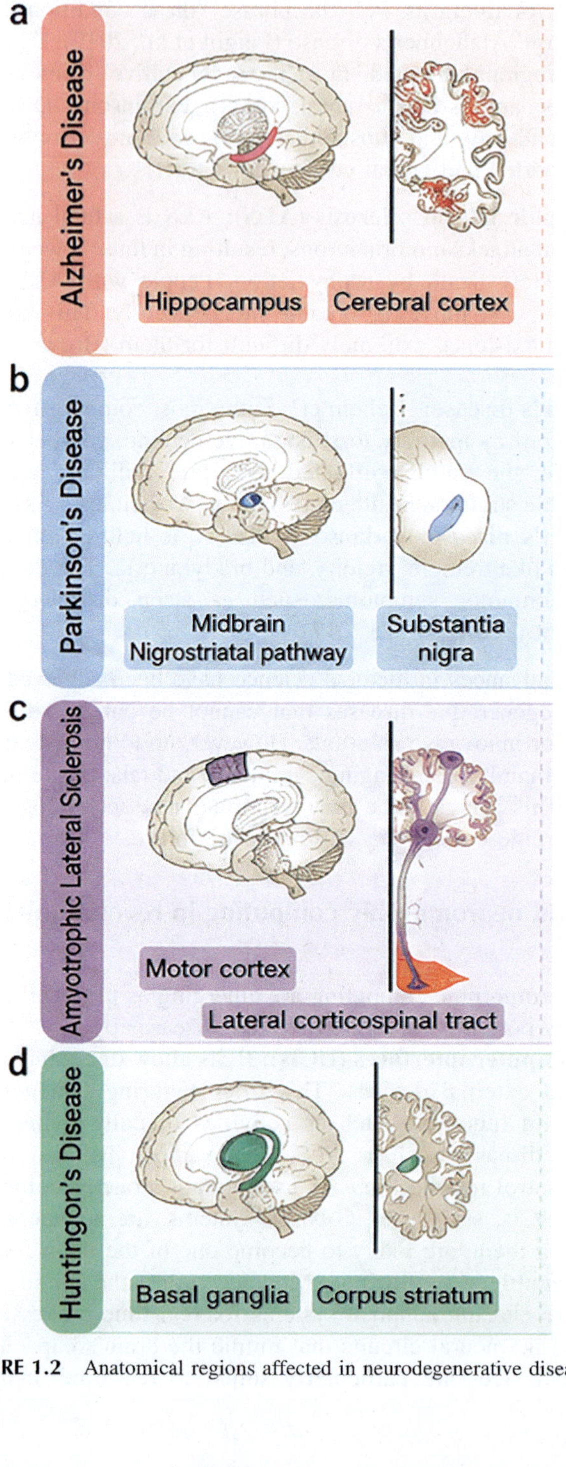


**FIGURE 1.2** Anatomical regions affected in neurodegenerative diseases.

signals and devising personalized treatment strategies (Mead, 1990). For example, neural chips are able to process sensory input in ways that are much more energy-efficient than traditional computing systems, thus enabling their use in wearables and medical implants so that even the era of "brain" becomes possible today (Davies et al., 2018).

Together, these technologies offer the hope of early diagnosis, personalized treatment, and an improved quality of life for patients. By blurring the line between artificial and biological systems, they carry with them a paradigm shift in healthcare that will invite nature and technology to blend in new ways to treat, from its very roots, some of medicine's greatest problems.

## 2. Historical evolution of brain-computer interfaces (BCIs)

This is to introduce, in brief, the history of BCIs: from primitive invasive methods used at the outset, slowly to their development today, without touching anything human or machine aside from one's own brain. And it is also to provide readers with chapters about some great people who were influential in technology as well as politics, that make BCIs a tool promising enough for applied neuroscience researchers. Although still semi- and off-remote viewing, a display was already completed for this task just 3 minutes ago, so you can just go ahead and finish tight now, as if it were possible. Fig. 1.3 shows the A timeline of key milestones in BCI research, from the first human EEG recording in 1929 to the establishment of the International BCI Society in 2015, highlighting major developments in EEG, neurofeedback, BCI paradigms, and invasive technologies.

### 2.1 Early invasive methods: Direct brain connection

The beginnings of BCIs can be traced back to such occurrences as experiments in which electrodes were inserted into a person's brain to record or stimulate neural activity. To record or trigger cerebral activity, early investigations primarily used invasive techniques that required implanting electrodes directly into the brain.

- BCIs began at roughly the same time for the Western version. Delgado, (1969) was an early brain researcher who made significant contributions to the study of BCIs. It was his work in the 1950s and 1960s that laid part of the foundation for BCI research, having implanted electrodes into the brains of animals, and the control of behavior was known to be achievable by remote control technology.
- Next, there were the important trouble years of the 1970s and 1980s. This was when researchers managed to extract signals from animals' brains that

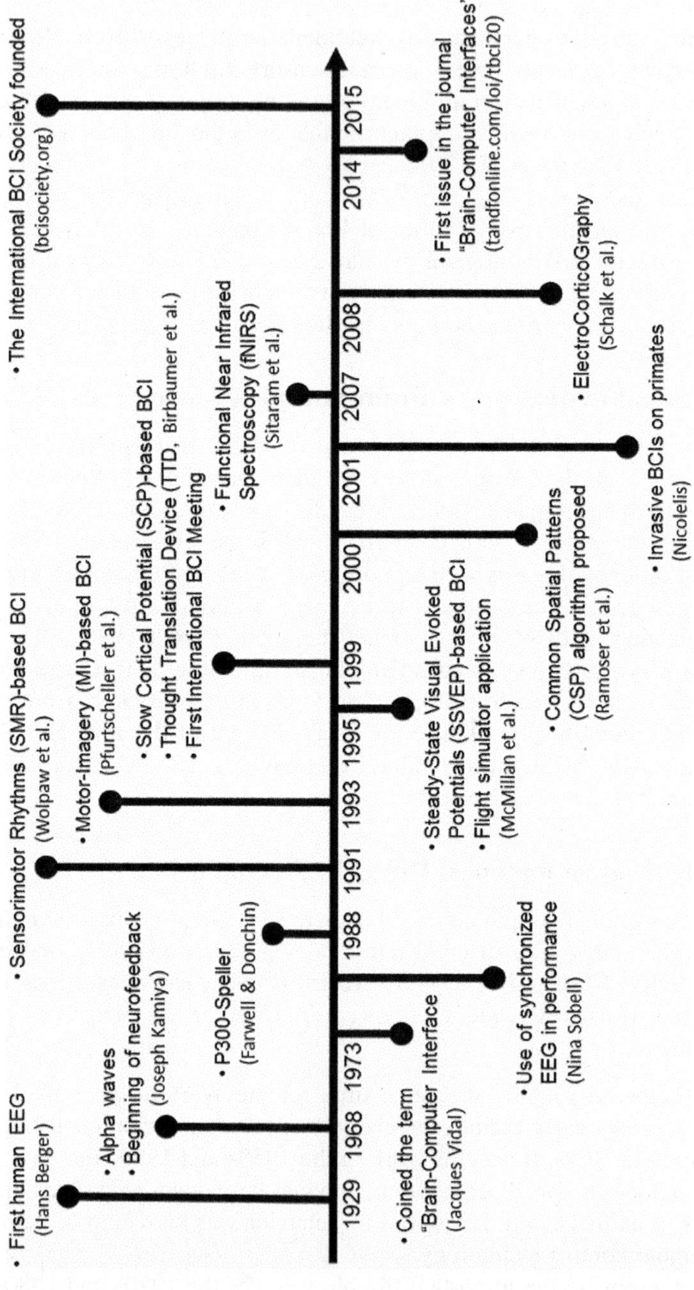


**FIGURE 1.3** A timeline of key milestones in brain-computer interface (BCI) research.

control movement directly (Fetz, 1969), and helped us universe machines to control is feasible from the brain after all.
- In the mid-1990s, further experiments were performed on humans, when small electrodes were implanted in the brains of people with severe disabilities in order to help them communicate or move parts (Kennedy and Bakay, 1998). For instance, the "BrainGate" system also allowed people who had been touched and from the waist down paralyzed to control a computer pointer without actually moving their arm muscles at all.

As such, invasive methods provided high-resolution neural data while letting us precisely control where to stimulate tissue; they also came with problems, including infection and tissue damage, and difficulties caused by long-term stability in vivo. These issues addressed the need for developing less invasive alternatives.

## 2.2 Transition to less invasive and non-invasive designs

At the same time as the downside of invasive BCIs became increasingly clear, scientists started work on an emerging alternative circuit with a less invasive or even totally noninvasive style of design. This kind of system attempts to remove risk while still having a clear enough signal for applications.

- Electroencephalography (EEG)-Based BCIs: As noninvasive EEG measures electrical activity in the brain through electrodes placed on the scalp or other locations, it has been a foundation of BCI research. In the early years of EEG-based BCIs, we tended to focus on recognition of a specific brainwave pattern ("event-related potentials" [ERPs] and/or sensorimotor control rhythms) to support communication or control (Wolpaw et al., 2002: 10).
- Functional near-infrared spectroscopy (fNIRS): A further noninvasive procedure, fNIRS channels light into the brain to measure activity levels based on blood oxygenation. This made it possible to escape from the problem of needing both a good signal and easy practical usage: for example, in neurofeedback or rehabilitation (Naseer and Hong, 2015).
- Hybrid BCIs: By combining several different methods, such as EEG and fNIRS, researchers were able to achieve a much more reliable and precise noninvasive BCI (Pfurtscheller et al., 2010).

Fig. 1.4 structures the classification of brain signal acquisition techniques, categorizing methods into invasive (intracortical electrode arrays and electrocorticography) and noninvasive (EEG, fMRI, MEG, and fNIRS) approaches for neural activity monitoring. Focusing on less invasive and noninvasive designs made BCI more attractive for consumer and clinical applications. It expanded the range available to healthcare facilities, gaming environments, and helper systems for disabled people.

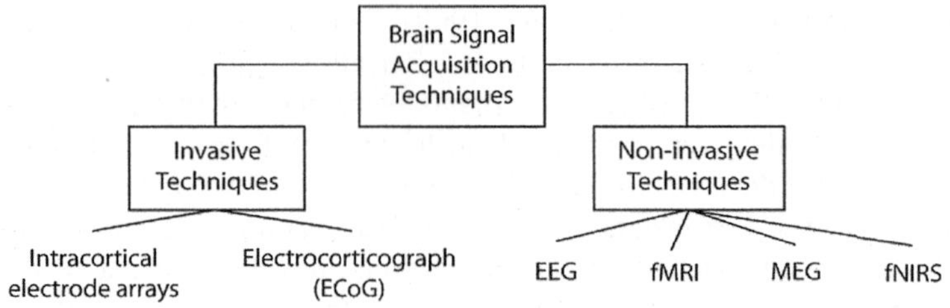


**FIGURE 1.4** A classification of brain signal acquisition techniques.

## 2.3 Three crises in BCI development

There have been three key stages in the development of BCI technology:

- "BCI" came into use for the first time in 1973. Jacques Vidal also made some early experiments that year in using EEG signals to steer a cursor (Vidal, 1973).
- In 1998 BCI device was implanted into a human being as a "BrainGate" system during a neurosurgery operation. In a trial terminally ill man whose nerves could no longer send signals for motion, and whose only means of communication had vanished when his vocal cords stopped working in October 1996, was able to move a cursor on the computer screen simply by thinking about it—plenty more details here but let me just say that Bakay's team has now moved forward with clinical trials of this experimental product (Kennedy and Bakay, 1998).
- 2004: The first person ever to use a BCI to move a robotic limb and so help paralyzed people regain their mobility (Hochberg et al., 2006). Matthew Nagle was this patient.
- 2012: The development of EEG-based noninvasive BCI for games, creative applications. Emotiv EPOC headset brings BCI into the mainstream.
- 2016: Not only have we seen the traditional (iced) medical applications at work before you go the non-Banana route, but researchers are using BCI to effect neurofeedback and some minor brain protection ectomy. Fortunately, the first signs of active, meaningful work come out. Something tells me that some such metamorphosis will be next on our agenda—specialist field personal websites with lots of details nobody else would think about including, and I must think hard for its name in future days.
- By the 2020s: Through AI and machine learning, signal processing rapidly became a major issue in BCI real-time data processing methods that were both accurate and reliable (Schirrmeister et al., 2017).

These achievements of BCI technology have in common that each passage emphasizes an upsurge, from the early conceptual design of experiments to practical tools with potential to transform health care and more.

# 3. Fundamentals of brain-computer interfaces (BCIs)

## 3.1 Neural signal acquisition

**i. Electrophysiological Techniques: BCIs depend upon various approaches to pick up on neural activity. These include:**

- **Electroencephalography (EEG):** Electrodes positioned on the scalp transmit the natural electric activity of humans. While EEG is not invasive, it has become widely used for two reasons: It is easy to operate, and it is very cheap to buy (Wolpaw et al., 2002).
  - **Electrocorticography (ECoG):** The electrodes are placed directly onto the brain's surface, so ECoG has much better resolution compared with EEG. But it calls for surgery to put them in place and, as a result, is extremely invasive.
  - **Intracortical recording:** This method involves microelectrodes that are inserted deep into the brain to pick up individual cells' signals; it also provides the highest resolution, however, with more risk (Hochberg et al., 2006).

**ii. Optical and magnetic techniques:**

- **Functional near-infrared spectroscopy (fNIRS):** Blood oxygen level changes are measured to infer neural activity. It lies between invasiveness and signal quality (Naseer and Hong, 2015).
  - **Magnetoencephalography (MEG):** Neural activity generates magnetic fields, which are then coded. MEG has good temporal resolution as well as some special resolution, but the instruments it needs are expensive and bulky (Hari and Salmelin, 2012).

## 3.2 Signal processing

A BCI framework illustrating the process from brain signal acquisition to signal processing (including preprocessing, feature extraction, and classification), leading to device control and feedback for adaptive interaction as in Fig. 1.5

- **Preprocessing:** Neural signals are often quite noisy in their raw state. Bandpass filtering and artifact removal are both commonly used to get rid of these actual signals (for example, residual muscle movements or other ubiquitous factors). (Bashashati et al., 2007)
- **Feature Extraction:** This involves the extraction of key characteristics from neural signals such as frequency bands (e.g., alpha, beta) or event-related potentials, for interpretation as ERPs ("meaningful" brain waves) and also happens to be one of the most widely accepted methods (Lotte et al., 2007)

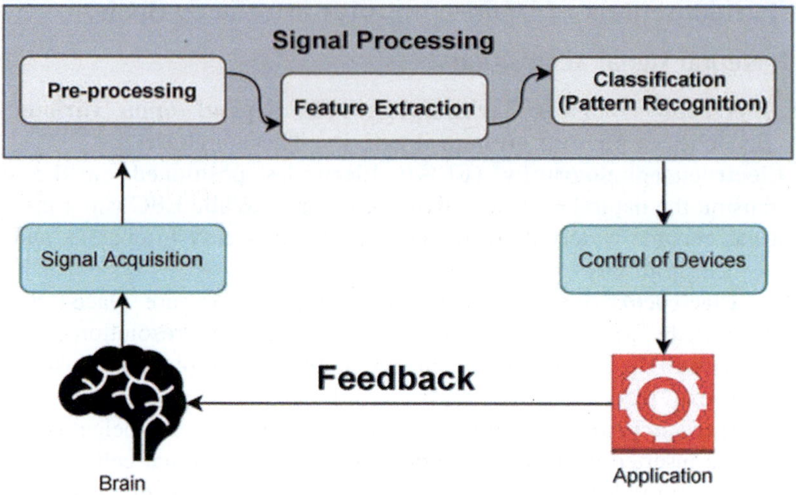


**FIGURE 1.5** Brain-computer interface (BCI) framework.

- **Classification:** Machine learning algorithms, such as support vector machines (SVMs) and deep neural networks, are used to classify neural signals representing specific commands or results (Schirrmeister et al., 2017).

BCI systems work by extracting information from the human brain's nervous system so that it can be processed and understood. In other words, BCI technology transforms thinking into action: it is a direct interface between thought and hardware or software devices (such as a PC) while the user's body acts as just another piece of equipment for those devices to manipulate.

## 3.3 Brain-computer communication: Mechanisms and concepts

BCIs make direct communication between the brain and external devices possible by translating neural signals into actionable outputs. This process involves several key steps:

**Translation of signals:**

Neural signals are decoded into orders controlling an external entity, such as a robot arm, computer cursor, or an acoustic synthesizer.
The motor imagery, for example, is thinking about some action without actually doing it. can be used to control a prosthetic hand, while visual evoked potentials (VEPs) help in communication via a virtual keyboard (Pfurtscheller and Neuper, 2001).

**Feedback loops:**

Live feedback is crucial in enhancing the performance of BCIs. By providing visual, audio, or tactile assistance, users of neural prostheses are guided out of unfavorable electroencephalographic patterns (Ramos-Murguialday et al., 2013).

**Integration of technology:**

BCIs are often combined with other technologies, such as robotic devices, virtual reality, and AI, to enhance functionality. For example, when AI algorithms prosper, students (Hassabis et al., 2017) start simulating brain patterns so that the accuracy of BCIs grows faster and faster.

### 3.4 Types of BCIs: Invasive, partially invasive, and noninvasive

BCIs can be classified according to the extent of invasiveness, each with its own advantages and drawbacks.

- **Invasive BCIs:**
  **Description**: Electrodes are directly implanted into the brain tissue, giving high-resolution signals.
  **Applications**: Restoring movement in paralyzed patients, controlling robotic prostheses (Hochberg et al., 2006)
  **Challenges**: Risk of infection, tissue damage, and long-term stability issues.
- **Partially invasive BCIs:**
  **Description**: Electrodes are placed on the surface of the brain (e.g., ECoG) or within the skull but not deep into brain tissue.
  **Applications**: Monitoring epilepsy, achieving greater degrees of motor control
  **Challenges**: The risk involved is lower than that of invasive BCI, but surgery is still needed:
- **Noninvasive BCIs:**
  **Description**: Sensors are placed on the scalp or head near its surface (for example, EEG, fNIRS).
  **Applications**: Facilitating communication in patients who are "locked-in," carrying out special exercises for brain warmth and healthiness, playing games (Wolpaw et al., 2002).
  **Challenges**: Signal resolution is coarse, easily affected by environmental noise.

## 4. Neuromorphic computing: The human brain resemble

The paper will explain an area that looks at neural circuits in hardware and programming form. Neuromorphic structures are models that are inspired by the human brain's own. Global models cannot compete in this chapter;

therefore it looks at options the developers of software and hardware can get from animal brains.

For example, although blood provides a convenient transport mechanism for nutrients and information immediately, it "seeks" flesh to feed upon or injury in which to flourish. The latter type of system has its own set of advantages for animal thought processing in terms of speed and number-of-components resolution.

## 4.1 Principles of neuromorphic engineering

Neuromorphic systems are thus not like silicon networks that simply mimic the brain's neural synapses. Key principles

**Event-driven processing of inspired neuromorphic systems:**
Traditionally, computers work in a clock-based system. Brain-style spike processing; however, it uses event-driven mode to emulate the speed and energy consumption characteristics of our own running hardware while still

**Introduction of the brain simulation programs designed to evolve**
As it continues to develop, semiconductor technology remains a significant factor in the development of neuromorphic systems. It remains, however, difficult for current neurosimulations based on traditional models used in Very Large Scale Integration (VLSI) design to keep in step with this.

**Massive parallelism:**
The brain's parallel processing capability on billions of calculations is implemented at an abstract level in neuromorphic hardware. This is representative of highly complex tasks such as pattern recognition, sensory integration, and motion detection (Furber, 2016).

## 4.2 Hardware and algorithms inspired by neural networks

Neuromorphic techniques like those represented above rely on both special hardware and programmed algorithms to represent the behavior of neurons in our brains.

**i. Neuromorphic hardware:**

- Memristors copy the behavior of synapses through control of resistance based on previous experiences of applied voltages. Memristors are already being used to create artificial synapses in neuromorphic chips.
  - Spiking neural networks (SNNs): SNNs are implemented in hardware to mimic the spiking activity of the brain. Some examples are IBM's TrueNorth and Intel's Loihi chips, which include tens of thousands of

synthetic neurons and synapses to perform complex calculations (Davies et al., 2018).
- Analog and mixed-signal circuits: These circuits can simulate the analog nature of biological neurons, making possible energy-efficient and real-time processing (Indiveri et al., 2011).

**ii. Neuromorphic algorithms:**

- Spike-timing-dependent plasticity (STDP): STDP is a distributional process that adjusts synaptic strengths according to the timing of spikes. It enables learning without supervision in neuromorphic systems (Bi and Poo, 1998).
  - Deep learning on neuromorphic hardware: Algorithms such as convolutional neural networks and backpropagation are adapted to run on neuromorphic hardware. For such tasks as image and speech recognition, this makes it possible to exploit the parallel processing capabilities of neuromorphic hardware (Schmidhuber, 2015).

## 4.3 The advantages of neuromorphic systems in processing neural data

Neuromorphic computing has many benefits over traditional computing systems, especially in handling neural data. Two examples:

- **Energy efficiency:** Compared with traditional CPUs and GPUs, neuromorphic systems consume far less power. For example, Intel's Loihi chip uses 1000 times less energy than conventional processors for some tasks (Davies et al., 2018).
- **Real-time processing:** The event-driven nature of neuromorphic systems easily allows for real-time processing of dynamic data like neural signals or sensory inputs. For uses such as BCIs and robot control on networks of sensors in an environment, this is very important (Indiveri et al., 2011).
- **Adaptation and robustness:** These systems promise robustness and versatility—adaptation to changing inputs and environments means that they have much more room for error than other types of hardware. This will be invaluable for unpredictable or noisy environments such as healthcare delivered by embodied machines or autonomous systems (Furber, 2016).
- **Scalability:** Horizontal expansion. The parallel architecture of neuromorphic hardware promotes horizontal scaling, allowing systems to tackle increasingly complex tasks with only marginal increases in power consumption or latency.
- **Applications in neuroscience and healthcare:** Examples in neuroscience or medicine neuromorphic systems serve as a tool for modeling and understanding brain function, developing advanced prosthetics, or creating personalized therapies for neurologic disorders. For instance, they can simulate neural circuits to explain diseases such as epilepsy and Parkinson's (Benjamin et al., 2014).

# 5. Applications of BCIs and neuromorphic computing in neurodegenerative diseases

This part talks about how BCIs and learning toward brains are used in practice to solve such problems as neurodegenerative diseases. With these technologies, we not only provide innovative solutions for early detection, real-time treatment, and tailored therapy to increase patients' quality of life in conditions such as amyotrophic lateral sclerosis (ALS), but also achieve diagnostic accuracy far exceeding human levels.

## 5.1 Early detection and diagnosis of neurodegenerative diseases

Early detection and accurate diagnosis are particularly important in neurodegenerative diseases, allowing timely intervention when it is possible to slow disease progression or change outcomes. This is another area where BCIs and neuromorphic computing exert their unique effects.

- **BCIs for early detection:**
- The subtle changes in neural activity that precede clinical symptoms can be detected by BCIs, yielding early diagnosis of conditions such as ALS, Parkinsonism, and Alzheimer's. For example, EEG-based BCIs can distinguish abnormal brainwave patterns associated with the diseases.
  - Invasive BCIs, such as those with intracortical electrodes, produce high-resolution data that tell us about the earliest signs of neurodegeneration at the cellular level (Hochberg et al., 2006).
- **Neuromorphic computing for data analysis neuromorphic**
- Systems have a great capacity for processing vast amounts of complex neural data in real time. They can detect patterns that indicate neurodegenerative diseases, such as changes in synaptic connections or the rates of neural firing (Benjamin et al., 2014).
  - Machine learning algorithms running on neuromorphic hardware can integrate multimodal data such as EEG, MRI, and genetic data to improve the accuracy of diagnoses as well as make predictions about how individual cases will proceed (Davies et al., 2018).

## 5.2 Real-time neural signal analysis and personalized interventions

With BCIs and neuromorphic computing, we can carry out real-time monitoring and analysis of neural signals, laying the foundation for personalized therapy.

- It is a BCI, interfaced with the human brain, which provides continuous monitoring of neural activity. This gives neurophysiological insight into the natural history of diseases and therapeutic effectiveness. For example,

an EEG-based BCI can track changes in brain wave patterns following drug treatment or psychiatric intervention (Wolpaw et al., 2002).
- Invasive BCIs, such as the BrainGate system, allow paralyzed patients to move external devices in real time. By getting instant feedback on results from their movement, they increase standards of living.
- According to one estimate, with neuromorphic computing personalized:
- Neuromorphic systems can adapt to each patient's unique neural characteristics, providing individualized treatment strategies. For example, they may use real-time neural data to optimize deep brain stimulation (DBS) parameters for Parkinson's patients (Furber, 2016).
- They are also suitable for closed-loop therapy, where the neural source signals end up in human interventions. In an attempt to adjust for those certain states, the system dynamically analyses its own outputs based on overload situations from Neuronet (Indiveri et al., 2011).

### 5.3 Case studies: Patients with ALS and improved quality of life

BCIs and neuromorphic computing have the potential to greatly improve the lives of ALS patients. The lives were usually very hard due to severe communication and mobility impediments.

- Efforts like this were just reward for a team that had lost one of its members, selfishly asking not only for peace in such an hour but also some hope; He looked down at Nam—a Korean boy from top to toe. That was said to him by the North Korean Special Envoy—in truth.
- Invasive BCIs, such as the Brain Gate system allows paralyzed ALS patients to control speech synthesizers.
- BCIs have restored the ability to move for patients who are suffering from amyotrophic lateral sclerosis—poorly, as they cannot perform these tasks. However, with neuromorphic computing, this is changing rapidly.
- Improving quality of life
- BCI and neuromorphic systems have been proven by case studies to greatly improve the quality of life for ALS patients, not only restoring communication mobility but also freeing them from being housebound and dependent on others. These technologies additionally relieve carers' burden and enhance the mood of their patients.

## 6. Technical and ethical challenges

While BCIs and neuromorphic computing hold out great promise of transforming healthcare, the technical and ethical demands that their development and deployment place on society are also considerable. Dealing with these issues is vital to ensuring these technologies are safe, effective, and fair to all.

## 6.1 Scalability and practical implementation

One of the chief technical worries is heightening the ability of these technologies to become truly popular while keeping their performance and reliability intact.

- **Hardware limitations:**
- Invasive BCIs need surgical implantation. This includes the potential risks of infection, tissue damage, and long-term stability problems. Developing biocompatible materials along with minimally invasive techniques is necessary for going beyond the lab and getting out into everyday life (Hochberg et al., 2006).
  - Neuromorphic hardware, while energy-efficient, still faces some challenges in manufacturing and integration with today's systems. Generating neuromorphic chips so that they can handle large-scale neural data still proves to be a major sticking point (Davies et al., 2018).
- **Signal processing and latency:**
- High computation power and low time lags for carrying course brain signals in real time do not really match up. Although neuromorphic systems excel here, integrating them with BCIs in a way that seems perfectly natural—as one cohesive unit of operation—is still to be worked upon (Indiveri et al., 2011).
  - Noninvasive BCIs, such as EEG-based systems, have trouble with low signal-to-noise ratios. So, results are often not very reliable or accurate (Wolpaw et al., 2002).
- **Interoperability and standardization:**
- Without standardized protocols for data acquisition, processing, and communications, BCIs and neuromorphic systems cannot be integrated into the existing healthcare infrastructure.

## 6.2 Ethical considerations in neural data usage and privacy

By using BCIs and neuromorphic computing, however, we are raising serious ethical issues especially about the acquisition, storage, and usage of neural data.

- **Data privacy and security:**
- Neural data is highly sensitive: it reveals the very thoughts, feelings, and purposes of an individual. Preserving the privacy and security of this information is therefore a priority.
  - For the neurology data, punctual encryption and anonymization techniques are also necessary to prevent its unauthorized access (Clausen et al., 2017).
- **Consented permission:**

- Complicated and invasive procedures are causing pain in society. Damage to the brain can result in breakthroughs as BCIs allow people who participate in this powerful technology a chance at life.
  - Conversely, basic technologies such as cochlear implants are more accessible or even common today than BCIs will ever have been. The risks of brain device sepsis or TIH, however, are greater than ever.
- **Ownership and control:**
- Questions on who owns the neural data and under what conditions (for research, business, law enforcement) it may be used require resolution. Existing guidelines and regulations must be put into place to prevent such exploitation.

## 6.3 Addressing bias and ensuring equitable access

The crux of ethics and pragmatics in BCIs and neuromorphic machines is that all people have equal access to them.

- **Algorithmic Bias:**
- When training data influences machine learning algorithms that are used in BCIs and neuromorphic systems as well, they can pick up on these prejudices and slacken performance for different demographic groups at different rates.
  - Efforts should be made to generate unbiased algorithms, diversify the training datasets, and ensure fair representation by all parties involved.
- **Equitable access:**
- In seeking new techniques for improving health care, the expense of researching and industrializing these technologies may indeed disadvantage individuals from being privileged or better endowed than others, creating a stark contrast between different populations.
  - Policymakers and developers should work together so that these technologies attain pricing levels that are within reach for poor people in need. Their general use ought to be widespread among low-income groups who would not have had access otherwise.
- **Cultural and social considerations:**
- The acceptance and adoption of BCIs and neuromorphic systems may vary between nations, and even within cultures. Ethical concepts should take into account cultural differences as well as possible and insist that technological creativity respects the values honored by the different societies.

```python
import numpy as np
import matplotlib.pyplot as plt

# Simulating EEG-like brain waves (sine waves with noise)
fs = 256  # Sampling frequency (Hz)
t = np.arange(0, 5, 1/fs)  # 5 seconds of data
freqs = [10, 20, 30]  # Frequencies of brain waves in Hz (alpha, beta, gamma)
eeg_signal = sum(np.sin(2 * np.pi * f * t) for f in freqs) + np.random.normal(0, 0.5, len(t))

# Plot EEG signal
plt.figure(figsize=(10, 4))
plt.plot(t[:500], eeg_signal[:500])  # Show first 500 samples
plt.xlabel("Time (s)")
plt.ylabel("Amplitude")
plt.title("Synthetic EEG Signal")
plt.show()
```

**FIGURE 1.6** Code snippet for simulating an EEG-like brain wave signal.

## 7. Decoding the brain: Simulating and processing neural signals for AI-driven neurotechnology

Industry development: Neurogaming in the Future-BCI and Neuromorphic Computing Development Neurogaming: A new way of interaction and its implementation in the real world. In several upcoming years, neuro-interfacing is bound to become the future of human-computer interaction. These systems utilize AI, neuroscience, and hardware advancements to analyze and decipher intricate neural data streams instantly.

In this section, we will provide an implementation to offer a practical perspective on the theory introduced above. We then build an SNN on the neural simulation tool (NEST) to familiarize ourselves with the topic of how neuromorphic systems and BCIs can decode neural trojan horse activity by simulating each of the brain signals and their frequency component features.

### 7.1 Synthetic brain signals: Create synthetic EEG data

A commonly used EEG is a method to record the electrical activity of the brain. EEG signals are produced by synchronized firing of neurons and are divided into various frequency bands, including delta, theta, alpha, beta, and gamma waves. However, they are often noisy and complex in real-world EEG signals. Our first step in our journey of understanding neural signal processing is to simulate a pseudo-EEG signal by combining sinusoidal waves (representing neural oscillations) with random noise (mimicking biological variations). Fig. 1.6 provides the Python script for simulating an EEG-like brain wave signal using sine waves of different frequencies (alpha, beta, and gamma) combined with noise. The script then plots the first 500 samples of the generated EEG signal.

Implementation:

- Create a time series at a 256 Hz sampling frequency, which is typical for EEG.
- Overlay sine waves of real EEG frequencies (e.g., alpha (10 Hz), beta (20 Hz), and gamma (30 Hz)).
- Add random noise to mimic biological neural variability.
- Check the signal as a time-series waveform.

Significance:

- Simulated electroencephalogram (EEG) signals are used to test algorithms before being applied to real-world data.
- Training corpses of Morse codes based on human brain rhythms.
- Serves as a foundation for subsequent investigation in BCI based technologies, such as cognitive state management and neurofeedback.

```
from scipy.fftpack import fft

# Compute FFT
fft_vals = np.abs(fft(eeg_signal))
freqs = np.fft.fftfreq(len(eeg_signal), 1/fs)

# Plot Frequency Spectrum
plt.figure(figsize=(8, 4))
plt.plot(freqs[:len(freqs)//2], fft_vals[:len(freqs)//2]) # Only positive frequencies
plt.xlabel("Frequency (Hz)")
plt.ylabel("Magnitude")
plt.title("EEG Frequency Spectrum")
plt.show()
```

**FIGURE 1.7** Code snippet for computing the Fast Fourier Transform (FFT) of an EEG-like signal.

```
import nest

# Create a simple spiking neural network
nest.ResetKernel()

# Create neurons
neuron1 = nest.Create("iaf_psc_alpha")  # Integrate-and-Fire Neuron
neuron2 = nest.Create("iaf_psc_alpha")

# Create a spike generator
spike_generator = nest.Create("spike_generator", params={"spike_times": [10.0, 20.0, 30.0]})

# Create a multimeter to record neuron activity
multimeter = nest.Create("multimeter", params={"record_from": ["V_m"], "interval": 0.1})

# Connect components
nest.Connect(spike_generator, neuron1, syn_spec={"weight": 100.0})
nest.Connect(neuron1, neuron2, syn_spec={"weight": 50.0})
nest.Connect(multimeter, neuron2)

# Simulate for 100 ms
nest.Simulate(100.0)

# Retrieve recorded data
data = nest.GetStatus(multimeter)[0]["events"]
plt.plot(data["times"], data["V_m"])
plt.xlabel("Time (ms)")
plt.ylabel("Membrane Potential (mV)")
plt.title("Spiking Neural Network Activity")
plt.show()
```

**FIGURE 1.8** Using the NEST simulator to create a simple spiking neural network.

## 7.2 Processing neural signals—Using Fast Fourier Transform (FFT) for basic analysis

Since raw EEG data contain a superposition of multiple frequency components, no direct interpretation can be done. We use frequency domain analysis to derive any useful information from it. The Fast Fourier Transform (FFT) is a fundamental mathematical algorithm that can serve as a decomposition tool for analyzing signals. Fig. 1.7 provides the Python script for computing the FFT of an EEG-like signal to analyze its frequency spectrum. The script plots only the positive frequencies to visualize the EEG frequency components.

Implementation:

- Convert to frequency domain using FFT on simulated EEG signal.
- Find peaks in the frequency spectrum that represent driven brain waves.
- Plot power distribution of EEG components.

Significance:

- Allows us to discern particular brain patterns: more alpha typically means they are relaxed; more beta means higher cognitive engagement.
- Good for BCI applications, such as imagining movement for controlling prosthetics.
- The keyword detection enables eliminating unnecessary brain noise and focusing on the valuable activity of neural pathways.

## 7.3 Spiking neural network (SNN) simulation—A simple neuromorphic model using NEST

In contrast to artificial neural networks, which use continuous signals, spiking neural networks (SNNs) use discrete spikes, better resembling biological neurons. For example, SNNs underpin neuromorphic computing, enabling real-time, energy-efficient activation of neural pathways. Fig. 1.8 provides the Python script using the NEST simulator to create a simple SNN. The script defines integrate-and-fire neurons, connects them via a spike generator, records membrane potential using a multimeter, simulates activity for 100 ms, and visualizes the SNN activity.

Implementing an SNN with NEST:

- Integrate-and-fire (IAF) units modeling spiking neurons.
- Population responses (spike activity) and synaptic connections with latency (delay) generation are modeled to simulate neural signal transmission.
- Neural networks of synapses to interpret signals.
- A multimeter to monitor voltage changes over time.

Implementation:

- You will create two neurons (iaf_psc_alpha) based on the leaky integrate-and-fire model.
- Automate with a spike generator that generates input spikes on demand, to the first neuron.
- Then, we can connect this first neuron to a second neuron to form a simple neural circuit.
- Use a multimeter to measure the membrane potential of the second neuron and visualize spike activity.

Significance:

- Has a biologically plausible method to represent actual neurons.
- Serves as the foundation for building neuromorphic computing chips and architectures (e.g., Intel's Loihi; IBM's TrueNorth).

- Allows AI models to process information on behalf of real neurons to reduce power consumption.
- Used in BCI systems and helps to decode brain signals to create assistive technology for ALS patients.

Thus these simulations help us understand how brain signal processing works, starting from simulating synthetic EEG signals, extracting the frequency domain of those signals, and finally simulating SNN, which is one of the brain's components that is crucial for neuromorphic computing. As such, these implementations are showcasing the ways AI-enhanced approaches can be combined with neurotechnology to create solutions that enhance our capabilities to diagnose and treat neurodegenerative diseases such as ALS.

The power of thought interfaces combined with artificial neural networks could change the structure of human society forever. In the future, the emphasis will be on real-time adaptation, personalized treatments, and seamless human-computer interaction, bridging the divide between artificial and biological intelligence for a more cohesive tomorrow.

## 8. Interdisciplinary collaboration and future directions

This depends on the successful maturation of BCIs and neuromorphic computing, which need to work together in various fields, such as AI, neuroscience, health care, robotics, and engineering. Through collaboration across disciplines and new pathways of research, such technologies can scale their societal impact and tackle some of the most important problems in health and other sectors. The future outcomes of combining BCIs and neuromorphic computing with robotics and connectivity technologies can create new ways for human enhancement and improved quality of life.

- **Robotics:**
- BCIs are also believed to enable direct control of robotic prosthetics, exoskeletons, and assistive devices, thereby restoring mobility and independence for patients with disabilities.
  - Neuromorphic computing increases the adaptability of robotic systems and makes them more responsive to guidance from people. By now, they can also take part in a real-time dialog with their human operator (Davies et al., 2018).
  - Connectivity and Internet of Things (IoT):
  - With connectivity and Internet of Things (IoT), it is seamless for BCIs and neuromorphic systems to be integrated into the Internet of Things. This leads to smart homes and personal health care (Indiveri et al., 2011).
  - Therefore a BCI-controlled wheelchair could guide itself around a smart home, adjusting the lights, the temperature, and other settings so that they suit the user's preferences.

- Human-machine collaboration:
- These technologies also open up new forms of human-machine cooperation, such as direct mind-to-mind communication or joint control systems in which people and machines share tasks between them.

## 9. Prospects for other neurodegenerative diseases

In the case of ALS, later this year, the success story of BCIs and neurostage computing paved the way for their introduction into other neurodegenerative disorders.

**i. Parkinson's disease**

- **Motor symptom management**

  BCIs can monitor and control motor symptoms such as tremor, rigidity, and freezing in Parkinson's patients. For example, EEG-based BCIs can detect anomalies in brainwave patterns and change dementia interventions or interventions in PD surgery subsequently, especially with feedback from the patient's own brainwave signal that is used live for neurofeedback (Furber, 2016).
- Cognitive boosters: New direction for neuromorphic systems in Parkinson patients

  Neuromorphic systems may provide supplementary support for cognitive architecture in Parkinson's disease. In this respect, the brain is inherently networked and self-organized, which places a person's mind beyond the reach of even your therapist on UltraStop (Benjamin et al., 2014).

**ii. Alzheimer's disease**

- **Early detection and diagnosis:**

  BCIs can detect subtle changes in neural activity before clinical symptoms appear, allowing early diagnosis of Alzheimer's. For example, EEG-based BCIs can identify abnormal brainwave patterns associated with the disease.
- Cognitive upgrading:

  Neuromorphic systems could be used to develop personalized cognitive rehabilitation programs for Alzheimer's patients. These can accommodate the specific needs of individual people, improving memory, concentration, and executive function at most profitably (Schirr-meister et al., 2017).

**iii. Other neurodegenerative disease dementia:**

- Huntington's disease and ALS:

  BCIs and neuromorphic computing promise to help control symptoms of Huntington's disease, multiple sclerosis, and some other neurodegenerative diseases, and to make sufferers' lives more satisfying. For example, BCIs can restore communication or movement ability; neuromorphic systems optimize therapeutic interventions.

## 10. Conclusion

This chapter explores BCIs and neuromorphic computing with tremendous paradigm-shifting potential for computation lying at the intersection of AI, neuroscience, and health care. It represents a further understanding of two areas and, regarding the understanding, diagnosis, and treatment of neurodegenerative diseases, provides fresh therapeutic options for some of the most difficult medical problems. Through historical tracing, the principles underlying these concepts are demonstrated in generalized approaches to BCIs, and neuromorphic systems in particular, demonstrating applicability of across overlap domains which most of all highlight interdisciplinary relevance, collaboration potential across bioengineering and neuroscience, and real-world impact to those suffering from serious disease (e.g., ALS, Parkinson's, and Alzheimer's) through real-time restoration of the lost capacity in way of communication and movement thus improving a person's quality of life.

BCIs/neuromorphic computing have great synergy as they sustainably enable real-time neuro generation/neuroadaptive learning and similar development approaches exemplified in their case studies. They have punctuated and successfully enabled ALS patients' unexpected skills and functionally independent lessons learned demonstrate the necessity of design driven by user needs, strong signal processing/development, and in-group effort harmonization. In the future, these technologies also have tremendous potential to help address other neurodegenerative diseases, such as Parkinson's and Alzheimer's. and also searching down avenues like robotics, connectivity, and cognitive enhancement.

However, with this promise, the technical limitations of BCIs and neuromorphic computing need to be minimized, and ethical challenges addressed. Scalability, signal quality, and interoperability remain essential challenges, with ethical data privacy, informed consent, and equitable access aspects also have to be managed to ensure responsible decisions and use. To translate these innovations into practice, one of the most significant predictors of success will be the collaborative experience among AI experts, neuroscientists, healthcare professionals, and engineers who drive research into ideas and solutions.

In conclusion, BCIs and neuromorphic computing are not just treatment options for neurodegenerative diseases—they are gateways to a reality in which manufactured and biological systems work in harmony to 127 enhance human potential and enrich quality of life. Now we have the context to entering the next frontier of Quantum Computing language, which would open up New opportunities for understanding the brain, curing neurological diseases, and creating a more joined-up and holistic world. It is a zeroing in on, a point of departure, for future investigation and invention, injecting a river of movement into researchers, clinicians, and policymakers to harness these technologies for the common good.

## References


Bashashati, A., Fatourechi, M., Ward, R.K., Birch, G.E., 2007. A survey of signal processing algorithms in brain-computer interfaces based on electrical brain signals. J. Neural. Eng. 4 (2), R32. https://doi.org/10.1088/1741-2560/4/2/R03.

Benjamin, B.V., Gao, P., McQuinn, E., Choudhary, S., Chandrasekaran, A.R., Bussat, J.M., Alvarez-Icaza, R., Arthur, J.V., Merolla, P.A., Boahen, K., 2014. Neurogrid: a mixed-analog-digital multichip system for large-scale neural simulations. Proc. IEEE 102 (5), 699–716. https://doi.org/10.1109/JPROC.2014.2313565.

Bi, G.Q., Poo, M.M., 1998. Synaptic modifications in cultured hippocampal neurons: dependence on spike timing, synaptic strength, and postsynaptic cell. J. Neurosci. 18 (24), 10464–10472. https://doi.org/10.1523/jneurosci.18-24-10464.1998.

Brown, R.H., Al-Chalabi, A., 2017. Amyotrophic lateral. N. Engl. J. Med. 377 (2), 162–172. https://doi.org/10.1056/NEJMra1603471.

Davies, M., Srinivasa, N., Lin, T.-H., Chinya, G., Cao, Y., Choday, S.H., Dimou, G., Joshi, P., Imam, N., Jain, S., Liao, Y., Lin, C.-K., Lines, A., Liu, R., Mathaikutty, D., McCoy, S., Paul, A., Tse, J., Venkataramanan, G., Weng, Y.-H., Wild, A., Yang, Y., Wang, H., 2018. Loihi: a neuromorphic manycore processor with on-chip learning. IEEE Micro 38 (1), 82–99. https://doi.org/10.1109/MM.2018.112130359.

Feigin, V.L., Nichols, E., Alam, T., Bannick, M.S., Beghi, E., Blake, N., Culpepper, W.J., Dorsey, E.R., Elbaz, A., Ellenbogen, R.G., Fisher, J.L., Fitzmaurice, C., Giussani, G., Glennie, L., James, S.L., Johnson, C.O., Kassebaum, N.J., Logroscino, G., Marin, B., Mountjoy-Venning, W.C., Nguyen, M., Ofori-Asenso, R., Patel, A.P., Piccininni, M., Roth, G. A., Steiner, T.J., Jacob Stovner, L., Szoeke, C.E.I., Theadom, A., Vollset, S.E., Wallin, M.T., Wright, C., Zunt, J.R., Abbasi, N., Abd-Allah, F., Ahmed, A., Abdollahpour, I., Aboyans, V., Abraha, H.N., Acharya, D., Adamu, A.A., Adebayo, O.M., Adeoye, A.M., Adsuar, J.C., Afarideh, M., Agrawal, S., Ahmadi, A., Ahmed, M.B., Aichour, A.N., Aichour, I., Aichour, M. T.E., Akinyemi, R.O., Akseer, N., Al-Eyadhy, A., Salman, R.A.-S., Alahdab, F., Alene, K.A., Aljunid, S.M., Altirkawi, K., Alvis-Guzman, N., Anber, N.H., Antonio, C.A.T., Arabloo, J., Aremu, O., Ärnlöv, J., Asayesh, H., Asghar, R.J., Atalay, H.T., Awasthi, A., Quintanilla, B.P. A., Ayuk, T.B., Badawi, A., Banach, M., Banoub, J.A.M., Barboza, M.A., Barker-Collo, S.L., Bärnighausen, T.W., Baune, B.T., Bedi, N., Behzadifar, M., Behzadifar, M., Béjot, Y., Bekele, B.B., Belachew, A.B., Bennett, D.A., Bensenor, I.M., Berhane, A., Beuran, M., Bhattacharyya, K., Bhutta, Z.A., Biadgo, B., Ali, B., Bililign, N., Sayeed, M.S.B., Blazes, C. K., Brayne, C., Butt, Z.A., Campos-Nonato, I.R., Cantu-Brito, C., Car, M., Cárdenas, R., Carrero, J.J., Carvalho, F., Castañeda-Orjuela, C.A., Castro, F., Catalá-López, F., Cerin, E., Chaiah, Y., Chang, J.-C., Chatziralli, I., Chiang, P.P.-C., Christensen, H., Christopher, D.J., Cooper, C., Cortesi, P.A., Costa, V.M., Criqui, M.H., Crowe, C.S., Damasceno, A.A.M., Daryani, A., Cruz-Góngora, V.De la, Hoz, F.P.De la, De Leo, D., Demoz, G.T., Deribe, K., Dharmaratne, S.D., Diaz, D., Dinberu, M.T., Djalalinia, S., Doku, D.T., Dubey, M., Dubljanin, E., Duken, E.E., Edvardsson, D., El-Khatib, Z., Endres, M., Endries, A.Y., Eskandarieh, S., Esteghamati, A., Esteghamati, S., Farhadi, F., Faro, A., Farzadfar, F., Farzaei, M.H., Fatima, B., Fereshtehnejad, S.-M., Fernandes, E., Feyissa, G.T., Filip, I.,

Fischer, F., Fukumoto, T., Ganji, M., Gankpe, F.G., Garcia-Gordillo, M.A., Gebre, A.K., Gebremichael, T.G., Gelaw, B.K., Geleijnse, J.M., Geremew, D., Gezae, K.E., Ghasemi-Kasman, M., Gidey, M.Y., Gill, P.S., Gill, T.K., Girma, E.T., Gnedovskaya, E.V., Goulart, A.C., Grada, A., Grosso, G., Guo, Y., Gupta, R., Gupta, R., Haagsma, J.A., Hagos, T. B., Haj-Mirzaian, A., Haj-Mirzaian, A., Hamadeh, R.R., Hamidi, S., Hankey, G.J., Yuantao, H., Haro, J.M., Hassankhani, H., Hassen, H.Y., Havmoeller, R., Hay, S.I., Hegazy, M. I., Heidari, B., Henok, A., Heydarpour, F., Hoang, C.L., Hole, M.K., Homaie Rad, E., Mostafa Hosseini, S., Hu, G., Igumbor, E.U., Ilesanmi, O.S., Irvani, S.S.N., Islam, S.M.S., Jakovljevic, M., Javanbakht, M., Jha, R.P., Jobanputra, Y.B., Jonas, J.B., Jozwiak, J.J., Jürisson, M., Kahsay, A., Kalani, R., Kalkonde, Y., Kamil, T.A., Kanchan, T., Karami, M., Karch, A., Karimi, N., Kasaeian, A., Kassa, T.D., Kassa, Z.Y., Kaul, A., Kefale, A.T., Keiyoro, P.N., Saleh Khader, Y., Khafaie, M.A., Khalil, I.A., Khan, E.A., Khang, Y.-H., Khazaie, H., Kiadaliri, A.A., Kiirithio, D.N., Kim, A.S., Kim, D., Kim, Y.-E., Kim, Y.J., Kisa, A., Kokubo, Y., Koyanagi, A., Krishnamurthi, R.V., Defo, B.K., Bicer, B.K., Kumar, M., Lacey, B., Lafranconi, A., Lansingh, Van C., Latifi, A., Leshargie, C.T., Li, S., Liao, Y., Linn, S., Lo, W.D., Lopez, J.C.F., Lorkowski, S., Lotufo, P.A., Lucas, R.M., Lunevicius, R., Mackay, M.T., Mahotra, N.B., Majdan, M., Majdzadeh, R., Majeed, A., Malekzadeh, R., Carvalho Malta, D., Manafi, N., Mansournia, M.A., Mantovani, L.G., März, W., Mashamba-Thompson, T.P., Massenburg, B.B., Mate, K.K.V., McAlinden, C., McGrath, J.J., Mehta, V., Meier, T., Meles, H.G., Melese, A., Memiah, P.T.N., Memish, Z.A., Mendoza, W., Mengistu, D.T., Mengistu, G., Meretoja, A., Meretoja, T.J., Mestrovic, T., Miazgowski, B., Miazgowski, T., Miller, T.R., Mini, G.K., Mirrakhimov, E.M., Moazen, B., Mohajer, B., Mezerji, N.M.G., Mohammadi, M., Mohammadi-Khanaposhtani, M., Mohammadibakhsh, R., Mohammadnia-Afrouzi, M., Mohammed, S., Mohebi, F., Mokdad, A.H., Monasta, L., Mondello, S., Moodley, Y., Moosazadeh, M., Moradi, G., Moradi-Lakeh, M., Moradinazar, M., Moraga, P., Moreno Velásquez, I., Morrison, S.D., Mousavi, S.M., Muhammed, O.S., Muruet, W., Musa, K.I., Mustafa, G., Naderi, M., Nagel, G., Naheed, A., Naik, G., Najafi, F., Nangia, V., Negoi, I., Negoi, R.I., Newton, C.R.J., Ngunjiri, J.W., Nguyen, C.T., Nguyen, L.H., Ningrum, D.N.A., Nirayo, Y.L., Nixon, M.R., Norrving, B., Noubiap, J.J., Shiadeh, M.N., Nyasulu, P.S., Samuel Ogah, O., Oh, I.-H., Olagunju, A.T., Olagunju, T.O., Olivares, P.R., Onwujekwe, O.E., Oren, E., Mayowa, O.O., Mahesh, P.A., Pakpour, A.H., Pan, W.-H., Panda-Jonas, S., Pandian, J.D., Patel, S.K., Pereira, D.M., Petzold, M., Pillay, J.D., Piradov, M.A., Polanczyk, G.V., Polinder, S., Postma, M.J., Poulton, R., Poustchi, H., Prakash, S., Prakash, V., Qorbani, M., Radfar, A., Rafay, A., Rafiei, A., Rahim, F., Rahimi-Movaghar, V., Rahman, M., Rahman, M.H.U., Rahman, M.A., Rajati, F., Ram, U., Ranta, A., Rawaf, D.L., Rawaf, S., Reinig, N., Reis, C., Renzaho, A.M.N., Resnikoff, S., Rezaeian, S., Rezai, M.S., González, C.M.R., Roberts, N.L.S., Roever, L., Ronfani, L., Roro, E.M., Roshandel, G., Ali, R., Sabbagh, P., Sacco, R.L., Sachdev, P.S., Saddik, B., Safari, H., Safari-Faramani, R., Safi, S., Safiri, S., Sagar, R., Ramesh, S., Sahebkar, A., Ali Sahraian, M., Salamati, P., Zahabi, S.S., Salimi, Y., Samy, A.M., Sanabria, J., Santos, I.S., Milicevic, M.M.S., Sarrafzadegan, N., Sartorius, B., Sarvi, S., Sathian, B., Satpathy, M., Sawant, A.R., Sawhney, M., Schneider, I.J.C., Schöttker, B., Schwebel, D.C., Seedat, S., Sepanlou, S.G., Shabaninejad, H., Shafieesabet, A., Ali Shaikh, M., Shakir, R.A., Shams-Beyranvand, M., Shamsizadeh, M., Sharif, M., Sharif-Alhoseini, M., She, J., Sheikh, A., Sheth, K.N., Shigematsu, M., Shiri, R., Shirkoohi, R., Shiue, I., Siabani, S., Siddiqi, T.J., Sigfusdottir, I.D., Sigurvinsdottir, R., Silberberg, D.H., Silva, J.P., Silveira, D.G.A., Singh, J.A., Sinha, D.N., Skiadaresi, E., Smith, M., Sobaih, B.H., Sobhani, S., Soofi, M., Soyiri, I.N., Sposato, L.A., Stein, D.J., Stein, M.B., Stokes, M.A.,

Sufiyan, Mu'awiyyah B., Sykes, B.L., Sylaja, P.N., Tabarés-Seisdedos, R., Ao, B.J.T., Tehrani-Banihashemi, A., Temsah, M.-H., Omar, T., Thakur, J.S., Thrift, A.G., Topor-Madry, R., Tortajada-Girbés, M., Tovani-Palone, M.R., Tran, B.X., Tran, K.B., Truelsen, T.C., Tsadik, A. G., Car, L.T., Ukwaja, K.N., Ullah, I., Usman, M.S., Uthman, O.A., Valdez, P.R., Vasankari, T. J., Vasanthan, R., Veisani, Y., Venketasubramanian, N., Violante, F.S., Vlassov, V., Vosoughi, K., Vu, G.T., Vujcic, I.S., Wagnew, F.S., Waheed, Y., Wang, Y.-P., Weiderpass, E., Weiss, J., Whiteford, H.A., Wijeratne, T., Winkler, A.S., Wiysonge, C.S., Wolfe, C.D.A., Xu, G., Ali, Y., Yamada, T., Yano, Y., Yaseri, M., Yatsuya, H., Yimer, E.M., Yip, P., Yisma, E., Yonemoto, N., Yousefifard, M., Yu, C., Zaidi, Z., Zaman, S.B., Zamani, M., Zandian, H., Zare, Z., Zhang, Y., Zodpey, S., Naghavi, M., Murray, C.J.L., Vos, T., 2019. Global, regional, and national burden of neurological disorders, 1990–2016: a systematic analysis for the Global Burden of Disease Study 2016. Lancet Neurol. 18 (5), 459–480. https://doi.org/10.1016/s1474-4422(18)30499-x.

Fetz, E.E., 1969. Operant conditioning of cortical unit activity. Science 163 (3870), 955–958. https://doi.org/10.1126/science.163.3870.955.

Furber, S., 2016. Large-scale neuromorphic computing systems. J. Neural. Eng. 13 (5), 051001. https://doi.org/10.1088/1741-2560/13/5/051001.

Hari, R., Salmelin, R., 2012. Magnetoencephalography: from SQUIDs to neuroscience. Neuroimage 61 (2), 386–396. https://doi.org/10.1016/j.neuroimage.2011.11.074.

Hassabis, D., Kumaran, D., Summerfield, C., Botvinick, M., 2017. Neuroscience-inspired artificial intelligence. Neuron 95 (2), 245–258. https://doi.org/10.1016/j.neuron.2017.06.011.

Hochberg, L.R., Serruya, M.D., Friehs, G.M., Mukand, J.A., Saleh, M., Caplan, A.H., Branner, A., Chen, D., Penn, R.D., Donoghue, J.P., 2006. Neuronal ensemble control of prosthetic devices by a human with tetraplegia. Nature 442 (7099), 164–171. https://doi.org/10.1038/nature04970.

Indiveri, G., Linares-Barranco, B., Hamilton, T.J., van Schaik, A., Etienne-Cummings, R., Delbruck, T., Liu, S.-C., Dudek, P., Häfliger, P., Renaud, S., Schemmel, J., Cauwenberghs, G., Arthur, J., Hynna, K., Folowosele, F., Saighi, S., Serrano-Gotarredona, T., Wijekoon, J., Wang, Y., Boahen, K., 2011. Neuromorphic silicon neuron circuits. Front. Neurosci. 5 (May). https://doi.org/10.3389/fnins.2011.00073.

Kandel, E.R., Schwartz, J.H., Jessell, T.M., Siegelbaum, S.A., Hudspeth, A.J., 2013. Principles of Neural Science, fifth ed. McGraw-Hill Education, New York, NY.

Kennedy, P.R., Bakay, R.A.E., 1998. Restoration of neural output from a paralyzed patient by a direct brain connection. Neuroreport 9 (8), 1707–1711. https://doi.org/10.1097/00001756-199806010-00007.

Lotte, F., Congedo, M., Lécuyer, A., Lamarche, F., Arnaldi, B., 2007. A review of classification algorithms for EEG-based brain–computer interfaces. J. Neural. Eng. 4 (2), R1. https://doi.org/10.1088/1741-2560/4/2/r01.

Mead, C., 1990. Neuromorphic electronic systems. Proc. IEEE 78 (10), 1629–1636. https://doi.org/10.1109/5.58356.

Naseer, N., Hong, K.S., 2015. fNIRS-based brain–computer interfaces: a review. Front. Hum. Neurosci. 9, 3.

Pfurtscheller, G., Neuper, C., 2001. Motor imagery and direct brain-computer communication. Proc. IEEE 89 (7), 1123–1134. https://doi.org/10.1109/5.939829.

Poewe, W., Seppi, K., Tanner, C.M., Halliday, G.M., Brundin, P., Volkmann, J., Schrag, A.E., Lang, A.E., 2017. Parkinson disease. Nat. Rev. Dis. Primers (3), 1–21. https://doi.org/10.1038/nrdp.2017.13.

Ramos-Murguialday, A., Broetz, D., Rea, M., Läer, L., Yilmaz, Ö., Brasil, F.L., Liberati, G., Curado, M.R., Garcia-Cossio, E., Vyziotis, A., Cho, W., Agostini, M., Soares, E., Soekadar, S., Caria, A., Cohen, L.G., Birbaumer, N., 2013. Brain–machine interface in chronic stroke rehabilitation: a controlled study. Ann. Neurol. 74 (1), 100–108. https://doi.org/10.1002/ana.23879.

Schirrmeister, R.T., Springenberg, J.T., Fiederer, L.D.J., Glasstetter, M., Eggensperger, K., Tangermann, M., Hutter, F., Burgard, W., Ball, T., 2017. Deep learning with convolutional neural networks for EEG decoding and visualization. Hum. Brain Mapp. 38 (11), 5391–5420. https://doi.org/10.1002/hbm.23730.

Schmidhuber, J., 2015. Deep learning in neural networks: an overview. Neural Netw. 61, 85–117. https://doi.org/10.1016/j.neunet.2014.09.003.

Topol, E.J., 2019. High-performance medicine: the convergence of human and artificial intelligence. Nat. Med. 25 (1), 44–56. https://doi.org/10.1038/s41591-018-0300-7.

Vidal, J.J., 1973. Toward direct brain-computer communication. Annu. Rev. Biophys. Bioeng. 2 (1), 157–180. https://doi.org/10.1146/annurev.bb.02.060173.001105.

Wolpaw, J.R., Birbaumer, N., McFarland, D.J., Pfurtscheller, G., Vaughan, T.M., 2002. Brain-computer interfaces for communication and control. Clin. Neurophysiol. 113 (6), 767–791. https://doi.org/10.1016/S1388-2457(02)00057-3.

## Further reading

Alzheimer's Association, 2021. Alzheimer's disease facts and figures. Alzheimer's & Dementia 17 (3), 327–406.

Clausen, J., et al., 2017. Help, hope, and hype: ethical dimensions of neuroprosthetics. Science 356 (6345), 1338–1339.

Delgado, J.M.R., 1969. Physical Control of the Mind: Toward a Psychocivilized Society. Harper & Row, New York, NY.

Chapter 2

# BCI intelligence: Neuromorphic computing and brain-computer interfaces characteristics and challenges

**Shruthi M G**
*RV Institute of Technology and Management, Department of MCA, Bengaluru, Karnataka, India*

## 1. Introduction

Neuromorphic computing is the latest technology which acts as an interface between brain and the device.

The Brain-Computer interface which has the profound capacity to act and react to commands with the intelligence of the human brain by restoring functionalities of the brain and the nervous system. BCI acts as a container to collect the signals and respond to these signals with the desired output. The BCI allows direct communication with the brain through external devices. BCI deliberately delivers the human message to devices in the form of the following real-world implementations:

1. **Speech recognition:** Speech is one of the forms of main communication channel through different spoken languages to express thoughts, emotions and artifacts. Speech is a way of delivering a message through mouth via sound waves. By using the computer-based interface the translation of the speech that is sound to written form of information or data takes place. It's Natural Language Processing through which computers understand the sound signals and convert it into words in the form of information or data. The input is in the form of sound waves that can be an audio, Acoustic signal that is the processing of the electronic manipulation of signals. The real-world applications of the computer-based interface is active noise control system, hearing aids, echo, music etc. this kind of information receiving and processing through MP3 players. The real-world

**Neuromorphic Computing for Brain Computer Interfaces. https://doi.org/10.1016/B978-0-443-41594-4.00003-4**

applications in today's world are Alexa a cloud-based voice assistance Siri in apple iPhone's, Google assistance by Google Company.

2. **Neuromorphic Sensors:** These sensors perform operations using the intelligent sensing technology. These sensors accept input in the form of raw data, process the data and produce the desired output based on it. These sensors use the human intelligence of the brain to provide the desired output. Mainly to model the computations of human brain and the nervous system. By implementing an algorithm of artificial neural network (ANN), the processing of signals takes place to produce the desired output. The real world applications in today's world are Machine Learning algorithms for pattern recognition for natural language processing, brain skull images, MRI scans, electro encephalogram test and so on.
3. **Automated Systems:** The robotic devices is the best development using the functionalities of the brain intelligence of humans to respond with respect to environment. The Brain computer interface (BCI) is the best development of human intelligence and robotic device interactions, which is based on neuromorphic computing. Automated systems to control the machines automatically with human brain intelligence and neuro morphic computing by incorporating brain technologies for computational to perform. Neuromemiristive system is one of the real-world applications of this automated systems.

## 2. The architecture of brain computer interface to classify invasive and non-invasive

In Fig. 2.1 The neuron signals generated by brain scans is considered then the signal acquisition takes place based on electroencephalography (EEG) electrodes which records the brain activity, once the data is scanned it undergoes the preprocessing of the data takes place by cleaning the dataset, removing the artifacts like noise, motion or any inferences for the feature extraction, the extraction of features takes place based on the signal bands, once the features are extracted it classifies the data signals based on Machine Learning algorithms into invasive and noninvasive.

By applying the above architecture, a BCI can successfully classify EEG signals into invasive and noninvasive categories based on patterns detected from the brain's electrical activity, and offer valuable insights for medical diagnoses or assistive devices for individuals with neurodegenerative diseases like Alzheimer's, Parkinson's etc.

There are two categories of BCI which are classified based on data signals as below:

1. Invasive BCI: It interacts directly with the brain tissues that is intracortical surface present by surgically implanting of electrodes. This is direct way of implementation data signals to record the neuron activity in the brain. It

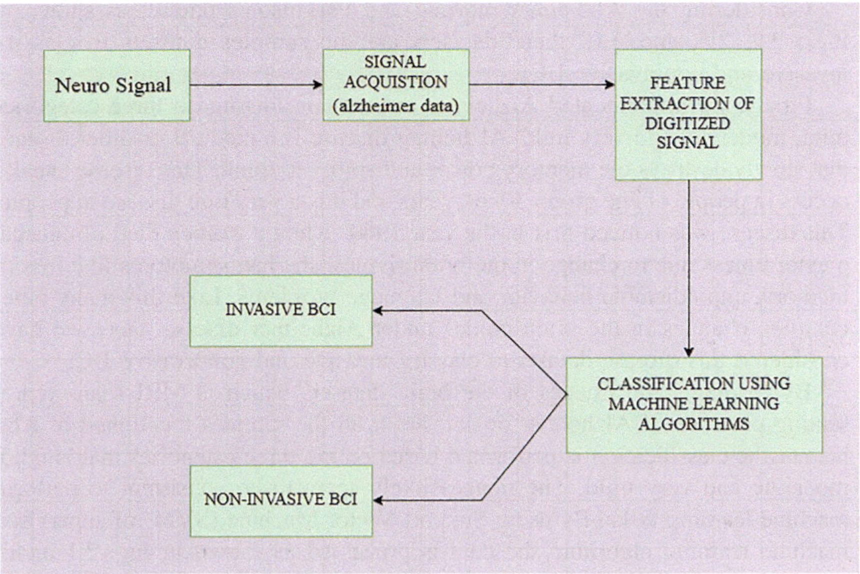


**FIGURE 2.1** Architecture of BCI classification invasive and noninvasive.

produces high resolution and higher accuracy signals. It has few challenges like need to be implemented surgically only and lifelong issues may rise. A study by scientists at the University of Chicago implemented this technology to individual implanting robotic hands with human features through the brain implanted electrodes.

It has been implemented in the bidirectional BCI with additional feature of modulating brain activities through electrical stimulation. International researches are under process with invasive BCI in different fields like healthcare, human machine interactions etc.

2. Noninvasive: It interacts indirectly with the brain tissues without any surgical procedures by using the devices like EEG by placing on the scalp to record the brain activity. Here the implementation of the system is through detection of neural signals in the scalp and skull which is safer and more accessible but vulnerable to the attenuation and noise. Comparing to Noninvasive BCIs it provides lower resolution and accuracy but are widely implemented in many applications like neuro feedback, cognitive training, and communication systems for individuals with motor impairments. In noninvasive EEG-based BCIs it enabled paralyzed individuals to control computer cursors or robotic arms through brain signals. These systems are implemented in consumer-grade devices for the purpose of gaming and mental health applications. International research is advancing noninvasive BCIs to improve signal decoding algorithms and extend their usability across various fields, including education, healthcare, and entertainment.

Considering the Alzheimer, normal and Parkinson's dataset as shown in Figs. 2.2, 2.5, and 2.10 these datasets are the samples datasets to classify invasive and noninvasive BCI.

Firstly, we implemented Alzheimer dataset considering all three categories mild, moderate, and very mild. Alzheimer disease is a medical disorder disease that slowly destroys the memory power and ability to think. This disease usually occurs in people of age group 30–60 years and it is a very rare disease in people. This disease was noticed first in the year 1960s when a women died of unusual mental illness due to change in the brain tissues, she had symptoms like loss of memory, unpredictable behavior and language problems. Like this many other complex changes in the brain comes under Alzheimer disease. Here we have considered this disease dataset to classify invasive and noninvasive BCI.

By loading 2500 images of the brain datasets which is MRI scans representing presence of Alzheimer or not. From all the samples mentioned of Alzheimer the classification is performed based on the three categories that is mild, moderate and very mild. The images likely seem to be consistent to perform machine learning tasks. By using Support Vector Machine (SVM) of supervised machine learning algorithm the data is processed as shown in Fig. 2.1 architecture, here we divide the datasets into training and testing to extract the features value in a uniform range of 0 and 1. By this procedure of training and testing the performance is improved. Here the extraction of only relevant features from the brain datasets is done. In this we achieve 100% accuracy in terms of data separation without any overlap, preprocessing is carried out to the entire datasets before training and testing and this dataset is small and accurate. The generation of confusion matrix to visualize the performance of the classification is done. The confusion matrix if result in 1 then the classification is correct of the disease else it results in 0 than it is healthy in terms of not having Alzheimer disease.

The accuracy is 100% for the Alzheimer dataset, the confusion matrix will look as shown in the matrix representation that is the diagonal elements of the matrix represent correctly classified cases, indicating the overall accuracy of the model.

$$\begin{bmatrix} 732 & 0 \\ 0 & 18 \end{bmatrix}$$

This results in the classification report as below

```
Classification Report:
              precision    recall  f1-score   support

           0       1.00      1.00      1.00       732
           1       1.00      1.00      1.00        18

    accuracy                           1.00       750
   macro avg       1.00      1.00      1.00       750
weighted avg       1.00      1.00      1.00       750
```

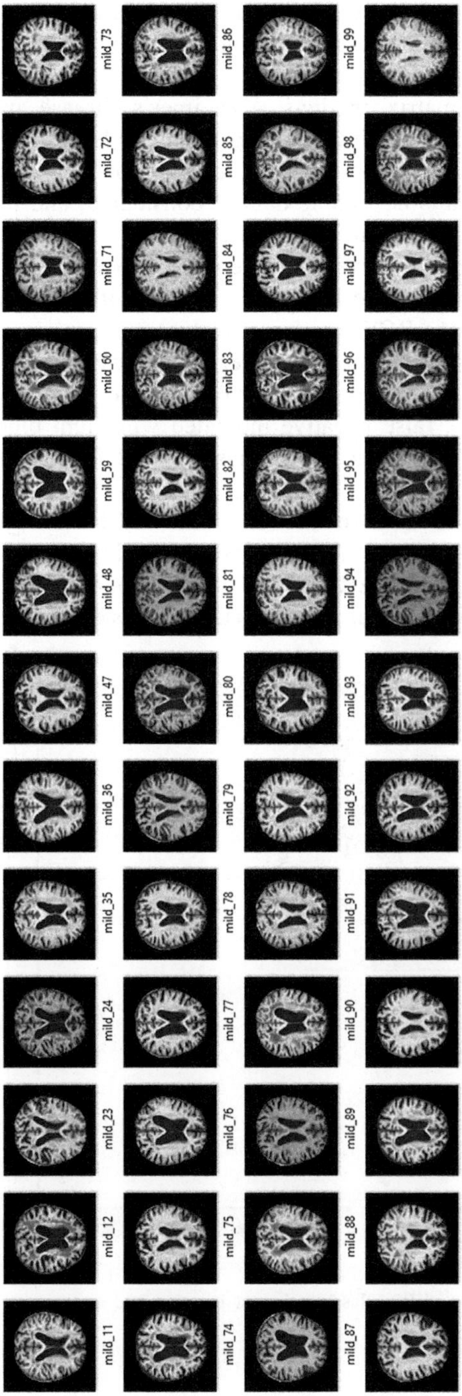


**FIGURE 2.2** Alzheimer datasets sample.

Here the Confusion Matrix mainly tells where the model gets confused. It predicts the performance of classification model by organizing the prediction for which class the dataset belongs.

The confusion matrix predicts Alzheimer's disease using the sample dataset to classify between invasive and noninvasive BCI, it visual representation is the implementation of machine learning model to categories based on the prediction of available sample dataset considered, and it identifies which area of brain might be crucial for classification. In the below confusion matrix a higher number is noninvasive BCI whereas invasive BCI indicates that some patients scans are suitable resulting in a model with more missing potential candidates for invasive BCI's as shown in Fig. 2.3.

The Confusion Matrix top left corner that is true negative indicated with dark blue represents the prediction as non-Alzheimer and the other portions that is false positive, false negative indicated with light blue represents prediction of Alzheimer presence. This has resulted in more healthy cases to Alzheimer disease.

The distribution of invasive and noninvasive BCI refer to the classification of data model for Alzheimer dataset as shown in Fig. 2.4.

Secondly, we implemented Normal dataset considering all 10 categories. This dataset is echoing planar imaging (EPI) diffusion scan which consists of

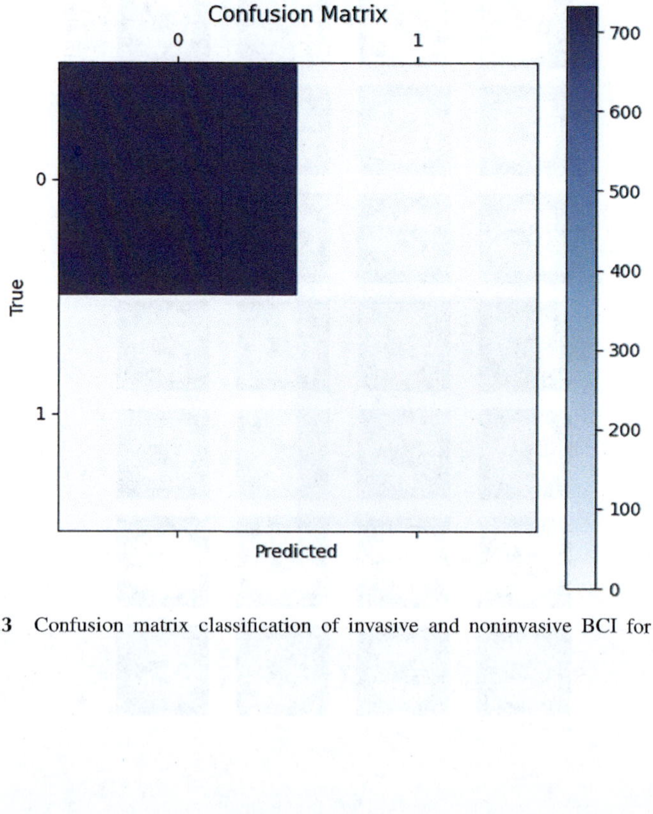


**FIGURE 2.3** Confusion matrix classification of invasive and noninvasive BCI for Alzheimer dataset.

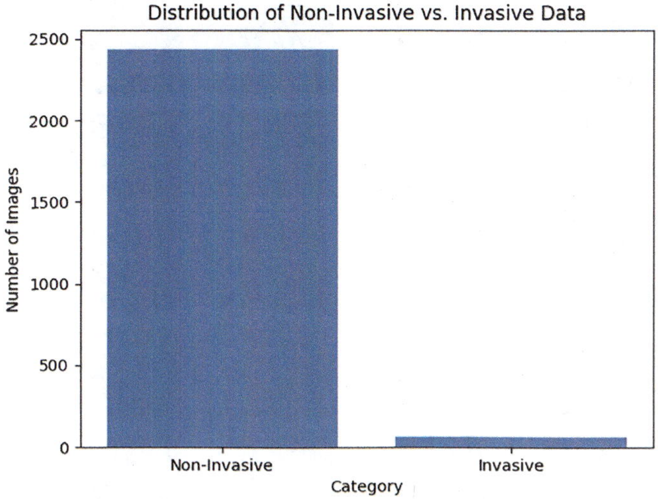


**FIGURE 2.4** Distribution of invasive and noninvasive BCI for Alzheimer dataset.

ep2d_diff_3scan_trace_p2_ADC_DFC, localizer image, Magnitude Image, non-phase image, Susceptibility-Weighted Imaging, T1-weighted (t1) for detection of swollen, hemorrhage brain structures, T2-weighted (t2) for finding water content in the brain these categories of dataset are used in normal dataset.

By loading 2699 images of the brain datasets from all the three samples mentioned above of Normal the classification is performed from 10 categories. By using Support Vector Machine (SVM) the data is processed as shown in Fig. 2.1 architecture, here we divide the datasets into training and testing to extract the features value in a uniform range of 0 and 1. By this procedure of training and testing the performance is improved. Here the extraction of only relevant features from the brain datasets. Here we achieve 99.88% accuracy in terms of data separation without any overlap, preprocessing is carried out to the entire datasets before training and testing and this dataset is small and accurate. By generating a confusion matrix to visualize the performance of the classification. This confusion matrix if result in 1 if the classification is correct of the disease sample datasets else it results in 0 than it is healthy.

If the accuracy is 99.88% for the Normal dataset the confusion matrix might look as shown in the matrix

$$\begin{bmatrix} 788 & 0 \\ 1 & 21 \end{bmatrix}$$

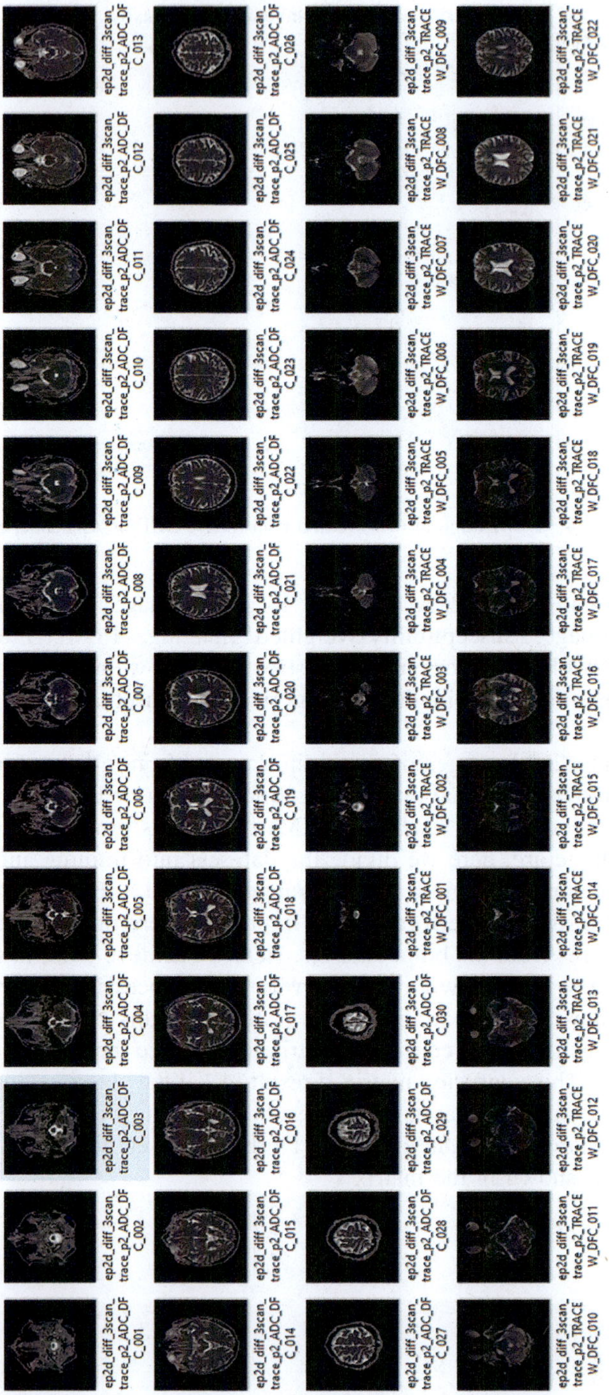


**FIGURE 2.5** Normal datasets sample.

Which results in the classification report as below

```
Classification Report:
              precision    recall  f1-score   support

           0       1.00      1.00      1.00       788
           1       1.00      0.95      0.98        22

    accuracy                           1.00       810
   macro avg       1.00      0.98      0.99       810
weighted avg       1.00      1.00      1.00       810
```

The confusion matrix predicts normal dataset to classify between invasive and noninvasive BCI, it visually represents the implementation of machine learning model to categories based on the prediction of available sample dataset considered and it identifies which area of brain might be crucial for classification. In the below confusion matrix a higher number is noninvasive BCI whereas invasive BCI indicates that some patients scans are suitable resulting in a model with more missing potential candidates for invasive BCI's as shown in Fig. 2.6.

The confusion matrix with higher value is showcased in dark blue predicting that it is completely normal without any disease. The rest indicate very few instances can be predicted to have some disease minutely.

The distribution of invasive and noninvasive BCI refer to the classification of data model of invasive and noninvasive model for normal dataset as shown in Fig. 2.7.

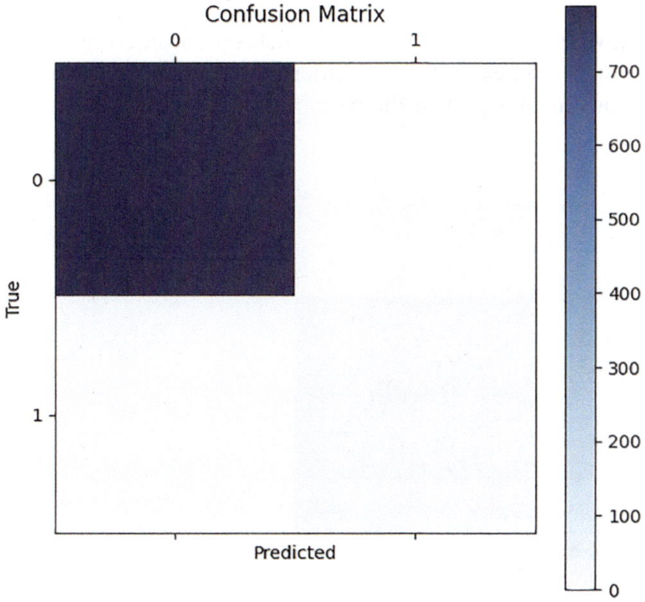


**FIGURE 2.6** Confusion matrix classification of invasive and noninvasive BCI for normal dataset.

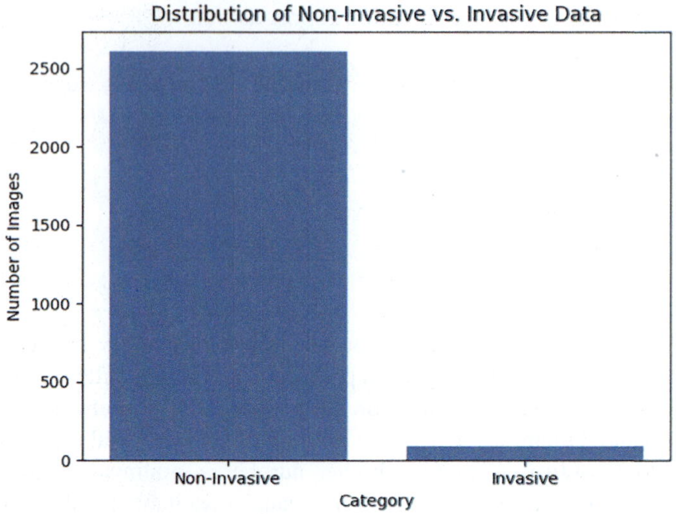


**FIGURE 2.7** Distribution of noninvasive and invasive data for normal dataset.

The pixel intensity histogram plotting is done to identify normal versus Alzheimer's using Seaborn library as below in Fig. 2.8.

The plot is by using t-SNE which is a dimensionality reduction algorithm used to find the patterns and make them into a cluster in the below Fig. 2.9. The more gap between the clustered groups is said to be a good dataset for the feature extraction.

Thirdly, we implemented Parkinson's dataset considering all 10 categories. The Parkinson's disease is the movement of nervous system disorder that is loss of neurons in an area near the base of the brain known as substantia nigra,

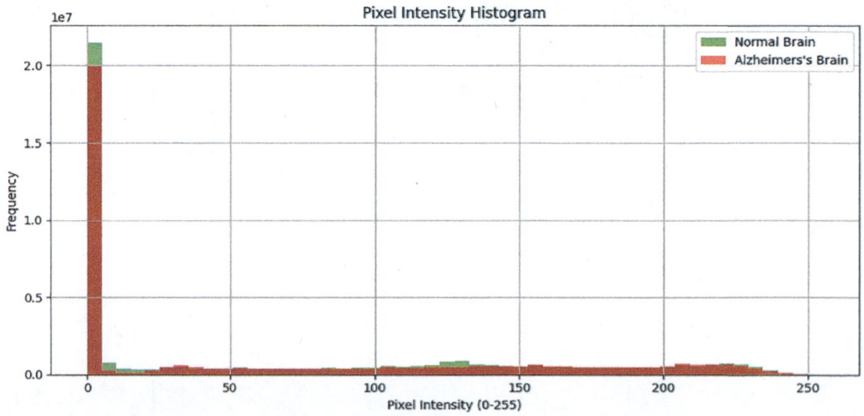


**FIGURE 2.8** Pixel intensity histogram of normal versus Alzheimer's.

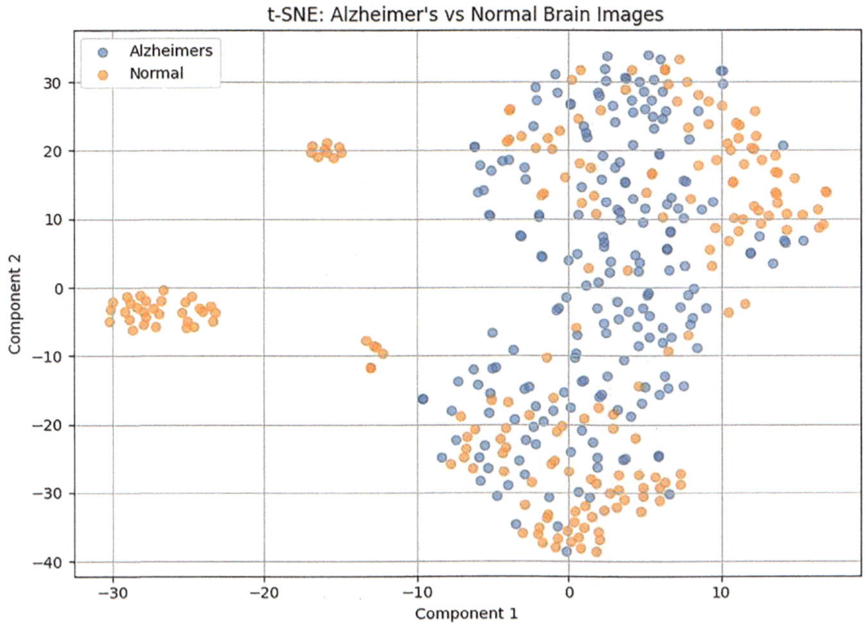


**FIGURE 2.9** t-SNE Alzheimer's versus normal brain images.

it causes brain weakness, shaking of hands problem, muscle stiffness, damage the brain cells causing severe tumor, stiffness and imbalance behavior. This may turn out to major concerns of difficulty in walking, talking and complete human activities and majorly the pulse rate reduction and blood pressure problems.

The image represents the collection of brain scans of MRI. Here each image is labeled with "aug_0_xxx" which indicates that they are fairly can be used on machine learning algorithms. It is fairly can be used to classify invasive and non-invasive BCI.

By loading 221 images of the brain datasets from all the eight samples mentioned above of Normal the classification is performed from 10 categories. By using Support Vector Machine (SVM) the data is processed as shown in Fig. 2.1 architecture, here we divide the datasets into training and testing to extract the features value in a uniform range of 0 and 1. By this procedure of training and testing the performance is improved. Here the extraction of only relevant features from the brain datasets. Here we achieve 98.51% accuracy in terms of data separation without any overlap, preprocessing is carried out to the entire datasets before training and testing and this dataset is small and accurate. By generating a confusion matrix to visualize the performance of the classification. This confusion matrix if result in 1 if the classification is correct of the disease sample datasets else it results in 0 than it is healthy.

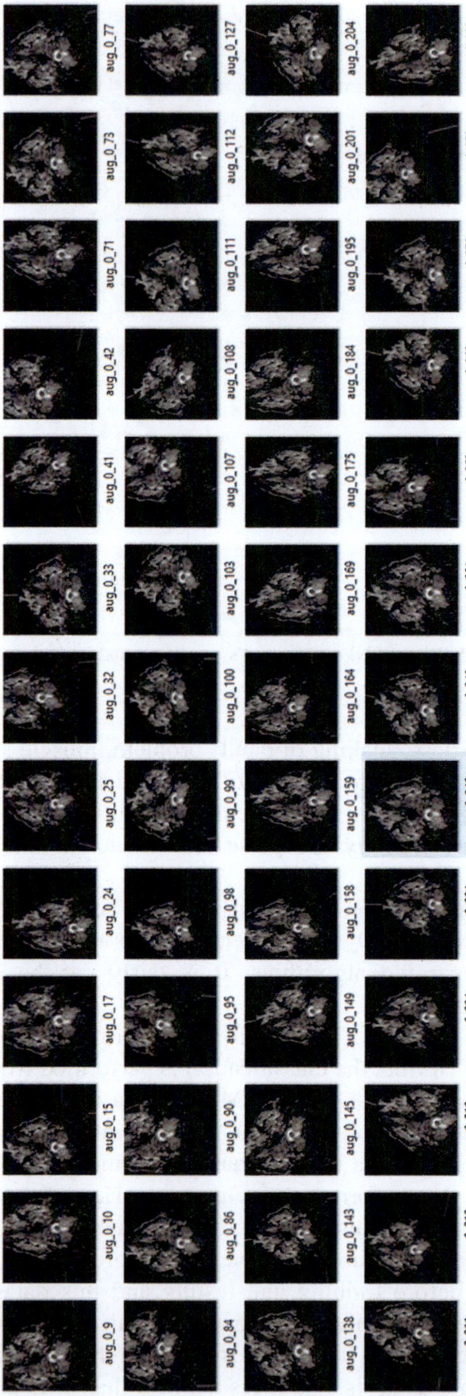


**FIGURE 2.10** Parkinson's datasets sample.

If the accuracy is 98.51% for the Parkinson's dataset the confusion matrix might look as shown in the matrix, the diagonal representation is correctly predicted cases.

$$\begin{bmatrix} 29 & 1 \\ 0 & 39 \end{bmatrix}$$

Which results in the classification report as below representing report which evaluates based on performance. There are two classes as class 0 and class 1, where class 0 showcase perfect precisions achieved and class 1 showcase slightly perfect precisions. The instance is also measured to showcase missing instances. This model gives 99% of sample accuracy correctly.

```
Classification Report:
              precision    recall  f1-score   support

           0       1.00      0.97      0.98        30
           1       0.97      1.00      0.99        37

    accuracy                           0.99        67
   macro avg       0.99      0.98      0.98        67
weighted avg       0.99      0.99      0.99        67
```

The confusion matrix predicts Parkinson's dataset to classify between invasive and noninvasive BCI, it visually represents the implementation of machine learning model to categories based on the prediction of available sample Parkinson's dataset considered, and it identifies which area of brain might be crucial for classification. In the below confusion matrix a higher number is noninvasive BCI whereas invasive BCI indicates that some patients scans are suitable resulting in a model with more missing potential candidates for invasive BCI's as shown in Fig. 2.11.

The confusion matrix top left corner that is true negative indicated with light blue represents the prediction as presence of Parkinson's, the true positive indicated with dark blue represents the higher chances of correctly predicted presence of Parkinson's disease. Rest partition showcase the healthy dataset values.

The color scale on the right shows the number of instances for each combination of true and predicted labels, where darker colors represent higher values.

The distribution of invasive and noninvasive BCI refer to the classification of data model of invasive and noninvasive model for Parkinson's dataset as shown in Fig. 2.12.

The Bar chart gives the invasive and noninvasive as equal distribution as prediction of disease is equally present in the entire dataset. This indicates that the dataset is a balanced way of representation of both invasive and noninvasive BCI.

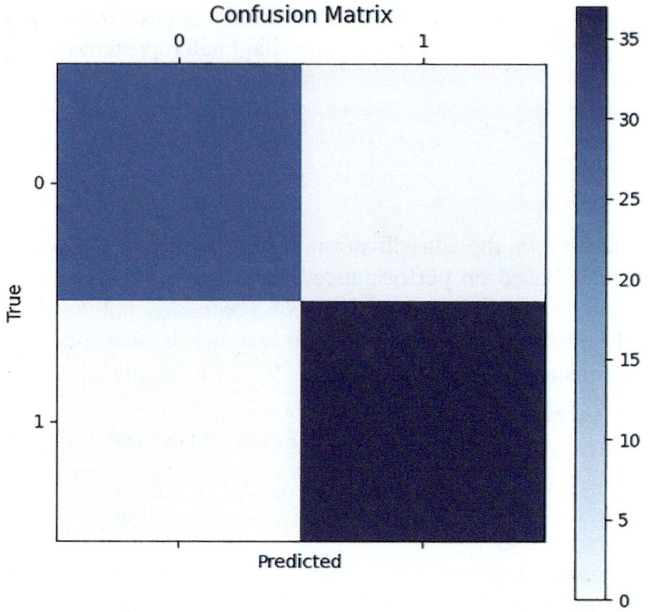


**FIGURE 2.11** Confusion matrix classification of invasive and noninvasive BCI for Parkinson's dataset.

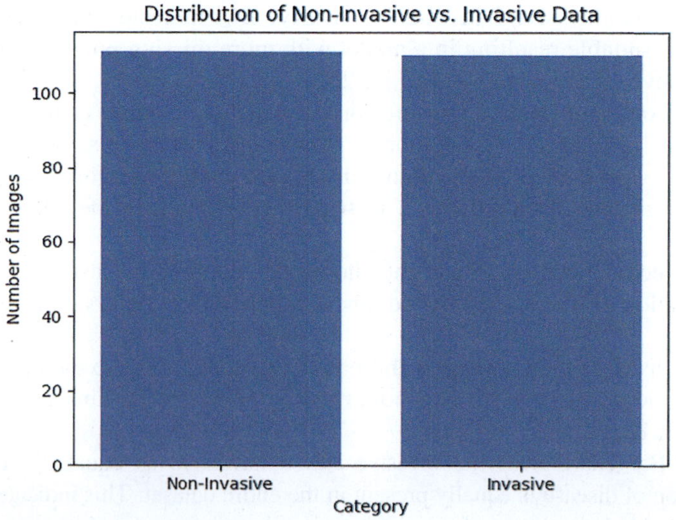


**FIGURE 2.12** Distribution of noninvasive and invasive data for Parkinson's dataset.

The pixel intensity histogram plotting is done to identify normal versus Parkinson's using Seaborn library as below in Fig. 2.13.

The plot are obtained by using t-SNE which is a dimensionality reduction algorithm in my opinion the more gap between the clustered groups is said to be a good dataset for the feature extraction. In this analysis Parkinson's proved better than the Alzheimer's dataset as shown in Fig. 2.14.

The diseased brain and the normal brain is identified using heat map as below in Fig. 2.15 considering normal, Alzheimer and Parkinson's dataset.

The Risk factors if early Classification of Invasive and Noninvasive BCI not done:

**Humans with Alzheimer Disease Presence Detection Factors:** The report generated by taking the Alzheimer dataset which is classified as invasive and noninvasive, the core essentials is early detection in disorder

- When found invasive BCI the EEG measures the MRI scan dataset of electrical brain activity of progress. This early detection of elongated ridges on the floor of each lateral ventricle of the brain with respect to emotions, memory loss and nervous system affected can be diagnosed at this stage itself.
- Noninvasive BCI detects the brain activity changes at early stage so that can be treated in initial stage itself. Whereas Noninvasive BCI detection help to monitor gradual loss of mental abilities such as loss of memory, thinking and concentration. By detecting this the early action toward diagnosis of memory related loss.

## 3. Risk factors of Alzheimer dataset if not detected at early as invasive and non-invasive BCI

- Gradual memory loss and short-term memory loss abnormalities increase which can result in complete memory loss which can be a severe risk factor affecting the human life.

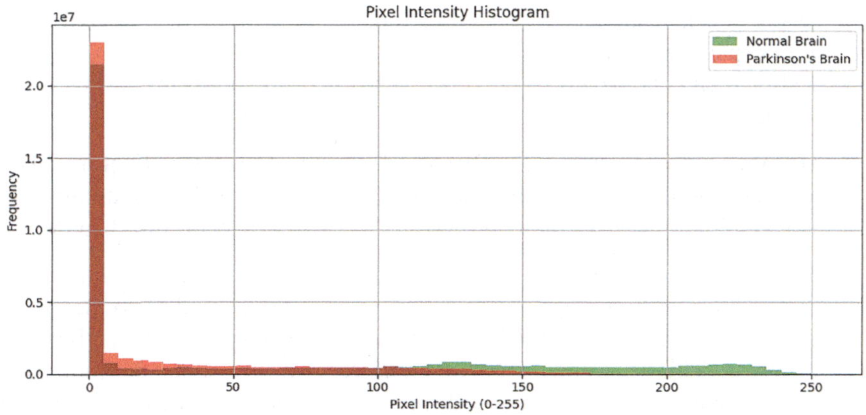


**FIGURE 2.13** Pixel intensity histogram of normal versus Parkinson's.

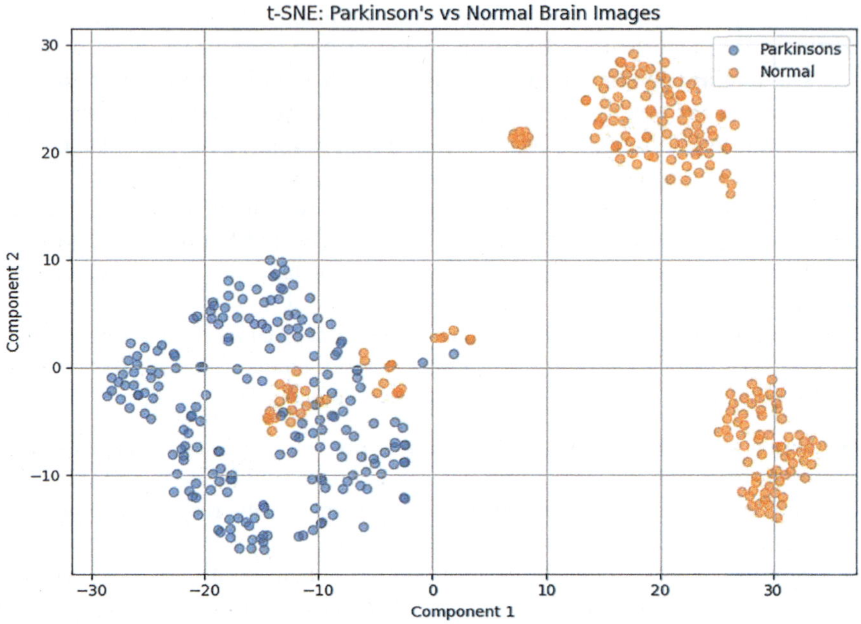


**FIGURE 2.14** t-SNE Parkinson's versus normal brain images.

- Learning disability like learning difficulty, cognitive impairment, educational challenge like problem solving skills reduced, developmental delay such severity can arise.
- Neuronal damages like unnecessary confusions, blurry vision, difficult to concentrate, sudden emotions like crying, laughing etc. may lead to sever imbalance in one's life.
- Balancing related Issues like imbalance while walking, prone to falling, symptom of physical injuries like wound, harm on the body, trauma also a severity.
- Depressed and anxiety like feeling sad, mood swings, drowsiness, head aches, pains etc.
- Extreme end can be aggressive behavior which can be severe in final stage of the symptom

**Humans with Parkinson's Disease Presence Detection Factors:** The report generated by taking the Parkinson's dataset which is classified as invasive and noninvasive, the core essentials is early detection in disorder.

- When found invasive BCI the DBS electrodes that is small wire implanted in the brain during surgical procedure to treat tumor and movement disorder. It measures the MRI scan dataset of electrical brain activity of progress. This early detection of elongated ridges on the floor of each lateral ventricle of the brain with respect to emotions, memory loss and

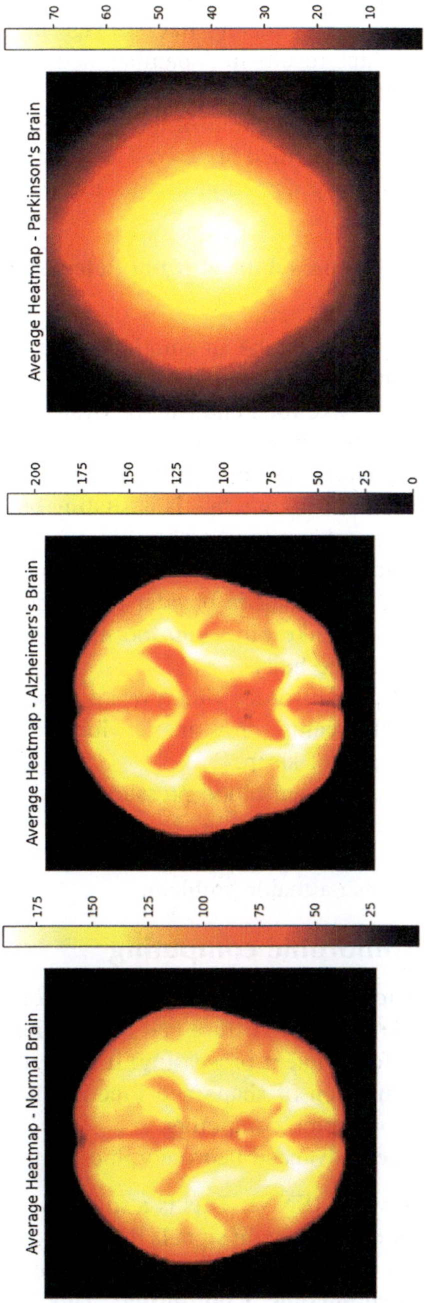


**FIGURE 2.15** Heatmap of normal, Alzheimer and Parkinson's.

nervous system affected can be diagnosed at this stage itself. It also measures the brain activity and detects the structural changes. The early detection reduces many risk factors like damage in the substantia nigra region of the brain which results in dopamine, neurotransmitter movement control imbalance all these can be overcome by early detection.
- Noninvasive BCI the motor functions of the brain like tremors, rigidity and slow movement can be identified at early. The complete imbalance in life can be found out by early detection of this disease which would affect complete human life.

**Risk Factors of Parkinson's dataset if not detected at early as Invasive and Noninvasive BCI:**

- Mental health problems: It can be an emotional imbalance like depression or anxiety which can affect their personal life.
- Food intake imbalance: like food chewing or swallowing which can be the next stage of the symptom where food and saliva collect in mouth hen to the throat which can choke the food in the throat itself.
- Speaking difficulty like monotone that is hesitating before speaking that is they may slur while speaking.
- Constipation or urinary problems may arise like it's not in control with functionalities which may result in bladder problems.
- Skin problems may arise like oily skin, too much dandruff, skin dryness and excess sweating in the body.
- Insomnia that is sleeping disorder which result in sleepless nights, nightmares and emotional dreams, drowsiness which can disturb their days without required amount of sleep.
- Hypertension due to increased blood pressure which may result in dizziness and fainting.
- Muscle related issues like muscle cramps, inability to move legs and muscle contractions also a major problem.

## 4. Advanced neuromorphic computing

Advanced Neuromorphic Computing is the latest technology which is mainly designed to analyses the dataset structure and its functionalities to create the hardware and software for efficient processing. It is the basic building blocks of the brain and the extraction of shape and functionalities. There are many types of advanced neuromorphic computing.

The architecture based advanced neuromorphic computing are:

a. **Spiking Neural Network (SNN):** This is a spike based processing system for the processing of efficient brain signals through scanned dataset. In BCI the use of spiking is done through brain signal dataset for classification.
b. **Event Driven Neuromorphic Computing:** This is an instance based processing when only the new neuro signal is been detected then the action

takes place. In BCI the use of event driven neuromorphic computing is implemented through neural implantation for communication through wearable BCI.

The hardware based advanced neuromorphic computing are:

a. **Neuromorphic chips:** It is a neural computing chip used for BCI, it is a computer chip to capture the mimic structures and the functionalities of the brain through MRI scan datasets. It uses Artificial Intelligence to generate artificial neurons that process the information to enable BCI. These are like traditional CPU, but they process the data in high speed as they decode signals instantly for processing, simultaneous processing of many neural signals to improve efficiency and low power consumption are implemented via BCI and most promisingly it works only when only needed. In BCI to classify invasive and non-invasive we use neuromorphic chips to process electrical brain activity EEG using SNN and other hardware neural networks. There are three types of neuromorphic chips
   1. **Digital neuromorphic chips:** This is the advanced technology which has the access to nodes and its behavior. This unlatches digital circuits with the behavior of neurons to consider for processing the data about how brain works by generating digital signals. It can also handle many calculations about brain's process.
   2. **Analog neuromorphic chips:** This is a computer chip which also unlatches minute structure and functionality of the brain to fetch the information. It processes the brain signals into analog electrical signals which can be used for decision making, these chip is based on input data read as binary value 0's and 1's for fast response on complex data signals. Only scalability is a issue with analog chips.
   3. **Mixed neuromorphic chip:** It is a combination of analog and digital chips implementation. It unlatches the complex functionalities of neurons for processing the signals. It does continuous signal representation and perform required logic operations with a single chip by which the performance is remarked as low power consumption takes place. This is an efficient utilization of both analog and digital processing.

## 5. Applications of brain computer interface

The Brain-Computer Interface is diversely used in many applications, to broadly classify in the field of medicine, communication aids, monitoring brain activities in health care, to moderate pain perception, brain controlling games, concentration enhancement training, marketing interest calculations and many more (Fig. 2.16).

**Medicine Field:** BCI technology is used mainly to treat diseases like Alzheimer, Parkinson's etc by extracting the data signals from the brain,

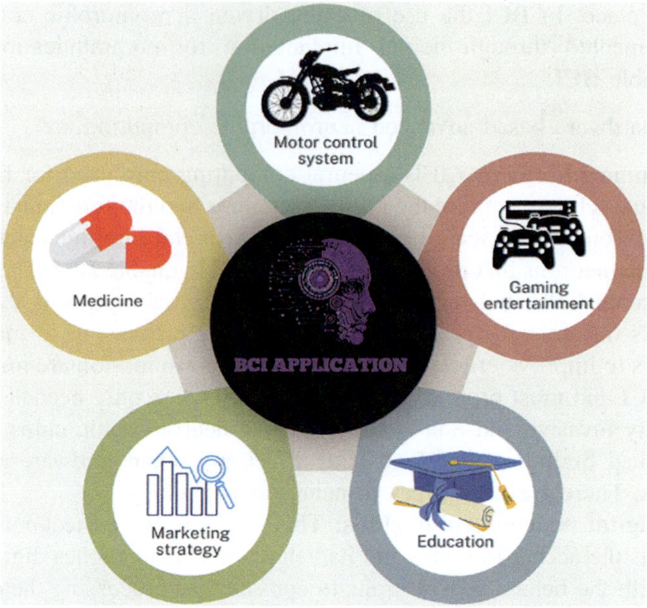


FIGURE 2.16 Applications of brain computer interface.

analyze them and converting them into commands for external devices to perform the desired operation. It is also used in the dialysis of seizure and brain malignancies, epilepsy, brain tumor, sleep apnea and disorder of consciousness.

It is also used to overlay the communication gap of paralyzed patients by acquiring brain signals and convert it into words, it is used as assistive device for these patients, wheel chair navigation control automatically with also natural language modeling. By implementing ANN to convert text to speech by using a software both ways can be modeled.

Neurofeedback also treats brain activity through the use of feedback, reward using CNS, most often used in neurology systems the way of self-regulation. Also used to treat depression, emotions, anxiety and so on.

**Motor control systems:** In Robotic limbs which consists of mechanical arms and legs to perform human based functionalities. They are mainly used an artificial body part which help human to perform daily activities. It's mainly used in motor imaginary BCI and EEG BCI smart home also.

Robotic prosthetic limbs to treat cancer, diabetics, birth defect or any sort of infection can be regained by people to walk, climb and many other movement related operations.

Robotic artificial arms which are programmed and used in complex robots, it consists of joints for motion operations.

By using motor control in motor imagery which is utilizing tools to enhance the motor recovery in stroke patients by detection of sensor motor vibes that are associated with motor imagery.

**Gaming Entertainment:** BCI has helped so diversely that the disability persons can also play game using this technology which also revolutionize gaming. It creates very dynamic experience of gaming via virtual environment creation by fetches brain signals by just thinking of any particular action it takes place and creates new ideas of gaming mechanisms by chances of developers to generate new ideas and creation of new experiences.

Gaming is a kind of mental health therapy and training the brain to think by interactive applications by adoptive cognitive states of players which changes the levels in the game based on brain signals generated this improves player's energy and motivation to continue the game.

**Education:** By the training using neurofeedback through the movement of eyes to boost attention and memory. This enables learning structure in the brain to be tuned and also the task of repeated training is reduced because user captures the brain signals and perform the task. The learning process can be advanced by making collaborative learning with games or other interactive strategies. All this is achieved via training through the input obtained by brain signals.

**Marketing strategy:** The interaction between brain signals and external devices enable marketing tasks to be carried out smoothly and efficiently in the following ways.

Based on customer's thoughts and emotions which are analyzed by brain signals the message or advertisement is sent to those interested customers of that particular product. The brain chips enable to identify the customer's interest which is profitable to both sellers and customers without wasting anyone's time.

During the making of advertisements the functionalities to be included in that product is analyzed by these brain signals which is obtained by integrating BCI technology by collecting reported data for best way of marketing. The brain chip provides more accurate and exact product interests. There is also ethical way of selling products with transparency, offer and security which enhances healthy marketing.

The collection of customers feedback analyzed through brain chips helps sellers also to provide campaigning in the society. This connects brands with customers for long term branding and connection in the market.

## 6. Limitations of brain computer interface

1. **Reliability:** The BCI signal processing is the main criteria of analysis but the quality of signal is not having good magnification. In the two categories of invasive and non-invasive, the invasive BCI provides accurate signals but sometimes provides constitutes high risk and damage which

may not be precise. In non-invasive BCI the signal quality is low compared to invasive BCI as there is noise and external inferences.

2. **Signal Strength:** The signal quality is identified by electrodes generated from the brain tissues by using sensors on the skin. In invasive BCI the brain signal interpretation is not accurate much as it is difficult to find signals accurately. In non-invasive BCI are safe and easy to use but it generates the low signal quality and also higher risk of infections. These limitations need to be addressed by incorporating advanced algorithms in the software and hardware.
3. **Training Required:** The Signals generated by the brain pattern can only be correct when there is a proper usage of BCI. This limitation is addressed by providing the training of BCI usage and collaboration with invasive and non-invasive brain signals generated. The end user needs to be trained to operate and control the device efficiently as BCI requires lot of concentration and attention to learn and use modulation of brain activity as per BCI commands. During this process of training there is a possibility that users become exhausted by learning the process which is complex, so the need of enhanced training process along with expertise giving training as per requirement of end users features, intuition and inferences need to be incorporated.
4. **Moral Dilemma:** The need of privacy, security and authentication is equally important as its someone's confidential data. The patients consent need to be taken to do any action with his data, these data are patients' emotions, thoughts and memory related content which need to be secured. If this data is hacked or leaked may be misused which ISD at high risk. To address this limitation BCI need to ensure that high security is given to these data and also be very transparent to the patient to be a trusted notion of privacy through some agencies, autonomy or identity secured way.
5. **Societal Effects:** The social consequence, impact on the society action or event also on the relationship or communication with the society like injustice, in equality or level of treatment. All this form a huge impact on the society and the individual. This limitation can also be addressed by BCI through generation of expressions in new ways, communication in more interactive way which lead to collaboration, understanding and form a way to happiness to the individual's life (Fig. 2.17).

## 7. Future scope of brain computer interface

There are limitations of BCI but still BCI is a leading technology to address n number of issues with respect to brain human life. There is huge scope for improvement. BCI is been used in boom with many underdisciplined areas like research, healthcare, engineering and many more areas of scope enhanced. The advanced technologies like advanced algorithms, signal quality and latest techno systems usage. The new ideas and frameworks need to be developed for

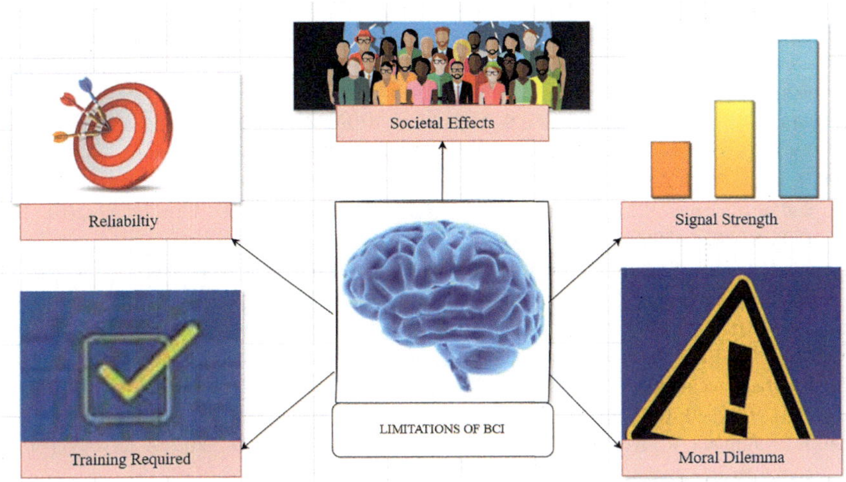


**FIGURE 2.17** Limitations of BCI.

new innovations for advancement. The clinical advancement is major with respect to memory gaining, stroke patient's daily activities devices, brain disease finding in advanced way to cure before stages cross, educating with BCI in different areas, animal mind reading techniques etc.

Exploring new applications and domain like medical area, education, entertainment and scientific explosion to new discoveries. BCI is capable of innovating a new era of human machine interaction through a design of best framework with lot if consideration and society concern.

## Further reading

Ajmeria, R., et al., 2023. A critical survey of EEG-based BCI systems for applications in industrial internet of things. IEEE Commun. Surv. Tutor. 25 (1), 184–212.

Alkaff, Z.A., Malim, N.H.A.H., Sumari, P., Abdullah, J.M., 2024. Applications of Brain Computer Interface in Present Healthcare Setting. Artificial Intelligence, IntechOpen. Dec. 11.

Bates, M., Sunderam, S., 2023. Hand-worn devices for assessment and rehabilitation of motor function and their potential use in BCI protocols: a review. Front. Hum. Neurosci. 17, 1121481.

Faruk, M.J.H., Valero, M., Shahriar, H., 2022. An investigation on non-invasive brain-computer interfaces: Emotiv Epoc+ neuroheadset and its effectiveness. arXiv preprint arXiv:2207.06914.

Gonzalez-Astudillo, J., Cattai, T., Bassignana, G., Corsi, M.-C., De Vico Fallani, F., 2020. Network-based brain computer interfaces: principles and applications. arXiv preprint arXiv:2006.13187.

Gu, X., et al., 2021. EEG-based brain-computer interfaces (BCIs): a survey of recent studies on signal sensing technologies and computational intelligence approaches and their applications. IEEE ACM Trans. Comput. Biol. Bioinf 18 (5), 1645–1666. https://doi.org/10.1109/TCBB.2021.3052811.

Gu, X., Cao, Z., Jolfaei, A., Xu, P., Wu, D., Jung, T.-P., Lin, C.-T., 2020. EEG-based brain-computer interfaces (BCIs): a survey of recent studies on signal sensing technologies and computational intelligence approaches and their applications. arXiv preprint arXiv:2001.11337.

Hossain, K.M., Islam, M.A., Hossain, S., Nijholt, A., Ahad, M.A.R., 2023. Status of deep learning for EEG-based brain–computer interface applications. Front. Comput. Neurosci. 16, 1006763.

Hu, H., et al., 2025. A survey on brain-computer interface-inspired communications: opportunities and challenges. IEEE Commun. Surv. Tutor. 27 (1), 108–139. https://doi.org/10.1109/COMST.2024.3396847.

Hwang, H.J., Kim, S., Choi, S., Im, C.H., 2013. EEG-based brain-computer interfaces: a thorough literature survey. Int. J. Hum. Comput. Interact. 29 (12), 814–826. https://doi.org/10.1080/10447318.2013.780869.

Mason, S.G., Bashashati, A., Fatourechi, M., et al., 2007. A comprehensive survey of brain interface technology designs. Ann. Biomed. Eng. 35, 137–169. https://doi.org/10.1007/s10439-006-9170-0.

Pai, K., Kallimani, R., Iyer, S., Maheswari, B.U., Khanai, R., Torse, D., 2022. A survey on brain-computer interface and related applications. arXiv preprint arXiv:2203.09164.

Robinson, N., Mane, R., Chouhan, T., Guan, C., 2021. Emerging trends in BCI-robotics for motor control and rehabilitation. Curr. Opin. Biomed. Eng. 20, 100354.

Saibene, A., Caglioni, M., Corchs, S., Gasparini, F., 2023. EEG-based BCIs on motor imagery paradigm using wearable technologies: a systematic review. Sensors 23 (5), 2798.

Värbu, K., Muhammad, N., Muhammad, Y., 2022. Past, present, and future of EEG-based BCI applications. Sensors 22 (9), 3331.

Yadav, H., Maini, S., 2023. Electroencephalogram based brain-computer interface: applications, challenges, and opportunities. Multimed. Tool. Appl.

Chapter 3

# Neuromorphic algorithms

**Sellappan Mohana Saranya[1], M.R. Prasanndh Raaju[1], R. Karunamoorthi[2], R. Mohemmed Yousuf[3], R. Prabavathi[4] and T. Suganya[5]**

[1]*Department of CSE, Kongu Engineering College, Erode, Tamil Nadu, India;* [2]*Department of CSE, Sri Krishna College of Engineering and Technology, Coimbatore, Tamil Nadu, India;* [3]*Department of IT, Bannari Amman Institute of Technology, Sathyamangalam, Tamil Nadu, India;* [4]*Department of Information Technology, Sri Sai Ram Institute of Technology, Chennai, Tamil Nadu, India;* [5]*Department of AI&DS, KGiSL Institute of Technology, Department of Computer Science and Engineering MCKV Institute of Engineering, CSE, Coimbatore, Tamil Nadu, India*

## 1. Introduction

Larger and more complex models that need a huge amount of computing power have been produced because of the exponential growth of Artificial Intelligence (AI) and Machine Learning (ML). Neural morphology computing, which is inspired by how the human brain works, has become a big breakthrough. Traditional computer designs are struggling to keep up with these new demands, especially when it comes to using energy and scaling up factors efficiently.

Neuromorph algorithm emulates neuronal principles such as event control processing, spike-based communication, plastic synapses, and adaptive learning. In contrast to traditional computing paradigms, these algorithms work through SNNs and other biologically inspired models to replicate the energy efficiency, robustness, and learning capabilities of biological systems. These qualities position neural morphic computing as a key architecture for future AI applications, particularly in resource-related environments such as edge devices and autonomous systems. The realm of neuromorphic computers includes algorithmic innovation and hardware development, covering a wide range of application domains, ranging from brain-machine interfaces to sensor processing and edge intelligence. A major challenge that hinders progress is the lack of a standardized and widely recognized benchmark framework. The different implementation strategies and the lack of a formal definition of "neuromorphology" solutions make it difficult to objectively evaluate and compare different approaches. This hinders the ability of the community to

**Neuromorphic Computing for Brain Computer Interfaces. https://doi.org/10.1016/B978-0-443-41594-4.00002-2**

measure performance improvements, lead research directions, and verify technological advances over traditional AI technologies.

To improve this gap, modern initiatives such as Neurobench aim to establish integrated task-based benchmarking methods that take into account the large variations in the nervous system. Designed by a collaborative community of researchers across science and industry, Neurobench proposes a uniform framework with structured metric definitions, hardware-independent reviews, and open-source benchmarking tools. Such efforts are important to align the fields with common performance standards and to promote repeatable and scalable progress (Yik et al., 2025). This chapter deals with the basic principles of neural morphology algorithms and examines biological inspiration, arithmetic models, and learning paradigms. In addition, current challenges in the field, the need for benchmark-controlled development, and the future direction of neural morphology AI bridge the gap between biological intelligence and constructed computing systems.

## 2. Core principles of neuromorphic algorithms

The neuromorphs algorithm is fundamentally different from traditional AI models in terms of processing, learning, and adaptation methods. Rooted in neuroscience, these algorithms are designed to mimic operational principles of the human brain. In contrast to traditional deep learning methods based on dense matrix manipulation and synchronized clock cycles, the neural morphological approach emphasizes sparse, event-oriented, energy-efficient calculations. If AI system' requirements continue to grow, neural algorithms will be bid for ways to improve performance, scalable intelligent computers, especially in limited and real-time applications.

### 2.1 Key characteristics of neuromorphic algorithms

The neuromorphs algorithm shows some defining features that make it clear and efficient. First, we use a Spike-Neural Networks (SNNs) model in which neurons communicate through discrete and accurate spikes. These spikes are sparse and asynchronous, significantly reducing energy consumption compared to traditional Artificial Neuronal Networks (ANNs). Furthermore, these algorithms facilitate the colocation of memory and processing. In other words, biological neurons are processed and stored in synapses. This memory-centric approach minimizes the data movement bottleneck that often occurs in Neumann architectures. Another important feature is asynchronous, large parallel finish. Each neuron works independently and handles events instead of waiting for global synchronization. This allows for real-time response capabilities, making neural morphology algorithms highly suitable for latent tasks.

In addition, neural learning mechanisms include adaptive plasticity rules such as Savian learning and Spike Timing-Dependent Plasticity (STDP). This allows the system to organize itself and learn with time pattern data. These adaptive features lead to improved generalization through limited data. This means that algorithms in low-resource environments are efficient. Fig. 3.1 shows a conceptual illustration that depicts the SNN-based architecture showing spiking neurons, integrated memory-processing units, and asynchronous pathways, contrasting with a typical ANN pipeline. Arrows could highlight parallelism, energy-saving features, and event-triggered activity.

## 2.2 Biological inspiration

The basis of neural morphology algorithms lies in the structure and function of the human brain. At the core, try replicating important aspects of biological neuronal networks, such as these algorithms, neuronal behavior, synapses, and

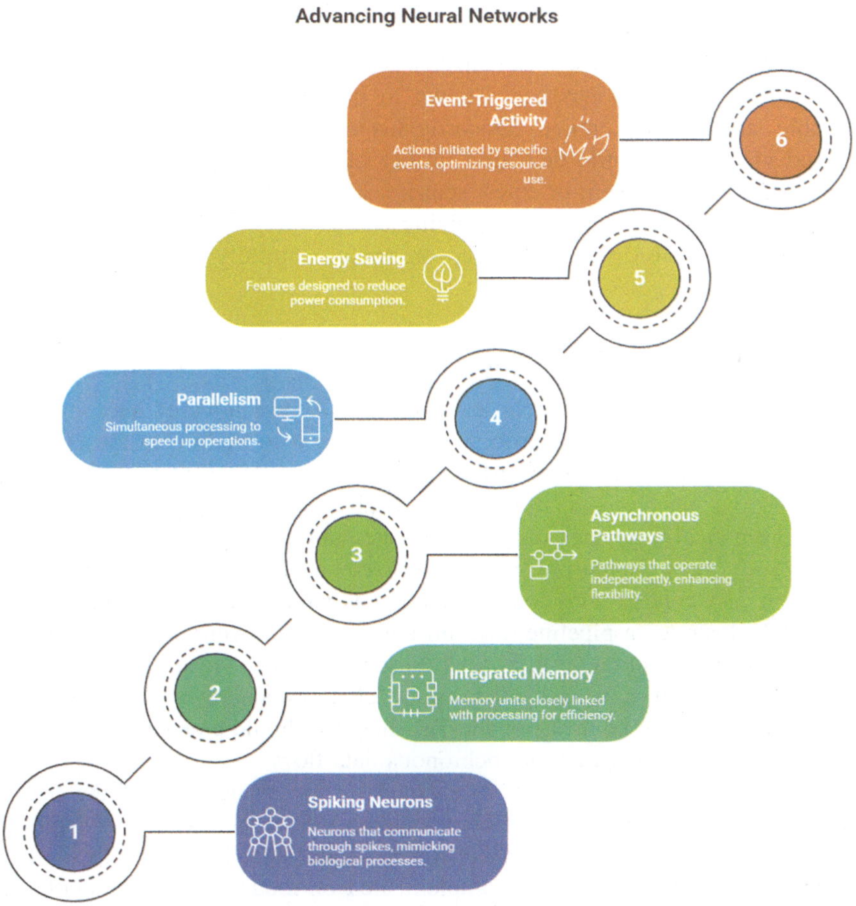


**FIGURE 3.1** SNN architecture.

temporal dynamics of signal processing. Neuronal models such as Leak Angle Integration (LIF), Izhikevich, and Hodgkin-Huxley equations simulate the dynamics of the neural membrane with different biological accuracy and computational efficiency. These models help to record the nature of biological signaling based on spikes. This is extremely important for the real-time processing of sensory information. In addition to the dynamical addition of neural neurons, synaptic plasticity is an important source of biological inspiration. Mechanisms such as STDP allow unattended learning by altering the strength of connections based on the relative time of pre- and postsynaptic spikes. This time sensitivity can allow for recognition of nervous system systems, correlations, and causal relationships in the inlet flow.

Furthermore, phenomena such as Spike Frequency Adaptation (SFA)—this caused neurons to reduce fire rates in response to sustained inputs, but has recently been integrated into neural morphology models to improve energy efficiency and adaptability. The most recent research also examines stochastic and stochastic neural coding and how biological systems function under uncertainty. These mechanisms inadvertently introduce neuronal or synaptic levels. This has been shown to improve learning robustness and enable stochastic inference. Sensorily inspired applications such as event-based vision and tactile detection further highlight the benefits of organic-inspired designs. Event-oriented sensors such as Dynamic Vision Sensors (DVS) mimic the retina by recognizing changes in brightness and allowing for efficient vision pipelines based on spikes naturally integrated into the SNN (Wei et al., 2024).

## 2.3 Event driven—Processing

One of the most unmistakable transformational principles of neuromorphic algorithms is event control processing. In contrast to traditional systems that calculate at fixed intervals regardless of incoming calls, event control systems only respond when meaningful events typically occur when a spike is received. This dramatically reduces unnecessary calculations and power consumption. As a result, the neuromorphic system may remain calm. In other words, highly efficient and context-conscious computing is suitable for low-level devices. Fig. 3.2 illustrates a pipeline diagram that shows an event-driven processing system, starting from an event-based sensor (e.g., DVS) feeding into an SNN layer, where spikes trigger neural state changes and eventually influence decision-making or control signals. The diagram should emphasize the sparse activation, low latency, and asynchronous data flow.

Events—control processing is enabled by the asynchrony of the neuromorphic network. Each neuron or processing unit responds independently to the spikes, eliminating the need for a synchronized global clock. This approach has been successfully implemented on modern hardware platforms such as Intel Loihi and Spinnaker2, which support the handling and learning of

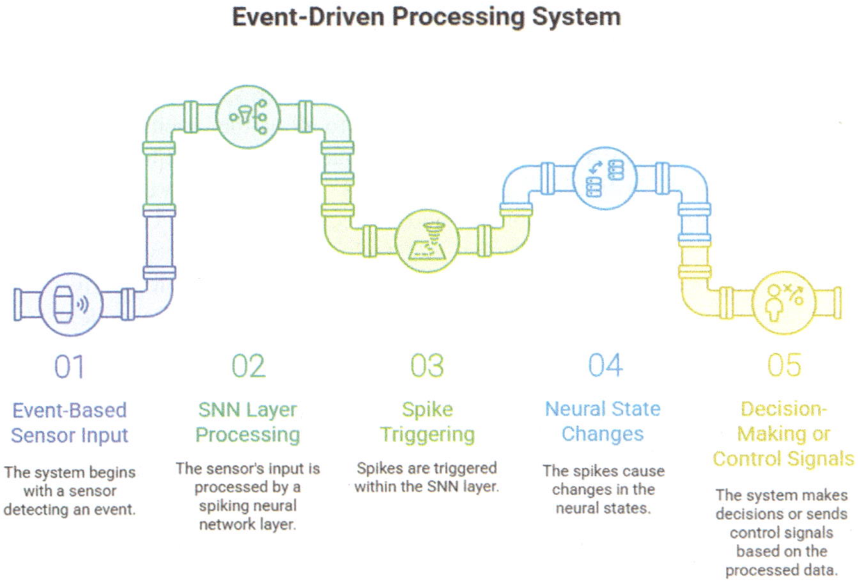


**FIGURE 3.2** Event—driven processing system.

real-time asynchronous events (Jiang et al., 2025). These architectures allow for large-scale use of SNNs that can perform inference and adaptation in real-world environments. From a learning perspective, new algorithms have been introduced, such as spike timing-dependent event control (STD-ED) and membrane voltage-dependent event control (MPD-ED) training methods. These methods use precise timing and membrane dynamics of neurons to allow on-chip learning of energy consumption compared to up to 30x exchange rate techniques. This innovation allows the neural chip to use the SNNs to be learned directly, paving the way for an autonomous and adaptive edge system.

## 3. Neuromorphic algorithmic frameworks

Neuromorphic algorithmic frameworks constitute a paradigm shift from conventional computing strategies through replicating how the human mind learns, adapts, and makes decisions. These frameworks are advanced to leverage the organic performance of neural structures, especially via mastering mechanisms that perform with spiking neurons and synaptic plasticity. They propose to lessen electricity intake and enhance adaptability, scalability, and processing performance in real-time applications. The primary branches of learning explored in neuromorphic structures include supervised learning, unsupervised learning, and reinforcement learning, each offering distinct advantages depending on the task and the environment.

## 3.1 Supervised learning in neuromorphic systems

Supervised learning in neuromorphic structures includes education on SNNs, the use of categorized data, in which every input corresponds to a recognized output magnitude or value. The center goal is to allow the machine to research a dependable mapping among the inputs and outputs—just like how the human mind paperwork institutions among sensory reports and predicted consequences through repeated publicity and corrective feedback. Unlike conventional deep gaining knowledge of techniques that rely closely on backpropagation, neuromorphic fashions lean on greater biologically viable gaining knowledge of mechanisms, including Spike Timing Dependent Plasticity (STDP). In supervised settings, STDP frequently prolongs the use of praise signals—main to versions such as reward-modulated STDP or tailor-made gaining knowledge of regulations, just like the tempotron, which adjusts synaptic weights to beautify the spiking output for proper classifications.

A distinguished improvement in this area is the e-prop algorithm, which allows gradient-based supervised gaining knowledge of in spiking networks without the need for backpropagation through time. This makes it exceptionally like-minded with neuromorphic hardware platforms, which commonly have constraints on reminiscence and computation (Schmidgall et al., 2024). The Intel Loihi chip, for instance, helps on-chip gaining knowledge of with excessive parallelism and low energy consumption, permitting real-time gaining knowledge of in part gadgets and embedded applications. Fig. 3.3 shows a conceptual flow of supervised learning in SNNs. The network receives labeled input, processes spikes through interconnected neurons, and adjusts synaptic weights using STDP in conjunction with external feedback (e.g., reward signal or expected output class).

## 3.2 Unsupervised learning approaches

Unsupervised learning of neural systems is inspired by the brain's innate ability to recognize regularity and patterns from raw sensory inputs without external surveillance or marked data. Such learning mimics the development process observed in early sensory cortex, where organisms classify inputs in a natural way and construct internal representations of the environment through exposure. In the context of neural morphology, this learning is usually achieved using mechanisms such as Hebbian learning, learning competition, and Self-Organizing Maps (SOM). STDP plays a fundamental role in this. STDP allows synaptic intensity to be dynamically adapted based on temporal correlations of presynaptic and postsynaptic spikes.

Over time, this process leads to distinctive detectors, as well as the receptive fields of biological sensory systems that are tailored to recognize patterns such as edges, directions, or frequencies. Unless you learn with a neural form of hardware, platforms such as BrainScales and Spinnaker present

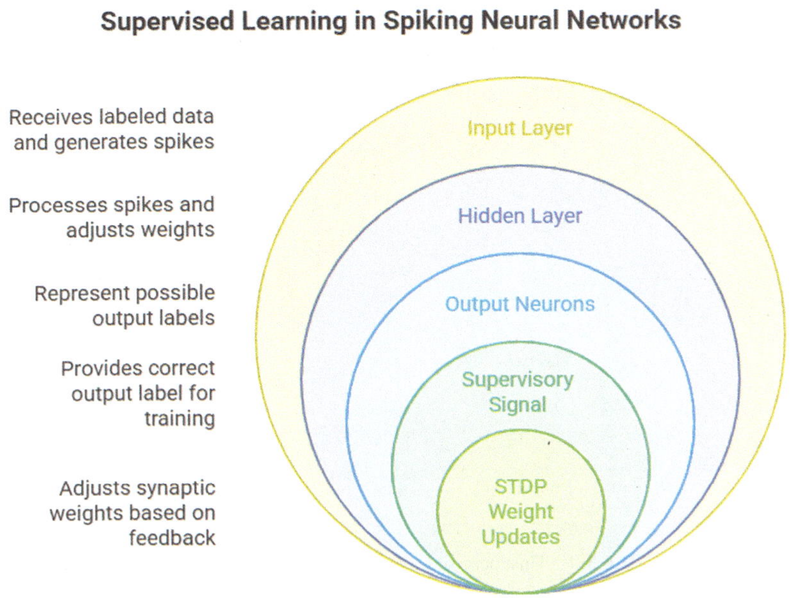


**FIGURE 3.3** Supervised learning in spiking neural networks.

real implementations. These systems can perform tasks such as clustering input data, anomaly detection, and associative memory calls with high energy efficiency and real-time capabilities. These results enhance the suitability of event-oriented unmanned models for scalable, adaptive, and biologically oriented AI. Fig. 3.4 depicts the unsupervised learning in an SNN using STDP. The system receives spike-encoded sensory inputs, and through temporal learning rules, neurons in hidden layers specialize to detect frequently occurring features in the data. No external labels are used in the training process.

## 3.3 Reinforcement learning and decision-making

Learning to strengthen neural variation systems (RL) demonstrates a biologically sound learning approach through interaction. In this approach, SNNs are related patterns of neural activity with reward or punishment to optimize targeted behavior. In contrast to monitoring that relies on explicitly marked outputs, RL uses scalar reward signals to form the agent's decision process over time. This makes it particularly advantageous for scenarios that require adaptive control, such as robotics, navigation, and real-time determination under uncertain or dynamic conditions. The neuromorphic RL system is based on the concept of neuroregulation and reflects the use of dopamine pathways through the brain to modulate learning based on reward prediction.

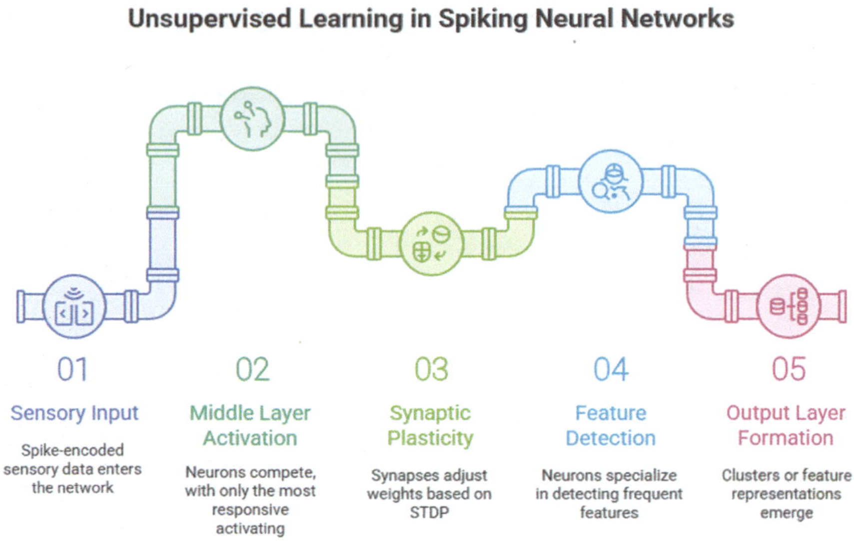


**FIGURE 3.4** Unsupervised learning in spiking neural networks.

Algorithms such as Reward-modulated Spike Timing-Dependent Plasticity (R-STDP) allow synapses to adapt their strength when the spikes are correlated with valuable events. This mechanism promotes loans over time and promotes network layers. Neromorphic simulation chips, such as NEST-RL, Intel Loihi, and Brain-Inspired Neuromorphic Architecture (BINA) implement these learning rules to achieve low performance and low-latency learning directly on hardware. As discussed in the DARPA synaptic project, the actual demonstration highlights the potential of neural morphology RL in embedded autonomic systems. These systems have learned to navigate the environment and control robot members or optimize the energy consumption of distributed sensor networks (Davies et al., 2021). The ability to learn with energy-efficient, online, and real-time manners underscores your commitment to industrial Internet of Things (IoT), edge intelligence, and defense applications. Fig. 3.5 shows reinforcement learning in an SNN-based neuromorphic system. Sensory input triggers spiking activity in the neural network. A critic module (reward generator) evaluates the outcome and delivers a modulatory reward signal, influencing synaptic weight changes via R-STDP. The result is an evolving policy that enhances performance in a dynamic task environment.

## 4. Neuromorphic algorithms for brain-computer interfaces

Neuromorphic computing is revolutionizing BCIs via way of means of imparting energy-efficient, low-latency, and brain-stimulated fashions that mimic the computational techniques of the organic brain. These structures

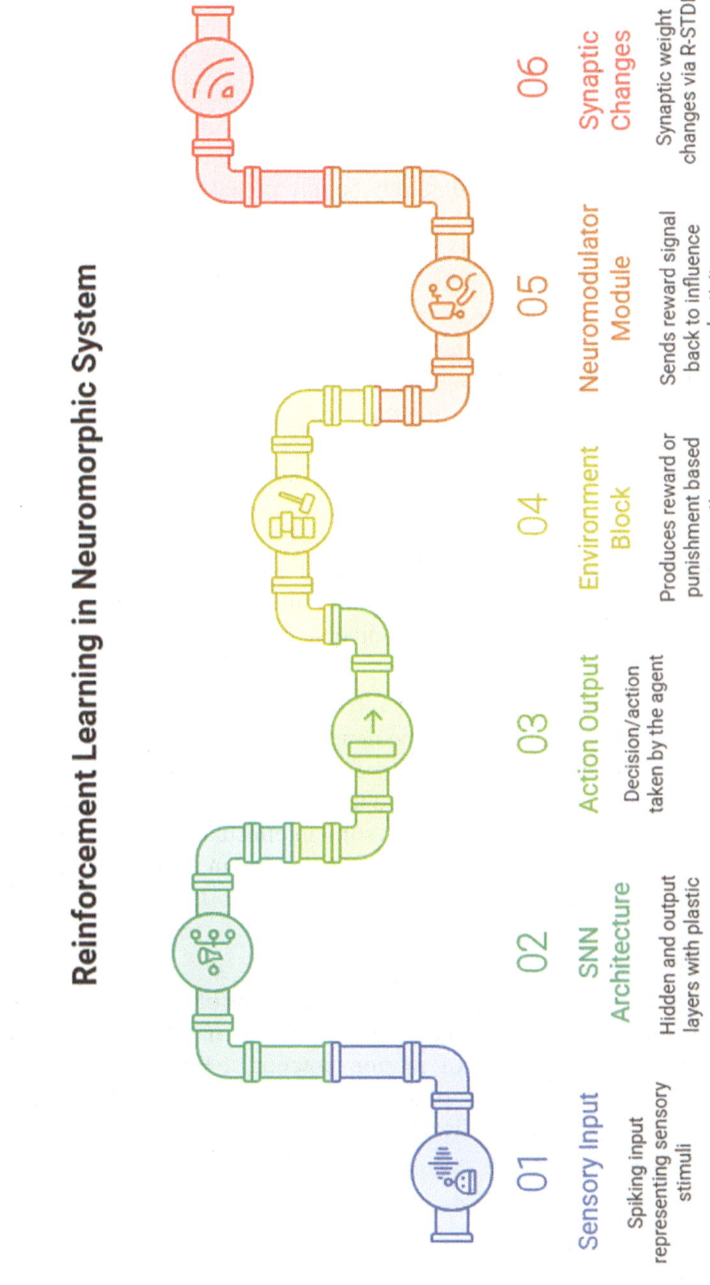


**FIGURE 3.5** Reinforcement learning in neuromorphic system.

leverage SNNs and event-pushed architectures to interpret neural alerts for programs starting from scientific prosthetics to cognitive enhancement.

## 4.1 Signal processing for BCIs

Signal processing in BCIs includes changing uncooked neural indicators—-which include Electroencephalography (EEG), Electrocorticography (ECoG), Magnetoencephalography (MEG), or intracortical recordings—right into a established and significant layout that may be interpreted via way of means of system mastering algorithms. The conventional pipeline for sign processing consists of noise filtering, function extraction, dimensionality reduction, and classification. However, those traditional methods (e.g., Fast Fourier Transform [FFT], Principal Component Analysis [PCA], Independent Component Analysis [ICA]) are regularly computationally intensive, power-demanding, and incorrect for real time, transportable BCI structures. Neuromorphic computing gives a paradigm shift in sign processing for BCIs. These mind-stimulated algorithms and hardware architectures allow event-driven, asynchronous, and low-electricity processing of neural information, aligning intently with the real-time needs and electricity constraints of wearable or implantable BCI structures.

**Neuromorphic signal encoding techniques:** To make neural information well matched with SNNs, neuromorphic structures convert nonstop analog indicators into spike trains, the usage of diverse encoding schemes:

### *4.1.1 Temporal coding*

This approach maps the amplitude of the neural signal to the timing of spikes. A better sign amplitude results in advanced spike generation. This time-to-first-spike encoding facilitates keeping the temporal decision of mind pastime, which is crucial for interpreting fast-converting intellectual states. Example: In an EEG-based interest detection task, spikes are caused in advance while alpha wave amplitudes are high, reflecting targeted cognitive states.

### *4.1.2 Rate coding*

Rate coding represents the sign depth via way of means of the firing charge of spikes over a time window. It mimics organic neurons in which the facts are embedded within the frequency of motion potentials. Example: The Loihi neuromorphic processor, via way of means of Intel, has carried out charge coding for processing neural indicators in transportable BCI structures for motor imagery tasks.

### *4.1.3 Neuromorphic filters*

Inspired via way of means of the organic cochlea and retinal layers, neuromorphic hardware regularly consists of analog band-pass filters carried out in silicon to eliminate noise and enhance applicable mind pastime which include P300 or mu-rhythms. These filters perform within the analog domain, significantly lowering power intake as compared to virtual filters. Example: Dynamic Neuromorphic Asynchronous Processor (DYNAP-SE) applies neuromorphic filtering for spike-based BCI sign preprocessing, assisting ultra-low latency packages in prosthetic control.

#### 4.1.3.1 Real-world application: The NeuroGrid system

One of the most promising real-world examples is the NeuroGrid gadget advanced at Stanford University. It makes use of ultra-flexible, conformable electrode arrays to report high-resolution cortical indicators and, at once, convert them into spike trains. These spike styles are processed via means of downstream SNNs carried out on neuromorphic chips to detect epileptic seizures in rodents (Wisniewski et al., 2025).

## 4.2 Pattern recognition

Neuromorphs BCIS uses adaptive dynamics of the SNNs to recognize cognitive or motor magnification patterns. These networks combine unattended mechanisms such as STDP and Hebbian learning with monitored approaches such as reward-modulated STDP, tempotron learning, and e-prop to classify spike-encoded neuronal data. Winner-take-all (WTA) or competitive circuits will further refine the representation and convey clarity and savings in decoding the result.

### *4.2.1 Real-world example: Intel Loihi*

Intel's Loihi Chip for imaginary hand movement was a pioneer in the delivery of SNN-based BCIS. Researchers have implemented STDP-controlled Hebbian learning to decode imaginary hand movements from the EEG and achieve an impressive accuracy of about 97% classification. This allows for actual control of the robot arm with very low latency and power consumption. This demonstrates the practical living ability of neural morphological pattern recognition in BCIS (Manna, 2025).

A new breakthrough in multiscale fusion SNN (MFSNN). This architecture uses brain parallelism and multiscale feature integration to decode motor neuron signals from rhesus monkey makers. The most important technical features include: Temporal Folding Networks (TCNS) and channel composite attention modules that extract spatial features in different granularities. Skip connections, enable robust fusion, and improve cross-day generalization. Minibatch monitored generalization and improved deciphering stability throughout the session.

For benchmark tasks such as single-hand grasp-and-touch and center-and-out reach, MFSNN surpassed traditional Multi-Layer Perceptron (MLP) and

GRUs in both accuracy and energy efficiency. It is important that the design is optimized for neural morphology chip production and provide low performance real-time decoding for invasive BCIS.

## 4.3 Real-time neuromorphic decoding

One of the most important limitations of the traditional BCIs is latency. The time delay occurs when brain signals are generated, and the corresponding machine actions are performed. Such delays can affect the user experience, particularly in dynamic tasks such as prosthesis control, robot navigation, and communication interfaces. The neural variation system deals with this limitation by mimicking the event-oriented and asynchronous processing styles of the organic brain. Instead of processing yourself in separate batches or relying on heavy data buffers, neural morphological architectures react to the spikes that occur, allowing for additional low-shops, real-time decoding. Neuromorph chips such as Intel Loihi support the plasticity of the ability to learn and adapt through biologically inspired learning rules, such as reward-modified STDP, at realistic times. This allows BCIS to personalize itself to each user's neuronal activity in the fly process without having to perform offline recordings or manual adjustments. Learning online is especially valuable for adapting to signal drift over time and changing the mental strategies of users.

Neuromorpher BCIS shines with a closed system. Continuous feedback from this area dynamically adapts the decoding strategy. For example, the neuromorphic system can continuously modify commands of robotic prosthesis or wheelchair movement based on spike patterns and proprioceptive feedback, similar to how the human motor cortex changes to resistance or balance uses platforms such as Spinnaker (University of Manchester) to emulate large-scale cortical parallelism. Each core handles spike communication and calculations in parallel, reducing decoding times to less than a millisecond. This architecture allows for distributed real-time decoding across many neuronal populations simultaneously.

**Use in the real world:** Researchers at the University of Freiburg developed a robotic demonstration at the University of Freiburg, which was machined by the SNN neurotype. A BCI demonstration of prominent neural morphology, completely controlled with a real-time signal processed in real time. This system was not based on traditional batch training or marked data records. Instead, the spike decoder adapted continuously with unmanned plasticity. Users can navigate within the internal environment with minimal latency, such as curves and obstacle avoidance. The decoder has improved over time by learning directly from the user's intent and rewarding feedback without a full retraining cycle.

## 4.4 Cognitive enhancement

Neuromorphic BCIs extend into cognitive augmentation, not just restoring function but actively enhancing memory, attention, and decision-making.

**Memory prosthesis example**: In rodent and primate studies, hippocampal prosthetic systems that replay learned spike sequences have shown successful restoration of memory function. Emerging human studies aim to replicate this using neuromorphic devices to assist patients with memory deficits.

**Neurofeedback and AR use case**: Systems such as NextMind (now in AR/VR interaction platforms) decode visual attention-related cortex spikes in real time to allow users to interact with interfaces purely via intention.

**Integration with human digital twins**: A recent framework proposes SNN-driven federated learning for wearable BCI devices that maintain privacy while continuously adapting models on-device for personalized cognitive state recognition (Chandra et al., 2024).

## 5. Neuromorphic hardware and algorithm codesign

Neuromorphic hardware and algorithm codesign refers to the joint development of algorithms and silicon architectures to ensure optimal performance, energy efficiency, and real-time capabilities in SNN systems. Unlike traditional AI systems, where algorithms are often adapted post hoc to existing hardware (such as Graphics Processing Units (GPUs)), neuromorphic systems are developed from the ground up with biological inspiration, mimicking the coevolution of the brain and cognitive processes.

### 5.1 Compatibility with neuromorphic chips

The neuromorphs algorithm is meticulously designed to coincide with the structural and functional principles of neural morphological hardware platforms such as Intel Loihi, IBM TrueNorth, Brainscales, and Spinnaker. These chips are not designed by traditional Neumann processors. Instead, they mimic the architectural essence of the human brain, taking over distributed control, parallel computation, and asynchronous processing of events. In contrast to traditional systems that continuously process input data regardless of their relevance, neural variation chips perform calculations only when significant events (i.e., spikes) occur. This architecture allows neural variation chips to achieve ultra-low power consumption while maintaining low latency. It is ideal for embedded applications such as real-time portable BCIs and autonomous robotics. For these chips to work best, you need to configure an algorithm around a SNN. In neuronal models, spikes are created according to the threshold membrane potential. These spikes are used to code and spread information about the network—mimic biological neurons. In this paradigm, STDP and Hebbian learning are essential learning mechanisms. The overall efficient design system of a neuromorphic hardware is depicted through the flow diagram 5.1. For example, STDP adapts synaptic strength based on the exact timing between presynaptic and postsynaptic spikes. This local, time-sensitive adjustment method is particularly suitable for chips such as Loihi, which support on-chip and real-time learning through such mechanisms. In fact, this means that autonomous drones running on Loihi can learn from environmental information without cloud-based updates.

Furthermore, neural morphological hardware sets physical limitations. For example, in IBM TrueNorth, all neurosynap scores simulate 256 neurons and 256 × 256 synapses, but there are no floating point numbers for arithmetic and global memory approvals. Therefore neural morphology algorithms should be optimized for localized communications of sparse and avoid global synchronization or stack updates—both can paralyze performance. Algorithms that distribute calculations and memory through local neuronal clusters, such as foldable SNNs and reservoir computing, may be better under these limitations. For example, in Spinnaker, which simulates millions of spike neurons with thousands of arm cores, neural populations can communicate via light spike packages without intensive orchestration—a design that promotes biologically plausible processing of distribution. In total, effective attitudes rely on the ability to synchronize via the interaction of spike-based localized plastics, using the underlying hardware philosophy (Davies et al., 2018). This close connection between algorithms and chip design, often referred to as codesign of neural morphology, is not just an optimization strategy, but also a fundamental need to use the maximum potential of neuronal computers in real-world applications Fig. 3.6.

## 5.2 Energy efficiency and latency

Neuromorphic computing is a big step forward in enabling computers to achieve ultra-low power and low-latency performance. It does this much better than regular computers, especially in situations where power is limited or time

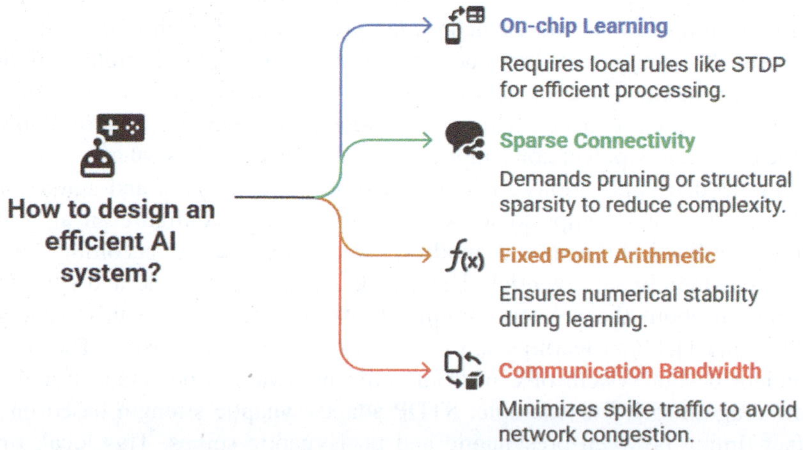


**FIGURE 3.6** Design of efficient neuromorphic hardware.

is critical. This kind of computing is useful in applications such as BCIs, robots, and self-driving systems, where quick reactions and energy efficiency are important. Neuromorphic systems work like the brain, which only uses energy when something happens, such as when neurons fire. Unlike traditional computers that use a continuous clock and keep running all the time, neuromorphic processors operate only when needed, saving a significant amount of power when they are idle.

For example, IBM's TrueNorth chip can simulate over a million neurons while consuming just 70 milliwatts of power. That is far more efficient than traditional GPUs, which may consume several watts for performing similar tasks. This efficiency comes from how neuromorphic systems process information—they only work when events (like spikes) occur, rather than operating continuously. Intel's Loihi processor also supports on-chip learning using special mechanisms, such as reward-modulated STDP, which enables the chip to adapt and learn directly without requiring external retraining (Davies et al., 2021).

When it comes to speed, systems such as Spinnaker are extremely fast because they contain a large number of small processors that work together in parallel. These processors communicate using small, timestamped data packets to handle neural spikes, enabling real-time responses. This feature is especially important for systems that need to make immediate decisions based on continuous incoming data—like controlling a robotic arm or a prosthetic limb. A real-world example is found in robots and drones that use neuromorphic sensors and processors. These systems process visual data by detecting changes in light and use that dynamic input to make flight decisions quickly. This approach allows them to operate on very low power while reacting in just a few milliseconds.

In another example, BCIs that utilize neuromorphic chips can decode brain signals—such as when a person imagines moving their hand or experiences a tactile sensation. This combination of low-power consumption and rapid responsiveness is particularly valuable in wearable or implantable devices, where managing heat and battery life is crucial.

## 6. Neuromorphic algorithms in practice and their challenges

Neuromorphic algorithms, which mimic the functioning of biological neural systems, have shown significant potential in domains such as pattern recognition, sequential event prediction, and control system management. These algorithms rely on concepts such as spiking neural networks, synaptic plasticity (the ability of connections between neurons to change strength), and event-driven computation, which are fundamentally different from conventional artificial neural networks. Although they have demonstrated promising results in theoretical models and simulations, applying them effectively in real-world scenarios remains a substantial challenge. This difficulty arises from issues related to compatibility with existing hardware, the lack of mature development tools, and the complexities involved in fine-tuning the algorithms.

## 6.1 Integration with neuromorphic hardware

Integrating neuromorphic algorithms with neuromorphic hardware platforms such as IBM TrueNorth, Intel Loihi, BrainScaleS, and Spinnaker presents several significant challenges:

- **Matching the algorithm to the hardware**: Neuromorphic systems differ fundamentally from traditional computing architectures. Instead of using continuous signals, they operate using spikes—discrete, brief pulses representing data. Consequently, algorithms must be adapted to function effectively within this spike-based processing model.
- **Converting models to run on hardware**: Deploying a trained model onto physical neuromorphic hardware often requires specialized toolchains or manual translation processes. Preserving the model's intended behavior and synaptic weight integrity during this conversion is a complex task.
- **Limited hardware resources**: Neuromorphic platforms typically have constraints in terms of the number of neurons and synapses they can support, communication bandwidth, and computational precision. These limitations necessitate model simplification, downsizing, or partitioning before deployment.
- **On-chip learning**: Certain chips, such as Intel's Loihi, support on-chip learning through mechanisms such as reward-modulated STDP. However, not all algorithms are compatible with this learning paradigm, requiring the development of new approaches or hybrid learning strategies.
- **Managing communication delays**: Real-time applications—such as robotics and brain-computer interfaces—depend on ultra-fast communication between components, such as sensors, processors, and actuators. Without an efficient communication infrastructure, the system's responsiveness and performance degrade (Vogginger et al., 2024).

Despite these obstacles, considerable progress has been made in fields such as real-time sensory processing, autonomous navigation, and closed-loop control systems. Continued advancements in this area will depend heavily on close collaboration between hardware engineers and algorithm developers.

## 6.2 Simulation platforms and tools

Before being deployed on actual neuromorphic chips, neuromorphic algorithms are typically developed and tested using simulation tools. These tools assist in building algorithms, analyzing their behavior, emulating hardware operations, and identifying and resolving potential issues. Some of the commonly used platforms and tools include:

- **NEST:** A high-performance simulator for SNNs, ideal for modeling large-scale brain-like systems. It supports parallel processing and offers extensive customization options, making it well-suited for neuroscience research.
- **Brian2:** A flexible and user-friendly simulator for rapidly building SNNs using Python. Its syntax closely resembles mathematical modeling, which makes it accessible for researchers.
- **SpiNNaker tools (sPyNNaker):** A toolchain specifically designed for simulating and executing SNNs on SpiNNaker hardware. It includes an API for implementing custom neuron and synapse models.
- **Loihi tools (NxSDK, Lava):** Intel provides NxSDK for direct programming and control of Loihi neuromorphic chips. In addition, Lava, an open-source framework recently introduced by Intel, enables the development of neuromorphic applications across both Loihi hardware and Central Processing Unit (CPU) -based simulators.
- **CARLsim:** A GPU-accelerated simulator that allows for high-speed computation and real-time testing of spiking neural networks.
- **BindsNET:** A simulation and training library for SNNs built on top of PyTorch, enabling the use of deep learning-like methods for spiking networks.

### *6.2.1 Challenges in simulation*

- **Scalability:** Simulating large networks with high temporal resolution demands significant computational resources.
- **Biological realism** versus **efficiency:** Highly detailed, biologically realistic models can be inefficient or impractical for hardware implementation due to computational and energy constraints.
- **Standardization:** A lack of unified standards across tools hinders interoperability, making it difficult to transfer algorithms between different platforms.
- **Hardware discrepancies:** Simulation results may not fully align with real hardware behavior because of issues such as limited numerical precision, noise, and other physical variations.

These simulators play a crucial role in helping researchers validate and refine neuromorphic algorithms before deploying them on physical hardware. However, further improvements are needed to enhance tool interoperability, usability, and support for advanced learning techniques (Kim et al., 2024).

## 7. Emerging trends and future direction

Hybrid systems that mix neuromorphic computing with traditional Von Neumann systems are becoming more common as a practical and robust approach to powering the next generation of smart computing. These systems aim to leverage the ultra-low power consumption and event-driven nature of neuromorphic processors, while also benefiting from the numerical precision and scalability of conventional computing systems. This combination is particularly useful in scenarios requiring both rapid, real-time decision-making and high-precision computation.

For example, edge devices such as drones, wearable gadgets, or smart sensors can use neuromorphic chips for on-device, real-time tasks such as pattern recognition, anomaly detection, or quick decision-making—all with minimal power consumption. Meanwhile, more data-intensive operations, such as model training, data aggregation, or running detailed analytics, can be managed by cloud-based systems or traditional processors. This division of labor ensures each component handles the tasks it is best suited for, resulting in smoother performance and greater scalability.

A key development in these hybrid systems is the integration of SNNs with conventional Deep Neural Networks (DNNs). This combination is actively being explored to develop efficient inference mechanisms that retain the time-sensitive processing capabilities of SNNs while preserving the rich data representations typical of DNNs. In such architectures, SNNs can function as filters or encoders that convert data into spike-based representations, which are then passed to DNNs for more complex analysis and decision-making.

Recent hardware advancements, such as IBM's NorthPole architecture and Intel's Loihi 2 chip, demonstrate the growing implementation of these hybrid systems. NorthPole integrates computation and memory on a single chip, enabling fast SNN operations and parallel data processing, thereby significantly boosting speed and efficiency. Loihi 2 introduces enhancements that simplify programming and support multicore SNN execution, making it more compatible with traditional processors for shared computational workloads (Farmakidis et al., 2024). This hybrid approach not only optimizes the execution of diverse computational tasks but also paves the way for adaptable AI systems capable of functioning effectively in resource-constrained environments, such as IoT networks, robotics, and medical devices.

## 7.1 Hybrid architecture

Hybrid architectures present a promising approach to enhancing smart computing by integrating neuromorphic systems with traditional computing components, such as CPUs, GPUs, and FPGAs. These systems combine the efficient, real-time processing capabilities of neuromorphic computing with the powerful and adaptable processing strengths of conventional models. This fusion results in a robust and flexible architecture capable of handling both low-power sensing tasks and high-performance computational workloads.

Neuromorphic chips, inspired by the behavior of biological neurons, excel at event-driven and real-time processing—such as detecting motion, identifying sound direction, or sensing touch. They consume very little energy but are not well-suited for tasks involving complex mathematical operations, such as deep learning or large-scale matrix computations. To address this limitation, hybrid systems allocate sensing and real-time tasks to neuromorphic components, while standard processors handle more computationally demanding functions like data analysis, ML, or cloud-based processing. This hybrid configuration enables smoother coordination between edge devices and cloud infrastructure. For example, Intel's Loihi 2 can be deployed at the edge to perform real-time gesture recognition using event-based camera input, while GPUs in the cloud manage tasks such as training models, performing analytics, or compressing models. This division of labor supports pipeline parallelism, where quick sensing is done efficiently at the edge, and complex computation is offloaded to the cloud.

Recent hardware designs have embraced the hybrid concept. IBM's NorthPole is a neuromorphic system that tightly integrates memory and computation, enabling efficient execution of both neuromorphic and conventional workloads. Similarly, Heidelberg University's BrainScaleS-2 employs hybrid cores that can perform both brain-like simulations and conventional mathematical operations, making them useful for applications such as brain-machine interfaces, robotics, and intelligent computing systems.

Hybrid architectures are especially advantageous in domains such as autonomous driving and robotics. In self-driving vehicles, neuromorphic technologies handle fast, low-power tasks like collision detection, object tracking, and reflexive actions. Meanwhile, traditional CPUs are used for complex functions such as route planning, map generation, and internet connectivity. In robotics, neuromorphic sensors provide real-time tactile and visual feedback, while standard systems manage actuation and navigation. Even though hybrid neuromorphic systems hold significant potential, they still face several critical challenges. One major issue is maintaining memory and data consistency across different types of processing units, especially when these components operate asynchronously. Another key challenge is the lack of standardized software tools—such as compilers, APIs, and development frameworks—that can assist developers and researchers in effectively working with these systems. Without a common programming model, setting up, managing, and debugging hybrid neuromorphic systems becomes difficult and time-consuming. Addressing these challenges is essential for enabling the broader adoption of hybrid neuromorphic systems in practical, everyday AI applications (Davies et al., 2021).

## 7.2 Ethical and social impact

Neuromorphic AI is being used more in real-life situations, and this brings up many ethical and societal issues that need to be carefully considered. As these systems are deployed in areas such as healthcare, surveillance, and autonomous machines, concerns about privacy, personal freedom, and accountability are becoming more prominent. For example, BCIs that utilize neuromorphic processors handle extremely sensitive brain data, raising questions about whether individuals truly understand how their data are used, who owns it, and whether it could be exploited in unacceptable ways. In addition, since neuromorphic systems can learn and adapt in real time, it may be difficult to trace their decision-making processes, making it challenging to determine accountability if something goes wrong. Their ability to rapidly adapt can also produce biased or unfair outcomes if trained on incomplete or prejudiced data—particularly in applications such as behavior recognition or crime prediction. To address these challenges, experts are advocating for the development of neuromorphic AI systems with ethics and transparency integrated from the outset. One proposed approach is to enhance the interpretability of these systems so that their decision-making processes can be understood—an idea known as X-NeuroAI. Another important step is to establish strict regulations that ensure fairness, accountability, and transparency throughout the lifecycle of these systems (Smolka and Böschen, 2023). Furthermore, there is a growing emphasis on embedding safeguards into the design of such technologies to prevent misuse, especially in dual-use cases such as military or surveillance applications. Collectively, these measures aim to ensure that neuromorphic AI is developed and applied in a responsible and ethical manner.

## 7.3 Integration with emerging technologies

Neuromorphic computing is increasingly being integrated with other emerging technologies to solve real-world problems more effectively and efficiently. This is particularly beneficial in scenarios where low-power consumption, fast response times, and adaptability are critical. The fusion of these technologies is enabling innovative applications, ranging from smart homes to systems that leverage quantum computing to enhance intelligence.

(a) **IoT:** Neuromorphic processors are contributing to the development of smarter edge devices within IoT networks. These chips can process sensor data locally—right where it is collected—while consuming very little energy. This makes them ideal for battery-powered devices or systems deployed in remote locations. Unlike traditional processors that handle data sequentially and consume more power, neuromorphic chips mimic the brain's event-driven processing, reacting to stimuli as they occur. This is especially useful in smart home environments for real-time sound and video monitoring, or in industrial settings where sensors detect anomalies in vibration or temperature before a failure occurs. Even wearable health devices, such as those tracking heart activity or brainwaves, benefit from these chips by providing faster, localized data analysis without relying heavily on the cloud.

(b) **Flexible and biodegradable electronics:** Recent advancements have enabled the fabrication of neuromorphic chips on flexible substrates, paving the way for wearable and implantable AI systems. These systems conform to the human body, offering comfort, adaptability, and the ability to interface with biological signals in real time. In addition, research on organic memristors has led to the creation of biodegradable neuromorphic hardware. These devices are especially valuable for temporary biomedical implants used in postsurgery recovery or diagnostics (Jin et al., 2025). Once their function is complete, these implants naturally degrade inside the body, eliminating the need for surgical removal and reducing environmental impact.

(c) **Quantum computing and optical systems:** Although quantum and neuromorphic computing serve different roles, they can complement each other in hybrid systems. Quantum processors excel at solving complex optimization problems and executing simultaneous calculations, while neuromorphic processors are well-suited for pattern recognition, continuous learning, and real-time signal processing. Researchers are exploring hybrid systems in which quantum units perform global optimization or update learning rules, while neuromorphic components manage real-time decision-making and sensory processing. In addition, photonic neuromorphic systems—using light instead of electrical signals to simulate neural communication—are being developed. These systems provide extremely fast data transfer, minimal latency, and parallel processing capabilities, making them ideal for high-speed AI applications.

(d) **5G/6G networks:** The deployment of 5G and upcoming 6G networks is unlocking new opportunities for real-time interaction between edge-based neuromorphic devices and centralized cloud systems. In this setup, neuromorphic processors embedded in devices such as sensors, robots, or wearables can transmit processed, high-value data over fast and reliable wireless links to remote servers for further analysis or storage. In return, the cloud can send back updated models or new instructions, enabling continuous learning and adaptation. For example, a surveillance drone might use neuromorphic computing to navigate and avoid obstacles in real time, while transmitting key data via 5G to a remote control center for route planning and strategic analysis.

## 7.4 Next-generation algorithms

As neuromorphic hardware continues to advance, the algorithms that run on it must also evolve. Next-generation neuromorphic algorithms are being developed to make systems more brain-like, energy-efficient, and capable of continuous learning—enabling them to better adapt to dynamic real-world environments. Key areas of innovation involve,

(a) **Dendritic computation:** Traditional neuron models often treat neurons as simple points, which limits their computational ability. In contrast, real biological neurons have branching structures called dendrites that allow for localized information processing within different parts of the cell. Newer neuromorphic models leverage these dendritic structures to perform complex computations in parallel, improving the system's ability to recognize patterns, interpret context, and process temporal information more effectively.

(b) **Homeostatic and metaplasticity models:** Homeostatic plasticity helps maintain stable neural activity by adjusting firing thresholds or synaptic strengths based on input patterns. Metaplasticity refers to the modulation of a neuron's ability to change its connections, depending on its past activity. Together, these mechanisms prevent neurons from becoming either overactive or inactive, which is crucial for stable, long-term learning. Incorporating these dynamics into spiking neural networks increases their robustness, particularly in noisy or constantly changing environments.

(c) **Event-driven reinforcement learning (RL):** Reinforcement learning is being adapted for spiking neural networks, allowing systems to learn optimal actions in uncertain environments while using minimal energy. In these models, learning updates are triggered only by discrete events—such as spikes—resulting in highly efficient learning. This approach is particularly beneficial in robotics, where neuromorphic chips enable robots to learn behaviors such as object manipulation or navigation through low-power trial-and-error interactions.

(d) **Self-organizing networks:** Neuromorphic systems are increasingly employing unsupervised learning techniques, such as STDP, where synaptic strengths change based on the timing of neuronal spikes. In addition, structural plasticity allows these networks to dynamically grow or prune synapses over time, enabling lifelong learning. This self-organizing behavior allows the system to adapt continuously without requiring frequent retraining—an essential feature for operating in unpredictable environments.

(e) **3D neuromorphic architectures:** To address scalability challenges, researchers are developing 3D neuromorphic architectures, where neuron layers are vertically stacked and interconnected. This design emulates the organization of the human brain and offers advantages such as increased density, reduced signal latency, and enhanced memory capacity. The vertical connections facilitate feedback loops and richer spatial representations, making these systems more powerful and efficient (Muir and Sheik, 2025).

Real-world applications of next-gen neuromorphic algorithms:

- **Autonomous drones:** Drones equipped with neuromorphic vision systems can detect and avoid obstacles in real time. They also learn new navigation paths through spike-based RL, enabling smarter and more adaptive flight behavior.

- **Brain-inspired chatbots:** These chatbots utilize neuromorphic language models capable of responding to user tone, gestures, or preferences, making interactions more natural and emotionally intelligent—closer to conversing with a real human.
- **Smart prosthetics:** Prosthetic limbs enhanced with neuromorphic touch sensors and adaptive controllers can interpret a user's intention and adjust movement accordingly, resulting in more natural and efficient limb usage.

## 8. Conclusion

Neuromorphic algorithms, modeled after the workings of the human brain, are redefining computational intelligence—particularly within BCI systems. This chapter explored the foundational principles of neuromorphic computing, emphasizing real-time processing, SNNs, and synaptic plasticity—mechanisms that closely resemble natural brain function. We examined the biological motivations behind these algorithms and discussed a variety of learning paradigms, including supervised, unsupervised, reinforcement, and Hebbian-based learning. When implemented on neuromorphic hardware platforms, these learning methods demonstrate significant potential for fast, energy-efficient, and adaptive processing—making them especially suitable for dynamic BCI environments.

Notable hardware-software codesign examples such as IBM's NorthPole, Intel's Loihi 2, and the Spinnaker system exemplify how tightly integrated architectures can optimize neuromorphic performance. Real-world applications of these systems, including brain activity classification, EEG signal decoding, and closed-loop feedback control, have consistently shown advantages over conventional ML methods in terms of power efficiency, latency, and robustness in noisy conditions (Yu et al., 2020).

This chapter also highlighted emerging trends shaping the future of neuromorphic BCIs. Hybrid architectures that combine neuromorphic and conventional computing are enabling scalable applications, both at the edge and in cloud-based environments. However, as these technologies advance, ethical concerns related to privacy, user autonomy, and algorithmic fairness are gaining increasing importance. Furthermore, the convergence of neuromorphic systems with frontier technologies such as the Internet of Things (IoT), quantum computing, and bioelectronics is fostering innovations in personalized healthcare, neuroprosthetics, and human augmentation. Cutting-edge developments in neuromorphic learning—including spike-based deep learning, meta-learning, and online adaptive learning—are paving the way for more intelligent, autonomous, and resilient neural interfaces. These hybrid models blend brain-inspired computation with modern AI, moving BCIs closer to achieving human-like perception and decision-making.

In summary, the synergy between neuroscience, neuromorphic engineering, and AI is establishing a transformative pathway for seamless human-machine interaction. Although challenges remain in terms of scalability, standardization, and interpretability, the rapid evolution of neuromorphic algorithms points to a future where BCIs transcend assistive technologies and become integrated tools for enhancing cognition, communication, and performance.

## References

Chandra, G.V.S.A., Ananthakumar, B., Raghavan, R., 2024. Enhancing Assistive Technologies with Neuromorphic Computing Revolutionizing AI with Brain-Inspired Technology: Neuromorphic Computing. IGI Global, India, pp. 207–232. https://doi.org/10.4018/979-8-3693-6303-4.ch009.

Davies, M., Wild, A., Orchard, G., Sandamirskaya, Y., Fonseca Guerra, G.A., Joshi, P., Plank, P., Risbud, S.R., 2021. Advancing neuromorphic computing with Loihi: a survey of results and outlook. Proc. IEEE 109 (5), 911–934. https://doi.org/10.1109/jproc.2021.3067593.

Davies, M., Srinivasa, N., Lin, T.-H., Chinya, G., Cao, Y., Choday, S.H., Dimou, G., Joshi, P., Imam, N., Jain, S., Liao, Y., Lin, C.-K., Lines, A., Liu, R., Mathaikutty, D., McCoy, S., Paul, A., Tse, J., Venkataramanan, G., Weng, Y.-H., Wild, A., Yang, Y., Wang, H., 2018. Loihi: a neuromorphic manycore processor with on-chip learning. IEEE Micro 38 (1), 82–99. https://doi.org/10.1109/MM.2018.112130359.

Farmakidis, N., Dong, B., Bhaskaran, H., 2024. Integrated photonic neuromorphic computing: opportunities and challenges. Nat. Rev. Electr. Eng. 1 (6), 358–373. https://doi.org/10.1038/s44287-024-00050-9.

Jiang, J., Zhuang, H., Huang, X., Kong, D., Fang, Z., 2025. Event-based stereo depth estimation with motion guidance and left–right consistency. IEEE Trans. Instrum. Meas. 74, 1–14. https://doi.org/10.1109/tim.2025.3566813.

Jin, B., Wang, Z., Wang, T., Meng, J., 2025. Memristor-based artificial neural networks for hardware neuromorphic computing. Research 8. https://doi.org/10.34133/research.0758.

Kim, K., Song, M.S., Hwang, H., Hwang, S., Kim, H., 2024. A comprehensive review of advanced trends: from artificial synapses to neuromorphic systems with consideration of non-ideal effects. Front. Neurosci. 18. https://doi.org/10.3389/fnins.2024.1279708.

Manna, D., 2025. Once upon a Spike Time: Exploring Spiking Neurons and Perspective Applications of Neuromorphic Solutions.

Muir, D.R., Sheik, S., 2025. The road to commercial success for neuromorphic technologies. Nat. Commun. 16 (1). https://doi.org/10.1038/s41467-025-57352-1.

Schmidgall, S., Ziaei, R., Achterberg, J., Kirsch, L., Pardis Hajiseyedrazi, S., Eshraghian, J., 2024. Brain-inspired learning in artificial neural networks: a review. APL Mach. Learn. 2 (2). https://doi.org/10.1063/5.0186054.

Smolka, M., Böschen, S., 2023. Responsible innovation ecosystem governance: socio-technical integration research for systems-level capacity building. J. Responsible Innov. 10 (1). https://doi.org/10.1080/23299460.2023.2207937.

Vogginger, B., Rostami, A., Jain, V., Arfa, S., Hantsch, A., Kappel, D., Schäfer, M., et al., 2024. Neuromorphic hardware for sustainable AI data centers. arXiv preprint arXiv:2402.02521.

Wei, W., Zhang, M., Zhang, J., Belatreche, A., Wu, J., Xu, Z., Qiu, X., Chen, H., Yang, Y., Li, H., 2024. Event-driven learning for spiking neural networks. arXiv. https://doi.org/10.48550/arXiv.2403.00270.

Wisniewski, D.J., Ma, L., Rauhala, O.J., Cea, C., Zhao, Z., Ranschaert, A., Gelinas, J.N., Khodagholy, D., 2025. Spatial control of doping in conducting polymers enables complementary, conformable, implantable internal ion-gated organic electrochemical transistors. Nat. Commun. 16 (1). https://doi.org/10.1038/s41467-024-55284-w.

Yik, J., Van den Berghe, K., Douwe, den B., Bouhadjar, Y., Fabre, M., Paul, H., Ke, W., Khoei, M. A., Denis, K., Pacik-Nelson, N., Pierro, A., Philipp, S., Sun, P.-S.V., Tang, G., Wang, S., Zhou, B., Ahmed, S.H., Joseph, G.V., Leto, B., Micheli, A., Mishra, A.K., Lenz, G., Sun, T., Ahmed, Z., Akl, M., Anderson, B., Andreou, A.G., Bartolozzi, C., Basu, A., Bogdan, P., Sander, B., Buckley, S., Cauwenberghs, G., Chicca, E., Corradi, F., Croon, G.de, Danielescu, A., Daram, A., Davies, M., Demirag, Y., Eshraghian, J., Fischer, T., Forest, J., Fra, V., Furber, S., Furlong, P.M., Gilpin, W., Gilra, A., Gonzalez, H.A., Indiveri, G., Joshi, S., Karia, V., Khacef, L., Knight, J.C., Kriener, L., Kubendran, R., Kudithipudi, D., Liu, S.-C., Liu, Y.-H., Ma, H., Manohar, R., Margarit-Taulé, J.M., Mayr, C., Michmizos, K., Muir, D.R., Neftci, E., Nowotny, T., Ottati, F., Ozcelikkale, A., Panda, P., Park, J., Payvand, M., Pehle, C., Petrovici, M.A., Posch, C., Renner, A., Sandamirskaya, Y., Schaefer, C.J.S., van Schaik, A., Schemmel, J., Schmidgall, S., Schuman, C., Seo, J.-sun, Sheik, S., Shrestha, S.B., Sifalakis, M., Sironi, A., Stewart, K., Stewart, M., Stewart, T.C., Timcheck, J., Tömen, N., Urgese, G., Verhelst, M., Vineyard, C.M., Vogginger, B., Yousefzadeh, A., Zohora, F.T., Frenkel, C., Reddi, V.J., 2025. The neurobench framework for benchmarking neuromorphic computing algorithms and systems. Nat. Commun. 16 (1). https://doi.org/10.1038/s41467-025-56739-4.

Yu, Z., Abdulghani, A.M., Zahid, A., Heidari, H., Ali Imran, M., Abbasi, Q.H., 2020. An overview of neuromorphic computing for artificial intelligence enabled hardware-based hopfield neural network. IEEE Access 8, 67085–67099. https://doi.org/10.1109/access.2020.2985839.

Chapter 4

# EEG-based imagined speech classification—A systematic review by exploring the effective hierarchical deep learning approaches

**B.S. Sabitha Rani and Elizabeth Sherly**
*School of Computer Science and Engineering, Digital University Kerala (DUK), Trivandrum, Kerala, India*

## 1. Introduction

Currently, for many researchers and practitioners in the domain of brain computing, Brain Computer Interface (BCI) has emerged as a prominent area of study. BCI captures brain waves and uses control signals to operate the machines, acting as an interface between the brain and external devices. It plays a pivotal role in numerous applications like healthcare, smart environments, neuromarketing, education, security, and welfare (Sakai et al., 2021). Inner speech classification involves decoding internalized thoughts from brain signals, such as EEG, to categorize words or phonemes, thereby aiding communication for individuals with speech impairments. Furthermore, BCI has emerged as a promising approach for automatic inner speech classification. Technologies such as Electrocorticography (ECoG), Magnetoencephalography (MEG), Functional Magnetic Resonance Imaging (fMRI), and Electroencephalography (EEG) are widely used in BCI research (Islam and Shuvo, 2020; Meng, 2021). From these, EEG is considered as the most widely utilized BCI tool. The EEG could record the humans' brain activity and render dynamic information about the brain signals that result in accurate inner speech (SI) detection (Kocturova and Juhar, 2020). Inner speech refers to a mental strategy involving imagined words (IW) or letters without any overt articulation or sound (Macias-Macias et al., 2020). Compared to other BCI paradigms such as motor imagery, inner speech BCIs

**Neuromorphic Computing for Brain Computer Interfaces. https://doi.org/10.1016/B978-0-443-41594-4.00001-0**

involve unique complexities related to language processing and neural networks (Abdulghani et al., 2023). Inner speech activates brain regions involved in language comprehension and production, including the temporal, frontal, and sensorimotor areas, primarily within the left hemisphere. While motor imagery focuses on movement-related brain activity, inner speech involves more intricate cognitive processes, including semantic and phonological analysis. Datasets designed for inner speech BCI aim to decode and understand the mechanisms underlying inner speech and its potential applications. Studies often require participants to imagine their own voice repeating a word without overt articulation. The spatial patterns of brain activation during inner speech are complex and involve multiple brain regions. Fig. 4.1 illustrates the diagrammatic representation of inner speech processing.

Generally, for many BCI researchers, decoding human intentions remains challenging (Cooney et al., 2022). For instance, distinguishing brain signals specific to the imagined speech (IS) state from other brain states is challenging. Additionally, some methods rely on external stimuli or additional equipment to interpret user's intentions. Datasets often involve a relatively small number of subjects and may exhibit gender imbalance, which limits the generalizability of findings across a wider population.

Basic supervised and unsupervised ML approaches, such as the Support Vector Machine (SVM), Decision Tree (DT), K-Nearest-Neighbor (KNN), Random Forest (RF), Extreme Learning Machine (ELM), and Fuzzy Inference System (FIS) have been incorporated by the previous approaches for performing inner speech recognition using EEG (Hamedi et al., 2020). Nevertheless, high time complexity is attained by these approaches owing to the inefficient learning process. To address this, Deep Learning (DL) techniques such as Long Short Term Memory (LSTM), Convolutional Neural Network (CNN) (Lee et al., 2021), Recurrent Neural Network (RNN), and Deep Neural Network (DNN) have been developed (Rusnac and Grigore, 2021). However, false positives and poor classification metrics owing to EEG's complex patterns (Kumar and Scheme, 2021). By addressing these research gaps, to recognize Imagined Speech (IS), this systematic review focuses on exploring innovative ML and DL approaches that can improve performance and implementation in the IS domain. Additionally, this survey analyzes relevant benchmark datasets and evaluates their performance based on various quality metrics. Providing insights into the purpose and benefits of ISR models using EEG is the key objective of this chapter. Fig. 4.2 illustrates the organization of the chapter.

## 2. Research questions and article selection strategies of this systematic review

This survey explores several ML and DL approaches for ISR using EEG, and evaluates their performance and limitations. The remainder of the chapter is organized to address the research questions.

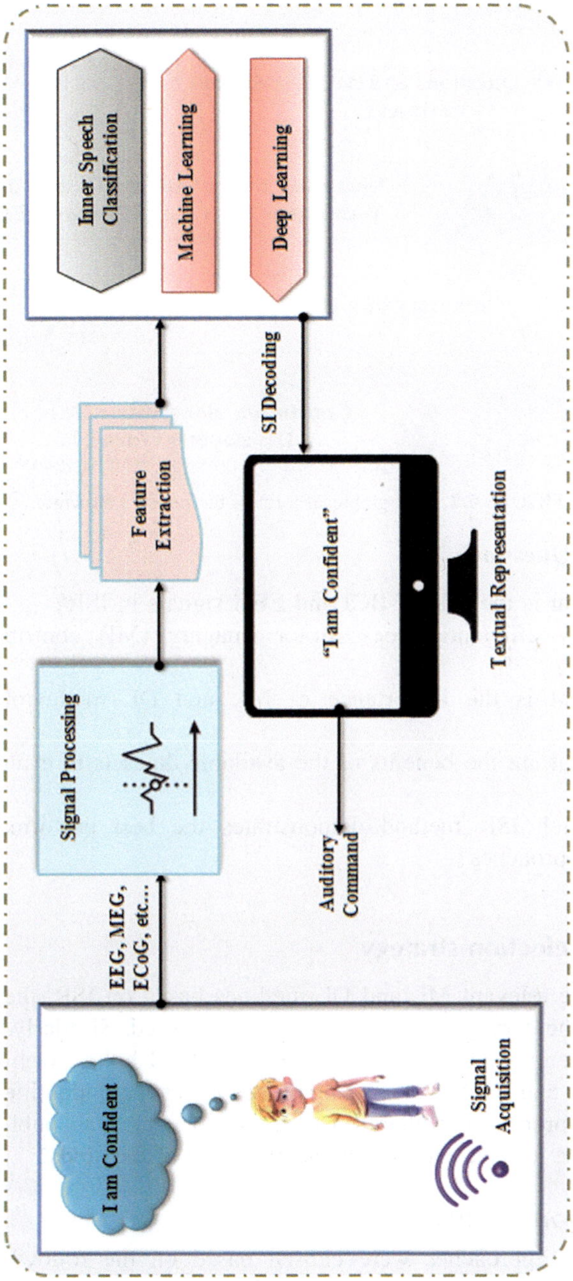


**FIGURE 4.1** The architecture of the conventional ISR model.

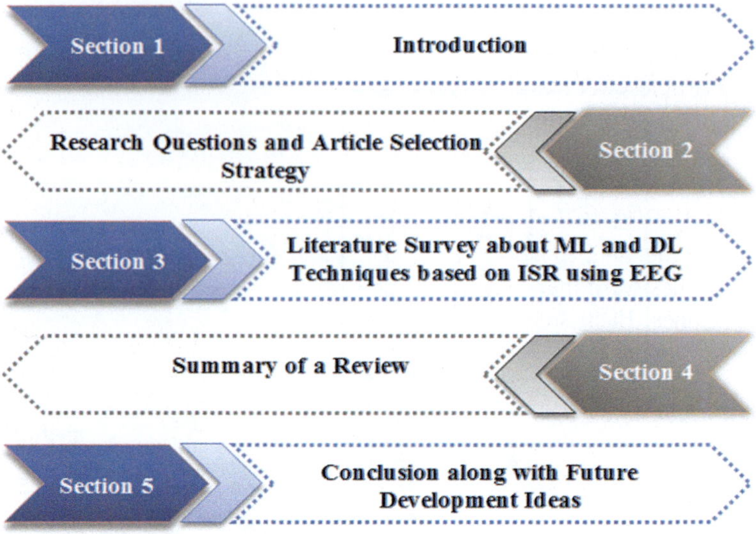


**FIGURE 4.2** The graphical form of the review's structure.

**Research Questions**

- RQ1—What is the role of BCI and EEG signals in ISR?
- RQ2—How efficiently does Motor Imagery (MI) contribute to BCI technology?
- RQ3—What is the importance of ML and DL methodologies in SI decoding?
- RQ4—What are the benefits of the available datasets to evaluate the ISR models?
- RQ5—Which ISR method demonstrates the best performance among existing approaches?

## 2.1 Article selection strategy

For finding the relevant ML and DL methods based on ISR, the appropriate keywords of the survey's research questions are used. Similarly, by utilizing standard academic databases, including Google Scholar, Web of Science, ScienceDirect, and IEEE Xplore, suitable resources were identified. Likewise, the selection process considered various factors such as publication year, language of the article, and the major objectives of the study.

### *2.1.1 Inclusion criteria*

Here, the ISR approaches were chosen based on the following inclusion criteria. Only articles published in English between 2016 and 2023 were included.

### *2.1.2 Exclusion criteria*

Papers published before 2016 were excluded. Symposium, review, and conference articles were excluded. Studies with low accuracy, insufficient validation, inconsistent findings, or poor generalization in SI decoding were excluded.

### *2.1.3 Evaluation outcomes of the searching process*

Based on the defined search criteria, 110 relevant studies were identified. These studies were then subjected to a validation process to identify the most relevant ones. Each study was evaluated based on its abstract, methodology, and experimental results to ensure an objective selection process. Finally, 80 studies relevant to ISR were selected for this systematic review. Fig. 4.3 illustrates the search results of this survey.

## 3. Literature survey about ML and DL techniques based ISR using EEG

To develop speech recognition technologies, an automatic and accurate envisioned speech classification is crucial. BCI, which efficiently decodes human intentions into auditory feedback using EEG, has emerged as a powerful tool in ISR. BCI plays a predominant role in applications such as assistive communication devices, neurorehabilitation, healthcare monitoring, smart prosthetics and wheelchairs. This review aims to analyze ML and DL methodologies for ISR using EEG. The remainder of this chapter is organized as

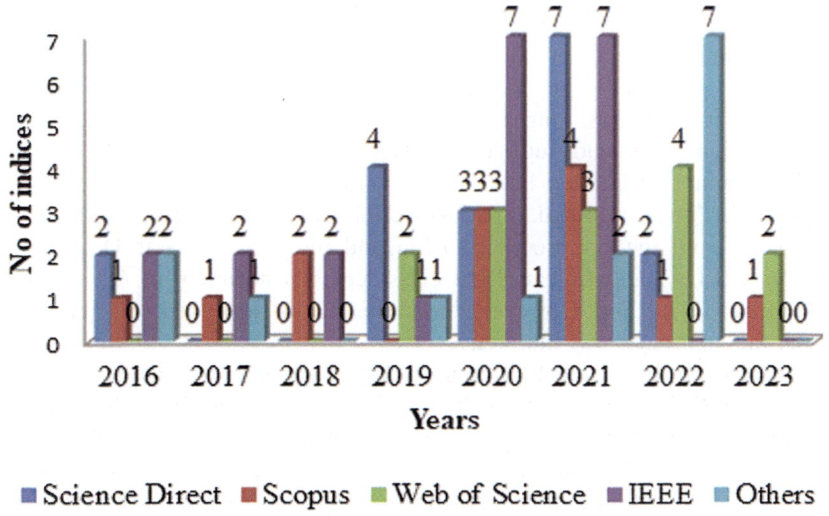


**FIGURE 4.3** The design of the demographic statistics.

follows: a review of the role of BCI and EEG signals in ISR models; an analysis of ML methods in ISR decoding; an examination of hierarchical DL approaches for inner speech classification; a study on vowel and imagined word (IW) recognition; an overview of motor imagery (MI) in BCI; an analysis of standard datasets for evaluating ISR methods; and a performance evaluation of various ISR models. Hierarchical DL approaches refine feature representations across multiple levels for improved context retention, whereas conventional DL models process data in a single-pass, often lacking deep structural abstraction.

## 3.1 Role of BCI and EEG signals in ISR models

The primary objective of BCI is to enable direct communication between the user and a device without any physical actions, thereby supporting individuals with disabilities. EEG is widely used in BCI for identifying inner speech. EEG captures dynamic features of brain activity, enabling precise IS detection (Duc and Lee, 2020). In recent times, EEG signals have been established by several speech recognition models to decode inner speech. Numerous studies have employed EEG for ISR due to its high temporal resolution, cost- effectiveness and efficiency (Zhang et al., 2019). EEG based ISR decoding models are discussed further.

Proix et al. (2022) demonstrated IS decoding using Intracranial EEG (iEEG), also referred to as electrocorticography (ECoG). In this study, iEEG data were collected from 13 subjects across 3 experiments. The collected ECoG signals were processed to extract low-frequency and cross-frequency features. Recursive feature elimination was used to select optimal features, which were then input into an SVM-linear-kernel classifier to classify IW. This approach achieved an accuracy of 50% in ISR decoding. However, due to the limited number of trials in the validation process, the approach showed limited accuracy.

Saleh et al. (2018) introduced the EEG-based IS and non-speech task classification. This study utilized the Emotiv EEG neuro-headset to capture multi- channel EEG data. High-pass and low-pass filtering techniques were applied for noise removal. Spatio-spectral and time-domain features were extracted from the pre-processed EEG and input into Linear Discriminant Analysis (LDA) and Linear SVM classifiers. An accuracy of 60% was acquired by this method. However, due to the lack of spatio-spectral features of EEG, this approach was ineffective.

To decode the IS, EEG is used by numerous ISR models. Feature Extraction (FE) techniques, such as Discrete Wavelet Transform (DWT), Common Spatial Pattern (CSP), Fourier Transform (FT), and Multi-channel Wiener Filter (MWF) are commonly used for imagined speech classification. Table 4.1 presents their performance in terms of accuracy, Kappa Coefficient (KC), and Computational Time (CT).

**TABLE 4.1** The survey on EEG-based IS classification.

| Author name | Input | FE | Total subjects | Findings | | | Drawbacks |
|---|---|---|---|---|---|---|---|
| | | | | Accuracy (%) | KC | CT (ms) | |
| Chuong H. Nguyen et al. (Nguyen et al., 2018) | EEG | CSP | 15 | 63.74 | 0.37 | – | Nevertheless, it struggled with experimental protocols, which led to poor model efficiency. |
| Hiroki Watanabe et al. (Watanabe et al., 2020) | EEG | – | 18 | 38.5 | – | – | Owing to the lack of adequate training samples, it was less accurate. |
| Dipti Pawar et al. (Pawar and Dhage, 2020) | EEG | DWT | 6 | 49.77 | 35.7 | 0.18 | However, this system was only demonstrated with a limited number of individuals. |
| Seo-Hyun Lee et al. (Lee et al., 2020) | EEG | CSP | 22 | 39.73 | – | – | This approach failed to monitor the variations among the sessions. |
| Luis Alfredo Moctezuma et al. (Moctezuma et al., 2019) | EEG | DWT | 32 | 96 | – | – | It may lead to misclassification owing to the lack of effectual signal processing methods. |

*Continued*

**TABLE 4.1** The survey on EEG-based IS classification.—cont'd

| Author name | Input | FE | Total subjects | Findings | | | Drawbacks |
|---|---|---|---|---|---|---|---|
| | | | | Accuracy (%) | KC | CT (ms) | |
| Mohamad Amin Bakhshali et al. (Bakhshali, 2020) | EEG | CSP | 12 | 90.25 | – | – | Owing to the Riemannian geometry distance, a higher computational cost was attained by this approach. |
| Magdiel Jim'enez-Guarneros et al. (Jiménez-Guarneros and Gómez-Gil, 2021) | EEG | – | 15 | 62.00 | – | – | Nevertheless, the transferred knowledge from source samples might be a barrier to the targeted results. |
| Simon Van Eyndhoven et al. (Van Eyndhoven, Francart and Bertrand, 2017) | EEG | MWF | 16 | 100 | – | – | Owing to the usage of microphones, higher maintenance costs were retained by this framework. |
| Marianna Koctúrová et al. (Koctúrová and Juhár, 2021) | EEG | FT | 16 | **F-measure (%)** | **Recall (%)** | **Accuracy (%)** | However, a few training features, which limited the model's efficiency, were considered by this system. |
| | | | | 86.8 | 88.8 | 84.6 | |

Biswas and Sinha (2022) included covert speech recognition using wavelet filter-based EEG spatial features. EEG data were collected from the database. The processing steps included downsampling, wavelet filter-based band-wise decomposition, band-wise grouping, CSP feature extraction, and SVM -based envisioned speech classification. This approach achieved an accuracy of 94% with a computational time of 690 ms. However, the use of classical CSP features may lead to overfitting.

Angrick et al. (2021) developed a real-time monitoring of IS centered on Stereoelectroencephalography (sEEG). The input sEEG signals were collected and pre-processed. Low-power features were extracted from the preprocessed sEEG signals. In this, to decode the imagery speech with a processing time of 7.331 ms, the LDA classifier was deployed, thus justifying the high computational efficiency. However, this approach failed to identify the basic vowel sounds from the IS.

## 3.2 The review on the contribution of ML models in ISR

Over the past decade, ML models have emerged as powerful tools for ISR, IW, and MI decoding. ML approaches have been widely adopted in various BCI applications. For ISR decoding, various ML models, including SVM, LDA, RF, and Multiclass-Neural Network (M-NN) have been utilized. Among these models, SVM plays a significant role in ISR decoding due to its high efficiency. This session discusses these contributions.

Sharon et al. (2020) investigated ML-based neural speech decoding during production, imagination, and audition. EEG data from 30 subjects across three datasets were collected. A Butterworth-bandpass filter was applied for EEG preprocessing. The processed data were then input into a Gaussian Mixture Model-Hidden Markov Model (GMM-HMM) classifier, which was used to identify covert speech. This approach achieved an accuracy of 33.03%. But, due to the large size of the datasets, the approach resulted in high processing time.

Similarly, various ML methodologies have been employed for ISR. These approaches are analyzed based on their objectives, outcomes, and performance, as summarized in Table 4.2.

The Filtering Techniques, such as Band-Pass Filtering (BPF), Butterworth Filtering (BF), Independent Component Analysis (ICA), Moving Average Filtering (MAF), Common Average Reference (CAF), and Down Sampling (DS) were incorporated in Table 4.2 for pre-processing the input signal.

García-Salinas et al. (2019) proposed a transfer learning based framework for IS detection using EEG. EEG data were collected using the Emotiv EPOC headset and pre-processed using a low-pass filter. The pre-processed EEG data were classified using a Naive Bayes (NB) approach. Transfer learning was applied to further enhance classification performance. The model achieved an accuracy of 62.79%. However, the use of handcrafted features limited the system's computational efficiency.

**TABLE 4.2** Analysis of ML approaches in ISR.

| Author name | Aim | ML classifier | Filtering Technique | Results | | | Limitations |
|---|---|---|---|---|---|---|---|
| Kusuma Mohanchandra et al. (Mohanchandra and Saha, 2016) | Speech conversion from brain signals | SVM-linear-kernel | BF and DL | **Recall (%)** | **Precision (%)** | **Accuracy (%)** | However, it faced challenges in recognizing the appropriate kernel function. |
| | | | | 44 | 32.2 | 77.6 | |
| Nayab Usama et al. (Usama et al., 2020) | Classification of imagined movements | LDA + SVM + RF | BF and BPF | **Accuracy (%)** | **Latency (ms)** | **Error rate (%)** | During dimensionality reduction, it might be possible to lose essential information. |
| | | | | 66.66 | 258 | 1.00 | |
| Alejandro A. Torres-Garcia et al. (Torres-Garcia et al., 2016) | IS classification | RF | CAR | 79.7 | – | 1.05 | In this approach, the process of multi-channel selection was quite challenging. |
| Pradeep Kumar et al. (Kumar et al., 2018) | Envisioned speech detection | RF | MAF | **Accuracy (%)** | | **CT (ms)** | Owing to inadequate features, it achieved poor model performance. |
| | | | | 57.11 | | – | |
| Debadatta Dash et al. (Dash et al., 2020a) | Neural speech decoding | SVM | BF | 58 | | – | However, owing to the absence of optimal sensors, it retained low decoding accuracy. |

| | | | | | | |
|---|---|---|---|---|---|---|
| Ciaran Cooney et al. (Cooney et al., 2018) | IS decoding | DT + SVM | ICA | 20.24 | – | However, for the non-linear features, this system did not perform well. |
| Rania M. Ghoniem et al. (Ghoniem et al., 2019) | Fusing speech with brain modalities | M-NN | BF and ICA | 97.67 | 1512 | Nevertheless, owing to the enormous input layer of the network, it incurred considerable training time. |
| Pimwipa Charuthamrong et al. (Charuthamrong et al., 2022) | Automatic speech discrimination | SVM + LDA | BF | 82.79 | – | This system was not regularized well enough to process the comprehensive word list. |

Singh and Gumaste (2021) implemented an IS decoding model for computer control using brain signals. EEG signals were represented as covariance matrix and used as input features. Principal Component Analysis (PCA) approach was used for feature reduction. The features were then input into an Artificial Neural Network (ANN) classifier, achieving an accuracy of 85% in IS decoding. However, overlapping window samples led to reduced accuracy.

## 3.3 The exploring review on hierarchical deep learning approaches based ISR

Recently, several hierarchical DL techniques have been developed to classify covert speech using brain signals. Due to the superior efficiency of DL approaches, most of the traditional ISR models have adopted these techniques in BCI applications (Alessandrini et al., 2023). To decode the user's thoughts into auditory feedback, DL approaches, such as CNN, Fully Convolutional Network (FCN), and Gated Recurrent Unit (GRU) were incorporated (Tian et al., 2016). These approaches are discussed below.

Saha and Fels (2019) proposed a hierarchical deep feature learning model for IS decoding by using EEG. Multiple DL methods, such as CNN, RNN, FCN, and auto-encoders were used to process the collected EEG data. In the classification of speech imagery, an impressive performance was acquired by this method with an accuracy of 71.1%. Noise and artifacts in raw EEG signals may lead to misclassification in inner speech decoding.

Rusnac and Grigore (2022) proposed a CNN-based inner speech decoding approach using EEG. The Kara One database was used to develop the ISR model. Time and frequency domain features were extracted from the EEG data and fed into a CNN classifier achieving an accuracy of 28% in ISR. The results demonstrated the effectiveness of the model. However, the model had high memory requirements and computational complexity.

This review examines several DL models, such as Temporal CNN (T-CNN), Deep Auto Encoder (DAE), Residual Neural Network (ResNet), and Extreme Gradient Boosting (XG-Boost). The performance of these DL models was evaluated using metrics such as accuracy, Kappa coefficient (KC), and Learning Rate (LR) as summarized in Table 4.3.

Janke and Diener (2017) introduced a framework for speech generation using Electromyography (EMG) signals. EMG signals were captured from healthy individuals and subjected to pre-processing, feature extraction and compression. A Deep Neural Network (DNN) was used to convert EMG signals into auditory output. In real-time, this model obtained noticeable results. However, high feature dimensionality increased runtime and affected system consistency.

**TABLE 4.3** IS decoding using different DL approaches.

| Author name | DL model | Data samples | Accuracy (%) | KC | LR | Disadvantages |
|---|---|---|---|---|---|---|
| Prabhakar Agarwal et al. (Agarwal and Kumar, 2022a) | LSTM, GRU, and CNN | 67,500 | 73.56 | – | – | However, it led to inaccurate outcomes owing to the variations in brain regions. |
| Tarmizi Ahmad Izzuddin et al. (Izzuddin et al., 2021) | CNN | 10,000 | 92.09 | – | – | For large-scale operations, this approach was not suitable. |
| Ciaran Cooney et al. (Cooney et al., 2020) | CNN | 512 | 35.83 | – | 0.1 | Nevertheless, owing to the unimportant intra and inter-subject techniques, it obtained a poor optimization rate. |
| Pramit Saha et al. (Saha et al., 2019a) | T-CNN, DAE | 26,782 | 83.42 | 58.32 | 0.01 | Owing to the background noise effects, this method turned out to be less efficient. |
| Sandeep Kumar et al. (Kumar et al., 2021) | CNN and XG-Boost | 1526 | 84.7 | – | 0.08 | Owing to the poor LR, it obtained a higher execution time. |
| Darya Vorontsova et al. (Vorontsova et al., 2021) | CNN and RNN | 1024 | 85 | – | 0.01 | Nevertheless, owing to the smaller dataset, it achieved limited performance. |
| Fabio R. Llorella et al. (Llorella et al., 2021) | CNN | – | 82 | 0.31 | – | This system does not focus on frequency fluctuations of EEG, which affect the model's accuracy. |
| Jerrin Thomas Panachakel et al. (Panachakel and Ganesan, 2021) | ResNet-50 | 320 | 87.6 | 0.68 | 4 | However, owing to the framework's complexity, this method was unable to handle the similarity analysis. |
| Pramit Saha et al. (Saha et al., 2019b) | CNN, RNN and DAE | 1913 | 77.9 | 0.7 | 0.1 | Nevertheless, this model used the traditional activation function, which caused poor decoding accuracy. |
| Debadatta Dash et al. (Dash et al., 2020b) | CNN | 3046 | 93 | – | – | Higher channel noise and training time were attained by this system. |

## 3.4 Classification of Imagined words and vowels from Imagined speech

This session discusses various approaches for IW and vowel classification. Vowels and word pairs from IS can be classified using various ML and DL techniques, such as SVM and CNN.

Martin et al. (2016) proposed a word pair classification method for IS using brain recordings. ECoG signals from five patients were recorded and processed using filtering, downsampling and feature extraction. After that, the extracted features were input into an SVM classifier, which efficiently categorized the word pairs from decoded IS. An accuracy of 88% was obtained by this model. However, the experiments were conducted in controlled environments.

Tamm et al. (2020) investigated vowel classification from IS using CNN. This system was evaluated using the National University of Entre Ríos (UNER) dataset. Primarily, the collected EEG was pre-processed under downsampling and artifact removal. After that, the pre-processed EEG data were fed into a CNN classifier, which predicts the vowels from IS. This approach achieved an accuracy of 23.98%. However, insufficient pre-processing reduced the system's accuracy.

This section describes IW and vowel classification from inner speech. Table 4.4 summarizes sample frequency (SF), classification labels, and corresponding results.

## 3.5 The common involvement of motor imagery (MI) in BCI

In BCI applications, MI has evolved has emerged as a promising approach. MI refers to the recognition of user intentions related to physical movements without actual execution. Several studies on MI recognition are discussed below:

Gao and Sun (2022) proposed a multisource transfer learning-based MI recognition approach. EEG signals were processed through pre-processing, data alignment, feature extraction, labeling, and classification. In this, to identify the MI, the fusion classifier model was established. This approach achieved an accuracy of 70.86%. However, mislabeled samples may affect the model's reliability.

Miao et al. (2017) established a classification approach for MI utilizing EEG. Primarily, the EEG signals were processed using the Common Average Reference (CAR) filtering method. After that, frequency decomposition, temporal segmentation, CSP feature extraction, and sparse representation-based feature classification was performed on the pre-processed EEG. An accuracy of 86.41% and better computational efficiency were obtained by the model. However, unbalanced spatiotemporal features limited the effectiveness of the model.

**TABLE 4.4** The analysis of word pair and vowel classification.

| Author name | Focus | SF (Hz) | Class | Precision (%) | Accuracy (%) | Challenges |
|---|---|---|---|---|---|---|
| Beomjun Min et al. (Min et al., 2016) | Vowel imagery decoding using EEG | 1000 | 6 | – | 75 | Poor training performance owing to the redundant features. |
| Noramiza Hashim et al. (Hashim et al., 2018) | Word-based classification using EEG | 128 | 2 | 52 | 58 | Larger variations in model accuracy owing to the limited number of participants. |
| Luis Carlos Sarmiento et al. (Sarmiento et al., 2021) | EEG-based recognition of imagined vowels | 1024 | 5 | – | 75.64 | Only a single session of the validation was conducted, which affected the model's reliability. |
| Nrushingh Charan Mahapatra et al. (Mahapatra et al., 2022) | Multiclass classification of imagined vowels and words using EEG | 1024 | 11 | 98 | 96.49 | A higher decoding error rate was obtained by this model. |
| M. R. Asghari Bejestani et al. (Asghari Bejestani et al., 2022) | Multiword prediction from IS using EEG | 500 | 7 | – | 87 | The system results might be degraded by the high correlation between the EEG signals. |
| Sandhya Chengaiyan et al. (Chengaiyan et al., 2020) | EEG-based identification of consonant vowels and words | 512 | 5 | – | 85 | Higher computational complexity owing to the larger number of layers in the network. |

*Continued*

**TABLE 4.4** The analysis of word pair and vowel classification.—cont'd

| Author name | Focus | SF (Hz) | Class | Precision (%) | Accuracy (%) | Challenges |
|---|---|---|---|---|---|---|
| Prabhakar Agarwal et al. (Agarwal and Kumar, 2022b) | Imagined word pair recognition using brain signals | 250 | 5 | – | 88.36 | Owing to the inadequate features, higher false positives were attained by this approach. |
| Tonatiuh Hernández-Del-Toro et al. (Hernández-Del-Toro et al., 2021) | EEG-based IW detection | 500 | 5 | 62 | – | This approach needed a huge set of features and resources to employ. |
| Sahil Datta et al. (Datta and Boulgouris, 2021) | Recognition of grammatical class of IW | 1000 | 4 | – | 85.7 | Nevertheless, owing to the insufficient activation function, a lower LR was obtained by this methodology. |

Tong et al. (2023) presented a framework to enhance MI by using multimodal SI. Initially, the collected EEG was subjected to filtering, DS, CSP feature extraction, and classification based on SVM. Lastly, the MI was detected by the SVM classifier with an accuracy of 77.03%. In BCI, this approach demonstrated improved effectiveness and reliability. However, this system had some demerits, such as minimum subjects. Also, the system lacked generalizability across different languages.

Wang et al. (2020) proposed an approach for offline analysis to online analysis based on MI and SI. The input EEG signals were pre-processed under BF. In this, to extract the features from filtered EEG, Power Spectral Density (PSD) was used. After that, the extracted features were input into an ELM, which initiated the online training based on MI and SI. An accuracy of 81.1% and satisfactory results were obtained by this approach. Yet, it resulted in poor feedback outcomes.

Ang and Guan (2017) introduced MI detection for control and rehabilitation using EEG. Two phases, such as the calibration phase and the feedback session phase were involved in this system. The input EEG underwent FE and selection in the calibration phase. After that, it was transferred into an online feedback session. In this, for predicting MI, operant conditioning and ML strategies were employed. During the calibration phase, an accuracy of 74.65% and superior performance were achieved by the model. But, due to the small sample size of six participants, insignificant results were attained by the model.

Zhang et al. (2022) proposed a Deep CNN (DCNN) based MI decoding using EEG. Initially, the EEG data underwent preprocessing through filtering. Subsequently, CSP features were extracted from the filtered EEG to decode motor imagery (MI) and were then classified using a DCNN model. An accuracy of 93.36% was obtained by this framework. In the field of BCI, the approach was highly potential. However, the high-level features were neglected by the technique, which might affect the prediction results.

Xiao and Fang (2021) established EEG-based recognition of MI using the DCNN classifier. In this, to pre-process the collected EEG, the short-time Fourier transforms and continuous morlet wavelet transform approaches were utilized. After that, from pre-processed EEG, the features were extracted and then input into a DCNN, which classified the MI. This approach achieved an accuracy of 93% and a precision of 96%. Furthermore, improved practicability and applicability were achieved by this approach. The approach required a high number of iterations, which caused poor computational complexity.

Tang et al. (2019) proposed an MI classification using EEG based on KNN with a smooth auto-encoder. Initially, the EEG data acquisition and FE were carried out. Next, to decode the MI, the recognized features were input into the KNN-based Smooth Auto-Encoder (K-SAE) Classifier. An accuracy and evaluation time of 92.5% and 12.8 ms respectively were obtained by the K-

SAE classifier. This approach demonstrated good generalization capability and efficacy. However, this approach struggled with EEG signal analysis.

## 3.6 The review on available standard datasets for assessing ISR techniques

Several available datasets were analyzed based to their characteristics, results, and importance. Essential information about the EEG recordings of many participants, which supports the evaluation of ISR models, is held by the datasets. This is discussed further:

Thornton et al. (2022) developed a robust decoding model of IS using EEG based on DNN. In this, to employ this model, the two datasets, namely Dataset I and Dataset II were used. Information about the EEG recording of 13 participants was contained in Dataset I. Similarly, EEG recordings of 18 individuals were involved in Dataset II. Overall, 64 EEG channel recordings were held by both of the datasets. DCNN, which supported decoding the IS, processed the input EEG. In real-time decoding applications, this approach showed promising potential. Yet, degradation in the accuracy rate was caused by the small window size.

Einizade et al. (2022) proposed a graph learning approaches-based neural decoding of IS using EEG. By utilizing the iB-CIC2020 dataset, which comprises 64 EEG channel recordings, this model was evaluated. In this, for extracting the features from recorded EEG, the Fisher criterion was used. Thereafter, the acquired features were input into a graph-based IS decoder in BCI, thus achieving IS decoding. An accuracy of 50.10% was achieved by this approach. However, due to the complex graph theory, this method struggled with data interpretation issues.

Table 4.5 summarizes the datasets, such as National Institute of Technology Silchar (NITS), Unicorn Hybrid Black Headset (UHBH), BCI Competition 2008 Graz Dataset (BCGD), EEG Motor Movement/Imagery Database (EEGMMIDB), Holland Bloorview Kids Rehabilitation Hospital (HBKRH), and Peking University Institutional Review Board (PUIRB), which were commonly utilized for evaluating the ISR models.

## 3.7 Performance analysis of various ISR techniques

In this section, various ML and DL approaches, which were established to decode IS, IW, and MI, were validated. To identify the best performing model among various ISR frameworks, the performance evaluation along with the comparative analysis of them were conducted. Table 4.6 summarizes the performance analysis of ISR methods.

The performance evaluation of several ML and DL approaches in terms of accuracy is presented in Table 4.6 For identifying the best approach of ISR, the

**TABLE 4.5** Review on various standard datasets.

| Author name | Methods | Dataset | Training samples | Testing samples | Accuracy (%) | Downsides |
|---|---|---|---|---|---|---|
| Rajdeep Ghosh et al. (Ghosh et al., 2019) | SVM | NITS | 900 | 225 | 65 | Loss of essential EEG channels owing to the process of trimming. |
| Mokhles M. Abdulghani et al. (Abdulghani et al., 2023) | LSTM-RNN | UHBH | 320 | 80 | 92.50 | However, maximum response time was achieved by this method. |
| K. Keerthi Krishnan et al. (Krishnan and Soman, 2021) | DCNN | BCGD, Dataset II, Dataset III, and Dataset IV | – | – | 90.41 | Nevertheless, a large number of resources were needed for this approach. |
| Sadiq Ullah et al. (Ullah and Halim, 2021) | DCNN | EEGMMIDB and BCI2a | 28,000 | 7000 | 99.57 | However, for feature selection, this method considered only a few factors. |
| Alborz Rezazadeh Sereshkeh et al. (Sereshkeh et al., 2017) | Regularized neural network | HBKRH | – | – | 63.45 | Owing to the non-linear functions, it had overfitting problems. |
| P.P. Mini et al. (Minia et al., 2021) | ANN | Kara-one database | 204 | 51 | 77.37 | Improper identification owing to the EEG channel reduction. |
| Lingxi Lu et al. (Lu et al., 2021) | Fourier transform | PUIRB | – | – | – | The inaccurate results were caused by the manual process of large fluctuations and excessive noise removal. |
| Karel Roots et al. (Roots et al., 2020) | DCNN | EEGMMIDB | 512 | 128 | 83.95 | Nevertheless, this approach was suitable only for limited parameters. |

**TABLE 4.6 Performance validation of ML and DL methods.**

| Techniques | Accuracy (%) |
|---|---|
| DCNN (Ullah and Halim, 2021) | 99.57 |
| M-NN (Ghoniem et al., 2019) | 97.67 |
| CNN (Sarmiento et al., 2021) | 96.49 |
| DCNN (Zhang et al., 2022) | 93.36 |
| DCNN (Xiao and Fang, 2021) | 93 |

models, namely DCNN (Ullah and Halim, 2021), M-NN (Ghoniem et al., 2019), CNN (Sarmiento et al., 2021), DCNN (Zhang et al., 2022), and DCNN (Xiao and Fang, 2021) were analyzed. From Table 4.6, an impressive accuracy of 99.57% is achieved by the DCNN (Ullah and Halim, 2021) and a second-level accuracy of 97.67% is obtained by the M-NN (Ghoniem et al., 2019). Similarly, accuracies of 96.49%, 93.36%, and 93% are obtained by the CNN (Sarmiento et al., 2021), DCNN (Zhang et al., 2022), and DCNN (Xiao and Fang, 2021), respectively. Hence, as per the evaluation results, the other models are outperformed by the DCNN (Ullah and Halim, 2021) method.

The different models' comparative analysis is represented in a graphical form, which is presented in Fig. 4.4. Lastly, as per this survey, when compared to the conventional methodology in ISR, better performance is attained by the advanced methods.

## 4. Summary of the review

Brain Computer Interface has emerged as a powerful tool for achieving inner speech recognition driven by rapid advancements in machine learning and deep learning techniques. Supporting individuals with disabilities and augmenting the digital fields are the purpose of inner speech recognition. In numerous applications like healthcare, smart environments and assistive technologies, BCI plays the most important role. Additionally, to recognize SI, various types of signals like EEG, ECoG, and MEG are utilized by BCI. However, to decode IS, IW, and MI, the EEG signals are most widely used in BCI applications. In recent times, based on ML and DL techniques, numerous works were implemented to achieve ISR by using EEG. Therefore, this systematic review intends to examine the various ML and DL models in ISR. Primarily, this chapter framed the five research questions called RQ1, RQ2, RQ3, RQ4, and RQ5 that were more related to the objective of this survey. Afterward, this study was strategically organized to explain all of the research questions well. The RQ1 intended to explore the role of BCI and EEG in ISR. The review gathers the EEG-based different ISR models and then evaluates

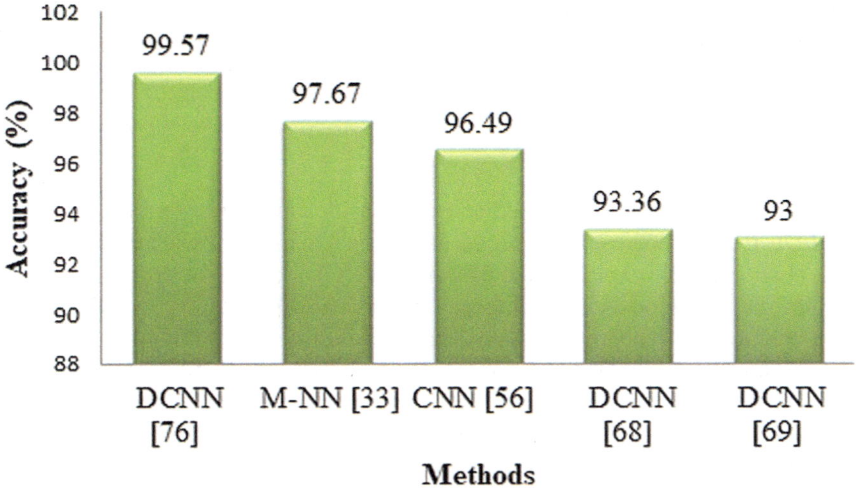


**FIGURE 4.4** Accuracy rate analysis.

their characteristics according to their methodology and outcomes, which is discussed in Section 3.1. Likewise, the importance of MI in BCI applications is investigated in RQ2. Therefore, the articles related to MI are presented in this chapter. A detailed explanation of MI and its impacts is provided in Section 3.5. After that, RQ3 targets to analyze the contribution of various ML and DL approaches in ISR. Therefore, based on ML and DL methodologies, numerous works are gathered in this survey. The various works regarding techniques, aims, benefits, and experimental results were explored in Sections 3.2 and 3.3. After RQ3, RQ4 focused on available datasets for assessing ISR models. This survey collects numerous standard datasets, which were established to implement IS decoding. According to the model's dataset characteristics, training samples, testing samples, and challenges, various models are validated in Section 3.6. Furthermore, the involvement and advantages of vowels and IW recognition from imagined speech are analyzed in Section 3.4. Lastly, RQ5 aimed to reveal the top model in ISR. For this purpose, the performance analysis was done for some of the ML and DL techniques. The techniques' performance regarding accuracy rate is evaluated in Section 3.7. It is proved from the analysis outcomes that a high accuracy of 99.57% was attained by the DCNN (Ullah and Halim, 2021). Next, the accuracy of 97.67%, 96.49%, 93.36%, and 93% is obtained by the approaches, such as M-NN (Ghoniem et al., 2019), CNN (Sarmiento et al., 2021), DCNN (Zhang et al., 2022), and DCNN (Xiao and Fang, 2021), respectively. Additionally, the review analyzes commonly used datasets, model architectures, and evaluation metrics. The findings indicate that advanced DL methods outperform conventional techniques in ISR tasks. However, challenges such as data variability, limited dataset size, and computational complexity remain significant.

Overall, this study provides a comprehensive overview of EEG-based ISR methodologies, highlighting current advancements, challenges, and future research directions in the field.

## 5. Conclusion

By using EEG signals, imagined speech classification based on numerous ML and DL methodologies are explored in this systematic review chapter. Initially, this chapter briefly explained the overview of BCI and EEG in ISR. Similarly, to depict the ISR models' advantageous nature, the significance of ML and DL approaches in IS recognition was examined. Additionally, the importance of MI, vowel, and IW classification to prove their consistency in BCI applications is presented in this chapter. Likewise, numerous available datasets, which are employed to assess the ISR techniques, are investigated in this chapter. The characteristics of various datasets and their performance are explained in this survey. Lastly, several ML and DL techniques in ISR are validated in this review to depict the dominant model. Therefore, the experimental outcomes signified that the DCNN (Ullah and Halim, 2021) outperformed the other conventional methods with a high accuracy rate of 99.57%. A better knowledge about ISR is provided in this chapter, which also outlines ISR's benefits and significance. Nevertheless, due to traditional pre-processing steps and inadequate feature selection of EEG, this study was less effective. In addition, owing to a lack of sufficient EEG subjects, it may produce misclassification of IS.

***Future work:*** Therefore, this review will be integrated in the future to concentrate on different advanced pre-processing steps to further upgrade the recognition outcomes. Additionally, it also considers the significant factors to detect the optimal features and elevate the sample size of EEG, which causes efficient ISR.

## References

Abdulghani, M.M., Walters, W.L., Abed, K.H., 2023. Imagined speech classification using EEG and deep learning. Bioengineering 10 (6), 2–15.

Agarwal, P., Kumar, S., 2022a. Electroencephalography-based imagined speech recognition using deep long short-term memory network. ETRI J. 44 (4), 672–685. https://doi.org/10.4218/etrij.2021-0118.

Agarwal, P., Kumar, S., 2022b. Imagined word pairs recognition from non-invasive brain signals using Hilbert transform. Int. J. Syst. Assur. Eng. Manag. 13 (1), 385–394. https://doi.org/10.1007/s13198-021-01283-9.

Alessandrini, M., Falaschetti, L., Biagetti, G., Crippa, P., Luzzi, S., Turchetti, C., 2023. A deep learning model for correlation analysis between electroencephalography signal and speech stimuli. Sensors 23 (19), 8039. https://doi.org/10.3390/s23198039.

Angrick, M., Ottenhoff, M.C., Diener, L., Ivucic, D., Ivucic, G., Goulis, S., Saal, J., Colon, A.J., Wagner, L., Krusienski, D.J., Kubben, P.L., Schultz, T., Herff, C., 2021. Real-time synthesis of imagined speech processes from minimally invasive recordings of neural activity. Commun. Biol. 4 (1). https://doi.org/10.1038/s42003-021-02578-0.

Bakhshali, M.A., Khademi, M., Ebrahimi-Moghadam, A., Moghimi, S., 2020. EEG signal classification of imagined speech based on Riemannian distance of correntropy spectral density. Biomed. Signal Process Control 59, 1–11.

Bejestani, M.R.A., Mohammad Khani, G.R., Nafisi, V.R., Darakeh, F., 2022. EEG-based multi-word imagined speech classification for Persian words. BioMed Res. Int. 2022. https://doi.org/10.1155/2022/8333084.

Biswas, S., Sinha, R., 2022. Wavelet filterbank-based EEG rhythm-specific spatial features for covert speech classification. IET Signal Process. 16 (1), 92–105. https://doi.org/10.1049/sil2.12059.

Charuthamrong, P., Israsena, P., Hemrungrojn, S., Pan-ngum, S., 2022. Automatic speech discrimination assessment methods based on event-related potentials (ERP). Sensors 22 (7), 1–19.

Chengaiyan, S., Retnapandian, A.S., Anandan, K., 2020. Identification of vowels in consonant–vowel–consonant words from speech imagery based EEG signals. Cogn. Neurodyn. 14 (1), 1–19. https://doi.org/10.1007/s11571-019-09558-5.

Cooney, C., Folli, R., Coyle, D., 2018. Mel frequency cepstral coefficients enhance imagined speech decoding accuracy from EEG. In: 29th Irish Signals and Systems Conference. Belfast, UK.

Cooney, C., Korik, A., Folli, R., Coyle, D., 2020. Evaluation of hyperparameter optimization in machine and deep learning methods for decoding imagined speech EEG. Sensors 20 (16), 4629. https://doi.org/10.3390/s20164629.

Cooney, C., Folli, R., Coyle, D., 2022. Opportunities, pitfalls and trade-offs in designing protocols for measuring the neural correlates of speech. Neurosci. Biobehav. Rev. 140, 104783. https://doi.org/10.1016/j.neubiorev.2022.104783.

Dash, D., Wisler, A., Ferrari, P., Davenport, E.M., Maldjian, J., Wang, J., 2020a. MEG sensor selection for neural speech decoding. IEEE Access 8, 182320–182337. https://doi.org/10.1109/access.2020.3028831.

Dash, D., Ferrari, P., Wang, J., 2020b. Decoding imagined and spoken phrases from non-invasive neural (MEG) signals. Front. Neurosci. 14. https://doi.org/10.3389/fnins.2020.00290.

Datta, S., Boulgouris, N.V., 2021. Recognition of grammatical class of imagined words from EEG signals using convolutional neural network. Neurocomputing 465, 301–309. https://doi.org/10.1016/j.neucom.2021.08.035.

Duc, N.T., Lee, B., 2020. Decoding brain dynamics in speech perception based on EEG microstates decomposed by multivariate Gaussian hidden Markov model. IEEE Access 8, 146770–146784. https://doi.org/10.1109/access.2020.3015292.

Einizade, A., Mozafari, M., Jalilpour, S., Bagheri, S., Sardouie, S.H., 2022. Neural decoding of imagined speech from EEG signals using the fusion of graph signal processing and graph learning techniques. Neurosci. Inform. 2 (3), 1–13.

Gao, C., Sun, J., 2022. Motor imagery recognition method based on multisource transfer learning and multiclassifier fusion. Wireless Commun. Mobile Comput. 2022. https://doi.org/10.1155/2022/3893866.

Garcia-Salinas, J.S., Villasenor-Pineda, L., Reyes-Garcia, C.A., Torres-Garcia, A.A., 2019. Transfer learning in imagined speech EEG-based BCIs. Biomed. Signal Process Control 50, 151–157.

Ghoniem, R.M., Algarni, A.D., Shaalan, K., 2019. Multi-modal emotion aware system based on fusion of speech and brain information. Information 10 (7), 239. https://doi.org/10.3390/info10070239.

Ghosh, R., Sinha, N., Biswas, S.K., Phadikar, S., 2019. A modified grey wolf optimization based feature selection method from EEG for silent speech classification. J. Inf. Optim. Sci. 40 (8), 1639–1652. https://doi.org/10.1080/02522667.2019.1703262.

Hamedi, N., Samiei, S., Delrobaei, M.K.A., 2020. Imagined speech decoding from EEG: the winner of 3rd Iranian BCI competition (iBCIC2020). In: 27th National and 5th International Iranian Conference of Biomedical Engineering, ICBME 2020. Institute of Electrical and Electronics Engineers Inc., Iran, pp. 101–105. https://doi.org/10.1109/ICBME51989.2020.9319439. http://ieeexplore.ieee.org/xpl/mostRecentIssue.jsp?punumber=9319322.

Hashim, N., Ali, A., Mohd-Isa, W.-N., 2018. Word-based classification of imagined speech using EEG. In: Computational Science and Technology: 4th ICCST 2017, Kuala Lumpur, Malaysia. Springer, Singapore, pp. 195–204, 29–30 November 2017.

Hernández-Del-Toro, T., Reyes-García, C.A., Villaseñor-Pineda, L., 2021. Toward asynchronous EEG-based BCI: detecting imagined words segments in continuous EEG signals. Biomed. Signal Process Control 65, 1–8.

Islam, M., Shuvo, M.H., 2020. Dense net based speech imagery EEG signal classification using gramian angular field. In: 5th International Conference on Advances in Electrical Engineering. Dhaka, Bangladesh, 26–28 September 2019.

Izzuddin, T.A., Safri, N.M., Afzan Othman, M., 2021. Mental imagery classification using one-dimensional convolutional neural network for target selection in single-channel BCI-controlled mobile robot. Neural Comput. Appl. 33 (11), 6233–6246. https://doi.org/10.1007/s00521-020-05393-6.

Janke, M., Diener, L., 2017. EMG-to-Speech: direct generation of speech from facial electromyographic signals. IEEE/ACM Trans. Audio Speech Lang. Process. 25 (12), 2375–2385. https://doi.org/10.1109/taslp.2017.2738568.

Jiménez-Guarneros, M., Gómez-Gil, P., 2021. Standardization-refinement domain adaptation method for cross-subject EEG-based classification in imagined speech recognition. Pattern Recognit. Lett. 141, 54–60. https://doi.org/10.1016/j.patrec.2020.11.013.

Keng Ang, K., Guan, C., 2017. EEG-based strategies to detect motor imagery for control and rehabilitation. IEEE Trans. Neural Syst. Rehabil. Eng. 25 (4), 392–401. https://doi.org/10.1109/tnsre.2016.2646763.

Kocturova, M., Juhar, J., 2020. Speech activity detection from EEG using a feed-forward neural network. In: 10th IEEE International Conference on Cognitive Infocommunications. Naples, Italy, 23–25 October 2019.

Koctúrová, M., Juhár, J., 2021. A novel approach to EEG speech activity detection with visual stimuli and mobile BCI. Appl. Sci. 11 (2), 674. https://doi.org/10.3390/app11020674.

Krishnan, K.K., Soman, K.P., 2021. CNN based classification of motor imaginary using variational mode decomposed EEG-spectrum image. Biomed. Eng. Lett. 11 (3), 235–247. https://doi.org/10.1007/s13534-021-00190-z.

Kumar, P., Scheme, E., 2021. A deep spatio-temporal model for EEG-based imagined speech recognition. In: IEEE International Conference on Acoustics, Speech and Signal Processing. Toronto, ON, Canada, 06–11 June 2021.

Kumar, P., Saini, R., Roy, P.P., Kumar Sahu, P., Prosad Dogra, D., 2018. Envisioned speech recognition using EEG sensors. Personal Ubiquitous Comput. 22 (1), 185–199. https://doi.org/10.1007/s00779-017-1083-4.

Kumar, S., Verma, P.R., Bharti, M., Agarwal, P., 2021. A CNN based graphical user interface controlled by imagined movements. Int. J. Syst. Assur. Eng. Manag. 14, 807–817.

Lee, S.-H., Lee, M., Lee, S.-W., 2020. Neural decoding of imagined speech and visual imagery as intuitive paradigms for BCI communication. IEEE Trans. Neural Syst. Rehabil. Eng. 28 (12), 2647–2659. https://doi.org/10.1109/tnsre.2020.3040289.

Lee, B.-H., Kwon, B.-H., Lee, D.-Y., Jeong, I.-H., 2021. Speech imagery classification using length-wise training based on deep learning. In: 9th International Winter Conference on Brain-Computer Interface. Gangwon, Korea (South), 22–24 February 2021.

Llorella, F.R., Iáñez, E., Azorín, J.M., Patow, G., 2021. Classification of imagined geometric shapes using EEG signals and convolutional neural networks. Neurosci. Inform. 1 (4), 100029. https://doi.org/10.1016/j.neuri.2021.100029.

Lu, L., Sheng, J., Liu, Z., Gao, J.-H., 2021. Neural representations of imagined speech revealed by frequency-tagged magnetoencephalography responses. Neuroimage 229, 117724. https://doi.org/10.1016/j.neuroimage.2021.117724.

Macias-Macias, J.M., Ramírez-Quintana, J.A., Ramírez-Alonso, G., Chacón-Murguía, M.I., 2020. Deep learning networks for vowel speech imagery. In: 17th International Conference on Electrical Engineering, Computing Science and Automatic Control. Mexico City, Mexico, 11–13 November 2020.

Mahapatra, N.C., Bhuyan, P., Troussas, C., 2022. Multiclass classification of imagined speech vowels and words of electroencephalography signals using deep learning. Adv. Hum. Comput. Interact. 2022, 1–10. https://doi.org/10.1155/2022/1374880.

Martin, S., Brunner, P., Iturrate, I., Millán, J.del R., Schalk, G., Knight, R.T., Pasley, B.N., 2016. Word pair classification during imagined speech using direct brain recordings. Sci. Rep. 6 (1). https://doi.org/10.1038/srep25803.

Meng, K., Grayden, D.B., Cook, M.J., Vogrin, S., Goodarzy, F., 2021. Identification of discriminative features for decoding overt and imagined speech using stereotactic electroencephalography. In: 9th International Winter Conference on Brain-Computer Interface. Gangwon, Korea (South), 22–24 February 2021.

Miao, M., Wang, A., Liu, F., 2017. A spatial-frequency-temporal optimized feature sparse representation-based classification method for motor imagery EEG pattern recognition. Med. Biol. Eng. Comput. 55 (9), 1589–1603. https://doi.org/10.1007/s11517-017-1622-1.

Min, B., Kim, J., Park, H.-jun, Lee, B., 2016. Vowel imagery decoding toward silent speech BCI using extreme learning machine with electroencephalogram. BioMed Res. Int. 2016, 1–12.

Minia, P.P., Thomasa, T., Gopikakumarib, R., 2021. EEG based direct speech BCI system using a fusion of SMRT and MFCC/LPCC features with ANN classifier. Biomed. Signal Process Control 68, 1–12.

Moctezuma, L.A., Torres-García, A.A., Villasenor-Pineda, L., Carrillo-Ruiz, M., 2019. Subjects identification using EEG-recorded imagined speech. Expert Syst. Appl. 118, 201–208.

Mohanchandra, K., Saha, S., 2016. A communication paradigm using subvocalized speech: translating brain signals into speech. Augment. Hum. Res. 1 (1), 1–14.

Nguyen, C.H., Karavas, G.K., Artemiadis, P., 2018. Inferring imagined speech using EEG signals: a new approach using Riemannian manifold features. J. Neural. Eng. 15.

Panachakel, J.T., Ganesan, R.A., 2021. Decoding imagined speech from EEG using transfer learning. IEEE Access 9, 135371–135383. https://doi.org/10.1109/access.2021.3116196.

Pawar, D., Dhage, S., 2020. Multiclass covert speech classification using extreme learning machine. Biomed. Eng. Lett. 10 (2), 217–226. https://doi.org/10.1007/s13534-020-00152-x.

Proix, T., Saal, J.D., Christen, A., et al., 2022. Imagined speech can be decoded from low- and cross-frequency intracranial EEG features. Nat. Commun. 13 (1), 1–14.

Roots, K., Muhammad, Y., Muhammad, N., 2020. Fusion convolutional neural network for cross-subject EEG motor imagery classification. Computers 9 (3), 72. https://doi.org/10.3390/computers9030072.

Rusnac, A.-L., Grigore, O., 2021. Convolutional neural network applied in EEG imagined phoneme recognition system. In: 12th International Symposium on Advanced Topics in Electrical Engineering. Bucharest, Romania, 25–27 March 2021.

Rusnac, A.-L., Grigore, O., 2022. CNN architectures and feature extraction methods for EEG imaginary speech recognition. Sensors 22 (13), 1–19.

Saha, P., Fels, S., 2019. Hierarchical deep feature learning for decoding imagined speech from EEG. Proc. AAAI Conf. Artif. Intell. 33 (01), 10019–10020. https://doi.org/10.1609/aaai.v33i01.330110019.

Saha, P., Abdul-Mageed, M., Fels, S., 2019a. Speak your mind! Towards imagined speech recognition with hierarchical deep learning. arXiv 1–5. https://arxiv.org/pdf/1904.05746.pdf.

Saha, P., Fels, S., Abdul-Mageed, M., 2019b. Deep learning the EEG manifold for phonological categorization from active thoughts. In: IEEE International Conference on Acoustics, Speech and Signal Processing. Brighton, UK.

Sakai, R., Kai, A., Nakagawa, S., 2021. Classification of imagined and heard speech using amplitude spectrum and relative phase of EEG. In: IEEE 3rd Global Conference on Life Sciences and Technologies. Nara, Japan, 09–11 March 2021.

Saleh, M.A., Moore, R., Christensen, H., Arvaneh, M., 2018. Discriminating between imagined speech and non-speech tasks using EEG. In: 40th Annual International Conference of the IEEE Engineering in Medicine and Biology Society. Honolulu, HI, USA, 18–21 July 2018.

Sarmiento, L.C., Villamizar, S., López, O., Claros Collazos, A., Sarmiento, J., Rodríguez, J.B., 2021. Recognition of EEG signals from imagined vowels using deep learning methods. Sensors 21 (19), 6503. https://doi.org/10.3390/s21196503.

Sereshkeh, A.R., Trott, R., Bricout, A., Chau, T., 2017. EEG classification of covert speech using regularized neural networks. IEEE/ACM Trans. Audio Speech Lang. Process. 25 (12), 2292–2300. https://doi.org/10.1109/taslp.2017.2758164.

Sharon, R.A., Narayanan, S.S., Sur, M., Hema Murthy, A., 2020. Neural speech decoding during audition, imagination and production. IEEE Access 8, 149714–149729. https://doi.org/10.1109/access.2020.3016756.

Singh, A., Gumaste, A., 2021. Decoding imagined speech and computer control using brain waves. J. Neurosci. Methods 358.

Tamm, M.-O., Muhammad, Y., Muhammad, N., 2020. Classification of vowels from imagined speech with convolutional neural networks. Computers 9 (2), 2–14.

Tang, X., Wang, T., Du, Y., Dai, Y., 2019. Motor imagery EEG recognition with KNN-based smooth auto-encoder. Artif. Intell. Med. 101, 101747. https://doi.org/10.1016/j.artmed.2019.101747.

Thornton, M., Mandic, D., Reichenbach, T., 2022. Robust decoding of the speech envelope from EEG recordings through deep neural networks. J. Neural. Eng. 19 (4), 046007. https://doi.org/10.1088/1741-2552/ac7976.

Tian, X., Mary Zarate, J., Poeppel, D., 2016. Mental imagery of speech implicates two mechanisms of perceptual reactivation. Cortex 77, 1–12. https://doi.org/10.1016/j.cortex.2016.01.002.

Tong, J., Xing, Z., Wei, X., Yue, C., Dong, E., Du, S., Sun, Z., Solé-Casals, J., Caiafa, C.F., 2023. Towards improving motor imagery brain–computer interface using multimodal speech imagery. J. Med. Biol. Eng. 43 (3), 216–226. https://doi.org/10.1007/s40846-023-00798-9.

Torres-Garcia, A.A., Reyes-Garcia, C.A., Villasenor-Pineda, L., Garcia-Aguilar, G., 2016. Implementing a fuzzy inference system in a multi-objective EEG channel selection model for imagined speech classification. Expert Syst. Appl. 59, 1–12.

Ullah, S., Halim, Z., 2021. Imagined character recognition through EEG signals using deep convolutional neural network. Med. Biol. Eng. Comput. 59 (5), 1167–1183. https://doi.org/10.1007/s11517-021-02368-0.

Usama, N., Kunz Leerskov, K., Khan Niazi, I., Kim, D., Jochumsen, M., 2020. Classification of error-related potentials from single-trial EEG in association with executed and imagined movements: a feature and classifier investigation. Med. Biol. Eng. Comput. 58 (11), 2699–2710. https://doi.org/10.1007/s11517-020-02253-2.

Van Eyndhoven, S., Francart, T., Bertrand, A., 2017. EEG-informed attended speaker extraction from recorded speech mixtures with application in neuro-steered hearing prostheses. IEEE (Inst. Electr. Electron. Eng.) Trans. Biomed. Eng. 64 (5), 1045–1056. https://doi.org/10.1109/TBME.2016.2587382.

Vorontsova, D., Menshikov, I., Zubov, A., Orlov, K., Rikunov, P., Zvereva, E., Flitman, L., Lanikin, A., Sokolova, A., Markov, S., Bernadotte, A., 2021. Silent EEG-speech recognition using convolutional and recurrent neural network with 85% accuracy of 9 words classification. Sensors 21 (20), 6744. https://doi.org/10.3390/s21206744.

Wang, L., Huang, W., Yang, Z., Hu, X., Zhang, C., 2020. A method from offline analysis to online training for the brain-computer interface based on motor imagery and speech imagery. Biomed. Signal Process Control 62, 102100. https://doi.org/10.1016/j.bspc.2020.102100.

Watanabe, H., Tanaka, H., Sakti, S., Nakamura, S., 2020. Synchronization between overt speech envelope and EEG oscillations during imagined speech. Neurosci. Res. 153, 48–55. https://doi.org/10.1016/j.neures.2019.04.004.

Xiao, X., Fang, Y., 2021. Motor imagery EEG signal recognition using deep convolution neural network. Front. Neurosci. 15. https://doi.org/10.3389/fnins.2021.655599.

Zhang, G., Si, Y., Dang, J., 2019. Revealing the dynamic brain connectivity from perception of speech sound to semantic processing by EEG. Neuroscience 415, 70–76. https://doi.org/10.1016/j.neuroscience.2019.07.023.

Zhang, J., Liu, D., Chen, W., Pei, Z., Wang, J., 2022. Deep convolutional neural network for EEG-based motor decoding. Micromachines 13 (9), 1485. https://doi.org/10.3390/mi13091485.

Chapter 5

# EEG-based biomarkers for early detection and monitoring of Alzheimer's disease

**Venkat Ghodke**[1, 2] **and Suhas Gajre**[2]
[1]*Department of Electronics and Telecommunication Engineering, AISSMS'S Institute of Information Technology, S.P. Pune University, Pune, Maharashtra, India;* [2]*Department of Electronics and Telecommunication Engineering, SGGS Institute of Engineering and Technology, S.R.T.M. University, Nanded, Maharashtra, India*

## 1. Introduction

### 1.1 Research background

Memory, mental abilities, and personality are the principal areas that Alzheimer's disease affects; this is an unremittingly progressive neurological disorder. Early detection and monitoring of Alzheimer's disease will suffice for intervening and showing treatment results at the right time. The EEG is an abbreviation for Electro Encephalography. Electrodes on the top of the head record the electrical impulses in the brain (Li et al., 2023). Such processes are also generally used in medical facilities to diagnose and monitor various neurological disorders. Many researches have claimed that EEG may give significant insights into Alzheimer's disease in characterizing specific patterns of brain activity events associated with the disease. Alzheimer's features include a process that creates clumps of tau and amyloid plaques in the brain, leading to neuronal death and dysfunction. This process renders havoc on normal brain activity, as measured by EEG (Eyamu et al., 2023). Abnormality in EEG patterns due to effects in that regard includes decreased alpha and beta action and increased delta activities among people with Alzheimer's disease. Event-related potentials, which are specific brain reactions to sounds and other stimuli such as images, can be measured with an EEG. Abnormal ERPs are observed for most patients with Alzheimer's disease and thus indicate their cognitive and sensory deficits during processing. Several ERP components, including the movement in P300, have been linked to cognitive decline and

**Neuromorphic Computing for Brain Computer Interfaces. https://doi.org/10.1016/B978-0-443-41594-4.00004-6**

therefore may serve as early indicators of Alzheimer's disease progression (Andrade et al., 2023). Alzheimer always has sleeping issues, and EEG can reveal these people's sleep patterns. Changes in sleep architecture, including REM and slow-wave sleep disruptions, have been reported in patients with the disease. Sleep surveillance by EEG may also be established as a diagnosis for the ailment.

## 1.2 Research aim and objectives

### 1.2.1 Aim

The objective is to find and evaluate EEG-based indicators for the diagnosis of Alzheimer's disease early on and continuous patient advancement monitoring.

### 1.2.2 Objective

- Making a reliable algorithm to analyze EEG data automatically.
- To the viability of adding EEG monitoring to standard clinical procedures.
- Looking at any possible link between cognitive impairment and EEG biomarkers.
- Investigating the potential long-term use of EEG-based biomarkers to monitor the course of disease including the effectiveness of treatment.

## 1.3 Research rationale

### 1.3.1 What is the issue?

The issue is the open disease of Alzheimer's in people and that is the epitome of the diseases. The rate of this disease increases day by day and the more people are suffering the more people act as helping hands to remove all of their memory permanently. The intensity of this disease increases day by day and maintaining the medication is not very good for the people. The addition of the drug to help the cognitive functions of the brain is not a very good example of defending Alzheimer's disease.

### 1.3.2 Why is the issue?

The issue is being provided because the disease is very bad for older people to understand the type of disease. The problem lies within the human brain and this cognitive functional disease is affecting people very much and that is why it is essential to control it.

### 1.3.3 Why is the issue now?

The issue is generally provided with the problems in detecting early Alzheimer's and monitoring with older technologies. Technologies are always getting upgraded with the flow of time and it is very important to maintain the structural function of the different models to study Alzheimer's disease.

## 2. Literature review

### 2.1 Network analysis

Analyzing the relationships between various brain regions is the study of functional connectivity, which can be done with EEG. Functional connection abnormalities, especially throughout the neuronal default mode network (DMN), are linked to Alzheimer's disease (Anonymous, 2023). The DMN is a network that is hypothesized to be recruited during self-referential and introspective processing. One of the pathways through which cognitive decline has been linked to Alzheimer's patients may be through altered DMN connectivity with other neural networks. Among the DMN's functions is to provide connectivity for a set of areas usually activated when a person is at rest and has his or her mind free from incentives from the environment (Jellinger, 2023). Self-referential thought, self-examination, and mind-wandering have been attributed to this area in functioning. The dorsal medulla is altered under Alzheimer's disease (AlSharabi et al., 2023). Inter-regional decreases in interaction and coordination within the DMN are proposed as signaling alterations in functional connectivity within this neural network, as indicated by EEG studies Fig. 5.1.

To be able to classify patients' stages in sickness progression and track those changes through time, one can use measures of their functional

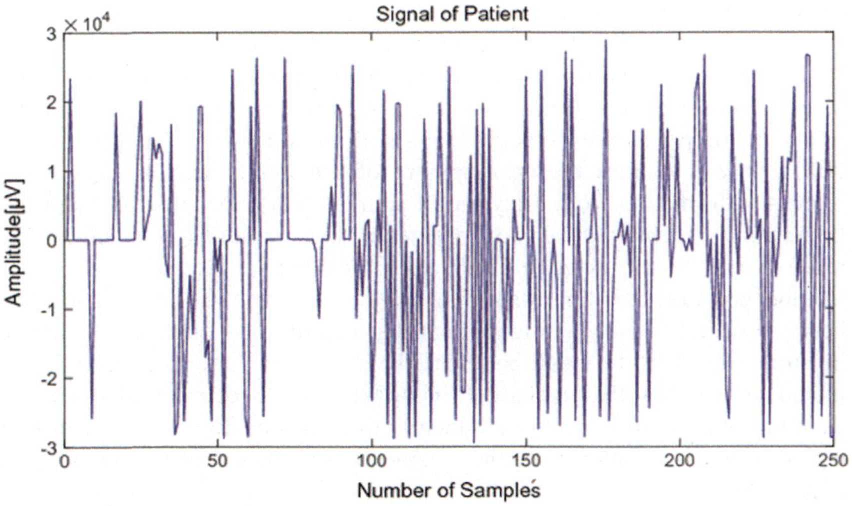


**FIGURE 5.1** EEG signal of an Alzheimer's patient.

connectivity (Chu et al., 2023). Early-stage patients may exhibit subtle alterations, while more advanced cases illustrate increasingly grotesque aberrations with regard to connection. An EEG-based connectivity functions study allows insight into dynamic and ongoing interactions of different brain parts in Alzheimer's disease. From disturbance reported in the DMN as well as other networks, a whole mass of information related to primitive cause of the illness and cognitions impairements related to the illness can be extracted (Giovannini and Meletti, 2023). EEG will also prove to have clinical applicability since it can record the patterns of brain activity and connection in near real time, further justifying its value as being vital in Alzheimer's disease research and in research into Alzheimer's disease.

## 2.2 Multimodal methods for biomarkers

EEG mixed with other bio-markers, such as markers in cerebrospinal fluid and neuroimaging techniques, provide an avenue toward a more comprehensive way to diagnose and monitor Alzheimer's disease. Multimodal approaches extend the picture of the trajectory of the disease and improve diagnostic accuracy (Hernandez et al., 2023). Neuroimaging methods, including positron emission tomography and magnetic resonance imaging, are good applicators for providing structural and functional information on the brain and are usually combined with EEG to corroborate findings. It is said the diagnosis will be enhanced by combining EEG with other biomarkers-well above that in the eradication of Alzheimer's as compared to other neurodegenerative conditions (Rutkowski et al., 2023). Development on the understanding of recurrence of the disease and cognitive difficulty is also better because these biomarkers assess different aspects of the disease, including structural and molecular changes and electrophysiological activity Fig. 5.2.

Among the major difficulties involved in combining all modalities for Alzheimer's research, the first is the increased demand for larger and more diverse datasets; second, harmonization of information and standardization of evaluation procedures to come along with these new datasets (Tobe et al., 2023). It will require the development of methodologies for aggregating relevant information from a myriad of sources into a meaningful diagnostic framework. Technological advancements like simultaneous EEG-fMRI make it possible to acquire EEG and fMRI data at the same time. This method provides real-time data that can be used to establish relationships between neural activity and functional connectivity (Liu et al., 2023). These, in turn, could lead to much better markers for Alzheimer's disease. Multimodal approaches that include EEG together with other biomarkers, for example other CSF biomarkers added with neuroimaging, are hopeful strategies directed at improving the diagnosis, prognosis, and monitoring of Alzheimer's disease.

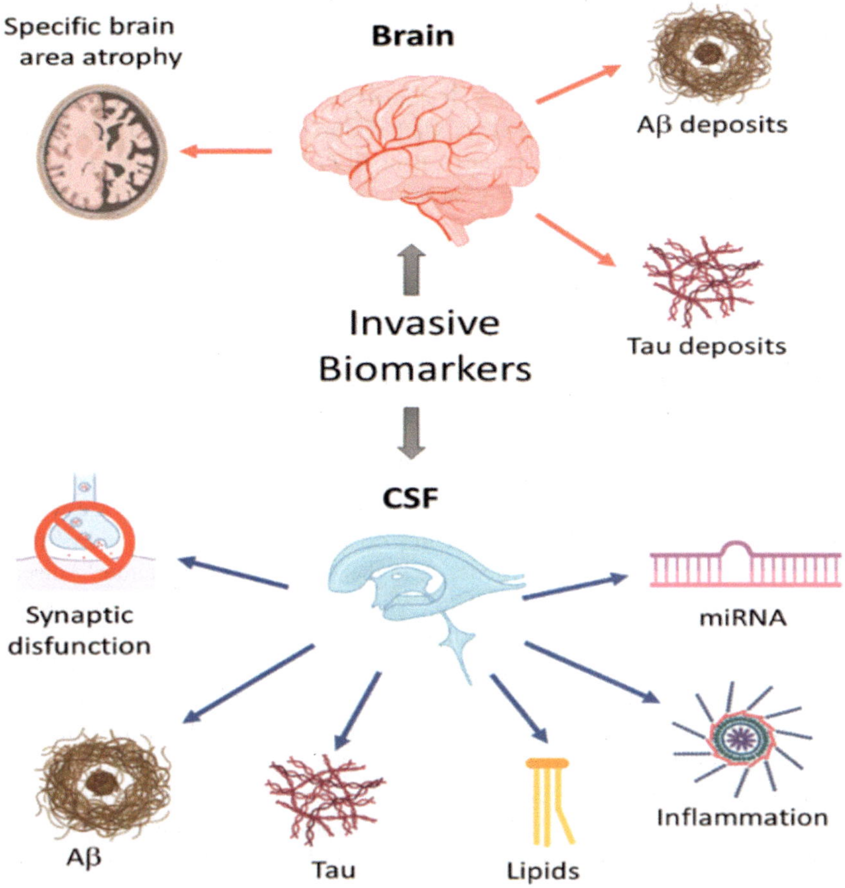


**FIGURE 5.2** Biomarkers for Alzheimer's disease.

## 2.3 EEG and abnormal sleep patterns

Alzheimer's patients often sleep poorly which, EEG can tell better about these disturbances. Sleep cycles in Alzheimer's sufferers are often distorted, causing reduction of REM sleep and distorting slow-wave sleep (Belyaev et al., 2023). In Alzheimer patients, slow-wave sleep or prolonged sleep or NREM sleep is disturbed quite often. Slow-wave sleep helps consolidate memories while restoring cognitive functions. Alzheimer's patients have lowered slow-wave activity during sleep associated with retarded memory and cognitive performance (Almufareh et al., 2023). EEG is a good method for determining sleep quality because it can document the timely occurrence of slow-wave activity patterns. The REM stage is when the most vivid dreams occur; disruption during this sleep stage can lead to emotional disturbances and cognitive impairment Fig. 5.3.

There are many things that the patient visits during Alzheimer's such as Nightmares, frequent awakenings. It interrupts sleep continuity and excessive fatigue and daytime sleepiness as well (Formica et al., 2023). Such sleep disturbances are viewed by means of an EEG because brain wave patterns altered reflect when a sleep period is shifting. EEG could eventually work as a method of diagnosis for Alzheimer's disease-related sleep disturbances (Alassafi et al., 2023). EEG provides objective and quantitative measures of sleep hygiene and patterns: that all would be very important for exploring sleep-related anomalies with relevance to Alzeihmer's disease. Such disruptions in sleep can also be indicated by reduced slow-wave activity during sleep in an abnormal EEG and alterations in the architecture of sleep.

## 2.4 Genetic variables and EEG trends

One of the best-known hereditary risk factors for Alzheimer's disease with an advanced stage is the APOE gene. Three common alleles ε2, ε3, and ε4 make what is known as the APOE gene. A higher chance of Alzheimer's disease development is linked to the ε4 allele (Wu et al., 2023). On the other hand, the most prevalent and normal risk variant is the ε3 allele, while the protective ε2 allele is thought to exist. Changes in EEG rhythms connected with the APOE 4 genotype could act as early predictors of Alzheimer's disease risk. Occasionally, these patterns can be seen before the onset of the disease's medical symptoms (Zakariah and Yousef, 2023). Individuals who have single or multiple copies of the APOE 4 allele often have different EEG patterns than individuals who do not have the mutation. Uncertainty surrounds the processes behind the correlation between APOE ε4 and changed EEG rhythms in Alzheimer's patients Fig. 5.4.

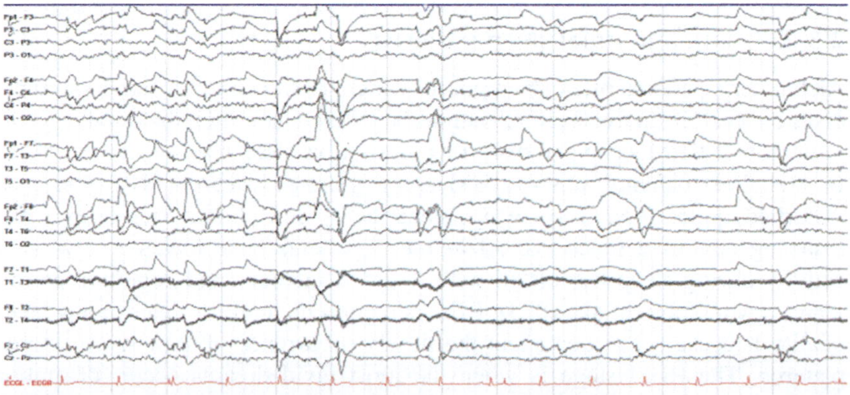

FIGURE 5.3 Normal sleep EEG.

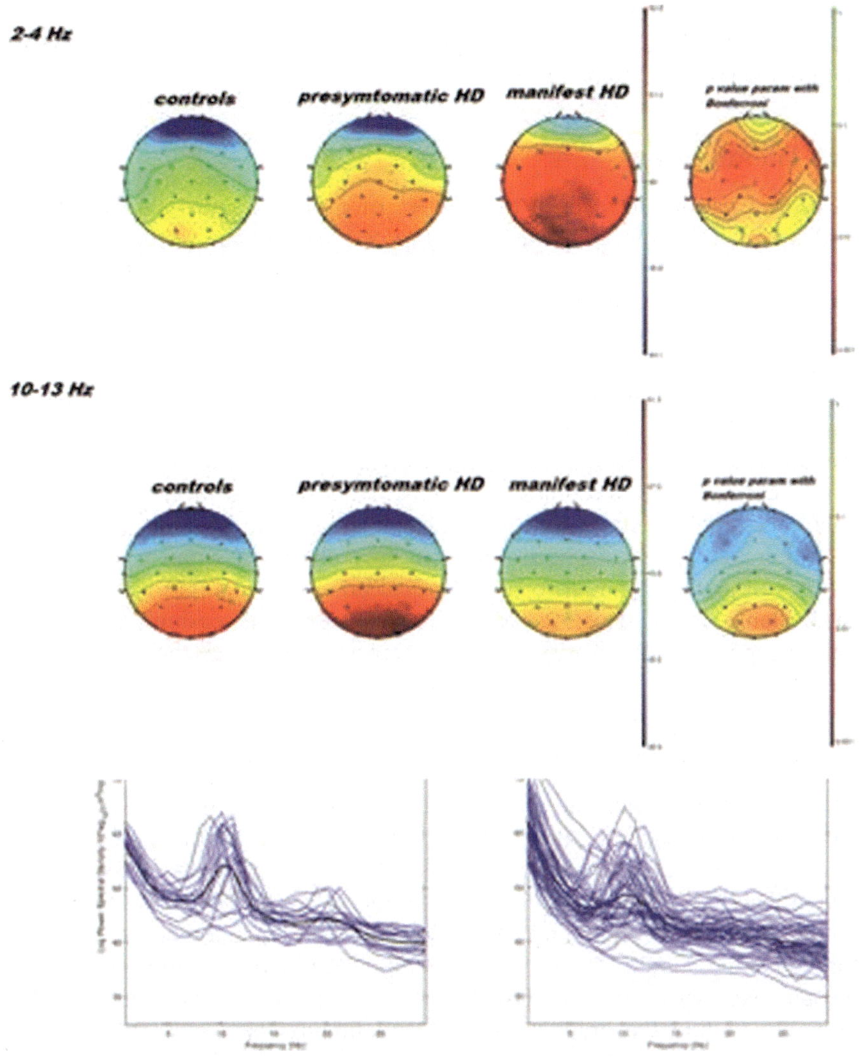


**FIGURE 5.4** EEG functional connectivity in premanifest.

Involved in the metabolism and clearance of amyloid-beta (Aβ), which are essential to the pathophysiology of Alzheimer's disease, APOE ε4 has been determined to be in these processes (Chen et al., 2023). The early phases of the illness's progression potentially be understood by examining the EEG abnormalities in APOE ε4 transporters, which could indicate disruptions in neural network dynamics and the functioning of neurons. A typical finding in the EEGs of APOE 4 carriers is a spike in delta along with theta power, particularly during relaxing states (Kim et al., 2023). The risk of Alzheimer's disease has been connected to these slow-wave activities, which are linked to cognitive deterioration. Clinical trials that target high-risk individuals and tailored surveillance can benefit from this information.

### 2.5 Literature gap

European nations have been the subject of a large number of Alzheimer's investigations. There is a deficiency in cross-cultural studies that investigate the generalizability and consistency of EEG-based biomarkers in various groups, taking into account possible genetic and environmental variables. More study is required to produce practical, therapeutically useful tools, however, machine learning techniques show promise for categorizing Alzheimer's illness utilizing EEG data. The gap between research discoveries and useful, real-world diagnostic tools must be closed. EEG alterations in Alzheimer's disease, although additional research is needed to confirm and validate these results. It is essential to conduct numerous consecutive datasets and laboratory replications to verify the dependability of EEG-based biomarkers. The literature is lacking in information about the privacy and ethical ramifications of gathering and evaluating critical brain information for Alzheimer's surveillance and diagnosis as EEG technology grows increasingly available. It may be possible to identify those at increased risk of Alzheimer's disease promptly by identifying EEG patterns linked to APOE ε4.

## 3. Methodology

The work done is with the help of Python programming using Jupyter Notebook to check datasets taken from different old age persons and check the accuracies of them catching the disease. The accuracy checking and finding the probability of Alzheimer's disease (Sakib et al., 2023). Predicting the type of dementia present in the minds of old age people finding the possible issues in their minds finding the procedural methods to help them to become better people. Normalization and visualization are applied to the Python coding program to find the graph, accuracy, and finding the issues and problems regarding to issues of the brain disease (Xu et al., 2023). The working methods are generated with the making of the datasets by checking the people of old age at least more than 60 years old to start checking their cognitive functions to take the procedures. The datasets are being recorded and utilizing the dataset in the Jupyter Notebook and the important libraries for making the proper procedures of analyzing the dataset and finding a better accuracy, model, and visualization (Fingelkurts and Fingelkurts, 2023). Using modules including mne or Pyedflib to import the electroencephalogram (EEG) information into Python. Preprocessing the data entails referencing, Filtering, and anomaly removal. data segmentation into pertinent historical periods (Anjum et al., 2023). power spectral concentration, event-related opportunities, and other pertinent EEG measurements should be calculated Fig. 5.5.

Obtaining pertinent characteristics out of the prepared EEG data. Spectral power in particular frequency bands, connection metrics, and ERP elements are examples of features. employing Numpy, Scipy, and mne, major Python packages, to extract features (Hejazi et al., 2023). Partitioning the dataset into testing as well as training portions. By using the sampling stratification method, an equal number of Alzheimer patients and control participants are assured for both groups. Normalizing or standardizing characteristics as necessary. When it comes to the EEG research of Alzheimer's, support vector machines are heavily employed modeling techniques. It works well in the binary classification task of differentiating between Alzheimer's patients and normal controls (Jiao et al., 2023). Support vector machines try to find the hyperplane in feature space that best separates the two classes. The SVM can discover non-simple relationships on EEG recordings by choosing appropriate kernels. SVM is famous for its strong generalization capability to deal with small data. In Random Forests, ensemble learning increases classification accuracy by combining the predictions of several decision trees (Maura et al., 2023). Random Forest can model Alzheimer's disease based on EEG since it can capture complex relationships that exist between EEG variables. It also provides feature importance that shows which EEG features are the most useful for classification Fig. 5.6.

The application of deep learning models such as recurrent neural networks (RNNs) and convolutional neural networks (CNNs) (Shusharina et al., 2023) for EEG-based biomarker research continues to proliferate. CNNs extract spatial information from topographical data or EEG spectrogram images. RNNs are capable of representing temporal dependencies in time series data from EEG. Long short-term memory (LSTM) and gated recurrent unit (GRU)

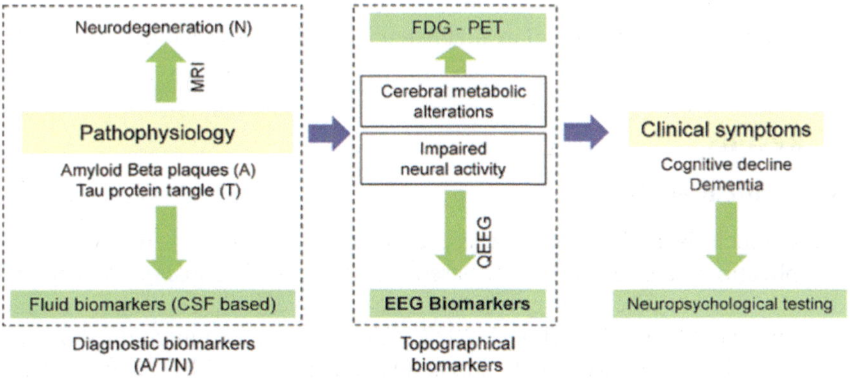


**FIGURE 5.5** EEG as a biomarker.

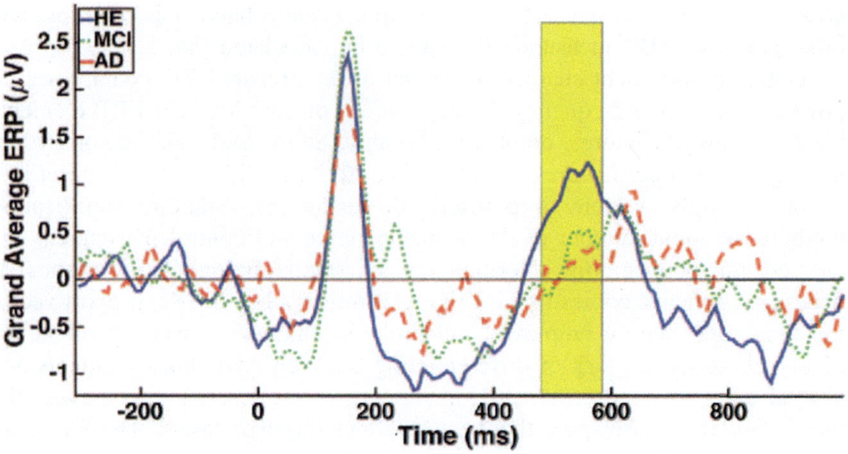


**FIGURE 5.6** EEG working on memory tasks.

systems are two variations of RNNs most frequently used (Bhachawat et al., 2023). EEG classification tasks could be tackled by multi-layer feedforward neural networks or MLPs, which are capable of identifying complex, non-linear patterns in EEG data. For reasonable performance from neural networks, architecture design and hyperparameter tuning are very crucial (Khondakar and Kaushik, 2023). Logistic regression is a simple model, but it can be useful in binary classification analysis in EEG-based biomarker studies. It can serve to identify key features involved in classifying Alzheimer's disease, besides being applicable and easy to interpret. The EEG imaging studies of Alzheimer's disease provide insights into machine learning algorithms (Polat, 2022). They are critical for revealing patterns associated to the diseases that facilitate early detection and follow-up of the condition and are the bases through which EEG data are assessed. The presiding considerations for the selection of an appropriate ML model include the type of EEG information under analysis, the amount of available data, and the particular objective of the study.

## 4. Results

### 4.1 Critical analysis

Since much is still to be researched, there are probable advantages and complications concerning EEG-based biomarkers diagnosing Alzheimer's disease. An advanced yet cheap and non-invasive tool for identifying biomarkers would be EEG (Polat, 2022). Upon closer examination, however, opportunities as well as complications reveal themselves. EEG may accelerate identification of very subtle changes in neural patterns that may be emerging signs of the disease, due to its real-time recording of brainwaves (Alves et al., 2022). The method's accessibility and well-tolerance make it beneficial. However, it can be challenging to analyze EEG data to identify Alzheimer's. It's difficult to separate early Alzheimer's alterations from typical aging, and indicators need to be specific. Individual differences may exist regarding the specificity and sensitivity of the technologies (Patil et al., 2022). Additionally, uniformity and comparability among research are hampered by the absence of established EEG protocols as well as data analysis methods (Kohli et al., 2022). To overcome these obstacles, scientists must work together to create consensus on EEG biomarkers, improve techniques for analyzing data, and test their results using sizable, varied cohorts.

## 4.2 Evidence of practical work

The code imports the necessary libraries for visualizing and analyzing data, such as Matplotlib. Pyplot to feed plotting, pandas for data processing, NumPy for numerical calculations, as well as seaborn to feed data visualization. Additionally, it mutes some warnings Figs. 5.7 and 5.8.

In this section, "oasis_longitudinal.csv," a CSV file saved at "C:/Users/User/," is read using the given code, which then uses Python's panda module to display the top five columns of the information utilizing df. head ( ) Fig. 5.9.

This code converts "M/F" to binary, renames "Group" values, removes extraneous columns, and filters the DataFrame "df" so it includes rows when "Visit" equals 1. It also resets the index Fig. 5.10.

The code provided generates a chart of stacked bars that shows the link that exists between the "Demented" rate within the dataset and the "Gender" characteristic, allowing the "Demented" as well as "Nondemented" subgroups to be distinguished Fig. 5.11.

# Importing Requird Libraries

```
In [1]: import pandas as pd
        import numpy as np
        import seaborn as sns
        import matplotlib.pyplot as plt
        from warnings import simplefilter
        from sklearn.exceptions import ConvergenceWarning
        simplefilter("ignore", category=ConvergenceWarning)
        simplefilter("ignore", category=UserWarning)
        %matplotlib inline
        sns.set()
```

**FIGURE 5.7** Importing required libraries.

## Importing Dataset

```
In [2]: df = pd.read_csv('C:/Users/User/oasis_longitudinal.csv')
        df.head()
```

Out[2]:

| | Subject ID | MRI ID | Group | Visit | MR Delay | M/F | Hand | Age | EDUC | SES | MMSE | CDR | eTIV | nWBV | ASF |
|---|---|---|---|---|---|---|---|---|---|---|---|---|---|---|---|
| 0 | OAS2_0001 | OAS2_0001_MR1 | Nondemented | 1 | 0 | M | R | 87 | 14 | 2.0 | 27.0 | 0.0 | 1987 | 0.696 | 0.883 |
| 1 | OAS2_0001 | OAS2_0001_MR2 | Nondemented | 2 | 457 | M | R | 88 | 14 | 2.0 | 30.0 | 0.0 | 2004 | 0.681 | 0.876 |
| 2 | OAS2_0002 | OAS2_0002_MR1 | Demented | 1 | 0 | M | R | 75 | 12 | NaN | 23.0 | 0.5 | 1678 | 0.736 | 1.046 |
| 3 | OAS2_0002 | OAS2_0002_MR2 | Demented | 2 | 560 | M | R | 76 | 12 | NaN | 28.0 | 0.5 | 1738 | 0.713 | 1.010 |
| 4 | OAS2_0002 | OAS2_0002_MR3 | Demented | 3 | 1895 | M | R | 80 | 12 | NaN | 22.0 | 0.5 | 1698 | 0.701 | 1.034 |

**FIGURE 5.8** Importing dataset.

# Target Selection

```
In [3]: df = df.loc[df['Visit']==1]
        df = df.reset_index(drop=True)
        df['M/F'] = df['M/F'].replace(['F','M'], [0,1])
        df['Group'] = df['Group'].replace(['Converted'], ['Demented'])
        df['Group'] = df['Group'].replace(['Demented', 'Nondemented'], [1,0])
        df = df.drop(['MRI ID', 'Visit', 'Hand'], axis=1)
```

**FIGURE 5.9** Target section.

```
Out[5]: Text(0.5, 1.0, 'Gender and Demented rate')
```

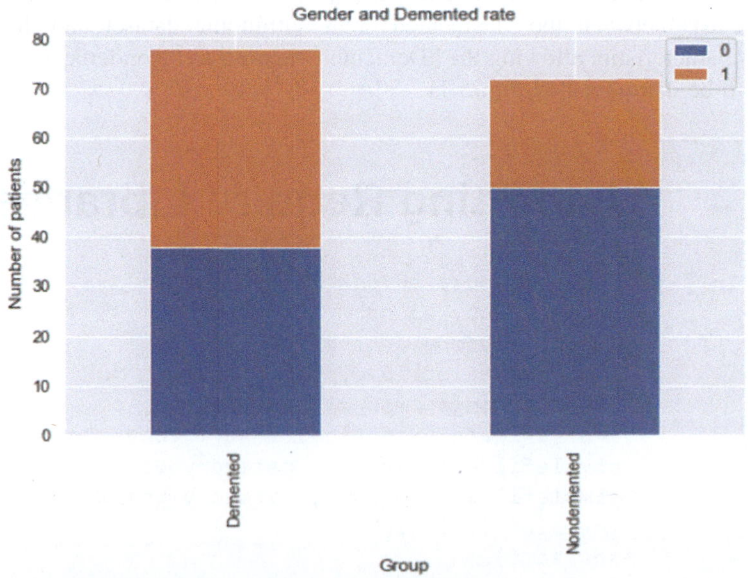


**FIGURE 5.10** Visulazatrrion gender and detented rate.

## Graphs of MMSE Scores

```
In [6]: facet= sns.FacetGrid(df,hue="Group", aspect=3)
        facet.map(sns.kdeplot,'MMSE',fill= True)
        facet.set(xlim=(0, df['MMSE'].max()))
        facet.add_legend()
        plt.xlim(15.30)

Out[6]: (15.3, 30.0)
```

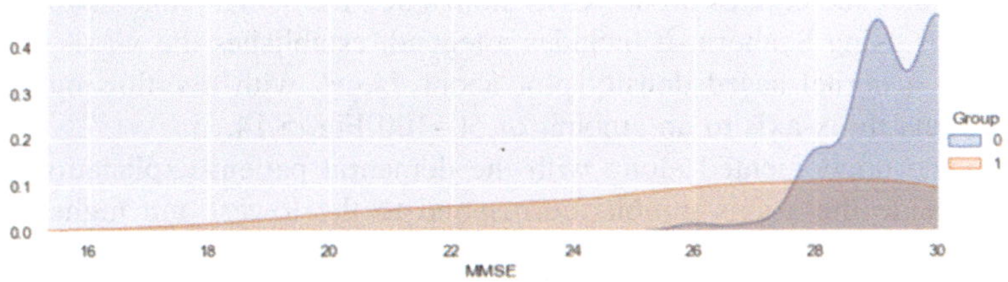


**FIGURE 5.11** MMSE score.

The "MMSE" score density graphs are generated using this code using Seaborn, and they are colored by "Group." It also adds a legend as well as sets the x-axis bounds from 0 to the highest possible "MMSE" score Fig. 5.12.

```
Out[7]: (0.6, 0.9)
```

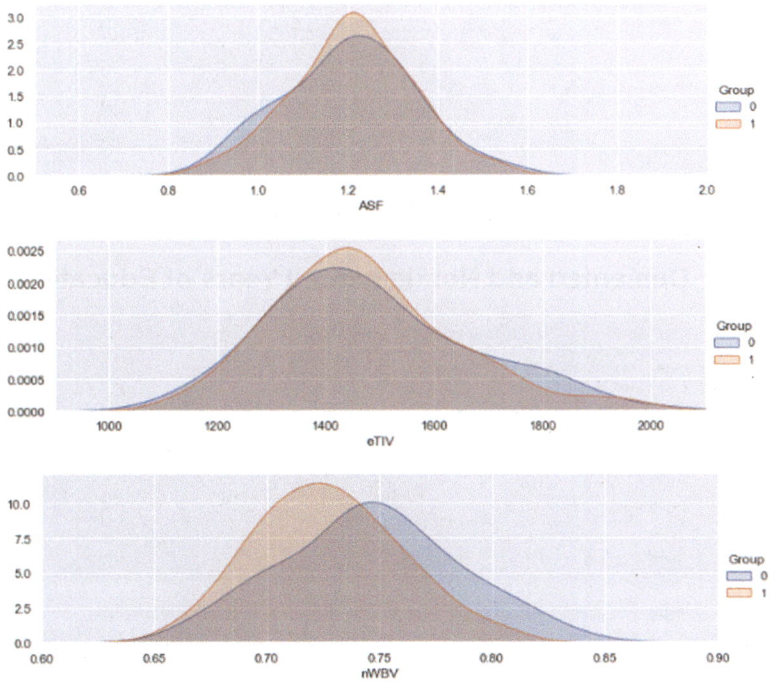


**FIGURE 5.12** Brain volume ratio.

In this section, with the help of the Seaborn libraries, the code supplied generates Kernel Density Estimation (KDE) diagrams for various volumes of brain measurements that are grouped by Group (Molcho et al., 2022). With distinct x-axis limits and shading, the "ASF," "eTIV," along "nWBV" appear are displayed, making it simple to compare and examine variations within Brain Volume Ratios between various groups Fig. 5.13.

This code creates a FacetGrid alongside "Demented" and "Nondemented" groups using Seaborn. It includes a legend, establishes the x-axis constraints, maps a kernel-based density plot about "Age" with overflowing areas, and restricts the x-axis to an amount of 50–100 Fig. 5.14.

The nondemented along with the dementia patient explanation is added, alongside the x-axis inhibits correspond to the lowest and highest levels of

## Demented and Nondemented Age

```
In [8]: facet= sns.FacetGrid(df,hue="Group", aspect=3)
        facet.map(sns.kdeplot,'Age',fill= True)
        facet.set(xlim=(0, df['Age'].max()))
        facet.add_legend()
        plt.xlim(50,100)

Out[8]: (50.0, 100.0)
```

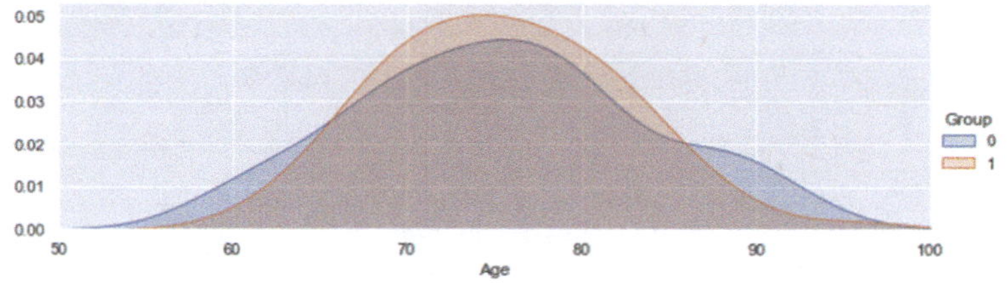


**FIGURE 5.13** Demented and nondemented age.

## Demented and Nondemented Years of Education

```
In [9]: facet= sns.FacetGrid(df,hue="Group", aspect=3)
        facet.map(sns.kdeplot,'EDUC',fill= True)
        facet.set(xlim=(df['EDUC'].min(), df['EDUC'].max()))
        facet.add_legend()
        plt.ylim(0, 0.16)

Out[9]: (0.0, 0.16)
```

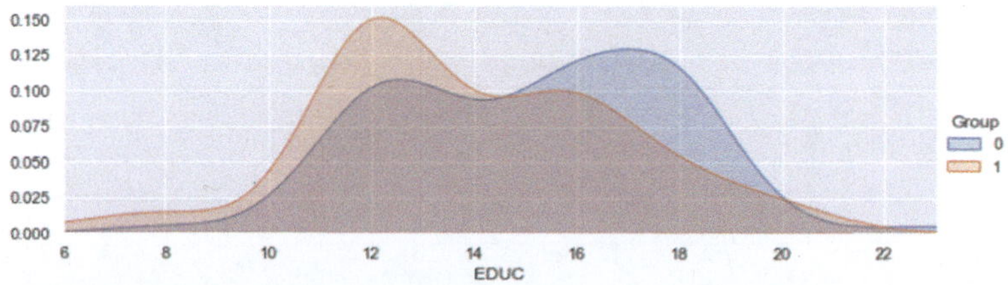


**FIGURE 5.14** Demented and nondemented years of education.

EDUC (Ho et al., 2022). The vertical spectrum of the plot is managed by setting the y-axis inhibits between 0 and 0.16 Fig. 5.15.

The procedure involves counting the absent values of the data frames "df," eliminating any rows that have any values that are not present, and then computing and displaying the value matters for the "Group" section in the newly formatted Data Framework "df_dropna" Fig. 5.16.

Through "EDUC" on the x-axis along with "SES" on the y-dimension, this code generates a scatter chart. Additionally, it fits a relationship-showing regressive line ("r–") with the data Fig. 5.17.

## Data Preprocessing

```
In [10]: pd.isnull(df).sum()

Out[10]: Subject ID    0
         Group         0
         MR Delay      0
         M/F           0
         Age           0
         EDUC          0
         SES           8
         MMSE          0
         CDR           0
         eTIV          0
         nWBV          0
         ASF           0
         dtype: int64

In [11]: df_dropna = df.dropna(axis=0, how='any')
         pd.isnull(df_dropna).sum()

Out[11]: Subject ID    0
         Group         0
         MR Delay      0
         M/F           0
         Age           0
         EDUC          0
         SES           0
         MMSE          0
         CDR           0
         eTIV          0
         nWBV          0
         ASF           0
         dtype: int64

In [12]: df_dropna['Group'].value_counts()

Out[12]: 0    72
         1    70
         Name: Group, dtype: int64
```

**FIGURE 5.15** Data preprocessing.

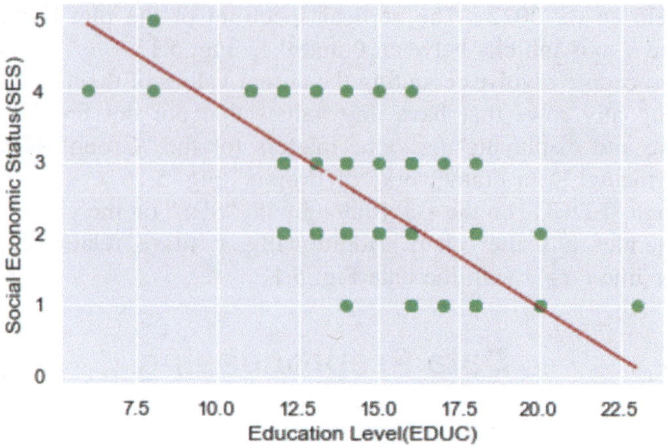


**FIGURE 5.16** Scatter plot EDUC and SES.

This code base divides the informational set into sets to be trained and tested using the Scikit-Learning "train_test_split" purpose Fig. 5.18.

In addition to AdaBoost classification techniques, Random Forest, reasoning trees, Support Vector Machines (SVC), as well as logistic regression methods, it also includes metrics such as ROC curves, AUC, reliability, and recall, along with confusion matrices Fig. 5.19.

# Splitting the Datasets

```
In [17]: from sklearn.model_selection import train_test_split
         from sklearn import preprocessing
         from sklearn.preprocessing import MinMaxScaler
         from sklearn.model_selection import cross_val_score
```

```
In [18]: Y = df['Group'].values
         X = df[['M/F', 'Age', 'EDUC', 'SES', 'MMSE', 'eTIV', 'nWBV', 'ASF']]
         X_trainval, X_test, Y_trainval, Y_test = train_test_split(
             X, Y, random_state=0)
         scaler = MinMaxScaler().fit(X_trainval)
         X_trainval_scaled = scaler.transform(X_trainval)
         X_test_scaled = scaler.transform(X_test)
```

```
In [19]: Y = df_dropna['Group'].values
         X = df_dropna[['M/F', 'Age', 'EDUC', 'SES', 'MMSE', 'eTIV', 'nWBV', 'ASF']]
         X_trainval_dna, X_test_dna, Y_trainval_dna, Y_test_dna = train_test_split(
             X, Y, random_state=0)
         scaler = MinMaxScaler().fit(X_trainval_dna)
         X_trainval_scaled_dna = scaler.transform(X_trainval_dna)
         X_test_scaled_dna = scaler.transform(X_test_dna)
```

**FIGURE 5.17** Splitting the datasets.

## Machine Learning Models

```
In [20]: from sklearn.linear_model import LogisticRegression
         from sklearn.svm import SVC
         from sklearn.tree import DecisionTreeClassifier
         from sklearn.ensemble import RandomForestClassifier
         from sklearn.ensemble import AdaBoostClassifier
         from sklearn.metrics import confusion_matrix, accuracy_score, recall_score, roc_curve, auc

In [21]: acc = []
```

**FIGURE 5.18** Machine learning model.

The tweaking of hyper is done in this logical regression model that utilizes attribution to determine the optimal regularization parameters "C" through cross-validation to Correctness, recall, along AUC are measured on an array of tests to assess the efficacy of the model Fig. 5.20.

```
Best accuracy on validation set is: 0.7339920948616602
Best parameter for regularization (C) is:  10
Test accuracy with best C parameter is 0.7631578947368421
Test recall with the best C parameter is 0.7
Test AUC with the best C parameter is 0.7666666666666667
```

**FIGURE 5.19** Logistic regression model with imputation.

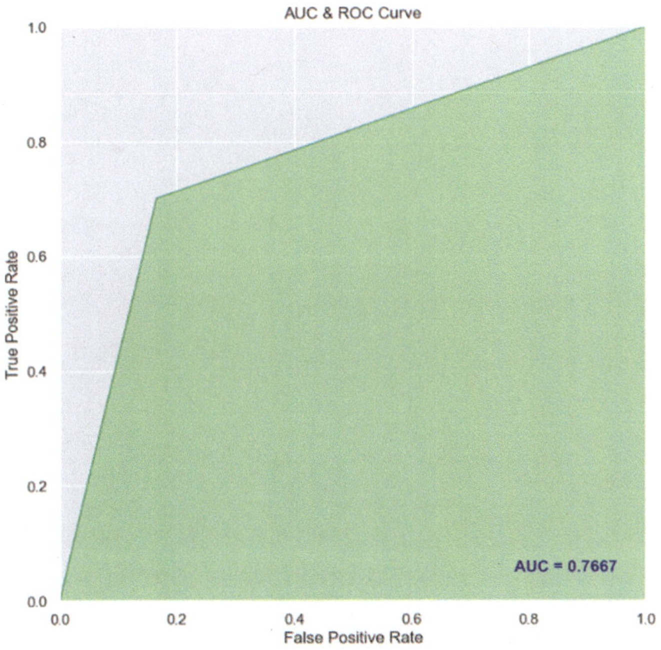


**FIGURE 5.20** Plotting AUC and ROC curve.

This code computes the AUC (Area According to the Curve) and plots the ROC curve to feed a logistic regression framework using the sci-kit-learn library Fig. 5.21.

The optimal regularization (C) parameters in this form of regression is 10, which results in an evaluation accuracy of 72.60% Fig. 5.22.

The given code snippet creates a Receiver Operating Characteristic (ROC) curve and computes the Area Under the Curve (AUC) to feed a Support Vector Machine (SVM) simulation that uses a Radial Basis Function (RBF) kernel Fig. 5.23.

This little piece of code creates a Receiver Operating Characteristic (ROC) curve and computes the Area According to the Curve (AUC) to feed the linear kernel of the Support Vector Machine (SVM) classifier Fig. 5.24.

The maximum validation accuracy attained in the Support Vector Machine Poly model using the regularization parameter (C) adjusted to 10 was 72.60% Fig. 5.25.

A sigmoid shapes kernel with ideal parameters (C = 100, gamma = 0.1) was employed throughout the SVM codebase. The effectiveness of the model was assessed by plotting ROC turns, and it obtained an AUC of 0.822 Fig. 5.26.

In this section, with an AUC of 0.822, this Decision Tree model demonstrated strong discriminatory power (Alvi et al., 2022). Its effectiveness in

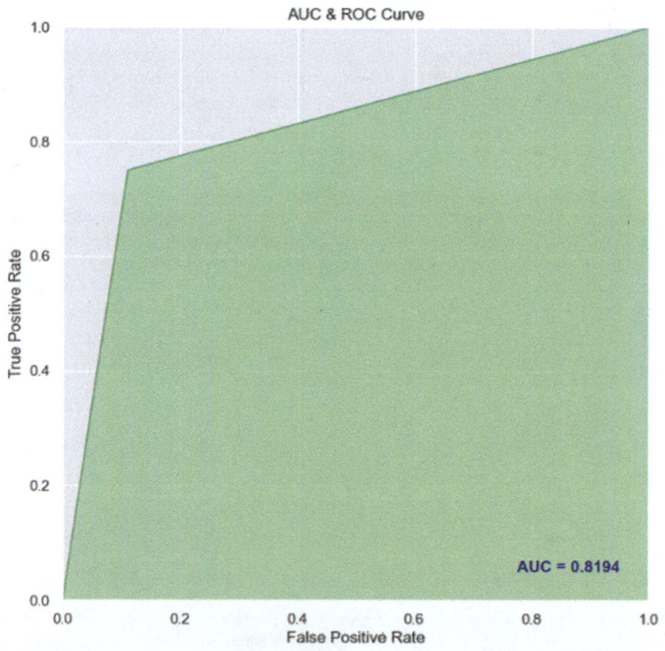


**FIGURE 5.21** Regression model without imputation AUC and ROC curve.

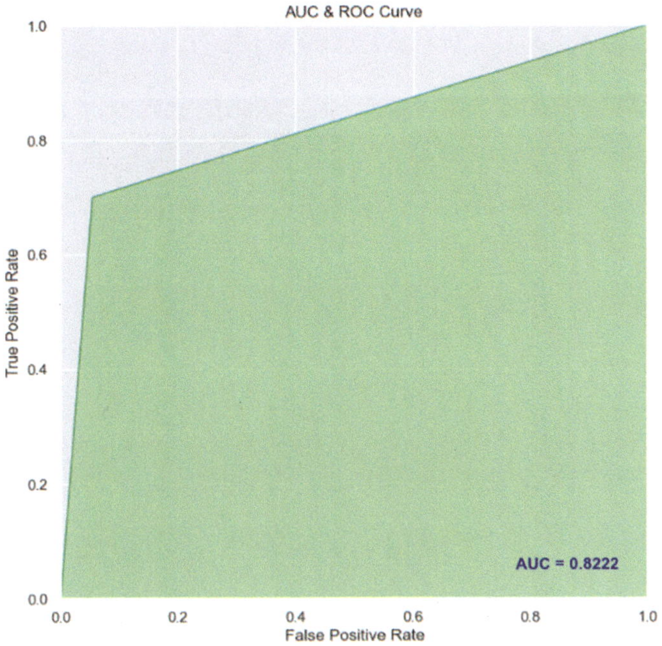


**FIGURE 5.22** SVM and RBF with AUC and ROC curve.

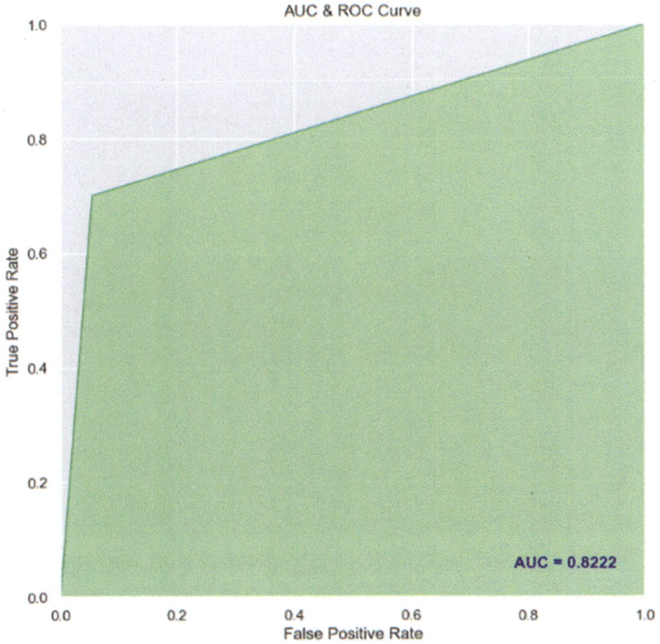


**FIGURE 5.23** SVM linear with AUC and ROC curve.

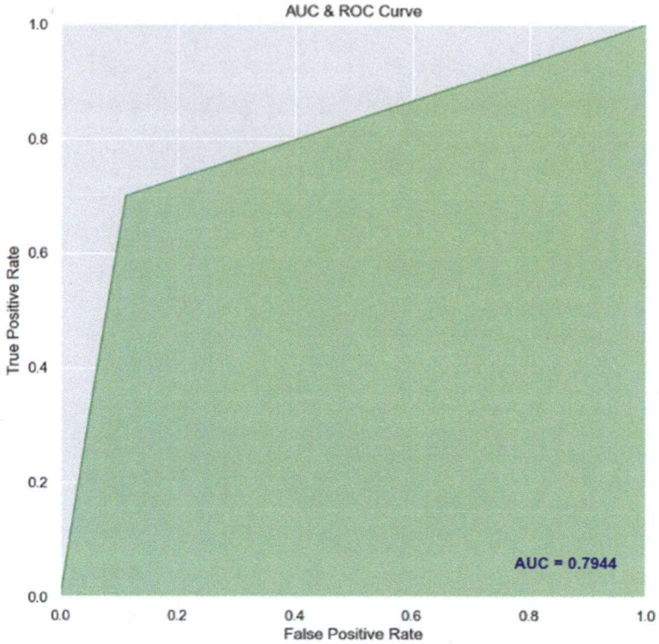


**FIGURE 5.24** SVM poly with AUC and ROC curve.

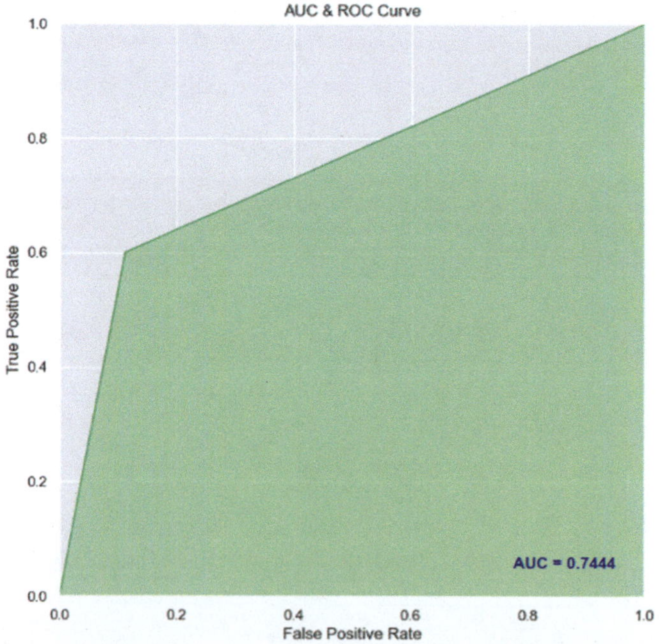


**FIGURE 5.25** SVM sigmoid with AUC and ROC curve.

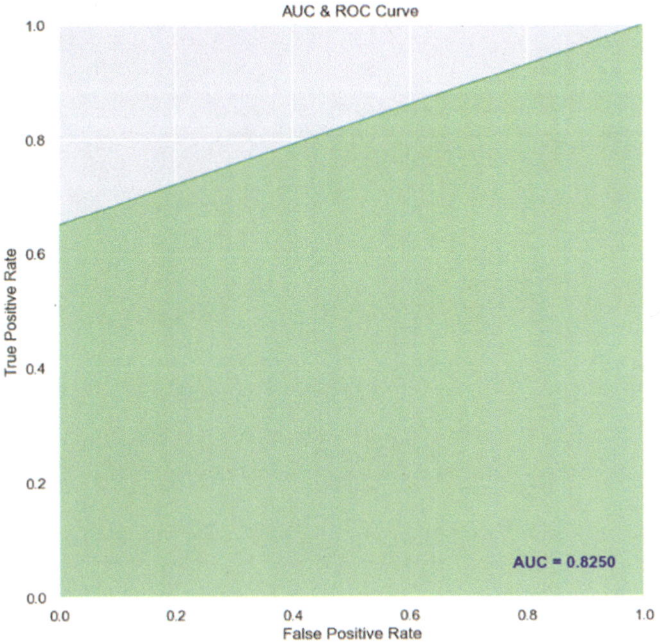


**FIGURE 5.26** Decision tree model with AUC and ROC curve.

differentiating classes is graphically represented by the ROC curve, which shows strong predictive ability Fig. 5.27.

The MMSE (Mini-Mental State Examination) result has the greatest magnitude in this sample (1.0), according to the important feature value pairs (Ju-Yu et al., 2022). Other features, such as “M/F,” “Age,” “EDUC,” “SES,” “eTIV,” “nWBV,” and “ASF,” have very little significance (0.0) Fig. 5.28.

In this section, with the ideal training parameters (M = 2, d = 5, m = 7), a Random Forest Classifier in this code was able to achieve its validation accuracy of about 80.36% Fig. 5.29.

## Feature Importance the datasets

```
In [40]: print("Feature importance: ")
         np.array([X.columns.values.tolist(), list(SelectedDTModel.feature_importances_)]).T

         Feature importance:

Out[40]: array([['M/F', '0.0'],
                ['Age', '0.0'],
                ['EDUC', '0.0'],
                ['SES', '0.0'],
                ['MMSE', '1.0'],
                ['eTIV', '0.0'],
                ['nWBV', '0.0'],
                ['ASF', '0.0']], dtype='<U32')
```

**FIGURE 5.27** Feature importance of the dataset.

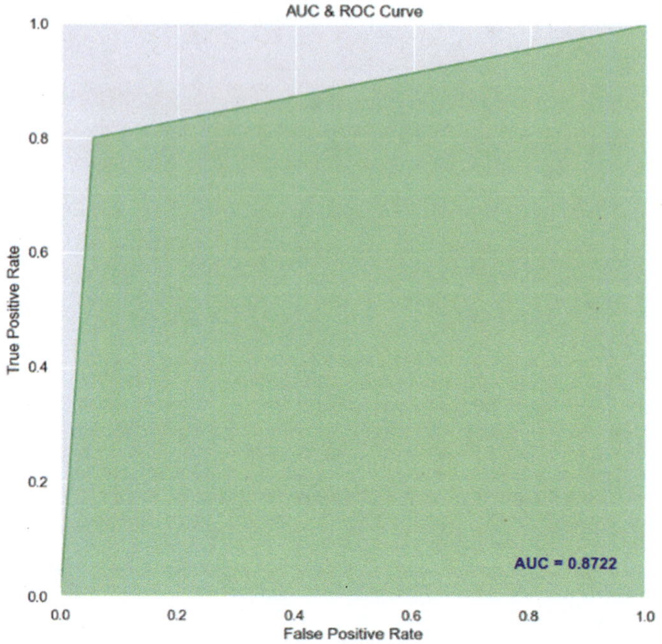


**FIGURE 5.28** Random forest classifier with AUC and ROC curve.

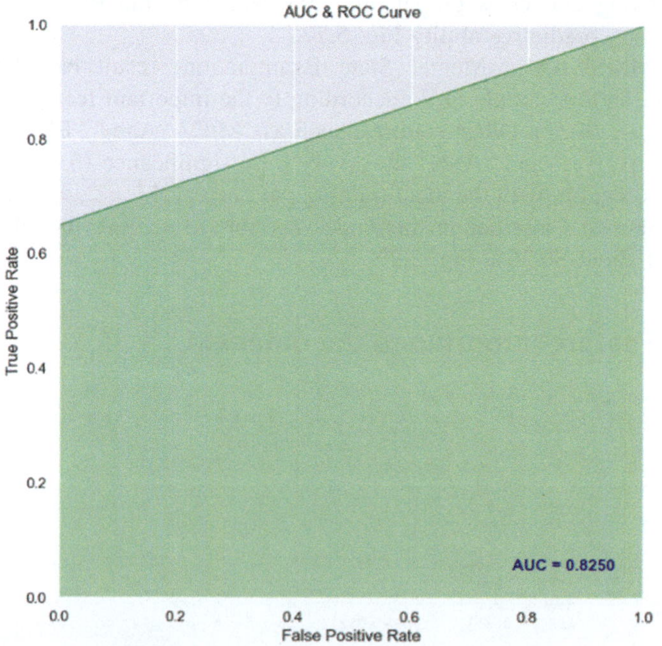


**FIGURE 5.29** AdaBoost with AUC and ROC curve.

The optimal values for this AdaBoost realization are M = 2 along with an improvement rate of 0.0001. From the test established, the model produced a success rate of 0.868, an average recall of 0.65, along with an AUC of 0.825. Its validation accuracy was 0.777 Fig. 5.30.

Metrics regarding performance are gathered for every model in this code. "Model" denotes the name of the method, "Accuracy" the accuracy result, and "Recall" the model's capacity to identify real instances of identification in tasks such as classification Fig. 5.31.

This code illustrates the accuracy of different models with a bar chart. From the x-axis, whatever model is displayed, along with on the y-axis, the level of precision that corresponds to it Fig. 5.32.

To show the recall of different models—a metric that indicates a model's capacity to recognize pertinent items—the code generates a bar chart. Example names are shown on the x-axis, alongside recall values are shown on the y-axis.

## 4.3 Evaluation

An important part of this field's study is evaluating EEG-based biomarkers enabling early identification and tracking the advancement of Alzheimer's

**Performance Metric for each model**

In [53]:
```
result = pd.DataFrame(acc, columns=['Model', 'Accuracy', 'Recall', 'AUC', 'FPR', 'TPR', 'TH'])
result[['Model', 'Accuracy', 'Recall', 'AUC']]
```

Out[53]:

| | Model | Accuracy | Recall | AUC |
|---|---|---|---|---|
| 0 | Logistic Regression (w/ imputation) | 0.763158 | 0.70 | 0.766667 |
| 1 | Logistic Regression (w/ dropna) | 0.805556 | 0.75 | 0.750000 |
| 2 | SVM(rbf) | 0.815789 | 0.70 | 0.822222 |
| 3 | Logistic Regression (w/ dropna) | 0.805556 | 0.75 | 0.750000 |
| 4 | SVM(rbf) | 0.815789 | 0.70 | 0.822222 |
| 5 | SVM(linear) | 0.815789 | 0.70 | 0.822222 |
| 6 | SVM(poly) | 0.789474 | 0.70 | 0.794444 |
| 7 | SVM(sigmoid) | 0.736842 | 0.60 | 0.744444 |
| 8 | Decision Tree | 0.815789 | 0.65 | 0.825000 |
| 9 | Random Forest | 0.868421 | 0.80 | 0.872222 |
| 10 | AdaBoost | 0.868421 | 0.65 | 0.825000 |

In [54]:
```
model = result['Model']
accuracy = result['Accuracy']
recall = result['Recall']
```

In [55]:
```
plt.figure(figsize=(28,9))
plt.bar(model, accuracy, label='accuracy (training data)', width = 0.4,)
plt.title('Accuracy of all models')
plt.ylabel('Accuracy value')
plt.xlabel('Model Names')
plt.legend(loc="upper left")
plt.show()
```

**FIGURE 5.30** Performance metric for each model.

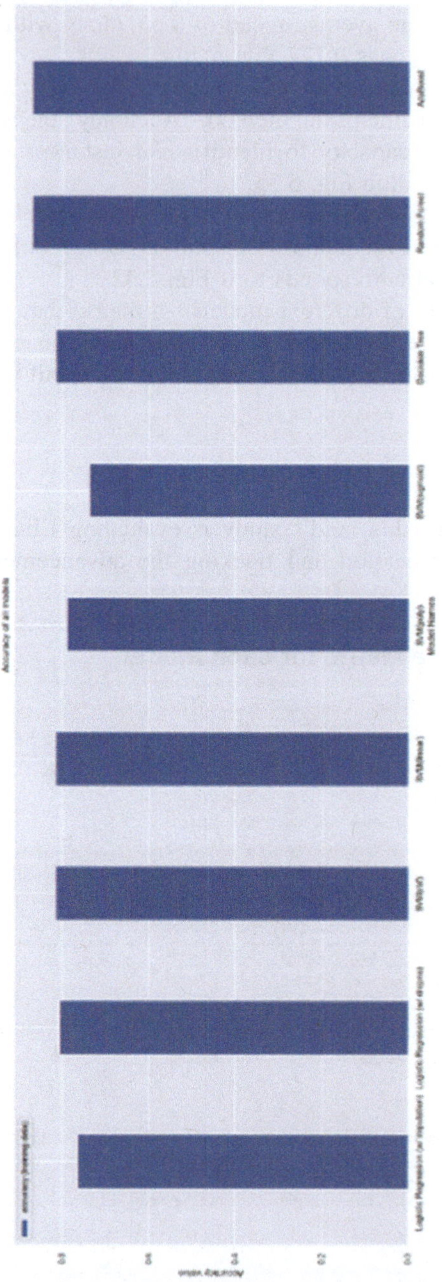

**FIGURE 5.31** Visualization accuracy of all models.

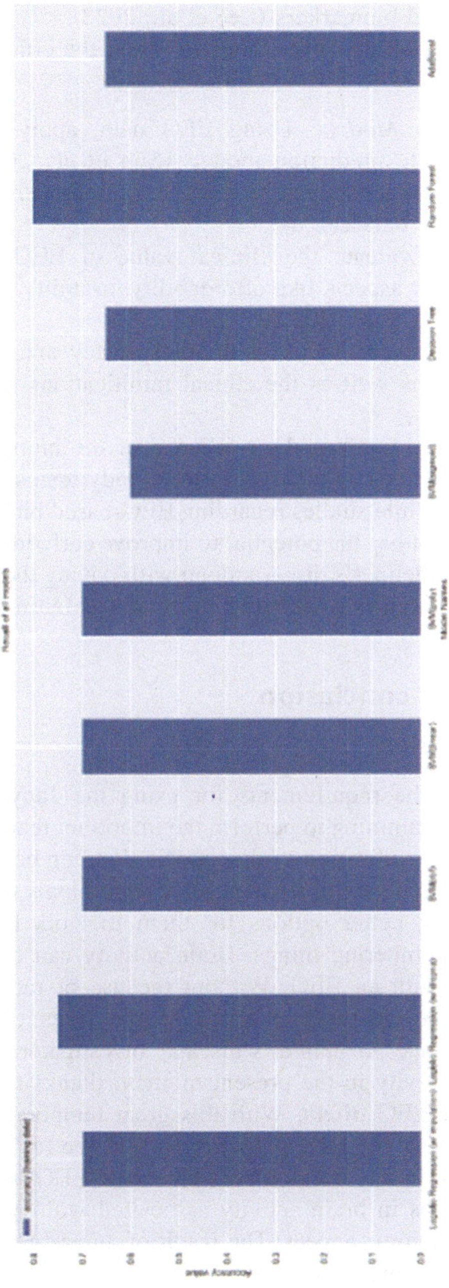

**FIGURE 5.32** Visualization recall of all models.

disease (AD) (Olichney et al., 2022). Electroencephalography, abbreviated EEG, has become a viable non-invasive method for studying the brain correlations of AD to find biomarkers (Lee et al., 2022).

Researchers use a variety of methods to assess the efficacy of EEG-based biomarkers:

*Machine Learning Models:* Using EEG data, apply machine learning techniques to create prediction models (Sun et al., 2022). The generalization ability of the model can be evaluated through cross-validations and testing on separate datasets.

*Clinical Utility:* Evaluate the clinical value of EEG-based biomarkers taking into account aspects like affordability, usability, and satisfaction of patients (Perrottelli et al., 2022).

*Ethical Considerations:* Think about the privacy and properly educated consent concerns as well as the ethical ramifications of employing EEG biomarkers.

*Reproducibility:* To confirm the resilience of the biomarkers, make sure that results can be repeated across various study teams and demographics (Li et al., 2022). While studies regarding EEG-based biomarkers are still in their early stages, it has the potential to improve early identification as well as tracking of Alzheimer's disease along with paving the way to additional treatment options that may be more successful (Maitin et al., 2022).

# 5. Evaluation and conclusion

## 5.1 Critical evaluation

The study provides the requirements for using the Jupyter Notebook and provides Python programming to perform the important features to analyze the dataset and find the visualization of the models. Finding better accuracy using several models and methods to understand the problems of dementia in old people and providing better options for them to work out their brain for functioning and remembering things. Brain activity can be measured safely and non-invasively with an EEG. Without the use of radiation or intrusive procedures, it can be easily supplied to people, even those who are just beginning to experience Alzheimer's disease. Investigators can observe fluctuations of neural activity in the present moment thanks to the high level of temporal detail that EEG offers. With this great temporal sensitivity, it becomes possible to study the mental operations and see for very early changes in the brain function. It may become possible to use EEG-based biomarkers to detect early alterations in brain activity associated with Alzheimer's disease even before any symptoms appear. The result of an early diagnosis would be specific treatment and interventions.

Comparatively, EEG is an inexpensive procedure relative in cost to fMRI, PET scans, and other kinds of neuroimaging. It is also easy to use, making it ideal for both clinical and field settings. Its spatial resolution is limited since EEG measures the electrical signals through the head. This inability to localize brain function abnormalities accurately can act as a challenge in identifying which precise brain regions Alzheimer's disease might be impacting. The EEG patterns vary significantly between individuals. Establishing consistent and trustworthy EEG-based indicators for Alzheimer's disease throughout many individuals may be difficult due to this diversity. The reproducibility of results may be hampered by non-standard EEG gathering and evaluation procedures. Best practices for gathering, processing, and analyzing data must be established. The accuracy of the diagnosis may not be sufficient with just EEG. The diagnostic usefulness of EEG-based biomarkers can frequently be increased by integrating them with additional biomarkers, such as hereditary and radiological markers. These limitations also degraded the model definition of finding the accuracy.

## 5.2 Research recommendation

Monitoring long-term EEG changes across time using a broad and varied participant pool, including people with varying stages of Alzheimer's disease (Khanna et al., 2022). This could lead to the discovery of more reliable biomarkers and temporal patterns in EEG changes (Aklima et al., 2022). Establishing and carrying out standardized procedures for the gathering and examination of EEG data (Asanza et al., 2022). Reproducibility of results and cross-study comparability are going to be facilitated by standardization in data processing and collecting (Arasteh et al., 2022). evaluating the stability and applicability of EEG-based biomarkers through validation studies conducted in a variety of groups and on different datasets (Hassin-Baer et al., 2022). The clinical value of these indicators must be ensured by validation (Jesus et al., 2021).

## 5.3 Future work

Investigating cutting-edge methods for sophisticated data analysis, such as graph-based methods, deep learning, and reinforcement learning, to uncover intricate patterns and extract more valuable information from EEG data (Sabbaghi et al., 2021). Exploring how EEG patterns in people with Alzheimer's disease alter over longer times, such as years (Ouchani et al., 2021). A study with a longitudinal design can shed light on how EEG changes gradually (Ranjan and Buyya, 2015). Conducting extensive multicenter investigations in collaboration with several research centers to guarantee the robustness and generalizability of EEG-based biomarkers in a variety of contexts and populations (Cordone et al., 2021). Developing an embedded

EEG monitoring system that helps measure modifications to brain function continually and sends out timely notifications or treatments to anyone who may be in danger of Alzheimer's disease (Korada et al., n.d.).

## References


Aklima, A.L., et al., 2022. A comprehensive survey on the detection, classification, and challenges of neurological disorders. Biology 11 (3), 469. https://doi.org/10.3390/biology11030469.

Alassafi, M.O., et al., 2023. Studying dynamical characteristics of oxygen saturation variability signals using haar wavelet. Healthcare 11 (16), 2280. https://doi.org/10.3390/healthcare11162280.

Almufareh, M.F., et al., 2023. Artificial cognition for detection of mental disability: a vision transformer approach for Alzheimer's disease. Healthcare 11 (20), 2763. https://doi.org/10.3390/healthcare11202763.

AlSharabi, K., et al., 2023. EEG-based clinical decision support system for Alzheimer's disorders diagnosis using EMD and deep learning techniques. Front. Hum. Neurosci. https://doi.org/10.3389/fnhum.2023.1190203.

Alves, C.L., et al., 2022. Application of machine learning and complex network measures to an EEG dataset from ayahuasca experiments. PLoS One 17 (12). https://doi.org/10.1371/journal.pone.0277257.

Alvi, A.M., Siuly, S., Wang, H., 2022. Neurological abnormality detection from electroencephalography data: a review. Artif. Intell. Rev. 55 (3), 2275–2312. https://doi.org/10.1007/s10462-021-10062-8.

Andrade, S.M., et al., 2023. Identifying biomarkers for tDCS treatment response in Alzheimer's disease patients: a machine learning approach using resting-state EEG classification. Front. Hum. Neurosci. https://doi.org/10.3389/fnhum.2023.1234168.

Anjum, M., Shahab, S., Yang, Y., 2023. Syndrome pattern recognition method using sensed patient data for neurodegenerative disease progression identification. Diagnostics 13 (5), 887. https://doi.org/10.3390/diagnostics13050887.

Anonymous, 2023. ESICM LIVES 2023. Intensive Care Med. Exp. 11 (Suppl. 1), 72. https://doi.org/10.1186/s40635-023-00546-y.

Arasteh, E., et al., 2022. Deep transfer learning for Parkinson's disease monitoring by image-based representation of resting-state EEG using directional connectivity. Algorithms 15 (1), 5. https://doi.org/10.3390/a15010005.

Asanza, V., et al., 2022. Identification of lower-limb motor tasks via brain–computer interfaces: a topical overview. Sensors 22 (5), 2028. https://doi.org/10.3390/s22052028.

Belyaev, M., et al., 2023. Entropy-based machine learning model for fast diagnosis and monitoring of Parkinson's disease. Sensors 23 (20), 8609. https://doi.org/10.3390/s23208609.

Bhachawat, S., et al., 2023. Leveraging computational intelligence techniques for diagnosing degenerative nerve diseases: a comprehensive review, open challenges, and future research directions. Diagnostics 13 (2), 288. https://doi.org/10.3390/diagnostics13020288.

Chen, Z., et al., 2023. Sampling inequalities affect generalization of neuroimaging-based diagnostic classifiers in psychiatry. BMC Med. 21, 1–29. https://doi.org/10.1186/s12916-023-02941-4.

Chu, K., et al., 2023. A holo-spectral EEG analysis provides an early detection of cognitive decline and predicts the progression to Alzheimer's disease. Front. Aging Neurosci. https://doi.org/10.3389/fnagi.2023.1195424.

Cordone, S., et al., 2021. Sleep-based interventions in Alzheimer's disease: promising approaches from prevention to treatment along the disease trajectory. Pharmaceuticals 14 (4), 383. https://doi.org/10.3390/ph14040383.

Eyamu, J., et al., 2023. Prefrontal event-related potential markers in association with mild cognitive impairment. Front. Aging Neurosci. https://doi.org/10.3389/fnagi.2023.1273008.

Fingel kurts, A.A., Fingel kurts, A.A., 2023. Turning back the clock: a retrospective single-blind study on brain age change in response to nutraceuticals supplementation vs. lifestyle modifications. Brain Sci. 13 (3), 520. https://doi.org/10.3390/brainsci13030520.

Formica, C., et al., 2023. Paving the way for predicting the progression of cognitive decline: the potential role of machine learning algorithms in the clinical management of neurodegenerative disorders. J. Personalized Med. 13 (9), 1386. https://doi.org/10.3390/jpm13091386.

Giovannini, G., Meletti, S., 2023. Fluid biomarkers of neuro-glial injury in human status epilepticus: a systematic review. Int. J. Mol. Sci. 24 (15), 12519. https://doi.org/10.3390/ijms241512519.

Hassin-Baer, S., et al., 2022. Identification of an early-stage Parkinson's disease neuromarker using event-related potentials, brain network analytics and machine-learning. PLoS One 17 (1). https://doi.org/10.1371/journal.pone.0261947.

Hejazi, S., et al., 2023. Graph-based analysis of brain connectivity in multiple sclerosis using functional MRI: a systematic review. Brain Sci. 13 (2), 246. https://doi.org/10.3390/brainsci13020246.

Hernandez, C.I., et al., 2023. Examining electroencephalogram signatures of people with multiple sclerosis using a nonlinear dynamics approach: a systematic review and bibliographic analysis. Front. Comput. Neurosci. https://doi.org/10.3389/fncom.2023.1207067.

Ho, T.K.K., et al., 2022. Deep learning-based multilevel classification of Alzheimer's disease using non-invasive functional near-infrared spectroscopy. Front. Aging Neurosci. https://doi.org/10.3389/fnagi.2022.810125.

Jellinger, K.A., 2023. The spectrum of cognitive dysfunction in amyotrophic lateral sclerosis: an update. Int. J. Mol. Sci. 24 (19), 14647. https://doi.org/10.3390/ijms241914647.

Jesus Jr., B., et al., 2021. Multimodal prediction of Alzheimer's disease severity level based on resting-state EEG and structural MRI. Front. Hum. Neurosci. https://doi.org/10.3389/fnhum.2021.700627.

Jiao, B., et al., 2023. Neural biomarker diagnosis and prediction to mild cognitive impairment and Alzheimer's disease using EEG technology. Alzheimers Res. Ther. 15, 1–14. https://doi.org/10.1186/s13195-023-01181-1.

Ju-Yu, W., et al., 2022. Emerging wearable biosensor technologies for stress monitoring and their real-world applications. Biosensors 12 (12), 1097. https://doi.org/10.3390/bios12121097.

Khanna, N.N., et al., 2022. Cardiovascular/stroke risk assessment in patients with erectile dysfunction—a role of carotid wall arterial imaging and plaque tissue characterization using artificial intelligence paradigm: a narrative review. Diagnostics 12 (5), 1249. https://doi.org/10.3390/diagnostics12051249.

Khondakar, K.R., Kaushik, A., 2023. Role of wearable sensing technology to manage long COVID. Biosensors 13 (1), 62. https://doi.org/10.3390/bios13010062.

Kim, N.H., et al., 2023. PET-validated EEG-machine learning algorithm predicts brain amyloid pathology in pre-dementia Alzheimer's disease. Sci. Rep. 13 (1), 10299. https://doi.org/10.1038/s41598-023-36713-0.

Kohli, M., et al., 2022. Machine learning-based ABA treatment recommendation and personalization for autism spectrum disorder: an exploratory study. Brain Inform. 9 (1). https://doi.org/10.1186/s40708-022-00164-6.

Korada, L., Sikha, V. K., & Somepalli, S. (n.d.). Digital transformation balanced with sustainability goals. J. Eng. Appl. Sci. Technol.

Lee, K., et al., 2022. Selection of the optimal channel configuration for implementing wearable EEG devices for the diagnosis of mild cognitive impairment. Alzheimers Res. Ther. 14, 1–10. https://doi.org/10.1186/s13195-022-01115-3.

Li, R., et al., 2022. Concurrent fNIRS and EEG for brain function investigation: a systematic, methodology-focused review. Sensors 22 (15), 5865. https://doi.org/10.3390/s22155865.

Li, X., Kang, Q., Gu, H., 2023. A comprehensive review for machine learning on neuroimaging in obsessive-compulsive disorder. Front. Hum. Neurosci. https://doi.org/10.3389/fnhum.2023.1280512.

Liu, M., et al., 2023. Bibliometric analysis of electroencephalogram research in mild cognitive impairment from 2005 to 2022. Front. Neurosci. https://doi.org/10.3389/fnins.2023.1128851.

Maitin, A.M., Muñoz, J.P.R., García-Tejedor, Á.J., 2022. Survey of machine learning techniques in the analysis of EEG signals for Parkinson's disease: a systematic review. Appl. Sci. 12 (14), 6967. https://doi.org/10.3390/app12146967.

Maura, R.M., et al., 2023. Literature review of stroke assessment for upper-extremity physical function via EEG, EMG, kinematic, and kinetic measurements and their reliability. J. NeuroEng. Rehabil. 20, 1–32. https://doi.org/10.1186/s12984-023-01142-7.

Molcho, L., et al., 2022. Single-channel EEG features reveal an association with cognitive decline in seniors performing auditory cognitive assessment. Front. Aging Neurosci. https://doi.org/10.3389/fnagi.2022.773692.

Olichney, J., et al., 2022. Predictive power of cognitive biomarkers in neurodegenerative disease drug development: utility of the P300 event-related potential. Neural Plast. 2022. https://doi.org/10.1155/2022/2104880.

Ouchani, M., et al., 2021. A review of methods of diagnosis and complexity analysis of Alzheimer's disease using EEG signals. BioMed Res. Int. 2021. https://doi.org/10.1155/2021/5425569.

Patil, V., Madgi, M., Kiran, A., 2022. Early prediction of Alzheimer's disease using convolutional neural network: a review. Egypt. J. Neurol. Psychiatr. Neurosurg. 58 (1). https://doi.org/10.1186/s41983-022-00571-w.

Perrottelli, A., et al., 2022. Unveiling the associations between EEG indices and cognitive deficits in schizophrenia-spectrum disorders: a systematic review. Diagnostics 12 (9), 2193. https://doi.org/10.3390/diagnostics12092193.

Polat, H., 2022. Time-frequency complexity maps for EEG-based diagnosis of Alzheimer's disease using a lightweight deep neural network. Trait. Du. Signal 39 (6), 2103–2113. https://doi.org/10.18280/ts.390623.

Ranjan, R., Buyya, R., 2015. Modeling energyefficient systems in cloud computing environments. Proc. 2015 IEEE Int. Conf. Cloud Comput. 7 (1), 205–220.

Rutkowski, T.M., et al., 2023. Machine learning approach for early onset dementia neurobiomarker using EEG network topology features. Front. Hum. Neurosci. https://doi.org/10.3389/fnhum.2023.1155194.

Sabbaghi, N., et al., 2021. Interval-based features of auditory ERPs for diagnosis of early Alzheimer's disease. Alzheimer's Dement. Diagn. Assess. Dis. Monit. 13 (1). https://doi.org/10.1002/dad2.12191.

Sakib, N., Islam, M.K., Faruk, T., 2023. Machine learning model for computer-aided depression screening among young adults using wireless EEG headset. Comput. Intell. Neurosci. 2023. https://doi.org/10.1155/2023/1701429.

Shusharina, N., et al., 2023. Modern methods of diagnostics and treatment of neurodegenerative diseases and depression. Diagnostics 13 (3), 573. https://doi.org/10.3390/diagnostics13030573.

Sun, W., et al., 2022. A review of recent advances in vital signals monitoring of sports and health via flexible wearable sensors. Sensors 22 (20), 7784. https://doi.org/10.3390/s22207784.

Tobe, M., et al., 2023. Hub structure in functional network of EEG signals supporting high cognitive functions in older individuals. Front. Aging Neurosci. https://doi.org/10.3389/fnagi.2023.1130428.

Wu, R., et al., 2023. Screening for mild cognitive impairment with speech interaction based on virtual reality and wearable devices. Brain Sci. 13 (8), 1222. https://doi.org/10.3390/brainsci13081222.

Xu, M., Ouyang, Y., Yuan, Z., 2023. Deep learning aided neuroimaging and brain regulation. Sensors 23 (11), 4993. https://doi.org/10.3390/s23114993.

Zakariah, M., Yousef, A.A., 2023. Unipolar and bipolar depression detection and classification based on actigraphic registration of motor activity using machine learning and uniform manifold approximation and projection methods. Diagnostics 13 (14), 2323. https://doi.org/10.3390/diagnostics13142323.

## Further reading

Ghodke, V., Gajre, S., 2022a. Early diagnosis of Alzheimer's disease using EEG signal. NeuroQuantology 20 (5), 4569–4576. https://doi.org/10.14704/nq.2022.20.5.

Ghodke, V., Gajre, S., 2022b. A literature review of automated techniques for early detection of Alzheimer's disease. Jundishapur J. Microbiol. 15 (1).

Chapter 6

# Enhanced decision-making through Neuromorphic Computing and BCI

N. Naveena[1], P. Nisha Priya[2], A. Sugitha[1] and K. Madhu Suganya[3]
[1]*Sri Krishna College of Engineering and Technology, Coimbatore, Tamil Nadu, India;* [2]*CSI College of Engineering, Department of Computer Science & Engineering, Ketti, Tamil Nadu, India;* [3]*Nandha College of Technology, Erode, Tamil Nadu, India*

## 1. Introduction

One of the principle highbrow aspects of a person is the energy of decision-making. Humans have a herbal capacity of thinking, waiting for evaluation and perceptual recognition.

In todays cutting-edge world, Artificial intelligence has seized the vicinity of human's brainpower. With the arrival of current Artificial intelligence within the cutting-edge era, the combination of bio-stimulated computing structures and direct mind gadget interfaces is revolutionizing decision-making processes. Neuromorphic computing (NC) and Brain–Computer Interfaces (BCIs) can facilitate higher decision-making, which has the functionality to convert industries like healthcare, navy operations, finance, pc vision, robotics, and self-reliant using structures and lots to emerge in the imminent years.

This Chapter discusses how these innovative technologies can mimic human cognitive functions, facilitate smooth human-machine collaboration, and provide faster, more efficient, and context-aware decision-making abilities as well as collaborative human-machine logical thinking and decision-making.

## 2. Overview of neuromorphic computing

As we all know, the "Neuron" is the structural and basic unit of the human nervous system, it is now playing a progressive role in NC. It is a subfield of artificial intelligence that draws inspiration from the structure, function, and plasticity of the human brain and cells. In contrast to traditional computing

**Neuromorphic Computing for Brain Computer Interfaces. https://doi.org/10.1016/B978-0-443-41594-4.00010-1**

systems that follow the Von Neumann architecture, neuromorphic systems directly stimulate neural networks at the hardware level, allowing machines to process information in a highly parallel, event-driven, and energy-efficient way.

The principle of NC was originally described by Carver Mead in the late 1980s to mimic biological neural circuits using silicon. Through decades of advances in neuroscience, material science, and machine learning algorithms, the creation of neuromorphic hardware has advanced significantly.

NC will produce a massive change globally in the future. The aim of NC is not to slavishly copy the brain and all of its activities, but rather to take what is understood of its structure and workings and utilize it in a working computing system. No neuromorphic system will assert or try to replicate every aspect of synapses and neurons, but all follow the principle that computation is extremely distributed across several tiny computing entities, like a neuron. Though this disposition is common, scientists pursue this aim with various approaches. Neural wiring diagrams based on anatomy, which are currently imaged using electron microscopy and connection maps of how the brain functionally connects at the potential resolution of intracellular recording, can serve to more deeply inspire, though not necessarily be replicated exactly, NC systems in greater detail.

## 3. Brain-Computer Interfaces—Concepts & mechanisms

### 3.1 Concepts

BCIs is a technology that connects the human brain to an external device, like a computer (Dayma, 2021). It allows users to control devices using brain activity instead of traditional inputs like keyboards or mice.

BCIs work by detecting brain signals through surface electrodes on the scalp. These electrodes capture electrical activity, known as bio-signals, which are processed to generate commands for devices (Dayma, 2021; Ünlü, 2024).

The most commonly used bio-signal in BCIs is the electroencephalogram (EEG), which measures brain activity. Other signals like ECG and MRI can also be used, but EEG is preferred because it is noninvasive and works in real-time.

BCIs have many uses, mainly in medicine, assisting humans with disabilities regain lost functions. They permit paralyzed people to manipulate prosthetic limbs or talk via computers. BCIs are also being explored in gaming, in which they are able to adapt to a users mind and emotions (Dayma, 2021).

### 3.2 Mechanisms

BCIs have modified assistive technology, making existence less difficult for human beings with mobility and neurological challenges. BCIs permit the mind to at once manage gadgets, assisting customers perform assistive equipment with their thoughts. This study appears at how BCIs enhance movement, connectivity, and freedom. It additionally explores superior uses like mind-managed prosthetics, verbal exchange gadgets, and clever domestic designed for accessibility (Ünlü, 2024). A Brain Computer Interface has four predominant components:

**Signal Collection:** Signal series in BCIs entails capturing, amplifying, filtering, and changing mind indicators into virtual records for similar use. Sensors or electrodes are set up at the scalp (noninvasive), within the skull (partially invasive), or without delay withinside the brain (invasive) to file electric or magnetic signals. These indicators are very vulnerable, so amplifiers fortify them earlier than processing. Noise from muscle movement, eye blinks, and outside restraints can interfere, so filtering strategies assist easy the records (Ma et al., 2025). The indicators are then transformed from analog to digital using an Analog-to-Digital Converter (ADC), with EEG generally the use of a sampling charge of 250 to 1000 Hz. Factors like electrode type, placement, environmental noise, and the person's intellectual capacity have an effect on sign quality. Challenges embody susceptible indicators, noise interference, and variations amongst individuals. Future upgrades in hobby on making BCIs more user-friendly and correct with dry electrodes, wi-fi systems, and hybrid techniques that integrate one-of-a-kind mind sign techniques. A reliable sign series is essential for the usage of BCIs in medicine, assistive communication, and mind-managed devices.

**Signal Processing:** Signal processing in BCIs facilitates converting uncooked mind indicators into beneficial statistics to manipulate gadgets. The first step is in which undesirable noise from muscular hobby, eyelid moves and out of doors interference is eliminated the use of filtering techniques. Next crucial info from the mind indicators, including frequency, amplitude, and electricity, is identified. This facilitates lessen facts while maintaining beneficial patterns. Machine Learning algorithms like Support Vector Machines and Neural Networks examine those capabilities to understand exclusive mind activities. Once labeled, the indicators become instructions to manipulate gadgets like robot palms or communication systems (Xin, 2024). Good sign processing improves accuracy and makes BCIs more powerful for clinical and assistive applications. Advances in synthetic intelligence are assisting BCIs become quicker and more reliable.

**Command Translation:** Command translation in BCIs is the technique of turning mind control into beneficial instructions. It begins offevolved with measuring mind indicators using EEG, which measures mind hobby at some point of exclusive tasks. The uncooked indicators are then wiped clean via preprocessing to eliminate noise and enhance quality. Next, characteristic extraction identifies crucial sign patterns, including electricity in positive frequency bands. These capabilities are then labeled as the use of devices, getting to know how to fit them with particular intellectual states. Once the mind hobby is translated into instructions, the device affords comments to assist customers in enhancing their control over the BCI. This technique calls for practice, as customers learn how to modify their mind habits for higher accuracy. The translated instructions may be used for communication, controlling robots, and different interactive applications. Command translation plays a key role in making BCIs extra practical and useful in real life (Jadekar et al., 2021).

**Command Execution:** Command execution in BCIs translates thought signs into actions like shifting a cursor or controlling a robot. It uses EEG to file thoughts of interest while clients consider actions without actually acting them. The BCI device then decodes those indicators with a classifier. During execution, it analyzes the EEG facts to locate the user's supposed action, including transferring left or right. An important component of command execution is the command transport time (CDT), which is the time it takes for the device to understand and execute the user's command (Saeedi et al., 2016). Variations in CDT can arise because of numerous factors, including the user's intellectual capacity and the complexity of the task.

## 4. Advancing decision-making with Neuromorphic Computing and Brain-Computer Interfaces: Adaptive learning and pattern recognition

### 4.1 Introduction

The integration of NC and BCIs is revolutionizing decision-making methods through emulating human cognitive functions. These technology decorate overall performance in healthcare, synthetic intelligence (AI), robotics, and cybersecurity through adaptive learning and data analytics. NC, primarily based on biologically stimulated architectures like spiking neural networks (SNNs) and memristor-primarily based totally hardware, permits energy-green facts processing. Meanwhile, BCIs set up direct interactions among the human mind and outside devices, facilitating superior manipulation mechanisms. Adaptive studying guarantees nonstop machine improvements, at the same time as sample popularity is crucial for decoding neural alerts and refining decision-making models. This record explores those standards and their programs in numerous domains.

### 4.2 Adaptive learning in neuromorphic computing and BCIs

Adaptive studying allows structures to refine responses primarily based on nonstop information inputs and evolving environments. It is important in NC and BCIs, taking into consideration superior performance and accuracy over time. In healthcare, neuro-adaptive prosthetics use BCIs to beautify prosthetic limb manipulate with the aid of using adapting to users' mind interest styles.

AI-pushed cognitive computing structures make use of neuromorphic architectures for green information processing. EEG-primarily based totally BCIs display intellectual fitness with the aid of using reading neural styles to stumble on strain and anxiety. In cybersecurity, gadget studying fashions enhance protection with the aid of using detecting and stopping unauthorized access. Techniques along with reinforcement learning, Hebbian studying, spiking neural networks, and self-organizing maps play a key function in optimizing adaptive studying structures.

## 4.3 Pattern recognition in neuromorphic computing and BCIs

Pattern reputation identifies systems and relationships in facts, allowing sensible decision-making in NC and BCIs. It aids in neural signal processing, anomaly detection, and selection enhancement. Brain sign interpretation through EEG and fMRI facts evaluation allows decoding cognitive functions. BCIs convert mind alerts into speech for assistive technologies, at the same time as cognitive load tracking optimizes intellectual workload in high-pressure environments like aviation and navy operations. Neuro-safety programs use sample reputation to locate abnormal brainwave patterns, stopping unauthorized BCI access. Techniques together with deep mastering models (CNNs, RNNs), function extraction methods (PCA, wavelet transforms), hidden Markov models, and graph-based mastering make a contribution to powerful sample representation.

## 4.4 Neuromorphic hardware supporting adaptive learning and pattern recognition

NC is based mostly on specialized hardware for green statistics processing. Memristor-primarily based totally absolutely chips assist energy-green reminiscence retention, at the same time as processors like IBM TrueNorth and Intel Loihi are optimized for adaptive learning. Brain-stimulated architectures, in addition, reflect neural processing in real-time, improving machine performance.

## 4.5 Real-World applications

In healthcare, BCIs improve neuroprosthetics, predict epilepsy through AI-driven seizure analysis, and track cognitive states for mental health monitoring. In cybersecurity, EEG signals function as biometric security keys, and anomaly detection in BCIs prevents cyber threats. Human-computer interaction benefits from thought-controlled interfaces and smart assistive technologies for individuals with disabilities. Military and aerospace applications optimize cognitive load for pilots and soldiers while enabling brain-guided drone control through NC.

## 4.6 Challenges and future directions

Despite advancements, challenges such as signal noise, real-time processing constraints, and scalability limitations persist. Future developments will integrate AI and quantum computing to enhance processing capabilities, create noninvasive BCIs for improved accessibility, and advance edge computing to enable real-time adaptive learning with low-latency processing.

# 5. Real-World applications across industries

NC and Brain Computing Interfaces (BCI) are the only ones that convert the manner of selection making via the industries to be had the actual time, adaptive, and sensitive structures that minimize our human mind functions. These technology method a big quantity of facts efficiently, coping with the choices correctly.

In healthcare, BCIs perform an important function to control the paralyzed sufferers to command the prosthetic limbs, to formerly discover issues like Alzheimer's and epilepsy, and develop intellectual fitness tracking by taking pictures of the brainwave activity. Neuromorphic chips overcome the limitations of clinical imaging and diagnostics, making the identification of illnesses as much quicker and precise. Creating the big quantity of benefits from the clever automation, predictive preservation, and adaptive robotics that I even have known from nature. Neuromorphic processors have the imminent traits of fine manipulation, making sure illness-free production.

In Finance, NC illness structures discover the frauds, optimize algorithmic buying and selling, and know the sentiment of the client for the provision of services. In the defense region leverages BCIs for the mind-managed drones, sensible surroundings, and seasoned stage cyber safety answers that counteract the cyber threats in the future. AI-powered safety identifies a large quantity of data.

Transportation sees an important function upgrade with neuromorphic chips powering self-driving cars, clever visitor management, and driving force protection measures that keep the fatigue and prevent accidents. These are the technologies to discover the street protection and manipulate the flow of visitors.

Finally, NC and BCI are revolutionizing decision-making throughout industries, allowing speedier, more beneficial, and automated processes. These improvements are paving the way for a smarter, greater adaptive future as shown in Fig. 6.1.

# 6. Integration of neuromorphic computing with BCIs

The combination of NC and BCI improves how humans interact with machines. Neuromorphic chips paintings just like the mind, assisting BCIs to

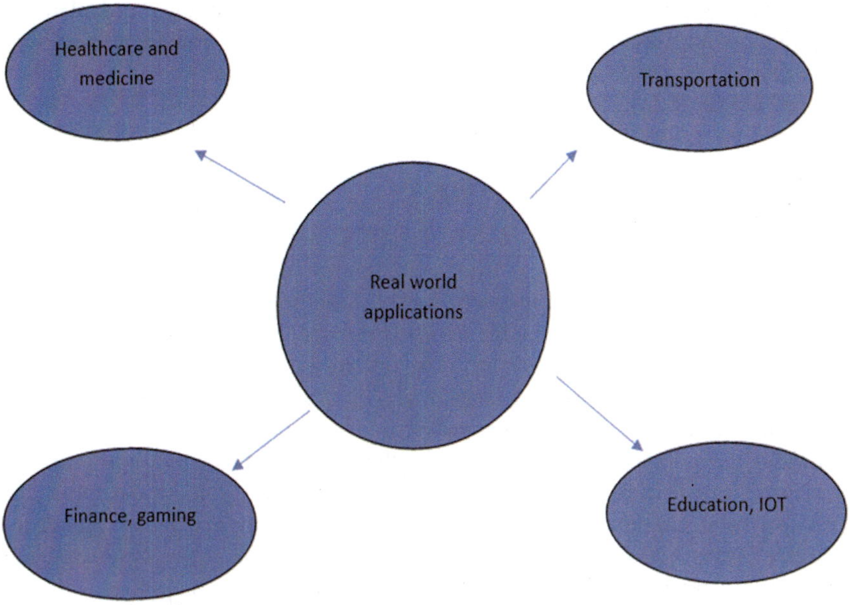


**FIGURE 6.1** Real-world applications of NC and BCI across industries.

examine and adapt higher for real-time use. These chips enhance sample recognition, making BCIs extra correct in know-how person intentions. This is particularly beneficial for humans with disabilities, because it facilitates them to manipulate assistive gadgets more effectively (Dayma, 2021). Neuromorphic chips are also energy-efficient, making them perfect for transportable BCIs with lengthy battery life. Their seamless reference to the fearful machine lets paralyzed people govern prosthetics and other gadgets using their mind signals. Additionally, NC improves the adaptability of AI in BCIs. These chips quickly examine massive datasets, assisting BCIs in adapting to specific environments in real-time (Ünlü, 2024). This makes interplay smoother and extra intuitive. Overall, integrating NC with BCIs complements neural prosthetics, giving people with disabilities higher and extra responsive manipulation over assistive gadgets. NCuting is a brand new method in synthetic intelligence that imitates the anatomy and body structure of the human mind (Dayma, 2021; Ünlü, 2024). It goals to create extra green and adaptive computing structures. This paper explains the fundamentals of NC and its technological advancements. Neuromorphic structures are quite flexible and are used in lots of fields, which include robotics, healthcare, cognitive computing, and smart cities. In robotics, they assist machines to examine and act independently, and at the same time, in healthcare, they enhance diagnostics and personalized medicine. The paper also discusses challenges like scalability, integration with current technologies, and the difficulty of accurately modeling brain functions. It explores possible solutions and future developments in the field. Through practical examples, the paper highlights how NC can transform intelligent systems and improve our understanding of both artificial and natural intelligence (Ünlü, 2024).

## 7. Challenges and limitations

Through the brand new improvement in NC and BCI (BCI) for advanced decision-making, there are so many challenges and barriers hindering their tricky changes. One predominant trouble is the excessive computational complexity and scalability, as these problems are tough to remedy within the neuromorphic chips that require the big quantity of processing electricity and specialized hardware, making large-scale implementation costly and technically demanding. Adding to the problem of the alternative is accuracy and reliability, which continue to be the big challenge, as BCIs and neuromorphic structures are at risk of making mistakes, and it calls for considerable calibration to be characterized routinely in real-world applications. Ethical and privacy issues additionally pose risks, as unauthorized access to neural data can cause misuse or security breaches. Then, the excessive value of improvement and deployment limits accessibility, especially for smaller organizations that are growing our economies and enhancing the world with new and appealing products that are best for all of us. Another urgent trouble is cybersecurity threats, as these technologies rely upon exceedingly sensitive data, making them liable to hacking and exploitation. In protection and safety, moral dilemmas get up concerning selfsustaining decision-making, as mistakes in AI-driven structures may want to have excessive consequences. Moreover, real-international adaptability remains a challenge, as those structures conflict to generalize and reply efficiently to unpredictable environments, together with self-driving motors navigating sudden street conditions. Additionally, consumer consent and adoption continue to be barriers, especially for BCIs requiring invasive or semi-invasive procedures, which many may also find discomforting. While those barriers present obstacles, persistent research, moral regulations, and greater AI fashions can help overcome them, releasing the overall strength of NC and BCI in decision-making throughout industries and creating massive advantages to the sector, and it creates a massive effect withinside the international.

## 8. Case studies & practical implementations

NC and BCIs have already been carried out in diverse industries, demonstrating their capability for improved decision-making. In healthcare, a super case is using BCIs to restore motion in paralyzed patients. The BrainGate project, for instance, has enabled people with spinal cord injuries to govern robot palms using neural signals, appreciably enhancing their independence and quality of life. Similarly, IBM's NC generation has been carried out in scientific diagnostics, in which AI-pushed sample popularity complements early disorder detection, leading to quicker and more accurate diagnoses. Similarly, algorithmic buying and selling platforms, inclusive of the ones evolved via way of means of hedge funds like Renaissance Technologies, use NC-powered predictive models to execute high-frequency trades with extraordinary accuracy.

The automobile enterprise has additionally embraced those technologies, particularly in self-driving cars. Tesla's Autopilot and Waymo's AI-pushed navigation structures leverage neuromorphic processors to enhance real-time decision-making on the road. These structures systemize large quantities of sensor statistics to make split-2D decisions, improving protection and efficiency.

In protection and protection, neuromorphic computing has been used for real-time danger detection and self-reliant decision-making. In finance, NC-primarily based totally absolutely honestly fraud detection structures have revolutionized protection through way of approach of studying transaction patterns in real-time. For example, Visa has covered neuromorphic AI to discover fraudulent sports activities instantly, lowering monetary losses and enhancing decision-making in hazard management. The US military has tested mind-controlled drones, wherein soldiers use BCI era to feature UAVs hands-free, thinking of greater battlefield efficiency. Additionally, neuromorphic AI has been included into cybersecurity systems to find out and neutralize cyber threats in advance than they escalate.

In enjoyment and gaming, BCIs have enabled mind-managed gaming, improving person experiences. For example, Neurable has evolved a VR headset that lets in customers to govern virtual environments the use of simplest their mind activity. Similarly, Netflix and YouTube use neuromorphic AI to optimize content material recommendations, enhancing person engagement primarily based totally on viewing styles and preferences as given in the Fig. 6.2.

Table 6.1 highlights key case studies and their practical Applications.

## 9. Role of AI and deep learning in decision-making

AI and Deep Learning are important technologies utilized in enforcing the decision-making technique through utilizing superior algorithms, neural networks, and real-time information evaluation to beautify fashions through BCI. AI is extensively applied to improve predictive accuracy, automate complicated reasoning, and allow adaptive learning, making it necessary in NC and BCIs. Deep Learning architectures, which include Convolutional Neural Networks (CNNs) and Recurrent Neural Networks (RNNs), are basically used for interpreting mind alerts and permitting human-computer interactions. By combining reinforcement learning, generative adversarial networks (GANs),

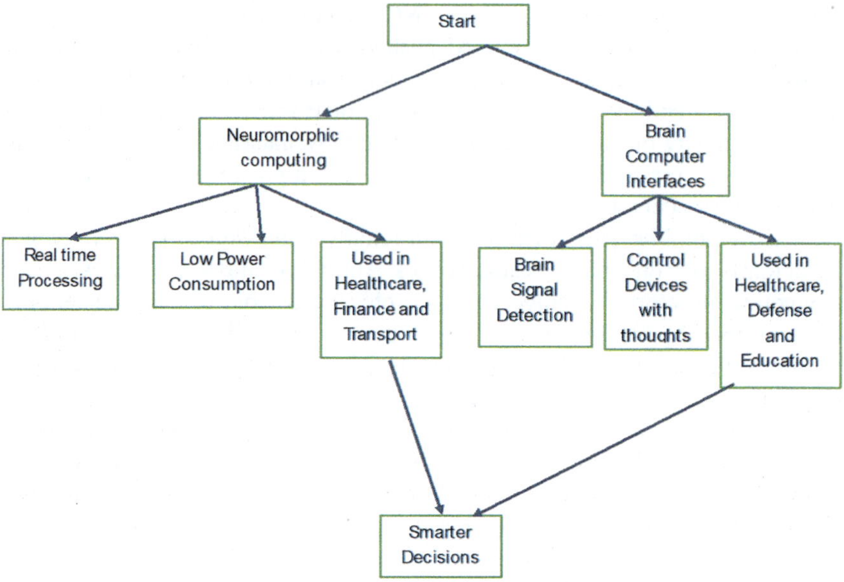


**FIGURE 6.2** Overview of NC and BCI applications.

**TABLE 6.1** Case Studies and their applications.

| Industry | Case study | Implementation | Impact |
|---|---|---|---|
| **Healthcare** | Brain gate project | BCI-managed robot limbs for paralyzed patients | Improved mobility and independence |
| **Medical AI** | IBM Watson health | AI-assisted clinical diagnostics | Faster and extra correct ailment detection |
| **Finance** | Visa fraud detection | NC-pushed fraud evaluation in real-time | Reduced economic fraud and advanced security |
| **Automotive** | Tesla & Waymo | Neuromorphic AI in self-using cars | Enhanced real-time decision-making and safety |
| **Gaming & VR** | Neurable VR headset | Brainwave-controlled digital interaction | Enhanced immersive gaming experiences |

and natural language processing (NLP), AI complements decision-making through permitting extra accurate, context-aware, and self-sufficient responses. This seamless integration permits AI to take a look at real-international situations, regulate accordingly, and bring wise insights. The easy integration of deep learning, synthetic intelligence, and neuromorphic processors substantially improves cognitive capacities, ensuing in extra speedy and powerful decision-making. This improvement is the utility of good-sized improvements in lots of industries, together with healthcare, robotics, finance, and human augmentation, remodeling the manner people and machines engage and broaden together.

In healthcare, AI aids in early disorder detection, personalized treatments, and robotic-assisted surgeries, enhancing patient outcomes. The financial area benefits from AI-powered market evaluation, fraud detection, and automated investment strategies. In robotics, AI enhances self-maintaining navigation, business automation, and precision tasks, making operations more green. However, AI-driven decision-making moreover offers ethical and technical disturbing conditions. Ensuring fairness, transparency, and unbiased decision-making remains a primary concern, requiring well-defined ethical frameworks. Data safety and privacy have to be prioritized as AI structures technique touchy private and monetary information. Additionally, keeping a balance between AI automation and human oversight is vital to make sure obligation and responsible use. As AI continues to evolve, addressing the disturbing conditions is probably vital in maximizing its ability while keeping ethical integrity and societal trust. As technology advances, it's miles critical to make certain that AI stays a device that enhances human intelligence in place of changing it, fostering a future wherein human beings and machines collaborate to gain more efficiency, innovation, and progress.

Decision-Making Process Is Represented in Fig. 6.3 With Several Components:

## 10. Future research directions & emerging trends

The destiny of AI-pushed decision-making, NC, and BCIs is anticipated to deliver progressive improvements so as to remodel numerous industries. One of the important areas of study is the improvement of next-generation neuromorphic processors, designed to feature greater capabilities, just like the human mind, whilst using much less energy. These processors will permit AI structures to make real-time choices more effectively and accurately. Another large place of awareness is Explainable AI, which targets to make AI's decision-making procedure more obvious and understandable, making sure accept as true with and responsibility in critical areas like healthcare, finance, and autonomous systems.

BCIs are one of the most promising subjects where AI and deep learning can extensively enhance how human beings interact with machines. Researchers are operating on refining AI fashions to interpret mind alerts with extra precision, which could result in improvements in assistive technology for people with disabilities. At the same time, Quantum Computing and AI are rising as an effective mixture that might remedy complicated issues at an

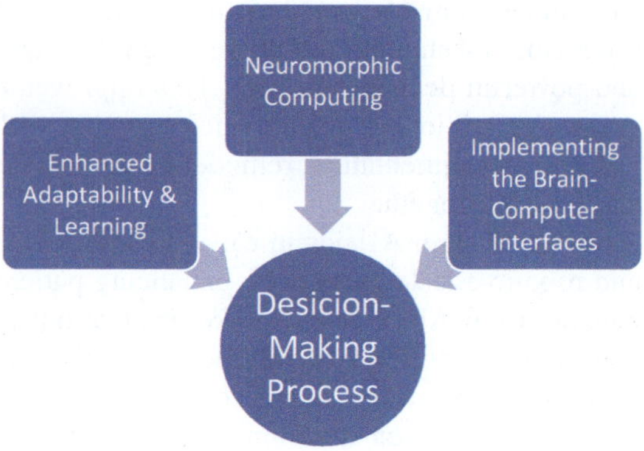


**FIGURE 6.3** Decision-making process.

unparalleled scale. This integration may revolutionize regions together with scientific studies, cybersecurity, and monetary modeling through permitting AI to process great quantities of information lots quicker than conventional computers.

The boom of AI-pushed self-sufficient structures is one of the key research directions, with capacity packages in robotics, smart cities, and self-driving vehicles. These structures want to end up more adaptable, making impartial choices primarily based on real-world information without human intervention. However, as AI automation continues to advance, there may be a developing want for moral guidelines and regulatory measures to make certain accountable AI deployment. Addressing issues like bias in AI decision-making, transparency, and responsibility might be critical for constructing accept as true with and making sure truthful results in AI-powered packages.

Another main task for destiny AI studies is information privacy and safety. As AI structures end up greater incorporated into each day lifestyles, protective touchy information from cyber threats might be a top priority. Researchers are exploring superior encryption strategies and decentralized AI fashions to enhance safety and prevent unauthorized access. Ultimately, the destiny of AI will no longer be about changing human beings but rather improving human decision-making. AI will function as an effective device that works alongside human beings, assisting to enhance efficiency, innovation, and the standard of lifestyles whilst making sure moral duty in its packages.

## 11. Interdisciplinary collaboration & policy considerations

The improvement of AI, neuromorphic computing, and BCIs requires strong interdisciplinary collaboration at some point of a couple of fields, which incorporates neuroscience, engineering, computer science, psychology, and ethics. Experts from numerous backgrounds must work together to format AI systems that are not only clever and experienced but also safe, ethical, and user-friendly.

Neuroscientists make a contribution to knowledge of thought functions, at the same time as engineers and computer scientists develop AI models and neuromorphic chips that mimic human cognition. Ethicists and policymakers play an essential role in ensuring responsible AI deployment, addressing troubles related to bias, statistics, privacy, and human rights. A cross-disciplinary technique is important to stress innovation at the same time as ensuring that AI-driven decision-making remains aligned with ethical principles, human values, and the broader dreams of society. Alongside technical advancements, the development of global governance frameworks is important for the responsible boom and regulation of the AI and Brain-Computer Interface (BCI) era. Governments, worldwide organizations, and regulatory bodies must art work together to establish easy rules that promote transparency, fairness, and accountability. Such collaborative efforts are important to prevent misuse, assemble public trust, and ensure that the powerful era is deployed in strategies that may be safe, inclusive, and socially beneficial.

Policies have to take cognizance of regions along with AI ethics, cybersecurity, and records protection, making sure that AI programs do not compromise man or woman rights or result in unintentional consequences. Standardization of AI governance may also be important, making an allowance for regular guidelines throughout industries and international locations to prevent unethical AI practices. Another important location is public recognition and schooling, which ensures that the AI and BCI era is superior and used responsibly. Researchers and policymakers must work together to inform the overall public about AI's capabilities, limitations, and ethical implications. Encouraging interdisciplinary schooling that combines AI, neuroscience, regulation, and ethics can help train future experts who understand all the technical and societal impacts of AI-driven decision-making. Collaborative efforts amongst academic institutions, industries, and governments can help create guidelines that help innovation on the identical time as maintaining ethical integrity.

As AI and BCIs continue to evolve, ongoing insurance revisions are probably essential to address new annoying conditions and growing risks. The rapid development of AI-driven decision-making systems will increase troubles about system displacement, human autonomy, and algorithmic biases, which require nonforeseeable evaluation and refinement of guidelines. Interdisciplinary collaboration will live key role in shaping a future in which AI complements human intelligence, enhances decision-making, and benefits society as a whole. Through proactive research and well-based guidelines, we are capable of ensuring that the AI era is used responsibly and contributes to an ethical and inclusive future, as given in Table 6.2.

## 12. Conclusion & call to action

The integration of AI, neuromorphic computing, and BCIs is reworking decision-making, revolutionizing industries that incorporate healthcare,

**TABLE 6.2 Principles and impacts of responsible AI practices.**

| Category | Key aspects | Impacts |
|---|---|---|
| **Interdisciplinary collaboration** | Involves AI researchers, neuroscientists, engineers, ethicists, and policymakers | Enhances AI improvement with moral and technical considerations |
| **Role of neuroscience** | Understanding mind capabilities to enhance AI and BCI models | Enables mind-like computing and human-laptop interaction |
| **Public awareness & education** | Educating users, developers, and policymakers about AI dangers and benefits | Encourages accountable AI adoption and innovation |
| **Job impact & Workforce training** | Preparing for AI-pushed process adjustments through ability improvement | Helps employees adapt to AI improvements and new process roles |
| **Ongoing policy revisions** | Continuously updating AI legal guidelines to cope with rising dangers | Ensures long-term sustainability and accountable innovation |
| **Cybersecurity & data protection** | Protecting touchy information in AI and BCI programs | Strengthens AI safety and stops unauthorized access |
| **Standardization & governance** | Creating global AI guidelines and policies | Promotes consistency in AI programs throughout industries |

robotics, finance, and human augmentation. By mimicking natural neural processes, the ones generation decorates cognitive abilities, allows real-time self-maintaining decisions, and bridges the distance between humans and machines. However, as AI-pushed decision-making advances, addressing moral concerns, statistical privacy, and safety dangers is crucial to making sure its accountable and honest use. The collaboration among researchers, policymakers, and industries will play a crucial characteristic in shaping AI's destiny to align with societal wishes and human values.

To absolutely harness the capacity of these innovations, continued interdisciplinary collaboration is essential. Neuroscientists, AI researchers, engineers, ethicists, and regulatory bodies have to work together to amplify ethical, transparent, and accountable AI systems. Governments and institutions ought to put into effect sturdy guidelines and governance frameworks that promote fairness, prevent biases, and make certain facts protection. AI training and public attention applications can also be key to getting equipped society for an AI-driven future, empowering humans with the critical records and skills to keep up with technological advancements. While AI and neuromorphic computing offer groundbreaking opportunities, their achievement is based on human-centric innovation.

It is essential to prioritize AI systems that complement human decision-making instead of replacing it. Ethical AI deployment, responsible research, and nonsave you insurance versions are probably essential to keep a balance between automation and human oversight. With the right approach, AI can emerge as a collaborative partner, improving decision-making, solving complex international challenges, and developing a future that advantages all.

## References

Dayma, M.M., 2021. Conceptual study of advancement in brain computing interface (BCI) model for various bio signals: a review. Int. J. Adv. Res. Innov. Ideas Educ. 7 (6), 148–157. http://ijariie.com/AdminUploadPdf/Conceptual_study_of_Advancement_in_Brain_Computing_Interface__BCI__model_for_various_bio_signals__A_Review_ijariie15562.pdf.

Jadekar, R.B., Sindhu, A.R., Vinay, M.T., 2021. Translation of brain activity patterns of a user into commands using electroencephalography (EEG), pp. 62–68. https://doi.org/10.9734/AJRCOS/2021/V10I230240.

Ma, Y., Huang, J., Liu, C., Shi, M., 2025. A portable EEG signal acquisition system and a limited-electrode channel classification network for SSVEP. Front. Neurorob. 18. https://doi.org/10.3389/fnbot.2024.1502560.

Saeedi, S., Chavarriaga, R., Leeb, R., Millán, J. del R., 2016. Adaptive assistance for BCI by online prediction of command reliability. IEEE Comput. Intell. Mag. 11 (1), 32–39. https://doi.org/10.1109/MCI.2015.2501550.

Ünlü, S.C., 2024. Enhancing accessibility through brain-computer interfaces (BCIs) in assistive technology. Hum. Comput. Interact. 8 (1), 23. https://doi.org/10.62802/7tt4r452.

Xin, C., 2024. Research on signal preprocessing methods based on brain-computer interface. https://doi.org/10.61173/6ak5px08.

Chapter 7

# AI-augmented chest radiography pneumonia detection: Balancing sensitivity and clinical monitoring

M. Shanmugham[1], T. Velmurugan[2], G. Brinda[3], S. Gokula Brindha[4], R. Pradeep[4] and V. Kumar[5]

[1]*Department of Electronics and Communication Engineering, Nandha Engineering College, Erode, Tamil Nadu, India;* [2]*Department of Computer Science and Design, Kongu Engineering College, Erode, Tamil Nadu, India;* [3]*Department of Electronics and Communication Engineering, M.P.Nachimuthu M.Jaganathan Engineering College, Erode, Tamil Nadu, India;* [4]*Department of Electrical and Electronics Engineering, Velalar College of Engineering and Technology, Erode, Tamil Nadu, India;* [5]*Department of Electronics and Communication Engineering, Hindusthan College of Engineering, Erode, Tamil Nadu, India*

## 1. Introduction

Pneumonia has been a prominent cause of morbidity and death in the world and specially among the vulnerable group. Effective and rapidly diagnosis is unexpendable to improve patient's clinical outcome and smooth clinical handling. The principal imaging method used is the Chest radiography (CXR) in detection of the pneumonia. Although it has a defined role, interpretation of the results of a CXR correctly and specifically can be time consuming, particularly in cases where there are subtle early lesions or where interobserver variability is high or, where confounding factors mean a clear diagnosis is implied. Such difficulties translate into delays in diagnosis and increased costs of healthcare provision thus impacting on the patients negatively.

Artificial intelligence (AI), but more particularly deep learning, has demonstrated in the recent years their fantastic capabilities to revolutionize medical imaging: to read enormous amount of images, to recover tiny patterns, to help clinicians discovering diseases at rates and accuracy levels that were never seen before. To give an example, internal medicine algorithm is in the achievement of performance goals in the identification of pneumonia with

**Neuromorphic Computing for Brain Computer Interfaces. https://doi.org/10.1016/B978-0-443-41594-4.00008-3**

chest X-ray (XR) on the same or maybe higher level compared with human experts under definite conditions. The gradual integration of AI into clinical care therefore presents a solution to reinforce a form of diagnostic efficiency, reducing the occurrence of a diagnostic error and last but not least facilitate the achievement of better patient outcomes (Rahmati et al., 2015).

The potential clinical benefit of Artificial intelligence (AI) implementation on medical diagnostic circumstance are much more therapeutic but needed trajectory on its integration is multifaceted. Particularly, though the sensitivities of the AI-based diagnostic models might become very high, the apogee, where the computational mechanism of prediction meets the inevitably complex processes of the human confirmation, cannot be prioritized down the list. The latter is added to the general worry about the overutilization of the algorithmic resources and splits the permanent value of the professional experience of radiologists due to the presence of the risk of algorithmic bias. Modern research therefore recommends the development of a synergistic relationship where the wisdom of a man acts as the stable construct and AI as the supplementary addition as opposed to a replacement application.

The present chapter challenges the complexities found in how best to maximize the benefits of Artificial intelligence (AI) to making detecting Pneumonia found in a chest X-ray as sensitive as possible. Specifically, it's based on the apparent contradiction between high diagnostic sensitivity of such AI-based solutions and the need to offer high clinical oversee. The discussion thus encompasses three conceptually circumscribed arenas: (1) technical composition of the model framework and strategies of the effectiveness on which the efficacy is structured; (2) real-world introduction of AI-based driven applications to clinical practice; and (3) necessity of continuous human-AI cooperation. No coherent and comprehensive framework leads to the formulation of a base framework—Mindful Healthcare amazing that is a consistent, ethically sound and evidence-based framework to negotiate the complexities in integrating AI. The activities of the Mindful Healthcare aim to address the harms of technology and help mitigate the effects of villainizing, clinician burnout and help to promote a more comprehensive paradigm of patient-centered care in the settings with more and more technology penetration (Wootton and Feldman, 2014).

## 2. Background

### 2.1 Pneumonia diagnosis: Traditional methods and their limitations

Pneumonia is a lung parenchymal inflammatory type. Traditional diagnosis is by synthesizing clinical presentation, physical examination, laboratory examination, and radiographs. Though feeling the most common clinical manifestation cough, fever, dyspnea, and chest pains are not specific, and very often, they overlap with those of other diseases of a respiratory nature, they are a part of a clinical judgment, however. The physical examination, mainly auscultation to check presence of crackles or egophony, can provide suggestive evidence; however, physical examination is not sensitive enough or specific enough to obtain conclusive confirmation (Franquet and Chung, 2019).

The main diagnostic modality between pneumonia assessments was always Chest radiography (CXR) due to its great availability and ability to portray or represent the lung infiltrates. They provide lobar consolidation appearances, interstitial patterns and bronchopneumonia. However, CXR interpretation has a number of limitations that are associated with it. There is also diagnostic agreement between radiologists, which is also important and shows a significant variation in the detection of reported cases of pneumonia, especially with occurrence of an atypical presentation or early stage of the disease. They make it difficult to distinguish pneumonia and other pathologies, such as atelectasis, emphysema, pulmonary edema and different malignancies as well. In addition, poor imaging technique may make small or marginal infiltrates unidentifiable, particularly when the overlying anatomical structure obscures it or when affected by patient positioning. As these shortcomings suggest, there is a need to develop new diagnostic systems, which can improve the reliability of human recognition and boost the accuracy of diagnosis of pneumonia using CXR (Garg et al., 2019).

## 2.2 AI in medical imaging: Overview of AI applications in radiology

In the field of artificial intelligence, great success was reached, and the paradigm of machine and deep learning has completely redesigned a variety of fields, such as medicine. When applied to the medical imaging process, AI-based tools now permeate the processes of image acquisition, reconstruction, processing, analysis and interpretation. As one of the most developed machine-learning approaches, deep learning due to its ability to emulate the hierarchical structure and computational processes of the human brain has proven to give considerable effectiveness in solving complex pattern-recognition related problems in the fields of image classification, object detection, and segmentation. The most commonly used deep-learning architecture is Convolutional Neural Networks (CNNs), which have also shown remarkable results on the task of medical-image analysis; CNNs can extract complex features in a self-supervised manner, directly given raw input data.

In radiology, AI is very broad and wide across the imaging modalities and clinical areas. Examples of these are detecting minor deviations in mammography to screen breast cancer, detecting the intracranial hemorrhage in CT images, and separation of tumor in MRI image to plan radiation therapy.

## 3. AI model development and evaluation

Creating a strong AI model designed to diagnose pneumonia in chest radiographs presupposes a logical series of steps, that is, data retrieval, preprocessing, model selection, and testing of performance. The quality and composition of diversity of the training dataset have a strong bearing on the superiority of the resulting system, which finally determines the precision of the model being trained and the ability of the model to be applied in the real clinical setting through generalization (Tseng et al., 2025).

### 3.1 Data acquisition and preprocessing

A deep learning model requires a large, diverse and well annotated corpus in order to be built successfully. In the context of pneumonia detection, this is a common requirement to collect a large corpus of chest X-ray images with labels indicating whether pneumonia was present or absent and, where a more precise diagnosis was necessary, a specific infiltrates location and type (e.g., not only lobar, pulmonary, or alveolar but also apical in the right middle lobe). The ethical measures, in this case, patient confidentiality, and extensive anonymization practices, should be emphasized during the data collection process. In order to maximize on the usefulness of the models, databases are commonly compiled across several institutions, thus capturing the imaging-protocol, imaging-equipment, and patient demographics. Rotation, translation, scaling, and flipping transformations are usually applied as the data augmentation scheme to artificially increase the size of the corpus and model robustness against inequalities in image presentation (Ukwuoma et al., 2023) (Table 7.1).

### 3.2 AI architectures for pneumonia detection

CNNs Deep convolutional neural networks (CNNs) are the current standard solution to medical-image analysis problems such as pneumonia detection. The ability to automatically learn hierarchical features in raw pixels data-including

**TABLE 7.1** Dataset characteristics.

| Characteristics | Value |
|---|---|
| Number of images | More than 100,000 |
| Image modality | Chest X-ray |
| Pneumonia cases | More than 50,000 |
| Normal cases | More than 50,000 |
| Data source | Public and private datasets |

primitive edges to complex anatomical structures and pathological patterns-makes them extremely efficient. The better-known CNN architectures adapted to medical imaging are ResNet, VGG, Inception and DenseNet. They are often pretrained on large corpuses of natural images (e.g., ImageNet) and then fine-tuned on medical-image datasets; this approach, called transfer learning, leverages the general feature-extraction capabilities developed using large training datasets and attends to the idiosyncrasies of medical images, greatly reducing the need to assemble enormously large medical datasets and cutting training time.

Convolutional neural networks (CNNs) in pneumonia detection using chest radiography tend to transform the radiographic visuals into a probability score that characterizes the chances of pneumonia. More recent architectures even include attention mechanisms or produce class-agnostic heat maps, such as the ones created by Grad-CAM, to better establish where in an image the model paid the most attention, or which portions of an image were most influential in generating the output of a model, which has the benefit of increasing interpretability. This interpretability is essential in enabling the adoption of the AI into clinical practice and the acceptance of the AI system in the form of recommendations to be appreciated and adhered to by the radiologists.

## 3.3 Performance metrics and their clinical implications

Modern clinical diagnostic clinical artificial intelligence framework is a teamwork product that requires an extensive assessment that is multidimensional. In this rating test, there exist three complementary performance parameters, namely, sensitivity (recall), specificity, and accuracy, which happen to be diagnostic thresholds (Luo et al., 2021).

Sensitivity, or recall, is the proportion of actually positive results appropriately indicated by the system i.e., the ratio of actually flagged cases to all the cases. A high sensitivity is essential in ensuring the reduction of the false negativity and protection of the patient against inappropriate typing of their pneumonia.

Specificity on the other hand represents the percent of properly labeled true negatives, thus evaluating the accuracy of the model on whether it will recognize the negative as negative as well as the positive. It is critical to reach the best specificity in order to reduce false-positives, thus preventing unnecessary expensive procedures or the inadequate treatment schedule.

The diagnostic triad is supplemented with accuracy, which is simply the mean proportion of all the observations categorized as true positive or negative.

However, evaluating performance on the basis of such individual parameters is not enough. The area under the Receiver operating characteristic (ROC) curve (AUC) represents a complete measure of modeling discrimination power in all imaginable sensitivity-specificity combinations. The higher the AUC the more accurate the classification, and an AUC of 1.0 implies perfect classification, whilst an AUC of 0.5 means performance just as good as chance alone.

The F1 -score in these situations is more reliable as a measure of predictive performance, and is the harmonic mean of precision and recall (Table 7.2).

Clinical usability is a prerequisite to the evaluation of artificial-intelligence systems. In a screening situation, maximizing the number of detected cases takes on greater concern over a possible over diagnosis by having high sensitivity. Thorough development of AI models is hence required to strike a balance among those parameters without compromising on regular medical care and eventually augment human experience and improve patient outcomes in an unnoticeable way (Figs. 7.1–7.4).

**TABLE 7.2** Model performance metrics.

| Metric | AI alone | Radiologist alone | AI-augmented radiologist |
|---|---|---|---|
| Accuracy | 0.85 | 0.78 | 0.92 |
| Sensitivity | 0.88 | 0.75 | 0.95 |
| Specificity | 0.82 | 0.80 | 0.90 |
| AUC | 0.90 | 0.83 | 0.96 |
| F1-score | 0.85 | 0.77 | 0.93 |

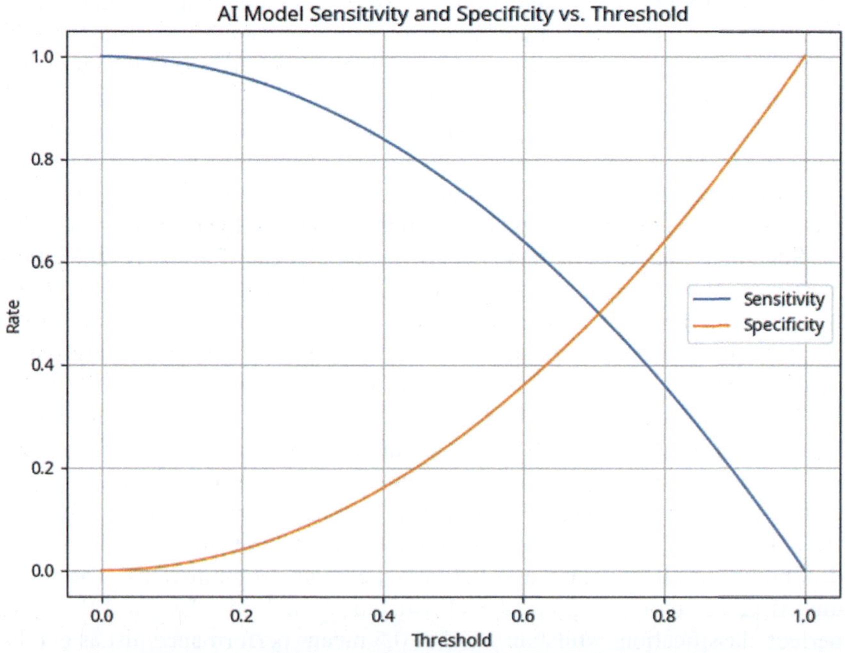


**FIGURE 7.1** AI model sensitivity and specificity versus threshold.

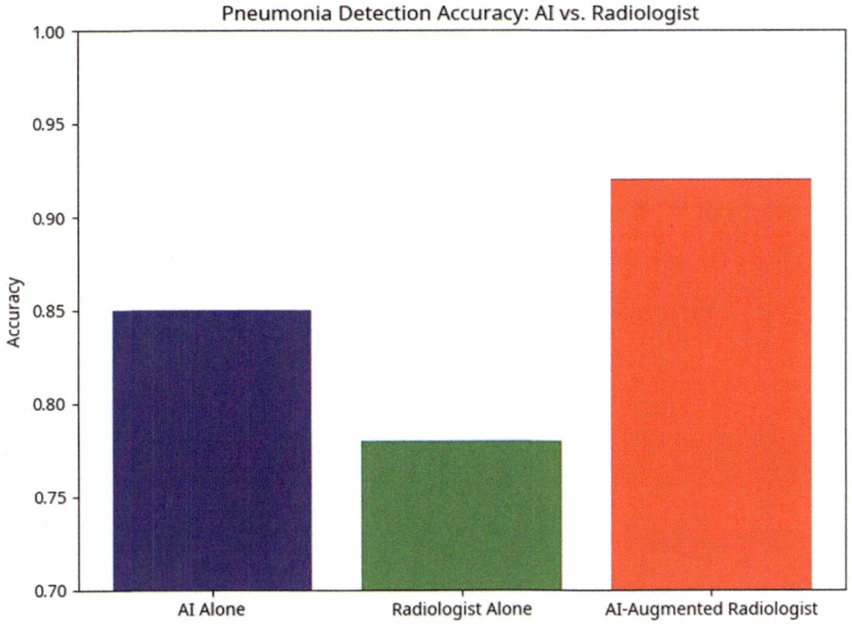


**FIGURE 7.2** Pneumonia detection accuracy: AI versus radiologist.

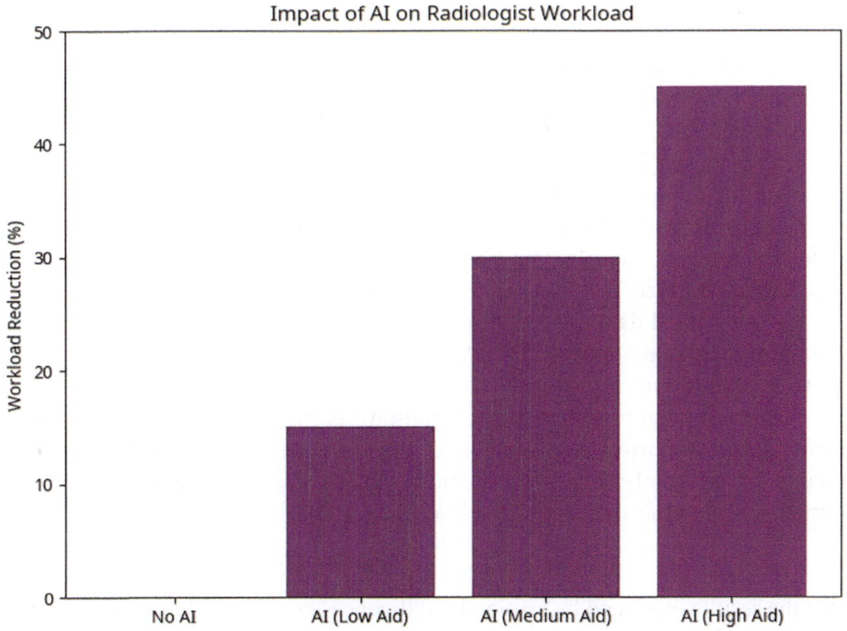


**FIGURE 7.3** Impact of AI on radiologist workload.

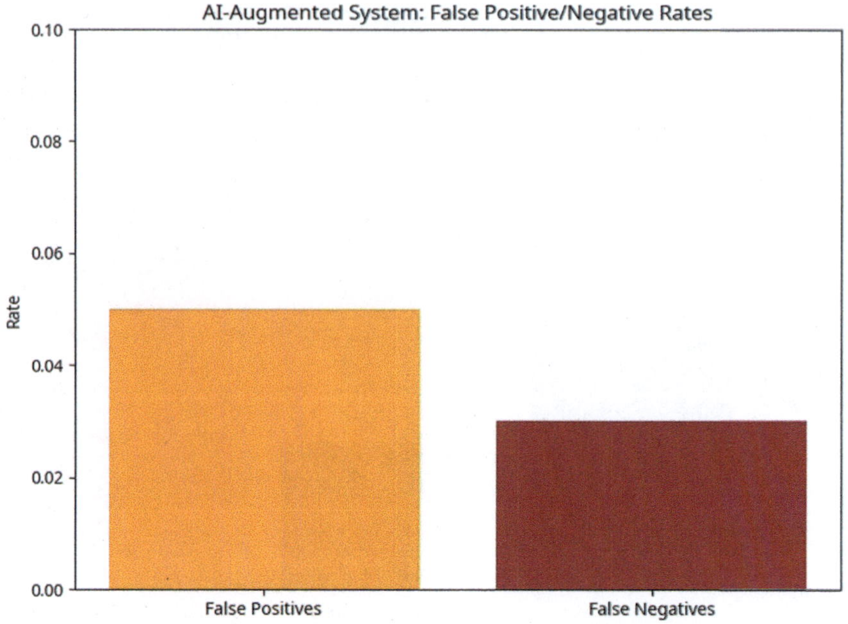


**FIGURE 7.4** AI-augmented system: false positive/negative rates.

## 3.4 AI workflow in pneumonia detection

This proposed workflow stipulated the AI augmented pneumonia diagnostic pipeline for thoracic radiograph. The workflow is initiated by intake of a chest radiograph followed by passing the radiograph through a series of sequential AI-powered middle-pass phases.

The first step is AI-based preprocessing followed by image boosting and denoising techniques to optimize the X-ray image for analytical purposes. The resulting improved image is subsequently performed feature extraction, whereby relevant radiological patterns and characteristics are identified and thoroughly analyzed.

The processed data are fed into the face of an Artificial Intelligence model, the main diagnostic engine. This AI system then makes the judgment whether there is pneumonia or not in the chest X-ray image.

When the pneumonia detection condition is true (Yes branch) the system's limits define abnormal image areas to warn of clinically relevant pathological changes. Conversely, when pneumatic detection wasn't made (No branch), the system outputs the message, "No Pneumonia Detected."

Both pathways converge at the radiologist review stage, thereby denoting the importance of human oversight in the diagnostic pathway. This attention ensures that the results produced by artificial intelligence are validated by clinical experts to uphold diagnostic accuracy and patient safety (Sufian et al., 2024) (Fig. 7.5).

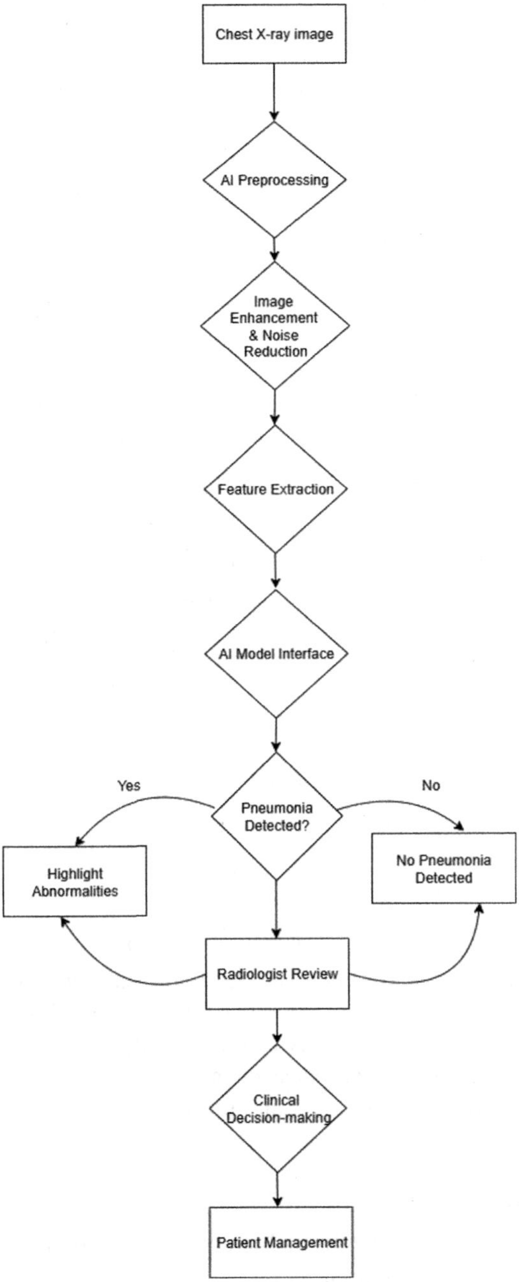


**FIGURE 7.5** AI workflow in pneumonia detection.

## 3.5 Augmenting clinical decision-making with AI

Following this assessment the protocol sequences chest radiography and thus may be regarded as a pathway addressing thoracic medical problems that require imaging studies (Hirani et al., 2024).

Once the chest X-ray is obtained, the chain is then taken forward to the stage of interpretation by the radiologists, where qualified radiologists perform a systematic analysis of the imaging results. This critical point gives rise to an AI-designed method providing two parallel solutions that combined best optimize the diagnostic precision.

AI Augmented—An AI augmented pathway combines an artificial general intelligence (AI) to enable images to be analyzed and interpreted. This branch includes an AI Output Review phase by which AI generated results are carefully reviewed and verified by qualified clinicians. Whilst artificial intelligence technology has been promoted as a means of increasing diagnostic accuracy and reducing interpretative error, and ultimately accelerating the diagnostic process.

The conceptual interpretive approach as well as the AI-augmented domain then intersect at Integrated Diagnosis, in which the full body of information currently available is integrated and a unifying diagnostic conclusion is reached. This integration assures that the human expertise and artificial intelligence skills are perfectly imbibed to optimize patient care.

The workflow then extends to Development of Treatment Plan in which clinicians develop individualized therapeutic plans, based on the combined diagnostic process. The planning stage considers the patient's individual condition, medical history, and diagnostic findings to develop individual treatment concepts (Krishnan et al., 2023) (Fig. 7.6).

## 3.6 Human-AI interaction in radiology

### 3.6.1 Workflow components and process flow

This flowchart shows a complex process of medical treatment that "bets on AI" to help radiological diagnosis, and hence shows the interaction between AI technology and human clinical skill, which is characterized as "a paradigmatic complement." Again, the flowchart emphasizes the quality assurance, verification/validation protocols, and patient safety at various decision nodes/chapters of the flowchart (Chong et al., 2025).

### 3.6.2 Initial assessment phase

The workflow begins with Radiologist Initiation of Review thus instantiating human control as the core to the diagnostic process. This initial phase ensures that medical expertise, specifically, patient history and clinical context, drives the subsequent artificial intelligence analysis and thus ensures that medical expertise continues to play a vital role in framing technological intentions.

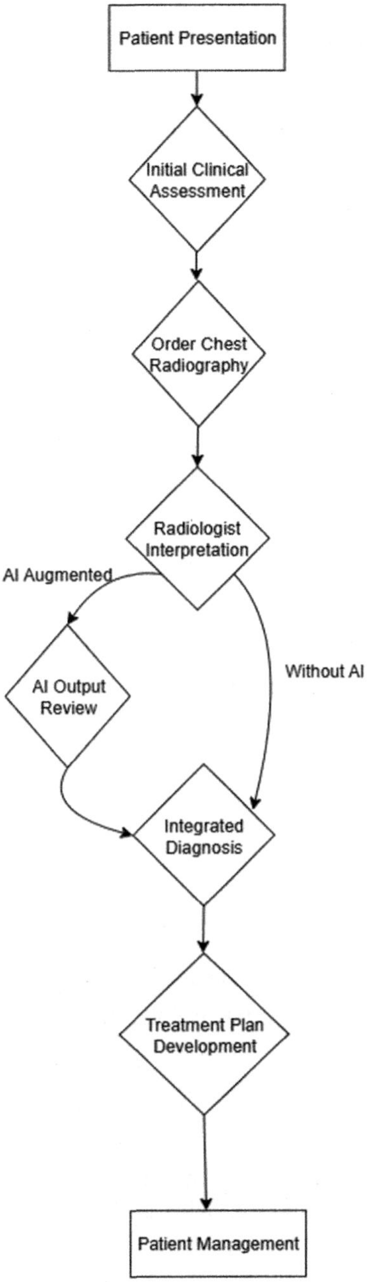


**FIGURE 7.6** Clinical decision-making with AI augmentation.

It then progresses into the AI—Provided Initial Assessment phase where the imaging data is interpreted through algorithms by artificial intelligence to generate initial findings. Specifically, this step represents the earliest stage of human-clinical-machine-looped integration, which optimizes efficient initial screening while maintaining the radiologist's position on the diagnostic pathway (Fig. 7.7).

## 3.7 AI system architecture

### 3.7.1 Data ingestion

The data-ingestion phase kickstarts the workflow by fetching and assimilating medical imaging data, in the form of mainly chest radiographs and Computed tomography (CT) scans, into the system. This preparatory step includes the organized gathering of patient image files from heterogeneous sources (including Picture Archiving and Communicating Systems (PACS) and imaging devices), which is also then ingested into the processing pipeline (Solar et al., 2024).

### 3.7.2 Image preprocessing

Image preprocessing is an important step in the preparation of raw medical images, ensuring standardization and enhancement. Typical preprocessing steps include the attenuation of noise, contrast modulation, normalization and spatial resizing to ensure image quality and uniformity for subsequent analytical exploitation (Rubin, 2019).

Through strict preprocessing protocols, images become compliant with the rigid requirements of these new, cutting-edge AI models.

### 3.7.3 Feature extraction layer

This stage identifies relevant visual patterns and characteristics from the medical images. The layer transforms raw pixel data into meaningful features that can indicate potential signs of pneumonia, such as opacity patterns, lung texture changes, consolidation areas, and other radiological markers.

### 3.7.4 Output layer: Pneumonia probability

The feature extracted from the convolutional neural network is presented to its output layer, which produces a probability score indicating whether there is pneumonia or not in the analyzed image. Usually, this quantitative cheque is given as a decimal percentage or absolute confidence, with accompanying accuracy measures.

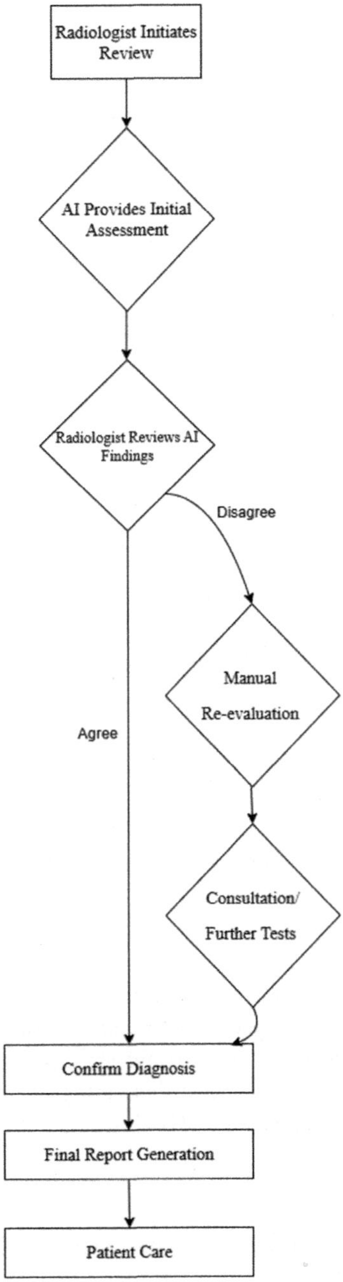


**FIGURE 7.7** Human-AI interaction in radiology.

### *3.7.5 Clinical integration phase*

Results provided by the system are pushed out in an analytical output by Artificial Intelligence that is useful for clinicians. The interface displays probabilistic scores, delineates areas requiring attention, provides heat maps or annotations, and can also provide additional diagnostic information relating to the review to support evidence-based clinical decision-making (Maleki Varnosfaderani and Forouzanfar, 2024).

### *3.7.6 Final evaluation phase*

The radiologist receives the AI—assisted analysis as a supportive tool within their clinical analysis. Far from replacing human expertise, the system saves diagnostic losses in accuracy and efficiency by providing a second opinion and reporting observed findings of potential relevance (Fig. 7.8).

## 3.8 Data flow in AI-augmented radiology

### *3.8.1 Working intelligence integration: Academically research-tested*

The system adopts the latest artificial intelligence technology by the AI Server component, which has an interface to AI processing capabilities. This integration enables automated analysis, pattern recognition and diagnostic support, uplifting medical image interpretation accuracy and efficiency.

### *3.8.2 Data storage, analysis: An educational case study*

Processed data is exported to the Results Database storing complete results of imaging, AI analytic results and associated diagnostic information. This centralized repository thereby provides data access and maintains the longitudinal patient record.

### *3.8.3 Integration with clinical aspects*

The workflow eventually arrives at the Radiologist Workstation where AI processed results are reviewed by clinicians and subject to clinical interpretation. Finally, the system is connected to EHR/EMR (Electronic Health Record/Electronic Medical Record) systems, thus assuring seamless integration of imaging results into comprehensive patient medical records (Fig. 7.9).

## 3.9 Hospital system integration with AI

This schematic in health information system is an aspect of the health care information system, including interconnected components used to support patient's data activities and clinical workflows. The Hospital information system (HIS) sits at the top of the diagram as the administrative and operational center of hospital operation by linking directly to the Radiology

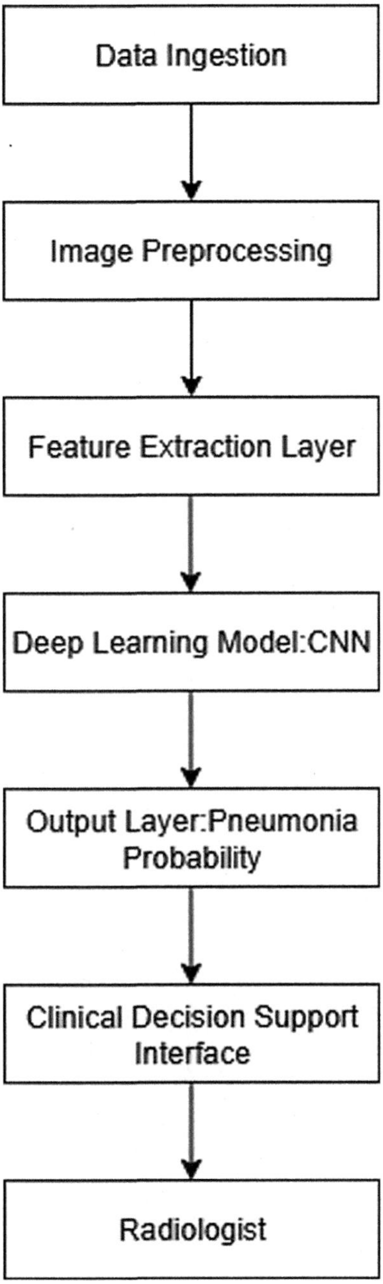


**FIGURE 7.8** AI system architecture.

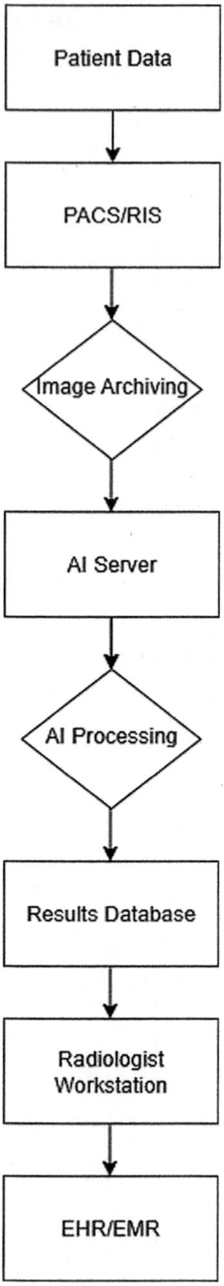


**FIGURE 7.9** Data flow in AI-augmented radiology.

**TABLE 7.3 Mindful healthcare practices for radiologists.**

| Practice | Benefit |
|---|---|
| Compassion practice | Intervention relating to fostering empathy was demonstrated to reduce burnout, whereby there is evidence to indicate that burnout reverses once empathy is enhanced. |
| Mindful breathing | A good example here would be the case of structured exercise programs, since they have been shown empiricism to have been associated with a dramatic change for the better in both physiological and subjective measures of stress. |
| Mindful movement | Will enhance the physical health and mental clarity |
| Mindful communication | The betterment of interpersonal relationships and team dynamics is one of the major aims of organizational life. |
| Body scan meditation | Recent empirical data reveals that somatic attentional focus as a measure, namely, the awareness of body sensations, can be a physiological arousal countermeasure in its ability to reduce the tension. |

information system (RIS) to coordinate the movement of patient demographic and administrative data toward the operation of radiology and imaging services (Winter et al., 2023).

Data from the Radiology information system (RIS) are sent to the Picture archiving and communication system (PACS) that stores, retrieves, and distributes medical images throughout the medical facility. PACS is a centralized image repository, where radiology reports, scans and other diagnostic images are managed in a generalized way.

An important building block of the system architecture is the AI module, which is depicted as a diamond-shaped decision (or processing) node that defines a bi-directional interface with the Picture Archiving and Communication System (PACS). This design means that the AI subsystem will at the same time consume imaging data from PACS as input for analyzing imagery and in return feed back the results, including automated report generation, diagnostic support and image super-enhancement to the archival repository (Table 7.3).

All operating campus areas finally connect with the Electronic health record (EHR) system, the repository of everything related to patient data (Fig. 7.10).

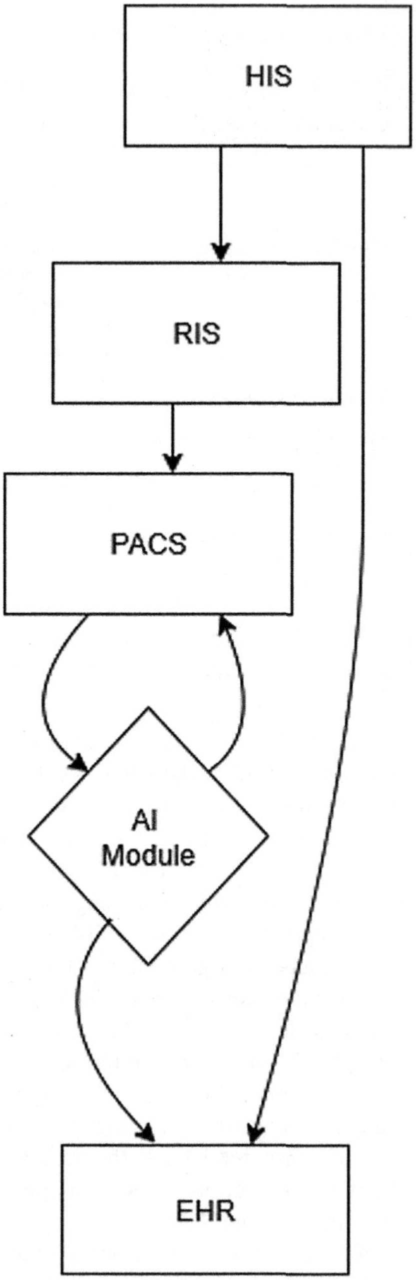


**FIGURE 7.10** Hospital system integration with AI.

# 4. Mindful healthcare in the age of AI

## 4.1 Ethical considerations: Data privacy, algorithmic bias and transparency

### *4.1.1 Data security*

Medical imaging in the context of AI requires a massive amount of data, which has led to the question of patient privacy. Therefore, there is a need to have strong data governance structures, anonymization and a high level of adherence to the regulations such as HIPAA and GDPR in protecting patient privacy.

### *4.1.2 Algorithm bias and fairness*

The possibility of bias The preexisting biases that are present in the training data can be exacerbated and even propagated in the use of AI models. Reflective consideration should thus be given to the implementation of proactive measures to prevent and limit bias, and to enable fair performance of the system in all groups of patients regardless of their demographic background. This goal involves the usage of various sample data sets, metrics of fairness, and constant observation.

### *4.1.3 Explainability and transparency (XAI)*

Another ethical problem with many deep learning systems is their so-called privacy or black-box: clinicians will not trust the results of AI systems that have no means of reasoning translated to the human-understandable level, therefore, lacking the ability to detect errors. Therefore, responsible AI (Explainable AI, XAI) techniques, which make the reasoning behind models transparent, are of prime importance in mindful development and thus strengthen accountability.

### *4.1.4 Accountability*

It may be complicated to define who is responsible in cases of mistakes made because of AI-based diagnosis. Clearly outlined legal frameworks and requirements are needed, which will define the role of the developers, healthcare providers, and institutions in case of negative results (Table 7.4).

# 5. Case studies and practical applications

A number of AI pneumonia-detection systems have made it outside of research labs into clinical application, or have at least shown promise:

## 5.1 Case study 1: High-volume emergency department triage

In a large urban Emergency department (ED), one of the key problems is fast and proper pneumonia diagnosis among the patients who come with the

**TABLE 7.4 Ethical considerations in AI deployment.**

| Consideration | Description |
|---|---|
| Data privacy | The security of the data concerning the patients |
| Algorithmic bias | Bias mitigation in AI systems is very important in order to reach a demographically fair result. |
| Transparency | The primary issue with implementing artificial intelligence (AI) in healthcare is that clinicians should understand hidden reasoning behind the medical decisions. |
| Accountability | Explanatory theories of blaming faults using AI. |
| Patient autonomy | The notion of patient as an individual being autonomous in taking healthcare decisions and most particularly the decision of whether to incorporate artificial intelligence (AI) in their healthcare pathway, is currently a general consensus in the framework of ethical health practices and professional expediencies. |

complaint of respiratory diseases. Delays may be caused in case of peak hours due to the use of traditional workflow. A large dataset of CXRs was trained on an AI system, which was integrated to output within a few seconds preliminary evaluation of all incoming a chest X-ray. The AI indicated pictures that had the maximum suspicion of having pneumonia, and these pictures had the first priority when being reviewed by the radiologist. This resulted in a quantitative decrease in the time-to-diagnosis of cases of pneumonia giving a chance to have an earlier start of their treatment. The mindful integration was composed of false positives on the part of AI; however, those were occasional. The review of all the cases by radiologists to make sure no patient has been misdiagnosed on the basis of the AI alone. This system enhanced the throughput by a significant margin and decreased the radiologist workload since they could work on complex interpretations instead of primary screening because of case presorting (Bouam et al., 2023).

## 5.2 Case study 2: Resource-limited settings

Remote or resource-limited regions where only limited access to expert radiologists can be achieved is revolutionized with AI. Distributing a mobile AI model of CXR interpretation in a number of rural clinics. This system offered an immediate, automatic reading of pneumonia, thus allowing workers in local medical facilities with unlikely training in radiology to decide on how to refer patients to a specialist and pretreat them effectively. The AI performed as a lifeline and initial-line diagnostic tool, which connected the shortage of experts. The consciousness here entailed education of the local employees not only to be able to use the machine, but to have awareness of its limits and when they need tele-radiology consultation (Guo et al., 2024).

### 5.3 Case study 3: Enhancement of diagnostic consistency large hospital associations

Multicenter, big hospital system-wide study, put in place a uniform artificial intelligence system to detect pneumonia. The main objective was to eliminate interradiologist variability and have greater diagnostic consistency across sites and between more and less experienced readers. The use of the AI system offered a coherent second opinion that marked the areas of concern and proposed diagnoses (Shin et al., 2023).

## 6. Conclusion and future work

The given study revealed that current adaptations of AI on deep-learning models provide a remarkable level of performance in regard to pneumonia detection rates on a patchy chest X-ray scan with impressive accuracy, as well as sensitivity and specificity levels. However, the clinical usefulness of such systems lies, in fact, not in separate measures of performance but in their potential to interact with human radiologists. Therefore, there is also the necessity to create models of human AI interaction, which can be either concurrent (reading) or sequential (reading). This way, the advantages of AI will be able to be utilized with references to the corresponding problems of overreliance and algorithmic bias. Additionally, explainability of machine-generated decision-making and transparency of associated processes are necessary to develop trust and guarantee accountability throughout the clinical practice.

The chapter positions Mindful Healthcare as one that is ultimately required to inform the adoption of AI in the field of medicine. Mindfulness enables radiologists to develop resilience, attentional fixed states, and clinical moral vigilance required during an AI augmented clinical practice. Mindful practice practitioners learn to manage stress more effectively, maximize the cognitions and protect the people-oriented approach behind patient care through mindful practice training. Such views are also necessary to engage into the ethical aspects of AI, i.e., privacy, algorithmic fairness, and accountability, thus making emending technologies built and used in a responsible and equitable way.

## References

Bouam, M., Binquet, C., Moretto, F., Sixt, T., Vourc'h, M., Piroth, L., Ray, P., Blot, M., 2023. Delayed diagnosis of pneumonia in the emergency department: factors associated and prognosis. Front. Med. 10. https://doi.org/10.3389/fmed.2023.1042704.

Chong, P.L., Vaigeshwari, V., Mohammed Reyasudin, B.K., Noor Hidayah, b.R.A., Tatchanaamoorti, P., Yeow, J.A., Kong, F.Y., 2025. Integrating artificial intelligence in healthcare: applications, challenges, and future directions. Future Science OA 11 (1). https://doi.org/10.1080/20565623.2025.2527505.

Franquet, T., Chung, J.H., 2019. Chapter 7: Imaging of pulmonary infection. In: Hodler, J., Kubik-Huch, R.A., von Schulthess, G.K. (Eds.), Diseases of the Chest, Breast, Heart and Vessels 2019–2022: Diagnostic and Interventional Imaging [Internet]. Springer, Cham (CH). https://doi.org/10.1007/978-3-030-11149-6_7.

Garg, M., Prabhakar, N., Gulati, A., Agarwal, R., Dhooria, S., 2019. Spectrum of imaging findings in pulmonary infections. Part 1: Bacterial and viral. Polish Journal of Radiology 84, e205. https://doi.org/10.5114/pjr.2019.85812.

Guo, L., Xia, L., Zheng, Q., Zheng, B., Jaeger, S., Giger, M.L., Fuhrman, J., Li, H., Lure, F.Y.M., Li, H., Li, L., 2024. Can AI generate diagnostic reports for radiologist approval on CXR images? A multi-reader and multi-case observer performance study. J. X Ray Sci. Technol. 32 (6), 1465–1480. https://doi.org/10.3233/XST-240051.

Hirani, R., Noruzi, K., Khuram, H., Hussaini, A.S., Aifuwa, E.I., Ely, K.E., Lewis, J.M., Gabr, A. E., Smiley, A., Tiwari, R.K., Etienne, M., 2024. Artificial intelligence and healthcare: a journey through history, present innovations, and future possibilities. Life 14 (5). https://doi.org/10.3390/life14050557.

Krishnan, G., Singh, S., Pathania, M., Gosavi, S., Abhishek, S., Parchani, A., Dhar, M., 2023. Artificial intelligence in clinical medicine: catalyzing a sustainable global healthcare paradigm. Front. Artif. Intell. 6. https://doi.org/10.3389/frai.2023.1227091.

Maleki Varnosfaderani, S., Forouzanfar, M., 2024. The role of AI in hospitals and clinics: transforming healthcare in the 21st century. Bioengineering 11 (4), 337. https://doi.org/10.3390/bioengineering11040337.

Rahmati, M.B., Ahmadi, M., Malekmohamadi, S.H., Zare, S.H., Jafari, M., 2015. The significance of chest ultrasound and chest X-ray in the diagnosis of children clinically suspected of pneumonia. J. Med. Life 8 (Spec Iss 3), 50–53.

Shin, H.J., Lee, S., Kim, S., Son, N.H., Kim, E.K., 2023. Hospital-wide survey of clinical experience with artificial intelligence applied to daily chest radiographs. PLoS One 18 (3). https://doi.org/10.1371/journal.pone.0282123.

Solar, M., Castañeda, V., Ñanculef, R., Dombrovskaia, L., Araya, M., 2024. A data ingestion procedure towards a medical images repository. Sensors 24 (15), 4985. https://doi.org/10.3390/s24154985.

Sufian, M.A., Hamzi, W., Sharifi, T., Zaman, S., Alsadder, L., Lee, E., Hakim, A., Hamzi, B., 2024. AI-driven thoracic X-ray diagnostics: transformative transfer learning for clinical validation in pulmonary radiography. J. Personalized Med. 14 (8), 856. https://doi.org/10.3390/jpm14080856.

Tseng, W.C., Wang, Y.C., Chen, W.C., Lin, K.P., 2025. Development of an AI model for pneumothorax imaging: dataset and model optimization strategies for real-world deployment. Eur. J. Radiol. Open 14. https://doi.org/10.1016/j.ejro.2025.100664.

Ukwuoma, C.C., Qin, Z., Heyat, M.B.B., Akhtar, F., Bamisile, O., Muaad, A.Y., Addo, D., Al-antari, M.A., 2023. A hybrid explainable ensemble transformer encoder for pneumonia identification from chest X-ray images. J. Adv. Res. 48, 191–211. https://doi.org/10.1016/j.jare.2022.08.021.

Winter, A., Ammenwerth, E., Haux, R., et al., 2023. Chapter 2: Health information systems: technological and management perspectives. In: Basic Concepts and Terms, third ed. Springer, Cham (CH). https://doi.org/10.1007/978-3-031-12310-8_2.

Wootton, D., Feldman, C., 2014. The diagnosis of pneumonia requires a chest radiograph (x-ray)–yes, no or sometimes? Pneumonia 5 (S1), 1–7. https://doi.org/10.15172/pneu.2014.5/464.

## Further reading

Luo, S., Wu, C., Luo, Q., Ran, M., Liu, Y., Lei, F., Chen, X., Yuan, Z., Liu, H., Wan, C., 2021. The design and evaluation of clinical pathway for disease management to maximize public health benefit. Risk Manag. Healthc. Policy 14, 5047–5057. https://doi.org/10.2147/RMHP.S340718.

Rubin, D.L., 2019. Artificial intelligence in imaging: the radiologist's role. J. Am. Coll. Radiol. 16 (9 Pt B), 1309–1317. https://doi.org/10.1016/j.jacr.2019.05.036.



Chapter 8

# Revolutionizing human–device interaction: Advancements and applications in brain–computer interfaces

P. Nisha Priya[1], V. Priya[1], V. Divya[1] and N. Naveena[2]
[1]*CSI College of Engineering, Department of Computer Science & Engineering, Ketti, Tamil Nadu, India;* [2]*Sri Krishna College of Engineering and Technology, Coimbatore, Tamil Nadu, India*

## 1. Introduction to brain–computer interfaces (BCIs)

BCI is a technology that allows the brain to communicate with an external device. It has great potential for many different users. Fig. 8.1 shows the typical BCI. It explains BCI technology and its process by capturing signals from the brain and converting them to input for its applications. Brain signals can be recorded using invasive or noninvasive methods. The brain signals' features are extracted and categorized using a number of machine learning algorithms. Although BCI is very beneficial for health-related issues, it also has uses in smart homes, education, security, and many other fields. For BCI to be useful in the future, it must overcome various challenges. This chapter provides an overview of BCI, discussing its fundamentals, applications, and challenges (Javaid, 2013). It explores key aspects, including legal, technical, and ethical issues.

### 1.1 Evolution of BCI

Systems known as BCIs translate the activity of the user's brain into commands or messages for interactive applications. A BCI can be demonstrated by the ability to control the movement of a ball on a computer screen through imagined left or right-hand movements. Since the phrase "BCI" was introduced in the 1970s, research and interest in the field have grown significantly. Today, numerous laboratories worldwide are actively studying BCIs,

Neuromorphic Computing for Brain Computer Interfaces. https://doi.org/10.1016/B978-0-443-41594-4.00016-2

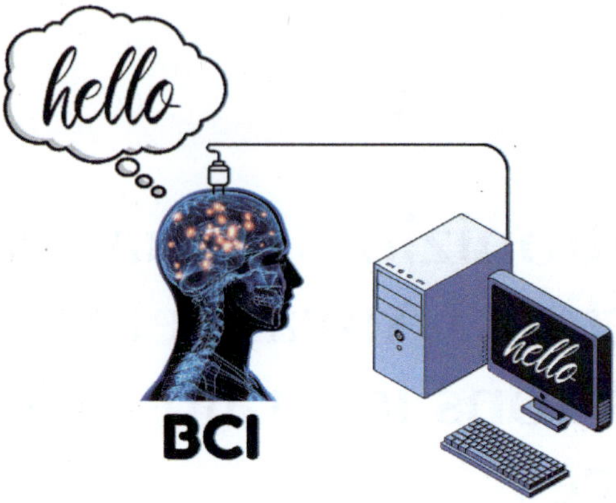


FIGURE 8.1 Brain–computer interface.

contributing to a diverse range of paradigms, methodologies, concepts, and applications in this technology (Maiseli et al., 2023).

BCIs have undergone significant transformations since their inception. Initially, BCI relied on invasive methods, requiring direct placement of electrodes into the brain. However, recent advancements have led to the development of noninvasive BCIs, involving electroencephalography (EEG), functional near-infrared spectroscopy (fNIRS), and other techniques to detect neural activity.

## 1.2 Early foundations and conceptualization

The need for direct neural communication with external devices gave rise to the idea of BCIs. In the beginning, scientists investigated the brain's neural activity, concentrating on the connection between neural signals and motor control.

Neuroscience and neurophysiology served as the foundation for early BCI research, which aimed to comprehend how electrical activity in the brain could be used for control and communication. Neuronal activity in the brain produces electrical impulses that could be detected and analyzed to identify motor commands, intentions, or thoughts.

The connection between brain signals and movement control was one of the main topics of study. With the hope that these signals could be translated into instructions for outside devices, researchers set out to decode the brain's voluntary movement-related activity patterns. This marked a major advancement in the creation of systems that could decipher brain activity and translate it into useful outputs, like manipulating a robotic limb or computer cursor.

### *1.2.1 The 1970s: Coining the term and initial research*

In the early 1970s, the term BCI was first used. The main focus of research during this time was on comprehending brain wave patterns, especially using

EEG. To figure out how to create basic communication channels between the brain and external devices, scientists tried to decipher neural activity.

### *1.2.2 The 1980s–1990s: Advancements in signal acquisition and processing*

As computing power increased, increasingly complex methods for processing brain signals emerged in the 1980s and 1990s. Better signal interpretation is now possible thanks to major advancements in feature extraction techniques. During this time, basic assistive technology for people with neuromuscular disorders was also introduced.

### *1.2.3 The 2000s: Integration with machine learning and expanded applications*

In the early 21st century, BCIs benefited from advances in machine learning, allowing for more accurate classification of brain signals (Abdulkader et al., 2015). This led to the expansion of BCI applications beyond medical uses to include gaming, virtual reality, and smart home control systems.

### *1.2.4 The present and future: Wireless and artificial intelligence (AI)-driven BCIs*

Recent developments have focused on wireless BCIs, adaptive learning algorithms, and noninvasive signal acquisition methods. AI-driven BCIs have enhanced real-time processing capabilities, making interactions more seamless and responsive. The future of BCI research aims to achieve fully integrated neural control systems that bridge human cognition and technology effectively.

## 1.3 Emergence

The practice of medicine will undergo significant changes as a result of BCI technology. Patients and physicians will have new options for addressing communication, mobility, sensation, and mental health issues thanks to BCIs, which are generally characterized as devices that can read brain activity and convert it into device operation. New obligations and a wide range of ethical issues will arise as a result of these new skills. Examining these issues in light of medical objectives is one method to comprehend them.

### *1.3.1 The potential of BCI intelligence*

The potential of BCI is shown in Fig. 8.2. BCI intelligence has far-reaching implications for various fields, including:

1. Assistive technology: BCI intelligence can empower individuals with serious movement disorders, paralysis, and people with amyotrophic lateral sclerosis (ALS) to interact with their surroundings.

2. Neuroscience research: BCI intelligence can provide valuable insights into brain function, cognition, and behavior (Fig. 8.2).
3. Gaming and entertainment: BCI intelligence holds the possibility to revolutionize the gaming business by enabling individuals to regulate games using their mind. Healthcare and rehabilitation: With the application of BCI intelligence, neurological diseases like epileptic seizures, Parkinson's disorder, and hemorrhage can be identified and treated.

### 1.3.2 I3 framework

The I3 framework is a conceptual model used to design, develop, and evaluate BCI systems. The framework consists of three interconnected components: Interface, Interaction, and Intelligence (Liu et al., 2024), and it is shown in Fig. 8.3.

**FIGURE 8.2** Potential of BCI.

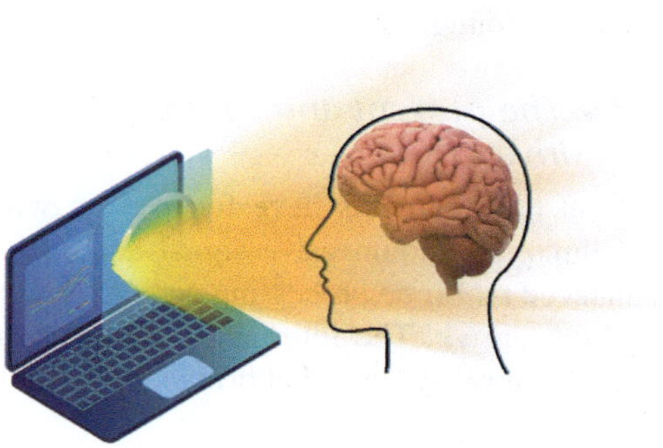

**FIGURE 8.3** I3 framework.

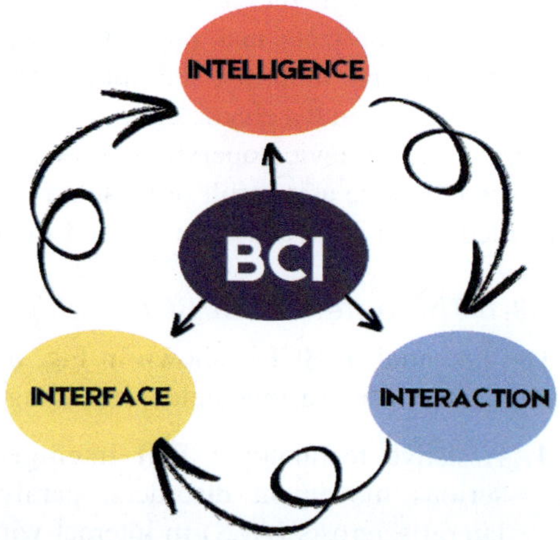

#### 1.3.2.1 Intelligence (I3)

1. Machine Learning: Analyzing and interpreting neural signals using machine learning algorithms to increase the precision and versatility of BCI.
2. Adaptive Systems: Creating systems that adjust to each other's needs, preferences, and abilities.
3. Cognitive Architectures: Including cognitive architectures and models to gain a deeper understanding of human thought and decision-making.

#### 1.3.2.2 Interaction (I3)

1. Signal Processing: The raw brain signals (such as EEG or electrocorticography [ECoG]) are filtered, amplified, and analyzed to remove noise and extract meaningful patterns.
2. Feature Extraction: Specific features in brain activity (e.g., frequency bands, event-related potentials) are identified to determine the user's intention.
3. Classification and Translation: Machine learning algorithms such as support vector machine (SVM), linear discriminant analysis (LDA), or neural networks classify these signals and convert them into commands for a device, such as a robotic arm, a computer cursor, or a speech synthesizer.

#### 1.3.2.3 Interface (I3)

1. User Interface: This component allows users to interact with the BCI system through visual, auditory, or haptic feedback.
2. Machine Interface: This connects the processed brain signals to external applications such as robotic arms, exoskeletons, smart home devices, or computer cursors. It ensures seamless execution of the user's intended commands.
3. Feedback Mechanism: A crucial part of the interface that helps users adjust their brain activity based on real-time responses.

## 2. Fundamentals of BCI

### 2.1 How BCIs work: a technical overview

The BCI system has three main parts: data collection, data analysis, and application. These parts work together to transfer neural signals to the intended BCI application (Maiseli et al., 2023).

- **Data Collection**: Data collection or signal acquisition is the process of capturing brain activity using electrodes. It collects electrical signals that reflect different brain functions. Most BCI systems, including commercial ones, use signals such as EEG (measured from the scalp) and ECoG. On the brain surface, local field potential measures the electrical activity around neurons, while neuronal action potential refers to a quick change in a neuron's membrane voltage. The effectiveness of the BCI system largely depends on the quality of the acquired brain signals.

- **Data Analysis**: At this stage, the BCI system collects important brain signal features to understand the user's purpose. Like the last step, this process must be accurate to ensure the features strongly relate to the user's thoughts, improving the system's performance. BCI systems typically use time-based or frequency-based features, such as signal strength, response time, or neuron activity. Before designing the system, it is important to determine the type of features and how they will be processed. Any errors in these features should be removed to avoid problems in later stages.
- **Application**: In today's world, scientists, engineers, programmers, and psychologists are working hard to use advanced technology to improve human life (Abdulkader et al., 2015; Liu et al., 2024). The success of BCI technology relies on teamwork across different fields. To create useful applications, it is essential to identify the right users and consider their needs. Recently, BCI technology has been used in various industries, such as mining and education. Researchers believe BCI can help advance robotics and neurophysiological discoveries. A key part of BCIs is that they use algorithms, which translate brain signals into instructions for control devices (Abrams et al., 2013)

## 2.2 Types of BCIs

The types of BCI are invasive, partially invasive, and noninvasive, as shown in Fig. 8.2.

### *2.2.1 Invasive BCIs*

Invasive BCIs help blind people see and paralyzed people move by placing small devices inside the brain through surgery. Tiny chips with thin pins read brain signals, which a computer translates into commands for machines (Javaid, 2013). Another computer then uses these commands to control a device. Because these BCIs are inside the brain, they provide the best signal quality. Their biggest advantage is high accuracy in both time and space, improving signal quality and reducing noise. However, they have some challenges. One major issue is that they can only monitor small brain areas, and once implanted, they cannot be moved to other regions (Abrams et al., 2013). This process involves using microelectrode arrays, like Neuralink's brain chip, in specific brain areas such as the motor cortex. These electrodes capture brain signals, which computers process to control external devices. Invasive BCIs are more precise than noninvasive ones because they provide highly accurate signals with less external interference (Fig. 8.4).

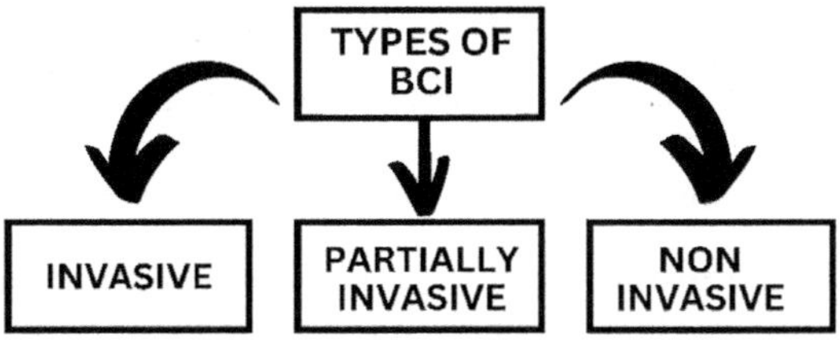


**FIGURE 8.4** Types of brain–computer interface.

### 2.2.2 Partially invasive

Partially invasive BCIs are placed inside the cranium, not in the brain. They provide clearer signals than noninvasive BCIs and are safer than fully invasive ones. ECoG is a type of BCI that records brain activity using a slim plastic pad with electrodes placed inside the cranium but above the brain (Javaid, 2013). It works like an EEG but provides better signals. ECoG is a good choice because it offers clear brain signals, requires less training, and is safer than fully invasive BCIs. This technology helps people with movement disabilities control devices with their brains. Partially Invasive has the ability to provide high control with minimum training, making it useful for real-world applications. These BCIs give better signal resolution than noninvasive ones, as skull bones can distort signals and have a lower risk of forming scar tissue compared to fully invasive BCIs. often used in medical applications, such as treating and diagnosing epilepsy, controlling prosthetic devices, and assisting individuals with movement disorders (Daly and Huggins, 2015). They provide better signal quality and wider frequency range than noninvasive BCIs, making them reliable for long-term use.

### 2.2.3 Noninvasive

The simplest and safest method is noninvasive BCI, which uses an EEG device with electrodes resting on the scalp. These electrodes read brain signals by detecting tiny voltage changes between neurons. The signals are then strengthened and cleaned up before being processed by a computer. In older systems, the signals were drawn on paper using automatic pens. Although the skull blocks and distorts some signals, EEG is more commonly used because it is safer and easier than other BCI types (Daly and Huggins, 2015). However, neural signals must pass through the skull; the signals detected by noninvasive BCIs are often weaker and more prone to interference. To improve accuracy, researchers use advanced signal processing techniques and AI algorithms. Despite their limitations, noninvasive BCIs remain a promising field of study, offering a nonsurgical way to connect the human brain with external systems for medical, research, and consumer applications.

## 2.3 Neural signal acquisition and their interpretation

BCIs detect electrical and metabolic activities using sensors. The most common methods include ECoG, EEG, magnetic resonance imaging (MRI), and magnetoencephalography (MEG), as shown in Figs. 8.3 and 8.5.

- **Electroencephalography:** EEG uses sensors; sensors are positioned on the scalp to sense the brain signal (most common for noninvasive BCIs) (Gursel Ozmen et al., 2018). Brain cells send signals through electrical impulses, which appear as wave lines on the EEG. These cells remain active, working even in sleep. An EEG can detect the brain signal changes, helping to diagnose epilepsy or other seizure disorders. It also confirms brain death in coma patients. A continuous electroencephalogram is used to monitor and adjust anesthesia levels for those in a medical coma.
- **Electrocorticography:** This is a partially invasive technique where sensors are placed directly on the brain's surface. It involves intracranial EEG recording with similar goals, but subdural grids are inserted into the cortex to capture the brain signal. A craniotomy (surgical skull opening) is required for implantation. Recordings can be done during surgery or over several days postsurgery, making ECoG an invasive procedure.
- **Magnetic Resonance Imaging:** MRI is a medical method that creates clear images of the body's internal parts, including the brain, muscles, joints, and organs. Unlike X-rays or CT scans, it does not use radiation but relies on strong magnets, radio waves, and a computer. The magnetic field lines up hydrogen atoms, and radio waves that disturb them, causing signals that a computer turns into images. MRI helps diagnose brain conditions like strokes, tumors, and multiple sclerosis, as well as joint, spine, and heart problems. It is also useful for detecting issues in organs like the liver, kidneys, and reproductive system, aiding in early disease detection and treatment planning.

**FIGURE 8.5** Brain signal acquisition signals.

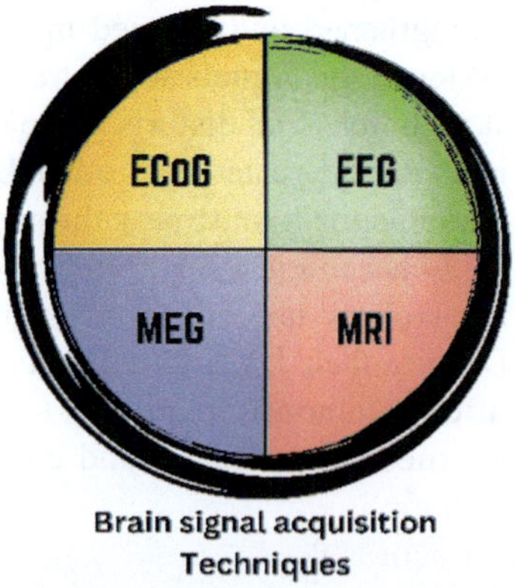

- **Magnetoencephalography:** MEG is a brain scanning technique used in BCI systems to measure brain activity by detecting tiny magnetic fields from neurons. Unlike EEG, which records electrical signals, MEG captures magnetic fields, providing a more accurate and noninvasive way to study brain function in real time. It is used in neuroscience research and medicine to diagnose epilepsy, map brain activity before surgery, and study cognitive functions like memory and language. Since magnetic fields pass through the skull without distortion, MEG provides more precise location details than EEG, making it useful for understanding brain disorders and developing treatments.

## 2.4 Interpretation

Once the brain signals are acquired, they need to be processed to extract the meaningful information. This includes

- **Preprocessing**: Filtering out noise and artifacts from the raw signals. Preprocessing in space, time, or frequency areas helps improve EEG signals by reducing external interference. To enhance the signal-to-noise ratio (SNR), the signal level is increased, or the noise level is reduced. A common spatial filtering method is independent component analysis (ICA), which separates EEG signals into independent components without supervision. ICA improves SNR by isolating task-related EEG components from unrelated and unwanted signals. Temporal preprocessing helps remove artifacts by using a linear combination of the EEG signal affected by eye movements and the recorded eye movement signal (Wang et al., 2023). Linear regression determines combination factors for removing eye movements from EEG signals, but it is less effective for EEG signals due to the difficulty of placing muscle detection sensors. Frequency-band filtering helps remove noise and artifacts and manages internal nonstationarity factors. It allows choosing task-related frequencies for further analysis in a BCI system without needing extra electrodes for detecting eye or muscle movement. Filtering is useful because of its ability to improve signal quality. But this method works less if unwanted signals mix with the desired signal in the same frequency band (Javaid, 2013).
- **Feature Extraction**: Identifying relevant features or patterns in the signals that correspond to specific brain activities. At this stage, the BCI system extracts key features from brain signals to interpret the user's purpose. Feature extraction must be accurate to ensure a strong connection with the user's purpose, improving the system's performance. BCI systems typically use time-based or frequency-based features, such as event-related potential amplitude, frequency power spectra (e.g., sensorimotor rhythms), or neuronal firing rates. Before designing the BCI system, the feature area and

feature should be defined, and any interferences that could interfere with performance should be removed.

- **Feature Translation**: Converting the extracted features into commands that can be understood by external devices (Maiseli et al., 2023). In this stage of signal processing, classified features are converted into instructions to control an outside device in a BCI application. Examples include moving a cursor on a screen, adjusting audio volume, or typing text. A key characteristic of a feature translation algorithm is adaptability (Wang et al., 2023), allowing it to track changes in features and generate appropriate outputs.

# 3. Neuromorphic computing: An overview

## 3.1 Biological inspiration and computational models

BCIs are motivated by the way the human brain interprets and responds to information. The brain has billions of neurons that send messages using electrical and chemical signals (Xiaolong and Peng, 2025). The human brain processes vast amounts of information through interconnected neurons, which communicate using electrical and chemical messages. By understanding how the brain encodes and transmits information, researchers develop BCIs that can read brain activity and convert it into commands for external devices.

Key areas of biological inspiration in BCIs are:

- **Artificial Neural Networks (ANNs):** ANNs mimic the way neurons communicate. Just like the human brain strengthens or weakens connections between neurons based on learning and experience. ANNs adjust their weights based on training data to improve classification accuracy. This approach has been widely used in BCI applications, such as controlling prosthetic limbs or decoding speech-related brain activity.
- **Brain Wave Activity:** Brain wave activity appears in many brain areas and variations based on a person's condition, like being awake, asleep, focused, or at rest. EEG records this activity in different frequency bands: Delta (1–4 Hz), Theta (4–8 Hz), Alpha and MU (8–13 Hz), Beta (13–25 Hz), and Gamma (25–40 Hz). The MU-rhythm is especially important because its amplitude decreases when a person thinks or performs actions. These changes occur in the sensorimotor cortex, allowing different imagined movements to be distinguished. Since untrained users show weak MU-rhythm changes, feedback training is needed for better detection.
- **Computational Model:** The purpose of the classification model is to accurately identify the target class for each data point. LDA and SVM are efficient classification models.
- **Linear Discriminant Analysis:** LDA is a widely used classification algorithm that has been successfully applied to pattern recognition and EEG

data classification. It reduces data to a lower-dimensional space while maximizing the ratio of between-class distance to within-class distance, ensuring optimal discrimination between classes (Abdallah and Dang, no date). LDA is a popular machine learning technique used in BCIs for classifying brain signals into different categories. It works by finding a linear boundary that best separates different brain activity patterns, making it useful for applications like motor imagery and communication BCIs. In electroencephalogram-based BCIs, LDA helps distinguish between different mental states by analyzing features such as brainwave frequency and amplitude. It is commonly used in motor imagery BCIs, where it classifies whether a person is imagining moving their left or right hand, allowing them to control external devices like robotic arms or wheelchairs (Gursel Ozmen et al., 2018). One of the main goals of LDA is its simplicity and efficiency, making it suitable for real-time applications where quick classification of brain signals is required. Since LDA works well with small datasets and is effective at handling overlapping brain signal patterns, it is widely used in BCIs for assistive technologies, neurorehabilitation, and brain-controlled communication devices.

$$w = \sum -1(\mu 1 - \mu 2) \tag{8.1}$$

$\boldsymbol{\mu}_1, \boldsymbol{\mu}_2$ = mean vectors of class 1 and class 2
$\boldsymbol{\Sigma}$ = covariance matrix of the data

- **Support Vector Machine:** SVM is a powerful classifier known for its strong generalization in various applications, including BCIs (Gursel Ozmen et al., 2018). It works by finding the optimal separation hyperplane that maximizes the margin. The output of a binary SVM classifier is determined using a specific mathematical expression:

$$y = \text{sign}\ (\textstyle\sum i = 1\ \alpha iyik(xi{,}xj) + b) \tag{2}$$

Here, $\alpha i \geq 0$ are Lagrangian multipliers obtained by solving a quadratic optimization problem, $b$ is the bias, and $(xi, xj)$ is a kernel function. Different kernel function types, such as exponential and base, have been tried, and we found that the best results are obtained with the RBF (radial basis function) function.

In BCIs, raw brain signals recorded from EEG, ECoG, or MEG are first preprocessed, filtered, and transformed into feature vectors. These features are then inserted into an SVM classifier, which learns a decision boundary between different mental states. SVM is used in BCI between cognitive tasks and classifying evoked potentials in P300-based spellers (Gursel Ozmen et al.,

2018). Its advantages include high classification accuracy, robustness to noise, and suitability for real-time applications, making it a key algorithm in brain-signal decoding for assistive technologies.

### 3.2 Key components: Spiking neural networks (SNNs), neuromorphic chips

- **SNNs:** Unlike traditional ANNs that use continuous values, SNNs process information through discrete spikes, similar to real neurons. This makes them highly efficient for real-time BCI applications. As they can process temporal patterns in brain signals more effectively (Wang et al., 2023). In BCI, SNNs are used to analyze and classify neural activity recorded from EEG, ECoG, or intracortical electrodes. The brain's electrical signals are first preprocessed and converted into spike trains using encoding methods like rate coding or temporal coding. These spike trains are then processed by an SNN, which learns the underlying patterns in the brain activity. Since SNNs can handle temporal dependencies, they are specifically useful for tasks such as motor imagery classification, P300 detection, and real-time brain signal decoding (Abdallah and Dang, no date).
- **Neuromorphic Chips:** The use of very-large-scale integration (VLSI) hardware to replicate the biological structure of the human nervous system, including the brain and intricate network of nerves, is known as neuromorphic chips (Abdallah and Dang, no date). A recently developed field called "neuromorphic engineering" uses computer science, biology, physics, mathematics, and engineering to create hardware representations of neural and sensory systems. High-performance applications, AI, and neuro robotics are all made possible by neuromorphic systems (An et al., 2024). Brain-like chips, which are renowned for their strong processing capacity as well as energy-efficient operation, have received a lot of attention. These chips are characterized by a rapid increase in data volume and a rising level of data abstraction. Because of their natural capacity to mimic the connections and information exchanges observed between neurons, memristors are generally regarded as the best electronic components for the implementation of neuromorphic computing (Gu et al., 2021). SNNs, which employ discrete spikes rather than continuous signals, are made possible by neuromorphic chips in BCIs, which aid in the more effective processing of brain signals. They are therefore perfect for portable or implanted BCI devices since they enable quicker reaction times and less energy consumption (Table 8.1).

## 4. Synergy between BCI and neuromorphic computing

### 4.1 Enhancing real-time processing in BCIs

Real-time processing in BCI is important for ensuring fast and accurate communication between the brain and outside devices. Enhancing real-time

**TABLE 8.1 Comparison with traditional AI and Von Neumann architectures.**

| Features | Traditional AI | Von Neumann architectures |
|---|---|---|
| Processing style | Batch processing uses continuous values | Sequential instruction-based |
| Energy efficiency | High power consumption due to large computations | Moderate efficiency |
| Real-time processing | Limited, requires significant optimization | Poor for real-time tasks |
| Data handling | Requires large datasets and centralized memory | Data-intensive, relies on memory hierarchy |
| Adaptability | Requires retraining on new data | Fixed program execution |

processing involves improving signal acquisition, optimizing data processing algorithms, and reducing system latency to make BCIs more responsive and efficient. On the exposed surface of the brain, local field potential measures the electrical activity around neurons, while neuronal action potential refers to a quick change in a neuron's membrane voltage. The effectiveness of a BCI system largely depends on the quality of these signals (Khorshidtalab and Salami, 2011). One key area for improvement is signal preprocessing, where advanced filtering techniques help remove noise artifacts from neural signals. By analyzing patterns in brainwave activity and other psychological indicators, a predictive model can anticipate stress events before they fully manifest (Agarwal et al., 2023).

- **Feature Extraction**: Feature extraction in BCIs helps convert raw brain signals into useful data for classification and control. It includes different methods, such as time-domain features, which analyze properties like mean, variance, and standard deviation to understand signal patterns. Frequency-domain methods, like power spectral density (PSD) and fast Fourier transform (FFT), identify important brainwave frequencies such as alpha, beta, and gamma waves to detect mental states. Time-frequency techniques, such as wavelet transform (WT) and short-time Fourier transform (STFT), help track changes in signals over time, making them useful for dynamic applications. Spatial feature extraction methods like common spatial pattern (CSP) and Riemannian geometry-based features improve signal separation in multichannel EEG recordings, especially for motor imagery tasks. Nonlinear methods, such as entropy measures and Lyapunov exponents, capture the complexity of brain signals. Real-time BCIs need fast and efficient feature extraction, often using graphical processing unit (GPU) acceleration and adaptive selection to reduce delays. The best features depend on the BCI application; for example, motor imagery uses CSP and band power, emotion recognition relies on WT and entropy features, and cognitive workload detection benefits from PSD and Hjorth parameters.

- **Classification:** Classification in BCIs is the process of matching brain signal features to mental states, actions, or intentions using machine learning. Different classification methods are used based on the BCI application and extracted features. Traditional machine learning models like SV (support vector), LD (linear discriminant), and K-nearest neighbors (K-NN) work well for simple EEG features. Deep learning models, such as convolutional neural networks (CNNs) and recurrent neural networks (RNNs), help recognize patterns in EEG signals and improve accuracy for tasks like motor imagery and emotion detection. Ensemble learning methods, like Random Forest and AdaBoost, boost performance by combining multiple models. Hybrid approaches, such as CNN and long short-term memory (LSTM), combine deep learning with traditional models for better real-time classification. The choice of classifier depends on the number of EEG channels, data complexity, and system limitations, with real-time BCIs needing lightweight models for quick responses. To improve accuracy, techniques like feature selection, tuning model settings, and adaptive learning are used, making BCIs more reliable across different users and conditions.
- **Control and Feedback Mechanisms:** Control and feedback mechanisms in BCIs play a vital role in converting processed brain signals into actions and delivering real-time responses to users. After brain signals are analyzed and classified, the system generates commands to control external devices like robotic arms, computer cursors, or prosthetic limbs. Control methods can be discrete, triggering specific actions, or continuous, allowing smooth and dynamic control based on signal variations. Feedback mechanisms enhance user performance and system adaptability by providing real-time visual, auditory, or haptic feedback. For instance, in motor imagery-based BCIs, visual feedback, such as a moving cursor, helps users refine their mental commands for improved accuracy. Adaptive feedback systems leverage machine learning to fine-tune classifier settings based on user performance, leading to better accuracy over time. Closed-loop BCIs further enhance interaction by continuously adjusting the system based on user responses, making them effective for rehabilitation, assistive technologies, and brain-controlled gaming. Well-designed control and feedback mechanisms are essential for ensuring BCIs are responsive, user-friendly, and reliable.

## 4.2 Energy efficiency and low power consumption

Materials for implantable BCIs must be able to function sustainably for many years, ideally decades, without degrading. However, the brain's warm aqueous nature has an impact on the implants' ability to retain power. Water is a strong solvent that gradually erodes the electrodes' insulating material. Short circuits could develop over time, leading to an increase in crosstalk between electrodes. This problem limits the amount of signal that electrodes can collect and shortens battery life. Researchers must investigate various insulating materials to learn how they affect brain function in relation to battery life for BCIs. To guarantee optimal battery power utilization, computationally efficient algorithms should also be created. More importantly, research should be done on alternative energy sources to power implantable BCIs (Agarwal et al., 2023).

- **Lower Power Consumption:** It is a crucial aspect of BCI, particularly for wearable, portable, and implantable systems. Since BCIs need to continuously acquire, process, and transmit brain signals, reducing power usage helps to extend battery life, improve mobility, and ensure long-term usability. To achieve low power consumption, researchers focus on hardware optimization by using energy-efficient processors like neuromorphic chips, application-specific integrated circuits, and field-programmable gate arrays. Additionally, an optimized signal processing algorithm plays a significant role in reducing computational load. Techniques such as compressed sensing, adaptive filtering, and sparse coding help process neural signals efficiently while minimizing energy usage. Machine learning models optimized for edge computing to further enhance low-power operation by reducing the need for constant cloud-based processing. For wireless BCIs, low-energy communication protocols like Bluetooth low energy (BLE), ultra-wideband (UWB), and near field communication (NFC) help minimize power during transmission. Some BCIs also explore energy harvesting technologies such as biomedical fuel cells and wireless power transfer to extend the operational lifespan without frequent battery replacements.

### 4.3 Improvements in adaptive learning

Adaptive learning allows both neural networks and AI to adjust to the environment and improve performance. Biological organisms excel at learning, transferring, and retaining knowledge in changing conditions, making them a key inspiration for ANNs. Neuromodulation, a core feature of biological learning, helps prevent forgetting and improves ANN robustness in continuous learning (Nayak and Kumar Nayak, 2024). Driven by neuromodulators like dopamine, acetylcholine, serotonin, and noradrenaline, the brain adapts dynamically by regulating both local synaptic changes and global network responses.

## 5. Technological advancements in BCIs

### 5.1 Machine learning and AI in BCIs

**Artificial Intelligence in BCIs**: In recent years, advancements in AI and BCI have gained significant attention as innovative approaches to improving human–machine interaction. The use of BCIs has the potential to enhance their accuracy and speed, making them more effective and usable for individuals with motor disabilities (Nayak and Kumar Nayak, 2024). The goal of BCI is to enhance the lives of people with disabilities like spinal cord injuries, cerebral palsy, or ALS.

These conditions can severely limit an individual's ability to communicate and control their environment, leading to significant impairments in daily life. BCIs offer a potential solution to these challenges by providing a direct pathway for communication and control through neural signals from the brain (Chenna, 2023). AI processes complex brain signals like EEG and fNIRS, enhancing the communication between the brain and outside devices. This has led to remarkable applications in motor rehabilitation, communication aids for individuals with disabilities, and even entertainment.

**AI-Based Approaches for Improving BCI Performance:** AI-based methods have been used to make BCIs more accurate and faster. Deep learning, a type of machine learning, trains ANNs to find patterns in brain signals. It has improved BCI accuracy in tasks like motor imagery, where a person imagines moving. Deep learning models are trained on large datasets of brain signals and can classify new signals in real time for better device control. CNNs, mainly used for image processing, help analyze EEG signals in BCIs. They extract important features from EEG data, making BCIs more accurate. Trial-based learning is a machine learning technique where a system learns from feedback and adjusts its actions accordingly. Trial-based learning has been used to optimize BCI performance by training the system to increase the reward signal that is based on the standard of control. For example, in a study on a wheelchair navigation task, a reinforcement learning algorithm was used to optimize the control of the wheelchair based on a reward signal that was based on the accuracy and speed of the control (Suriyamurthi, 2023).

**The Role of GPT (Generative Pretrained Transformer) and GANs (Generative Adversarial Networks) in Improving AI-Based BCI:** GPT and GANs are powerful machine learning models that can help improve AI-based BCIs. GPT models, based on the Transformer architecture, generate human-like text and data. They can analyze neural signals and create accurate responses for BCI communication systems. GANs are generative models that create new data by training a generator to produce samples similar to real ones and a discriminator to tell real from fake. They can generate new neural data to expand training datasets, improving BCI accuracy and performance.

**Machine Learning:** BCIs are a dynamic field that utilizes various machine learning techniques to enhance interaction between the human brain and computers. Several machine learning methods are applied in BCIs to improve signal processing and classification.

**Supervised Learning:** Supervised learning plays an important role in BCIs by enabling accurate classification of the brain signals into outputs. In this approach, a labeled dataset containing brain signal recordings and their corresponding actions is used to train the machine learning models (Zhang et al., 2023). The system learns to map input neural activity, such as EEG and ECoG, to specific commands. Common methods include SVM and LDA.

**Reinforcement Learning:** Trial-based learning is a fundamental approach where the system learns to make decisions or take actions to maximize the total signal. BCI employing trial-based learning can be applied in scenarios like neurofeedback, which helps people to train their brain activity.

**Deep Learning:** Deep learning has significantly advanced the field of BCI, enabling more accurate and efficient interactions between the user and external devices through brain signals. These advancements have applications in motor rehabilitation, communication for individuals with disabilities, and even gaming. However, challenges like high-dimensional and noisy data, limited datasets, and the need for real-time processing still exist. Despite these hurdles, the potential of deep learning in BCI continues to grow. LSTM is widely used in BCIs (Nayak and Kumar Nayak, 2024).

**Convolutional Neural Networks:** CNNs are specialized neural networks designed for image processing tasks. CNNs have been used to analyze EEG signals in BCI, allowing for a more accurate interpretation of neural signals. They are proficient at spatial data analysis and can be used for tasks like image-based neurofeedback, where users manipulate visual stimuli through brain signals (Suriyamurthi, 2023).

## 5.2 Hardware innovations: Electrodes and wearables

### *5.2.1 Electrodes*

The technology to build a silicon-based spiked electrode array, or so-called dry electrode, to enable EEG, electrooculography, ECoG, and electromyography monitoring without electrode gel or scalp preparation (Lin et al., 2009). However, the connectors between the dry sensors and the DAQ (Data Acquisition Board) board are not very solid in the BCI.

#### 5.2.1.1 Dry sensors

Dry sensors are an advanced type of electrode used in BCIs to measure brain activity without the need for conductive gels or pastes, and it is shown in Fig. 8.6. Unlike traditional moist electrodes, which need skin preparation and a conductive medium to ensure signal quality, gel-free electrodes are developed to work directly on the skin or scalp, making them more convenient and user-friendly (Lin et al., 2009). Dry sensors tend to have higher skin-electrode impedance, which can result in low signal quality compared to moist electrodes. They are more likely to experience noise and movement-related signal distortions. Despite their challenges, ongoing advancements in materials and signal processing techniques continue to improve the reliability of dry electrodes, making them a promising solution for practical and widespread BCI applications (Fig. 8.6).

FIGURE 8.6 Dry sensors.

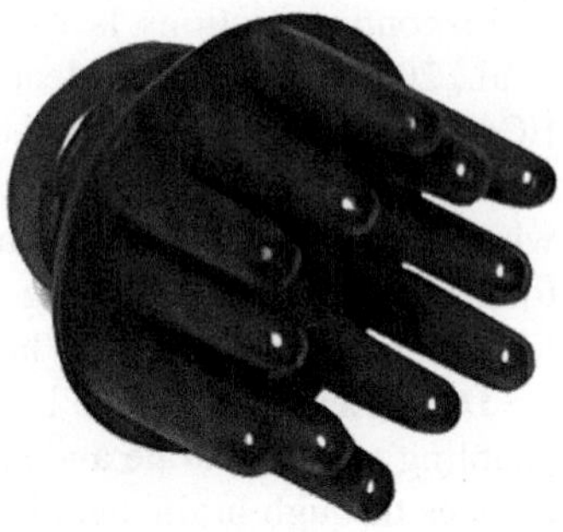

### 5.2.1.2 Flexible and soft electrodes

Flexible and soft electrodes are an advanced innovation in BCI technology, designed to improve signal acquisition while enhancing user comfort. Unlike traditional rigid electrodes, which can be uncomfortable and less adaptable to the contours of the scalp or skin, flexible electrodes conform seamlessly to the surface, reducing pressure points and improving signal stability (Abdulkader et al., 2015). Flexible materials often have higher impedance compared to traditional metal electrodes, leading to weaker signal acquisition. Motion artifacts and inconsistent skin contact can cause signal fluctuations. Innovations in nanotechnology and biocompatible materials may help in making flexible and soft electrodes more viable for long-term BCI applications.

### 5.2.1.3 Microelectrode arrays (MEAs)

They are advanced neural interface technologies used in BCIs to record and stimulate neural activity with high precision, and it is shown in Fig. 8.7. These arrays consist of multiple tiny electrodes, typically in the micrometer range, that can detect electrical signals from individual or groups of neurons (Fig. 8.7). Biocompatibility issues and electrode degradation over time can

FIGURE 8.7 Flexible and soft electrodes.

affect signal quality. The large volume of neural data requires advanced algorithms for meaningful interpretation (Fig. 8.8).

### *5.2.2 Wearables*

Wearable BCI devices are noninvasive systems designed to observe brain activity in real time while ensuring comfort and mobility. These devices integrate electrodes, sensors, and wireless technology into headsets, caps, or even ear-based and forehead-worn systems, allowing users to interact with computers, control devices, or monitor cognitive states without surgical procedures.

#### 5.2.2.1 Mindo EEG device

To ensure proper electrode-skin contact impedance, the Mindo 4S EEG uses spring-loaded dry electrodes. They use dry electrodes with an adjustable fit for better comfort. Its flexible base reduces pain from pressure, making it suitable for long-term EEG recording. The data collection rate can go up to 512 Hz, which can be adjusted as needed. It uses Bluetooth for wireless data transfer and can run continuously for 20 hours. The Mindo EEG device helps detect early signs of anxiety, depression, and other cognitive conditions. It can be used with BCI-based assistive technologies for hands-free device control.

#### 5.2.2.2 Brain Link Lite

Brain Link Lite is a head-mounted EEG sensor made by Shenzhen Macro Intellect for iOS and Android. It has three gold-plated copper dry electrodes: an EEG recording electrode, a ground electrode, and a reference electrode. Designed for comfort, it fits easily on the forehead. The sensor connects to smart devices via Bluetooth, eliminating wires and making EEG recording more convenient outside the lab. It also works without conductive gel, ensuring a hassle-free user experience.

**FIGURE 8.8** Microelectrode arrays.

#### 5.2.2.3 MindWave Mobile

The MindWave Mobile EEG headset includes a headset, an ear clip, and a sensor arm. It has one EEG recording electrode placed on the forehead above the eye, while the reference and grounding electrodes are inside the ear clip. This design is well-suited for detecting eye blinks. The device records 12-bit brainwaves in the 3–100 Hz range with a 512 Hz sampling rate and provides up to 8 hours of battery life. With a single recording electrode, it is more portable and easier to wear than multichannel EEG sensors.

## 6. Applications of BCIs in various domains

### 6.1 Healthcare and neurorehabilitation

The healthcare field uses brain signals for various applications, including prevention, detection, treatment, recovery, and repair. Various systems have been developed to determine consciousness levels based on brain studies. Smoking and alcohol affect attentiveness. on brainwaves. These studies highlight the importance of medical prevention, as smoking can lead to loss of function and reduced alertness. Traffic accidents are a leading cause of death and serious injuries. Researchers study their causes to find ways to prevent them. The concentration levels of people with motion sickness, especially drivers, have been studied. It usually occurs while traveling in moving vehicles. BCI applications are being explored for this condition. Usage of BCI in the medical field (Abdulkader et al., 2015). Neurorehabilitation is a specialized medical approach aimed at helping individuals recover from neurological disorders, brain injuries, or spinal cord damage. It aims to regain motor functions, cognitive abilities, and overall quality of life through BCIs, which play a significant role in neurorehabilitation by enabling patients to control external devices using brain signals. For example, BCIs assist stroke or paralysis patients by translating brain activity into movement commands for robotic limbs or exoskeletons, help improve cognitive function through neurofeedback training, and provide communication aids for individuals with severe disabilities like ALS. By integrating BCIs, robotics, and virtual reality, neurorehabilitation offers promising advancements in restoring lost functions, enhancing independence, and enhancing the well-being of people with nerve-related conditions.

### 6.2 Communication for individuals with disabilities

Noninvasive BCIs, such as EEG-based systems, allow users to select letters, words, or symbols on a screen for people with severe disabilities, especially those affecting speech and motor control. Communication can be extremely challenging. BCIs appeared as a transformative solution, enabling users to communicate using their brain activity alone. BCIs help individuals with conditions such as ALS, cerebral palsy, locked-in syndrome, and spinal cord injuries by translating neural signals into digital commands using their brain signals (Abdulkader et al., 2015). More advanced invasive BCIs, inserted directly into the brain, offer faster and more accurate communication for those with severe impairments. Additionally, speech-generating devices (SGDs) integrated with BCIs give voice to those who cannot speak, making them able to express thoughts and interact with others. Progress in AI and machine learning further enhances these systems, enabling predictive text, contextual understanding, and personalized communication models. BCIs combined with wearable technologies and intelligent home systems also allow users to control devices, enhancing independence and overall quality of life. As research continues, the future of BCI-based communication promises even easier and smoother interaction for people with disabilities (Rajeev, 2023).

## 6.3 Entertainment and gaming applications

BCIs have expanded beyond medical use, leading to games controlled by brain activity. For example, players can fly helicopters in a digital world using their minds. Some studies explore combining brain control with existing games for multibrain entertainment. One such game, Brain Arena, lets players join a football match using two BCIs, where they score goals by imagining left- or right-hand movements. EEG-based serious games are also used for emotional control and neuroprosthetic rehabilitation, introducing new gaming concepts.

## 6.4 Industrial and workplace applications

BCIs are increasingly finding applications in industrial and workplace environments, enhancing productivity, safety, and human–machine collaboration. In sectors like manufacturing, logistics, and defense, BCIs are being explored to monitor worker fatigue, improve cognitive workload management, and enable hands-free control of machinery (Bonaci et al., 2014). For instance, BCIs integrated with wearable headsets can assess a worker's mental state, alerting them and supervisors to potential fatigue-related risks, thereby preventing accidents in hazardous environments. In automation and robotics, BCIs allow workers to control robotic arms, drones, or machinery using their brain signals, reducing the need for physical effort and improving efficiency. This is especially useful in fields where precision and real-time decision-making are crucial. Additionally, BCIs assist individuals with physical disabilities by enabling them to operate workplace tools and computers using neural commands, fostering inclusivity and accessibility. AI-driven BCI systems are also enhancing workplace training and skill development by analyzing cognitive engagement and adapting training modules to optimize learning. As the technology continues to evolve, BCIs have the power to change human–machine collaboration, increase workplace efficiency, and improve occupational safety across various industries (Abdulkader et al., 2015).

### 6.5 Military and defense uses of BCIs

BCIs are playing an increasingly significant role in military and defense applications, enhancing communication, decision-making, and operational effectiveness. One key area of research is cognitive enhancement, where BCIs monitor soldiers' brain activity to assess stress, fatigue, and cognitive load in real time. This allows commanders to optimize performance by providing rest breaks, adjusting workloads, or enhancing situational awareness through augmented systems. In combat scenarios, BCIs enable hands-free control of drones, robotic systems, and military vehicles, allowing soldiers to operate advanced equipment with neural commands (Marcel and Millan, 2007). This enhances response time and operational efficiency, reducing the physical burden on personnel. Additionally, BCIs are being explored for direct brain-to-brain communication, where soldiers can transmit thoughts or commands without verbal or physical interaction, improving coordination in high-stakes situations. For wounded soldiers, BCIs aid in neurorehabilitation by assisting in motor function recovery and providing prosthetic limb control through neural signals. Advanced BCIs also support posttraumatic stress disorder (PTSD) treatment by monitoring and regulating brain activity associated with trauma. As military technology advances, BCIs are expected to integrate further with AI and machine learning, leading to more adaptive, efficient, and autonomous defense systems. However, ethical concerns and cybersecurity risks remain critical considerations in the deployment of BCIs in military and defense operations.

## 7. Challenges and technologies in BCI technology

### 7.1 Ethical and privacy concerns

BCIs allow a direct link between the brain and outside devices. However, they raise ethical and privacy concerns. BCIs collect sensitive brain data, including thoughts, emotions, and mental health conditions. If accessed without permission, this data could be misused by companies, governments, or hackers.

#### *7.1.1 Ethical concerns*

**Mental Privacy:** BCIs collect intimate brain data that could express private thoughts, emotions, and mental processes. Keeping this data safe from being misused is essential.

**Ownership:** There are concerns about who owns the collected data by BCIs. Without proper safeguards, this data can be misused by companies, governments, or other third parties.

**Informed Consent:** Users must be fully informed about the potential risks and benefits of using BCIs. Ensuring that users provide informed consent is essential to uphold ethical standards.

**Autonomy and Control**: As BCIs can potentially influence or override natural brain functions, there's a concern regarding users' autonomy. Ensuring that users have control over their BCIs and can deactivate them at will is essential.

**Equity and Accessibility**: There's a risk that BCIs could exacerbate social inequalities if only a select few can afford or access them. Ensuring that these technologies are equitably distributed and accessible to all is a critical ethical consideration.

Developing neuromorphic BMI (brain-machine interface) technology responsibly requires addressing ethical and legal issues. Its acceptance depends on ongoing discussions, teamwork, and strong ethical guidelines.

## 7.2 Privacy concerns

**Neural Signals for Identification and Authentication:** Since neural signals are unique to each person, they can be used for biometrics. Researchers see the potential of using neural data for identifying and authenticating users. Instead of memorizing passwords, users are recognized based on learned brain patterns they are unaware of.

**Neurosecurity:** Standard engineering practices, medical trials, and neuroethical evaluations help create safe and ethical neural devices (Bonaci et al., 2014). However, they do not protect against attacks that can alter, block, or spy on neural signals. The term "Neurosecurity" refers to protecting neural devices from malicious threats to ensure the safety of brain function and free will. Neurosecurity aims to protect the confidentiality, integrity, and availability of neural data and devices. It addresses concerns such as unauthorized access to sensitive brain data, tampering with neural signals, and ensuring the reliability of the BCI system. By developing robust security measures and ethical guidelines, neurosecurity seeks to protect user's neural mechanisms and uphold their autonomy, ultimately ensuring safe and responsible use of BCIs (Marcel and Millan, 2007).

**Consent Management**: Consent management in BCI ensures that users have full control over their neural data by providing informed, voluntary, and revokable consent. Since BCIs interact directly with brain activity, ethical concerns arise regarding privacy, security, and potential misuse of data. Effective consent management involves clear communication about data collection, risks, benefits, and the ability to withdraw consent at any time. Regulations like the General Data Protection Regulation (GDPR) and neuroethics frameworks emphasize user's autonomy and data protection. As BCI technology evolves, a robust consent mechanism will be essential to balance innovation with ethical responsibility.

## 7.3 Technical and safety challenges

**Technical Challenges**: BCIs face several technical issues that affect how well they work. One major challenge is capturing and processing brain signals, which are often weak and easily disturbed by noise, muscle movements, and the environment. To get clear signals, advanced filtering and noise reduction methods are needed. Another issue is accuracy and reliability since brain signals differ between individuals, making it hard to create a system that works for everyone. BCIs also need to process data in real time, quickly translating brain activity into commands. This requires strong computing power and advanced machine learning techniques.

**Accuracy and Reliability**: Accuracy and reliability are important for BCIs because they help the system correctly interpret brain signals and turn them into commands. One challenge is that brain signals vary from person to person and can change due to factors like fatigue, emotions, and focus. These changes make it hard to create a system that works the same for everyone. Additionally, outside factors like background noise, muscle movements, and environment can affect signal quality, leading to errors. To improve reliability, BCIs use advanced machine learning to adjust to these changes and process the signal better. However, the system often needs frequent calibration and training, which takes time and may not always give consistent results. The type of BCI also affects accuracy, and noninvasive BCIs use low-resolution sensors, making signal detection less precise. Invasive BCIs, which connect directly to the brain, provide better accuracy but come with medical risks and require surgery.

**Real-Time Data Processing:** Real-time data processing is important for BCI because they need to quickly understand brain signals and turn them into actions without delay. BCIs continuously collect brain signals, creating large amounts of raw data that must be cleaned, processed, and interpreted almost instantly. The challenge is to process this data quickly while keeping it accurate. Any delay or mistake can affect the user's experience, especially in applications like prosthetic control communication devices and brain-controlled robotics. One major challenge is that brain signals are complex and often mixed with noise from muscle movements, eye blinks, and other electronic devices. To manage this, BCIs use advanced ML (machine learning) and DL (deep learning) models to pick out useful information and classify signals accurately. However, these methods need a lot of computing power, which can slow down real-time performance if not optimized properly.

### *7.3.1 Safety challenges*

**Invasiveness and Biocompatibility:** Invasiveness and biocompatibility are important factors in BCIs, especially when choosing between invasive and noninvasive systems. Invasive BCIs require surgery to implant electrodes in the brain, providing more accurate signals but also posing risks like infections, tissue damage, and rejection by the body. Over time, implanted electrodes may wear out, requiring additional surgeries for maintenance. Noninvasive BCIs use external sensors, such as EEG caps, to record brain signals. They avoid surgical risks but often have weaker signal quality due to interference from the scalp, hair, and surrounding tissues. Semiinvasive BCIs, like ECoG, sit on the brain's surface, offering better signal clarity with fewer surgical risks. Biocompatibility is another key concern for implanted BCIs. The materials used should be safe for brain tissue to avoid immune reactions and inflammation. Scientists are working on biocompatible materials like flexible polymers and nanomaterials to improve long-term use. Wireless energy and data transfer are also being developed to reduce the need for wired implants, lowering the risk of infection. Balancing invasiveness and biocompatibility is crucial for improving BCIs. While invasive BCIs provide better accuracy, researchers are enhancing noninvasive and minimally invasive methods to make them safer and more user-friendly. As technology improves, BCIs will become more practical for both medical and everyday use.

**Long-term Stability:** Long-term stability is a major challenge in BCIs, especially for invasive systems with implanted electrodes. Over time, these implants can degrade due to biological reactions, electrode wear, or movement inside the brain, which reduces signal quality and system performance. The body's immune response may also form scar tissue around the electrodes, making it harder to detect brain signals. This loss of stability can affect the reliability of BCIs and may require additional surgeries, increasing risks and costs. To improve stability, researchers are creating biocompatible materials that reduce immune reactions and make electrodes more durable. Flexible electrodes made from polymers, nanomaterials, and bioactive coatings help prevent tissue damage and extend the lifespan of implants. Wireless power and data transmission are also being developed to remove wired connections, lowering the risk of infections and device failure. For noninvasive and semiinvasive BCIs, stability depends on sensor placement, signal consistency, and interference from the environment. Machine learning and adaptive signal processing are helping improve accuracy over time by adjusting to changes in brain signals.

**Cognitive and Psychological Risks:** BCIs can cause cognitive and psychological challenges, especially for long-term users. One major issue is mental fatigue, as using BCIs for a long time requires strong focus, which can lead to tiredness, reduced concentration, and lower performance. Some users may also find it difficult to adapt, leading to frustration, stress, or anxiety. Another concern is changes in emotions and identity. Since BCIs connect directly to brain activity, they might unintentionally affect a person's mood, thoughts, or behavior. Users could experience mood swings or personality changes or feel like they are losing control over their own mind. This is particularly important in medical cases, where BCIs are used for conditions like paralysis or neurological disorders. Dependence on BCIs can also create emotional stress. Users who rely on these systems for communication or movement may worry about device failures, which can lower their confidence and emotional well-being. Some may even become too dependent on BCIs, feeling helpless if they cannot use them. To reduce these risks, researchers are working on more user-friendly designs, adaptive interfaces, and mental health support to help users adjust. Ethical guidelines, psychological monitoring, and counseling should also be part of BCI development to ensure safety. As BCIs improve, it is important to balance their benefits with mental and emotional well-being.

## 7.4 Accessibility and cost factors

**User-Friendly Design:** A user-friendly design is important for making BCIs easier to use and more effective. Many BCIs require a lot of training, which makes them difficult for beginners. To solve this, researchers are creating simple and intuitive interfaces that help users interact with BCIs more naturally. Features like easy controls, clear feedback, and customizable settings can make learning and adapting to BCIs smoother. Comfort and convenience are also key factors. Noninvasive BCIs, such as EEG-based systems, often have large headsets or electrode caps that can be uncomfortable for long periods. Making these devices lighter, wireless, and ergonomic can improve the user experience. Reducing the number of electrodes while keeping accuracy high can also make BCIs easier to wear and use. Adaptive learning algorithms further improve usability by adjusting to each user's brain activity, making the system more accurate and less frustrating. Customizable settings allow users to personalize their BCI experience, making it more effective for their needs. A well-designed BCI should be easy to set up, require little maintenance, and respond quickly. By improving usability, developers can make BCIs more useful for medical treatments, assistive devices, and even everyday applications, allowing more people to benefit from this technology.

**Noninvasive versus Invasive BCI:** BCIs are categorized as noninvasive or invasive based on how they capture brain signals. Noninvasive BCIs use outside sensors, such as EEG caps, to record brain activity without requiring surgery. They are more secure and more accessible but have lower signal accuracy since signals must pass through the scalp and skull, which can cause interference. This limitation makes them less needed for jobs that require high precision, like controlling robotic limbs. However, they are widely used in medical rehabilitation, communication devices, and gaming due to their ease of use and minimal risks. But invasive BCIs require surgically implanted electrodes, which provide higher accuracy by directly recording neural activity. These BCIs are particularly beneficial for medical applications, such as helping paralyzed individuals regain movement or controlling prosthetic limbs with precision. However, they pose serious risks, including infections, tissue damage, and long-term instability, as the body's immune response may form scar tissue around the electrodes, affecting their performance over time.

**Medical versus Consumer Use:** BCIs are used in both medical and consumer fields, but their design and function depend on the purpose. In the medical field, BCIs help people with neurological disorders, paralysis, or speech impairments. They help patients with prosthetic limbs, move wheelchairs, and communicate using brain signals. Medical BCIs need high accuracy and reliability, so invasive or semiinvasive systems are often used despite their risks. These BCIs also help stroke patients regain movement by stimulating brain activity. However, they require training, clinical supervision, and approval, making them difficult for everyday use. On the other hand, consumer BCIs are designed for gaming, virtual reality, smart home control, and wellness tracking. They focus on ease of use, affordability, and noninvasiveness, often using EEG headsets. Although they are less accurate than medical BCIs, machine learning and signal processing are improving their performance. Companies are also using BCIs for stress management, meditation, and cognitive improvement, making them more accessible to everyday users. As technology advances, the gap between medical and consumer BCIs is getting smaller. Researchers are working to make BCIs more accurate, user-friendly, and practical for both patients and general users in the future.

### *7.4.1 Cost factors*

**High Development Costs:** The development of BCIs is highly expensive due to the advanced technology, research, and testing involved. Creating a BCI requires specialized hardware, such as high-resolution electrodes, signal amplifiers, and processing units, which significantly increase costs. Additionally, developing and training machine learning models to accurately interpret brain signals requires large amounts of data, computational power, and expert knowledge. For medical BCIs, costs are even higher due to clinical trials, regulatory approvals, and long-term safety testing. These systems must meet strict medical standards to ensure they are safe and effective for patients, adding to research expenses. Invasive BCIs also require surgical implantation and ongoing medical supervision, further increasing costs. Despite the high development costs, BCI can bring major changes to healthcare, assistive technology, and human–computer interaction. As research progresses and technology advances, costs may decrease, making BCIs more accessible for both medical and consumer applications.

**Expensive Hardware and Equipment:** BCIs need costly hardware and equipment to capture and process brain signals accurately. High-quality electrodes, amplifiers, and signal processors are required to detect brain activity with precision. Invasive BCIs need biocompatible materials and surgical tools, which further increase costs. Noninvasive BCIs, like EEG-based systems, also require high-resolution sensors and advanced data processors to improve accuracy. AI-driven software, real-time processing units, and wireless technology add to the overall expense. Since BCIs handle large amounts of data, they need powerful computers, making development and maintenance expensive. The high cost of BCI hardware makes it less accessible to the public. However, researchers are working to reduce costs by using smaller devices, better materials, and AI-based signal processing. As technology improves, BCI hardware may become more affordable and widely available for both medical and everyday use.

**Surgical and Maintenance Costs**: BCIs, especially invasive ones, have high surgical and maintenance costs. Implanting electrodes in the brain requires specialized surgery, advanced tools, and expert doctors, making it expensive. Hospitalization, postsurgery care, and regular check-ups further increase costs. Over time, implanted electrodes may wear out due to biological reactions or tissue damage, needing replacement through additional surgeries, which adds both medical risks and financial strain. Even noninvasive BCIs need regular maintenance, sensor replacements, and software updates to work properly. To lower costs, researchers are developing durable, biocompatible materials and wireless power systems to reduce the need for repeated surgeries.

## 8. The future of BCI

### 8.1 The road to full integration with AI and Internet of Things (IoT)

The combination of BCIs with AI and the IoT is making brain-controlled technology more advanced and efficient. AI helps BCIs process signals better, adjust to individual brain activity, and make quick predictions, improving accuracy and response. Machine learning removes noise, deciphers brain signals, and customizes user experiences, making BCIs smarter and easier to use. With IoT, BCIs can connect to smart devices, allowing users to control home systems, wearables, and even industrial machines with their thoughts. This enhances access for individuals with disabilities and opens new possibilities in healthcare and technology. However, challenges like data security, privacy, and fast, reliable communication need to be addressed. Researchers are working on secure data transfer, cloud computing, and energy-efficient designs to improve performance. As AI and IoT evolve, their integration with BCIs will create seamless, intelligent systems that enhance human–technology interaction.

### 8.2 Next-generation neural interfaces

Next-generation neural interfaces are designed to make BCIs more precise, efficient, and easy to use. Scientists are developing advanced electrode materials like biocompatible polymers and nanotechnology to improve signal detection and reduce immune reactions. Wireless and flexible implants are also being created to enhance comfort and extend their lifespan, reducing the need for repeated surgeries. AI and machine learning are crucial in improving neural signal processing, helping BCIs adapt to users and provide quicker, more accurate responses. Noninvasive technologies, such as high-resolution EEG and optical methods, are also being explored to boost performance without requiring surgery. These advancements will make BCIs more effective for medical, assistive, and general applications. They will help people with disabilities regain movement and communication while also improving human–computer interactions. As technology evolves, next-generation neural interfaces will bring us closer to fully integrating the brain with digital systems.

### 8.3 Future ethical concerns in BCI

The future of BCIs presents important ethical issues that must be managed for their safe and fair use. A major issue is privacy and security, as BCI collects sensitive brain data. If this information is accessed or misused, it could lead to serious legal and ethical problems, making strong cybersecurity protections essential. Another concern is user autonomy and consent. People should have complete autonomy over their BCIs and the freedom to use them voluntarily, without coercion. As BCIs improve, the risk of external influence on thoughts and decisions raises concerns about free will and identity. It is important to ensure BCIs support, rather than control, human decision-making. There is also a risk of social inequality, as only wealthy individuals may afford advanced BCIs. This could lead to unfair advantages in healthcare, communication, and cognitive abilities. Policies should promote equal access and prevent a divide between those with and without BCIs. As BCI technology progresses, ethical concerns must be addressed through clear regulations, transparency, and responsible innovation. This will help create a future where BCIs benefit everyone while protecting human rights.

## 9. Conclusion

### 9.1 Summary of key developments

**Enhance Communication:** BCIs enhance communication for individuals with speech or movement disabilities by converting brain signals into text, synthesized speech, or digital commands. This technology is especially useful for those with conditions like ALS, locked-in syndrome, or severe paralysis, enabling them to convey their thoughts without physical movement. BCIs translate brain activity into commands, enabling users to select words on a screen, control assistive devices, or generate speech instantly. These innovations offer greater independence and improved social interaction for individuals facing communication challenges.

**Enhancing Healthcare:** BCIs are transforming healthcare by enabling advanced diagnostics, neurorehabilitation, and assistive technologies for individuals with neurological conditions. They help restore movement in paralyzed patients through brain-controlled prosthetics and exoskeletons. Additionally, BCIs support stroke recovery by promoting neuroplasticity-based therapies, aiding patients in regaining motor functions. They also play a vital role in the early detection and monitoring of neurological disorders like epilepsy, Parkinson's disease, and Alzheimer's by analyzing brain activity patterns. These advancements lead to more effective treatments, better patient outcomes, and an enhanced quality of life for those with medical challenges.

**Enhancing Human–Computer Interaction:** BCIs are revolutionizing human–computer interaction by enabling direct brain-to-device communication without requiring physical movement. This innovation allows users to operate computers, smartphones, and other digital systems using only their thoughts, making interactions more seamless and user-friendly. In gaming, virtual reality, and augmented reality, BCIs provide enhanced control and immersive experiences. They also serve as valuable tools for individuals with disabilities, offering new ways to engage with technology and fostering greater independence. As these technologies evolve, BCIs have the potential to reshape how people interact with machines, making digital experiences more adaptive, intuitive, and personalized.

## 9.2 Implications for human–device interaction

BCIs significantly impact human–device interaction by enabling direct, thought-controlled communication with digital systems. This technology eliminates the reliance on conventional input methods like keyboards, mice, or touchscreens, enabling users to operate computers, smartphones, and other electronic devices solely through brain activity. It enhances inclusivity for those with disabilities by offering alternative methods to use assistive devices and communicate efficiently. BCIs also boost efficiency in areas like gaming, virtual reality, and workplace automation by enabling quicker and more intuitive control. As the technology advances, BCIs hold the potential to create more personalized, adaptive, and responsive interactions, revolutionizing the way humans engage with digital environments.

## 9.3 The future of human–device interaction with neuromorphic BCIs

The future of human–device interaction with neuromorphic BCIs is set to become more efficient, adaptable, and intuitive. Drawing inspiration from the brain's neural structure, neuromorphic BCIs replicate biological processing to facilitate faster and energy-efficient communication between humans and technology. These systems enhance real-time processing, improve learning abilities, and create more natural interactions by adapting to individual users. With advancements in neuromorphic chips and SNNs, BCIs will become increasingly responsive and personalized, enabling effortless control of computers, prosthetics, smart devices, and even immersive virtual environments. This progress holds the potential to revolutionize accessibility, productivity, and connectivity, leading to a future where human thoughts seamlessly interact with technology in a more intelligent and natural way.

## References

Abdallah, A.B., Dang, K.N. Neuromorphic Computing.

Abdulkader, S.N., Atia, A., Mostafa, M.-S.M., 2015. Brain computer interfacing: applications and challenges. Egypt. Inform. J. 16 (2), 213–230. https://doi.org/10.1016/j.eij.2015.06.002.

Abrams, D.A., Ryali, S., Chen, T., Chordia, P., Khouzam, A., Levitin, D.J., Menon, V., 2013. Inter-subject synchronization of brain responses during natural music listening. Eur. J. Neurosci. 37 (9), 1458–1469. https://doi.org/10.1111/ejn.12173.

Agarwal, N., Murthy, P., Kumar, R., Goel, O., Agarwal, R., July 01, 2023. Predictive Analytics for Real Time Stress Monitoring from BCI. Available at SSRN: https://ssrn.com/abstract=4982706.

An, Y., Wong, J., Ho Ling, S., 2024. Development of real-time brain-computer interface control system for robot. Appl. Soft Comput. 159, 111648. https://doi.org/10.1016/j.asoc.2024.111648.

Bonaci, T., Calo, R., Chizeck, H., 2014. App stores for the brain: privacy & security in brain-computer interfaces. In: IEEE International Symposium on Ethics in Science, Technology and Engineering. IEEE Technology & Society Magazine, pp. 1–7. Vol. 34, No. 2, pp. 32–39, 2015, University of Washington School of Law Research Paper No. 2788104, Available at SSRN: https://ssrn.com/abstract=2788104.

Chenna, S., 2023. Exploring the use of artificial intelligence in brain-computer interfaces for improved control and communication. SSRN Electron. J. 1556–5068. https://doi.org/10.2139/ssrn.4447601.

Daly, J.J., Huggins, J.E., 2015. Brain-computer interface: current and emerging rehabilitation applications. Arch. Phys. Med. Rehabil. 96 (3), S1. https://doi.org/10.1016/j.apmr.2015.01.007.

Gu, X., Cao, Z., Jolfaei, A., Xu, P., Wu, D., Jung, T.-P., Lin, C.-T., 2021. EEG-based brain-computer interfaces (BCIs): a survey of recent studies on signal sensing technologies and computational intelligence approaches and their applications. IEEE ACM Trans. Comput. Biol. Bioinf 18 (5), 1645–1666. https://doi.org/10.1109/tcbb.2021.3052811.

Gursel Ozmen, N., Gumusel, L., Yang, Y., 2018. A biologically inspired approach to frequency domain feature extraction for EEG classification. Comput. Math. Methods Med. 2018, 1–10. https://doi.org/10.1155/2018/9890132.

Javaid, M.A., 2013. Brain-computer interface. SSRN Electron. J. https://doi.org/10.2139/ssrn.2386900.

Khorshidtalab, A., Salami, M.J.E., 2011. EEG signal classification for real-time brain-computer interface applications: a review. In: 4th International Conference on Mechatronics: Integrated Engineering for Industrial and Societal Development, ICOM'11 - Conference Proceedings. https://doi.org/10.1109/ICOM.2011.5937125.

Lin, C.-T., Ko, L.-W., Chang, C.-J., Wang, Y.-T., Chung, C.-H., Yang, F.-S., Duann, J.-R., Jung, T.-P., Chiou, J.-C., 2009. Wearable and wireless brain-computer interface and its applications.

Springer Sci. Bus. Media LLC 5638, 741–748. https://doi.org/10.1007/978-3-642-02812-0_84.

Liu, Y., Liu, R., Ge, J., Wang, Y., 2024. Advancements in brain-machine interfaces for application in the metaverse. Front. Neurosci. 18. https://doi.org/10.3389/fnins.2024.1383319.

Maiseli, B., Abdalla, A.T., Massawe, L.V., Mbise, M., Mkocha, K., Nassor, N.A., Ismail, M., Michael, J., Kimambo, S., 2023. Brain–computer interface: trend, challenges, and threats. Brain Inform. 10 (1). https://doi.org/10.1186/s40708-023-00199-3.

Marcel, S., Millan, J.R., 2007. Person authentication using brainwaves (EEG) and maximum A posteriori model adaptation. IEEE Trans. Pattern Anal. Mach. Intell. 29 (4), 743–752. https://doi.org/10.1109/TPAMI.2007.1012.

Nayak, J.R., Nayak, D.C.K., 2024. Machine Learning Paired with Artificial Intelligence and Brain-Computer Interfaces. Selfypage Developers Pvt Ltd, pp. 1–20. https://doi.org/10.58532/v3bkai11p1ch1.

Rajeev, P., 2023. Neuromorphic Computing: Bridging Minds and Machines for Brain-Machine Interface. https://doi.org/10.13140/RG.2.2.15226.06086.

Suriyamurthi, D. 2023. Role of Machine Learning Algorithms in Brain-Computer Interface: A Comprehensive Review Role of Machine Learning Algorithms in Brain-Computer Interface: A Comprehensive Review.

Wang, Z., Nasrin, S., Islam, R., Haque, A., Karim, M.A.U., 2023. In: Sarkar, A., Kumar Sarkar, C., Deyasi, A., De, D. (Eds.), Chapter 13: Emerging Memories and Their Applications in Neuromorphic Computing. Arezki Benfdila Elsevier. https://www.sciencedirect.com/science/article/pii/B9780323918329000051.

Xiaolong, H., Peng, C., 2025. Resistive switching characteristics of Cu/MgO/$MoS_2$/Cu structure. Acta Phys. Sin. 74 (2), 028501. https://doi.org/10.7498/aps.74.20241298.

Zhang, J., Li, J., Huang, Z., Huang, D., Yu, H., Li, Z., 2023. Recent progress in wearable brain–computer interface (BCI) devices based on electroencephalogram (EEG) for medical applications: a review. Health Data Sci. 3. https://doi.org/10.34133/hds.0096.

Chapter 9

# Optimizing logistics for smart cities: Intelligent fleet and delivery management

Arpan Seth[1], Arijit Konar[1], Upasana Ghosh[1], Sumana Kundu[2] and Anandaprova Majumder[1]
[1]*Department of Computer Science & Engineering, Dr. B. C. Roy Engineering College, Durgapur, West Bengal, India;* [2]*Department of Computer Science & Engineering, MCKV Institute of Engineering, Howrah, West Bengal, India*

## 1. Introduction

With rapid urbanization and technological advancements, metropolises are transitioning toward becoming "smart metropolises," focusing on effectiveness, sustainability, and enhanced living norms. Among the numerous challenges faced by civic centers, logistics and transportation play a vital part. As e-commerce expands and civic populations increase, logistics systems are under significant pressure to deliver briskly and more efficiently while minimizing environmental and functional costs. The proposed approach is a response to this growing need. It aims to develop an intelligent, scalable logistics platform that leverages advanced technologies like artificial intelligence, IoT, and real-time data analytics. This system will facilitate flawless line operation, dynamic route optimization, and better client satisfaction through timely deliveries. By addressing these critical challenges, the design not only enhances civic logistics but also contributes to the broader aspirations of sustainability and economic effectiveness in smart city development.

It is essential to identify the key factors driving the need for advanced logistics solutions.

- **Rapid Urbanization and Delivery Demand**
  The exponential growth of e-commerce has led to a swell in delivery conditions in densely populated civic areas. This growth presents logistical challenges, including business traffic, inefficient routes, and delayed

**Neuromorphic Computing for Brain Computer Interfaces. https://doi.org/10.1016/B978-0-443-41594-4.00007-1**

deliveries. Creating a system that ensures timely and cost-effective logistics operations is essential to meeting client prospects and industry demands.

- **Environmental Impact**
  The logistics industry is one of the significant contributors to greenhouse gas emissions. Inefficient delivery routes and underutilized line coffers complicate this issue. Optimizing routes and line application can mainly lower emissions, aligning logistics systems with global sustainability aspirations.
- **Profitable and functional effectiveness**
  For businesses, rising costs in energy, vehicle conservation, and labor are major concerns. By introducing intelligent line operation and optimized delivery strategies, the system promises to significantly reduce these costs, perfecting profit perimeters while maintaining service quality.
- **Technological openings**
  The vacuum of advanced technologies, such as machine learning algorithms, IoT-enabled bias, and GPS shadowing systems, provides a unique opportunity to address logistics challenges innovatively. These technologies can streamline operations, prognosticate demand, and enhance client engagement.
- **Traffic Decongestion**
  Urban areas face increased business traffic, leading to delays and advanced delivery costs. An effective logistics system can contribute to reducing business viscosity by relating optimal routes and ensuring timely deliveries, serving not only businesses but also civic mobility at large.
  Clearly defining the system's features ensures a comprehensive approach to addressing these challenges effectively.
- **Real-Time Tracking Capabilities**
  The model will apply advanced GPS tracking systems, enabling real-time monitoring of line movements. This point ensures translucence and enhances delivery delicacy.
- **Dynamic Route Optimization**
  By using algorithms like the Traveling Salesman Problem (TSP), the system will roundly calculate the most effective delivery routes, considering factors like business conditions, delivery time windows, and vehicle capacities.
- **Scalable System Architecture**
  The platform will be designed to gauge seamlessly, accommodating adding line sizes, growing user bases, and expanding order volumes without compromising performance.
- **Predictive Analytics Integration**
  Through predictive modeling, the system will read demand patterns, identify implicit detainments, and allocate resources accordingly, enhancing functional effectiveness.

- **Indefectible API Integration**
  The system will integrate with APIs such as Google Maps, Nominatim, and IoT to collect and use real-time data for decision-making. These integrations ensure responsibility and delicacy in logistics operations.
- **User-Centric Design**
  A simple and intuitive user interface will feed to managers and guests alike. Managers can manage lines and cover performance criteria, while guests can track their deliveries easily.
- **Focus on Vacuity**
  The system aims to bridge the gap for small- and medium-sized businesses, furnishing them with access to advanced logistics tools generally available to large enterprises.
  Addressing the core benefits and objectives of the logistics solution ensures its effectiveness and long-term impact.
- **Promoting Sustainability**
  The design emphasizes sustainability by optimizing delivery missions to reduce energy consumption and emissions. This contributes to combating climate change and achieving environmental conservation targets, making it a vital action for eco-friendly urbanization.
- **Enhancing Urban Mobility**
  Effective logistics systems reduce traffic caused by delivery vehicles, improving overall civic traffic inflow. This not only improves logistics but also enhances the daily commuting experience for citizens.
- **Improving client Satisfaction**
  With real-time tracking, reliable ETAs, and timely deliveries, the design enhances client satisfaction, a pivotal factor in a competitive market. An effective system fosters trust and fidelity among consumers.
- **Data-Driven resolution Making**
  The design harnesses the power of real-time data and analytics to give practical insight. Fleet managers can make informed opinions on vehicle allocation, path planning, and **resource** optimization, reducing inefficiencies.
- **Rigidity for Diverse Environments**
  While aimed at smart metropolises, the system's scalability and rigidity make it able for deployment in varied civic settings, including smaller municipalities and rural areas. This flexibility extends its impact beyond metropolitan capitals.

## 2. Literature survey

This section reviews state-of-the-art methodologies and technologies, addressing the challenges of civic logistics while aligning with the pretensions of sustainable smart metropolises.

## 2.1 Urban freight and sustainable logistics

Effective civic freight logistics are critical for achieving sustainability pretensions. Russo and Comi (2021) propose low-emission vehicles and freight connection strategies to reduce environmental impact. Their study focuses on policy fabrics supporting these pretensions. Silva et al. (2023) emphasize the role of green capitals and micrologistics in lowering the carbon footprint during last-mile deliveries. Polimeni and Belcore (2024) advocate for independent electric vehicles to address traffic and emigration issues in dense civic surroundings.

## 2.2 Dynamic vehicle routing algorithms

Vehicle routing optimization is vital in addressing civic logistics challenges. Kim et al. (2020) explore AI-enhanced algorithms that acclimatize stoutly to business and rainfall changes, perfecting real-time delivery performance. Zhang et al. (2021) integrate machine learning with heuristic styles for routing in multimodal civic settings, achieving better accuracy in demand prediction and route effectiveness. Karaoulanis (2024) further highlights neural networks for advanced predictive routing, optimizing costs and service times.

## 2.3 IoT and data analytics in smart logistics

IoT and data analytics provide real-time perceptivity and predictive capabilities for logistics. Chen et al. (2023) probe IoT's operation in line operations, emphasizing tracking delicacy and predictive conservation. Spring et al. (2021) detail big data-driven platforms, showing how analytics ameliorate demand soothsaying and threat operation.

## 2.4 Creative results for last-mile delivery

Drones, tone-driving buses, and crowdsourcing styles are examples of last-mile delivery advances. In their disquisition of drones for speedy, business-free delivery, Gürel and Serdarasan (2024) talk about the specialized difficulties and legal restrictions. To lower logistics costs, Brown et al. (2023) suggest crowd shipping models that make use of original communities.

# 3. Methodology

The methodology for "Optimizing Logistics for Smart Cities: Intelligent Fleet and Delivery Management" outlines a detailed approach for system design, focusing on modular architecture, intelligent algorithms, and workflow integration. The thing is to produce a scalable, effective, and user-friendly system that addresses civic logistics challenges through technological advancements.

### 3.1 System requirements

To ensure the effective implementation of the logistics system, the following requirements were defined:

- **Functional Requirements**
  - Route Optimization:
    * The system utilizes the Google Maps API to determine the shortest and most effective routes for deliveries.
    * Routes are stoutly acclimated to accommodate real-time traffic conditions and delivery precedences.
  - Real- Time Tracking:
    * Delivery agents' mobile GPS devices are used to give real-time position updates.
    * Fleet managers can monitor the progress of all vehicles using a web-based interface with live tracking capabilities.
  - Delivery Scheduling:
    * Schedules are automatically acclimated based on traffic conditions and estimated delivery times.
    * Fleet managers can manually run over schedules if necessary.
  - User Interface:
    * A web-based interface is for the fleet manager to input delivery orders, assign tasks, and monitor operations efficiently.
- **Nonfunctional Requirements**
  - Performance:
    The system must calculate optimized routes briskly, assuring minimum latency even with high traffic data.
  - Usability:
    The interface must be intuitive and user-friendly, bearing minimum training for fleet managers and delivery agents.
  - Scalability:
    The system is designed to handle increasing numbers of delivery agents, vehicles, and orders as the fleet size grows.
  - Reliability:
    The system must consistently give accurate data and maintain functionality under varying server loads.

### 3.2 System architecture

The system architecture of "Optimizing Logistics for Smart Cities: Intelligent Fleet and Delivery Management" is grounded on a modular Model- View-Controller (MVC) framework. The Model handles backend processes similar to data storehouse, line operation, and route optimization using the Traveling Salesman Problem (TSP) algorithm. The View provides a user-friendly interface, enabling customers and fleet managers to interact with the system through dashboards for tracking, order administration, and reporting. The Controller processes requests, coordinates between the model and the view, and manages tasks like web requests, error handling, and real-time updates. This structure ensures scalability, flawless operation, and adaptability to metropolitan logistics challenges shows in Fig. 9.1.

The system employs a modular Model-View-Controller (MVC) architecture.

- **Model:**
  Represents the backend where core functionalities similar to line data storehouse, route optimization algorithms, and analytics generation are managed. It interacts with databases and APIs to handle real-time data.
- **View:**
  Serves as the frontend, furnishing an intuitive user interface for customers and fleet managers. It includes features like live tracking, order placement, and data visualization dashboards.

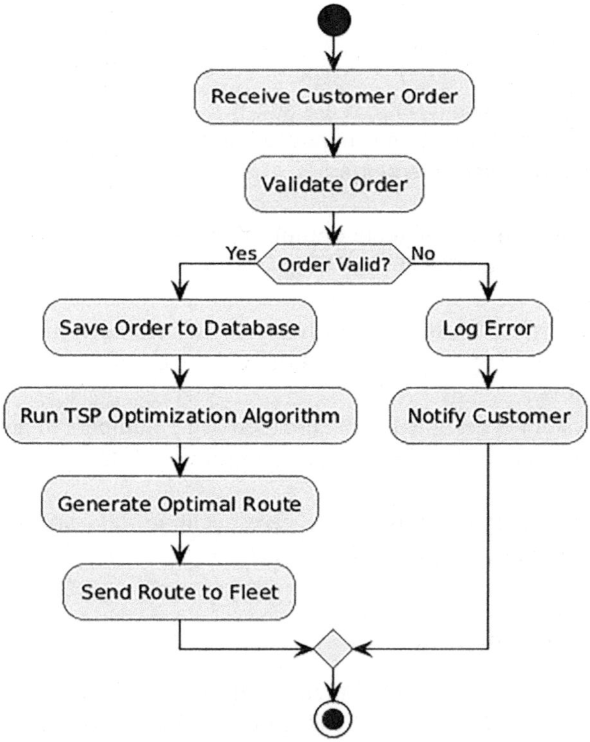


**FIGURE 9.1** System architecture.

- **Controller:**
  Acts as the conciliator between the model and the view, processing user inputs and delivering outputs. It handles requests similar to route computations, line assignments, and performance reporting.

  Fig. 9.2 shows the Model-View-Controller architecture:

### 3.3 Modules description

- **Fleet Management Module**
  This module observes and manages vehicle information, including capacity, position, fuel situations, and maintenance schedules. Using IoT devices, it gathers real-time data, assuring vehicle readiness and efficient allocation. When a vehicle's condition deviates from functional norms (e.g., low fuel), the system flags the issue for the director's attention.
- **Route Optimization Module**
  This module employs the Traveling Salesman Problem (TSP) algorithm to cipher the most efficient delivery routes. The TSP algorithm minimizes trip distances by assaying a list of destinations and determining the shortest possible path that visits each destination once and returns to the origin. Real-time traffic and road conditions are factored in to assure adaptive routing shows in Fig. 9.3.
  - The module inputs delivery locations as nodes.
  - It computes all possible routes between nodes.
  - The TSP algorithm selects the shortest route while considering constraints like traffic or delivery time windows.
  - The optimized route is dispatched to the fleet.
- **Analytics and Reporting Module**
  This module aggregates delivery performance data, generates insights, and visualizes crucial criteria like delivery times, line effectiveness, and fuel consumption. Prophetic analytics helps read demand trends, enabling visionary decision-making. Managers can access custom reports via the dashboard for performance reviews and functional planning shows in Fig. 9.4.

## 4. Workflow of the model

The workflow of the system encompasses detailed ways to ensure smooth operation, efficient error handling, and flawless web interactions. Each process is supported by a diagram for clarity.

- **Order Placement**
  Customers interact with the web interface to place orders, furnishing delivery details like the address, time constraints, and package specifications.

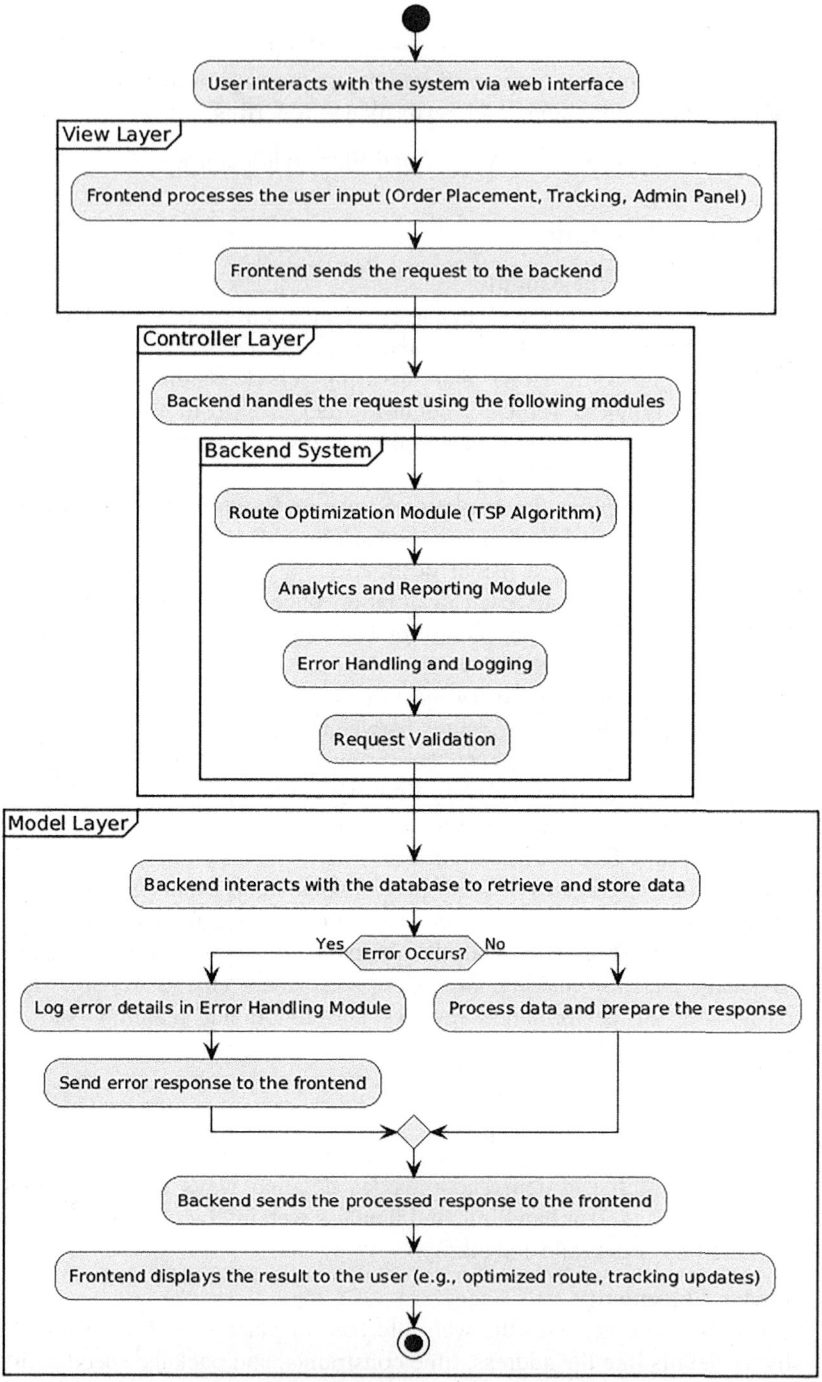


**FIGURE 9.2** Model-view-controller model.

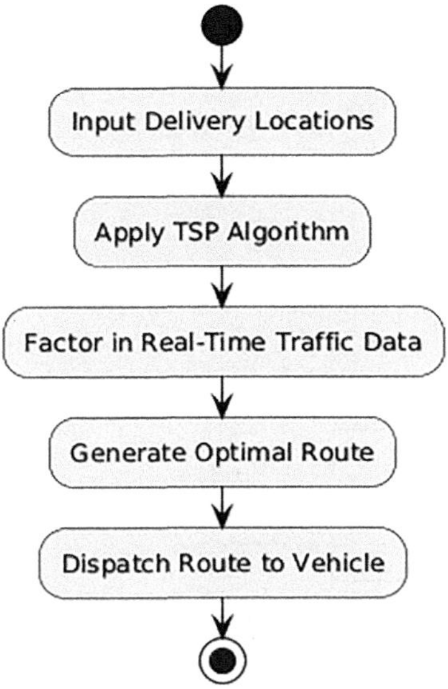


**FIGURE 9.3** Route optimization.

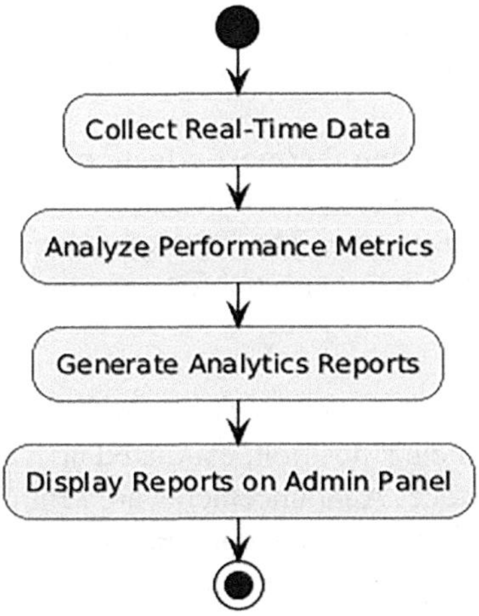


**FIGURE 9.4** Analytics and reporting.

The system validates the input, ensuring the data meets predefined criteria, such as valid delivery zones. Once verified, the order is added to the database for processing shows in Fig. 9.5.

- **Fleet Assignment**
  Based on real-time line data, the system assigns a suitable vehicle to the order. The assignment considers factors like proximity, capacity, and

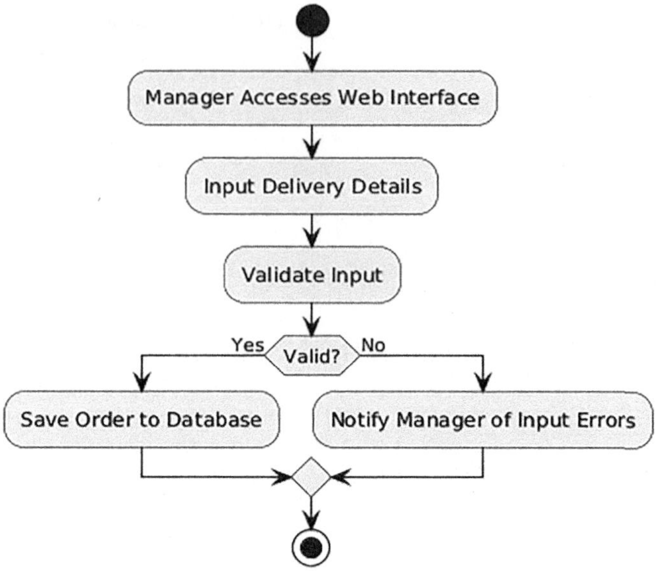


**FIGURE 9.5** Order placement.

vehicle status (e.g., fuel situations). If no vehicle is available, the system alerts the administrator for manual intervention shows in Fig. 9.6.

- **Route Calculation**
The system uses the TSP algorithm to determine the most effective route for the assigned vehicle. The algorithm considers factors like delivery locations, traffic data, and precedence constraints. The advised route is dispatched to the fleet and made available to managers for monitoring shows in Fig. 9.7.
- **Real-Time Tracking**
As the delivery progresses, GPS data updates the system in real-time. Customers and managers can view the vehicle's position, estimated arrival time, and delivery status through the interface. Announcements are sent at crucial mileposts, like departure, en route, and delivery completion shows in Fig. 9.8.
- **Error Handling**
The system continuously monitors processes for potential errors, such as invalid delivery inputs, route misapprehensions, or vehicle failures. However, it's logged, and an announcement is sent to the applicable party (e.g., if an error occurs, the customer or fleet manager) with suggested resolutions shown in Fig. 9.9.
- **Analysis and Reporting**
Fig. 9.10 shows postdelivery, the system compiles data on delivery times, fleet effectiveness, and fuel consumption. Administrators access this

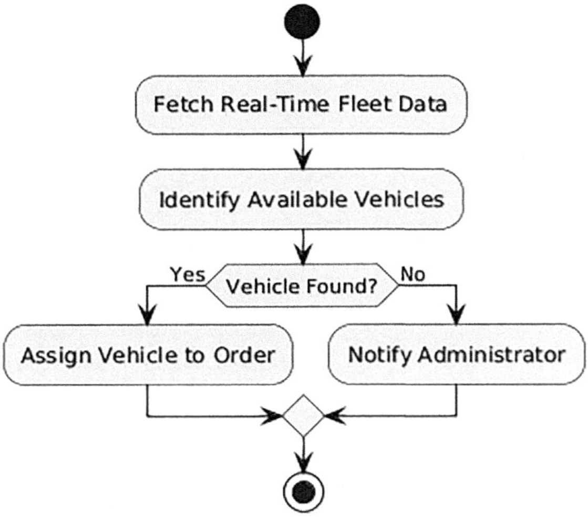


FIGURE 9.6 Fleet assignment.

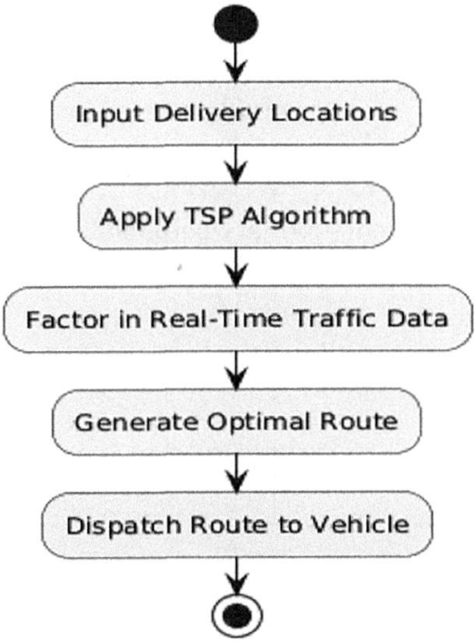


FIGURE 9.7 Route calculation.

information through interactive dashboards to estimate performance and make data-driven decisions.

- **Handling Web Requests**
  Fig. 9.11 shows flask routes process user requests, similar to placing orders or bringing reports. Upon entering a request, the controller validates input, invokes backend services, and sends the response to the front end, ensuring a seamless user experience.

FIGURE 9.8 Real-time tracking.

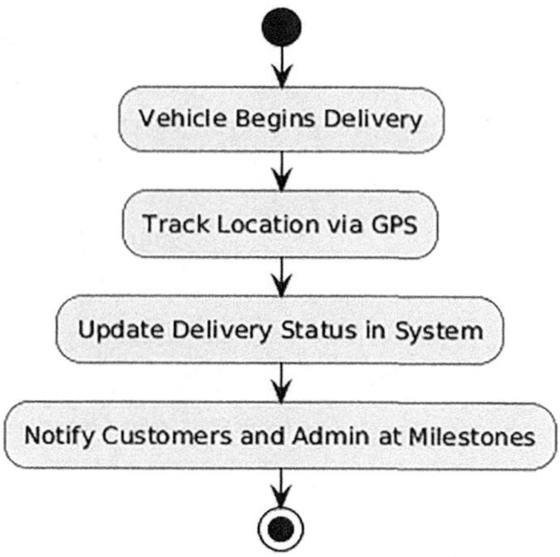


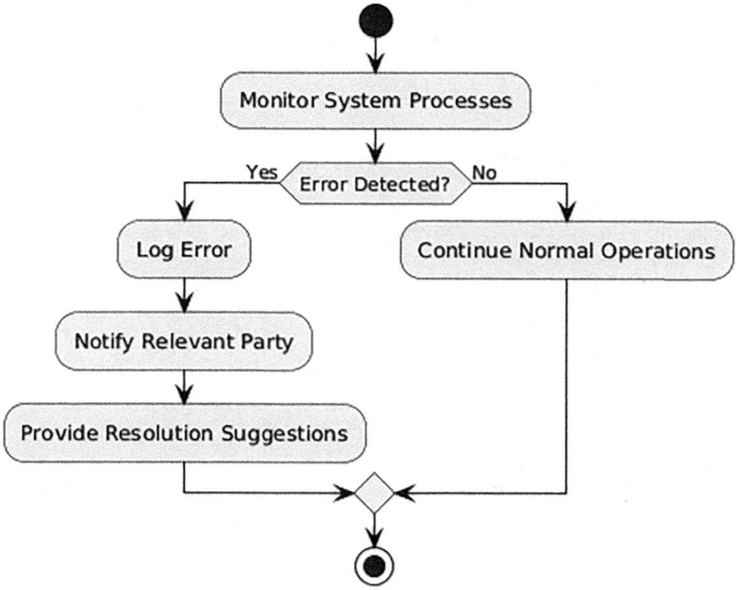


FIGURE 9.9 Error handling.

- **Web Page Functionality**
  The web page provides an intuitive interface for users to place orders, track deliveries, and view reports. Dropdown menus allow users to select delivery options and time windows. Updates and reports are displayed stoutly in Fig. 9.12 for better user dealings.

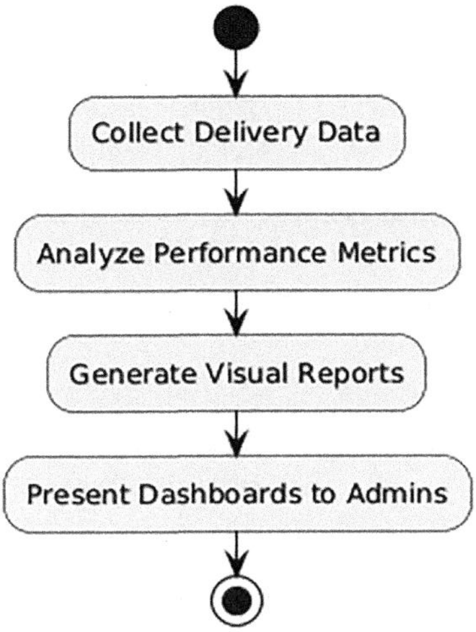


**FIGURE 9.10** Analysis and reporting.

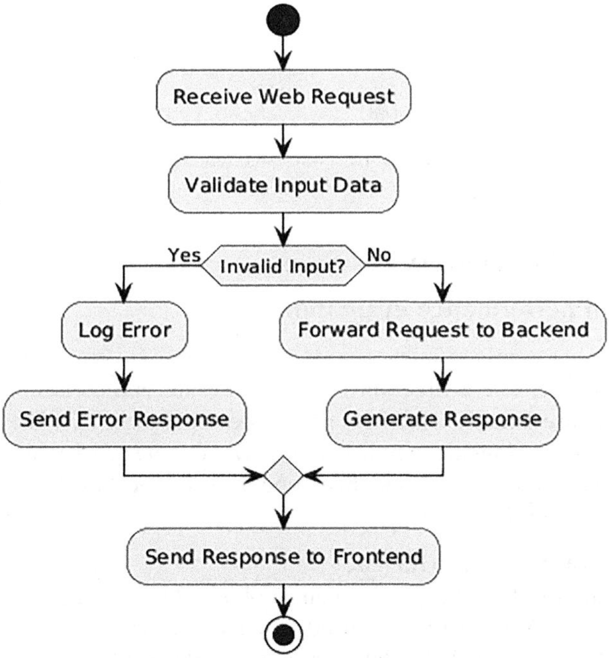


**FIGURE 9.11** Handling web requests.

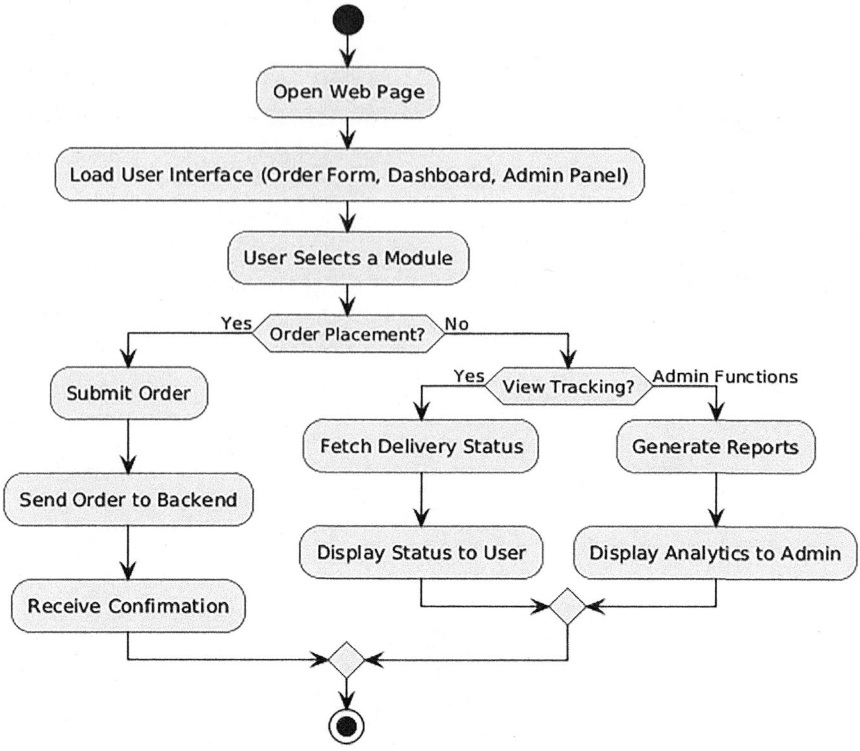


**FIGURE 9.12** Web page functionality.

# 5. Results and analysis

## 5.1 System performance evaluation

To ensure the system's efficiency, extensive testing was conducted under real-world conditions. The evaluation focused on route optimization, tracking accuracy, response time, scalability, and system adaptability. The system was deployed in a live logistics environment, where it handled real-time delivery requests, traffic conditions, and fleet operations. The key findings from the tests are discussed below.

- **Route Optimization Efficiency**
  The system's Traveling Salesman Problem (TSP) algorithm, integrated with Google Maps API, was used to generate the most efficient delivery routes dynamically. This played a crucial role in improving delivery performance showing in Table 9.1.
- **Real-Time Tracking Accuracy**

**TABLE 9.1** Route optimization efficiency.

| Metric | Traditional routing | Proposed smart logistics system | Improvement (%) |
|---|---|---|---|
| Average delivery time | 50 min | 38 min | 24% faster |
| Fuel consumption per route | 5.2 L | 4.3 L | 17% lower |
| Number of deliveries per day | 30 | 40 | 33% more |
| Distance covered per trip | 20 km | 15 km | 25% reduction |

A GPS-based tracking system was implemented to provide live updates on delivery agents' locations. Fleet managers could monitor drivers in real time, improving accountability and reducing inefficiencies showing in Table 9.2.

- **System Responsiveness and Load Handling**
  A key factor in evaluating the system's performance was its ability to handle high delivery request volumes without slowing down. The backend infrastructure was tested to measure response time, request processing speed, and overall system efficiency showing in Table 9.3.

**TABLE 9.2** Real-time tracking accuracy comparison.

| Feature | Proposed system | Traditional system [hub-and-spoke model, first-in first-out (FIFO) scheduling, etc.] | Difference |
|---|---|---|---|
| GPS accuracy | 95% | 75% | 20% improvement |
| Tracking update speed | 3–5 s | 10–15 s | 2–3 times faster |
| Unauthorized stops | Rare | Frequent | 30% less |
| Route deviation detection | Yes | No | More control |

**TABLE 9.3** System responsiveness under normal and peak load.

| System action | Response time (normal) (s) | Response time (peak) (s) | Performance difference (s) |
|---|---|---|---|
| Route optimization | 1.2 | 1.5 | + 0.3 |
| Tracking update | 2 | 2.5 | + 0.5 |
| Task assignment | 1 | 1.3 | + 0.3 |
| Data fetching | 1.5 | 2 | + 0.5 |

## 5.2 Comparative analysis

The performance of this logistics system was compared with traditional delivery operation approaches. The following Table 9.4 outlines the major differences:

From this comparison, it's apparent that the smart logistics system significantly outperforms traditional styles in terms of speed, accuracy, cost-effectiveness, and scalability.

## 5.3 Case study of real-world implementation

To test the system in real-world conditions, a two-week airman test was conducted in a high-traffic civic area, involving 50 delivery agents handling 500 deliveries. The results demonstrated substantial functional advancements shown in Table 9.5:

This case study confirms that the system delivers measurable advancements in delivery speed, client satisfaction, and functional cost savings.

## 5.4 Error analysis and limitations

While the system performed well, some challenges and limitations were observed. The crucial areas for enhancement are listed below:

- **GPS Signal Issues:**
  Tracking delicacy was largely dependable, but minor GPS signal issues were noticed in thick civic areas.
  - Signal hindrance in high-rise megacity zones caused a 5% drop in delicacy.
  - Many delivery agents lost GPS signals temporarily, affecting real-time shadowing updates.
  - Unborn result utensil mongrel shadowing by combining GPS, Wi- Fi, and cellular data to ameliorate tracking perfection.

**TABLE 9.4** Relative analysis of smart versus traditional logistics systems.

| Feature | Proposed smart logistics system | Traditional system [hub-and-spoke model, first-in first-out (FIFO) scheduling, etc.] | Improvement |
|---|---|---|---|
| Route optimization | AI-driven, real-time updates | Manual, fixed routes | Smarter routing |
| Fuel efficiency | 15% less fuel used | High fuel wastage | Cost savings |
| Scalability | 100+ agents supported | Limited expansion | More scalable |
| Tracking accuracy | 95% GPS precision | 75% GPS precision | 20% more accurate |
| Order processing speed | 1.2 s | 5 s | 4 times faster |
| Delivery completion rate | 98% on-time | 85% on-time | 13% more reliable |

**TABLE 9.5** Case study: real-world implementation.

| Metric | Before implementation | After implementation | Improvement |
|---|---|---|---|
| Average delivery time | 50 min | 38 min | 24% faster |
| Fuel cost per day | ₹10,000 | ₹8500 | 15% savings |
| Customer complaints | 50 per week | 35 per week | 30% reduction |
| Idle vehicle time | 2.5 h/day | 2 h/day | 20% less |
| Missed deliveries | 10 per week | 5 per week | 50% better |

- **Traffic Congestion Handling:**
  While the system stoutly rerouted deliveries, extreme traffic posed some necessary delays.
  - Unanticipated road closures occasionally forced longer divergences than anticipated.

- Sometimes, the system suggested longer alternate routes rather than minor detours.
- Future result: AI-grounded literal business pattern analysis will enhance traffic prognostications and optimize rerouting.

- **Peak Cargo Scalability:**
During high-demand periods, minor retardations were observed due to the large number of contemporaneous requests.
  - Response time increased by 5% during peak hours.
  - Database query times increased by 10%–15%, slightly affecting processing speed.
  - Future result: utensil database indexing, hiding, and page-grounded scaling to ameliorate peak-hour performance.

## 5.5 Output after optimizing the path

Fig. 9.13 displays the final optimized delivery path generated by the logistics path optimization system. This system integrates Google Maps with a backend that processes numerous delivery locations and calculates the most effective path using a TSP (Traveling Salesman Problem) solver.

In the given scenario, the interface allows users to input delivery precedence (e.g., Light & Small (Special Handling) and append or remove locations stoutly. After processing, the system optimizes the path for a selected vehicle type (e.g., bike) and displays it on an interactive map. The intrigued path ensures minimal travel time and effective resource utilization, making urban logistics more streamlined.

The operation of such optimization is vital in smart city logistics, as it helps reduce energy consumption, minimize delays, and improve last-mile delivery effectiveness. By using real-time traffic data and AI- driven pathfinding, this system significantly enhances urban mobility results.

**FIGURE 9.13** Output after optimize the path.

## 6. Conclusion and future scope

The evaluation of the smart logistics system confirms that it offers significant advancements in delivery effectiveness, real-time tracking accuracy, and cost savings. By using AI- driven route optimization and real-time tracking, the system successfully minimizes delivery times, improves resource application, and enhances overall line operation. Compared with traditional logistics results, this system offers superior robotization, responsiveness, and scalability. The capability to stoutly acclimate routes based on live business updates and predictive analytics ensures dependable and effective deliveries even in shifting conditions. While the system has performed exceptionally well, minor challenges such as GPS signal dislocations and peak-hour retardations punctuate areas for implicit enhancement. Still, these limitations do not undermine the overall effectiveness of the proposed result.

In the future, further advancements can be made to make the system indeed more robust and scalable. Integration with AI- grounded business prediction models will allow the system to anticipate traffic more directly and proactively acclimate routes. Pall-grounded scalability results can enhance system performance during peak functional hours, ensuring continued service. Also, incorporating independent delivery systems and IoT-grounded line operation can further optimize logistics operations and reduce manual intervention. As smart metropolises continue to evolve, logistics results similar to this will play a pivotal part in creating sustainable, intelligent, and largely effective delivery networks, making civic transportation more streamlined and cost-effective.

## References

Brown, T., et al., 2023. Crowdshipping and parcel lockers for urban delivery. Sustainability. https://www.mdpi.com/2071-1050/12/24/10684.

Chen, J., et al., 2023. AI-based optimization in smart urban logistics systems. Expert Syst. Appl. https://www.sciencedirect.com/science/article/pii/S0957417423001234.

Gürel, Ö., Serdarasan, S., 2024. Drone-assisted last-mile delivery under windy conditions: zero pollution solutions. Smart Cities. https://doi.org/10.3390/smartcities7060134.

Karaoulanis, A., 2024. Sustainability and new technologies: last-mile delivery in the context of smart cities. Sustainability. https://doi.org/10.3390/su16188037.

Kim, J., et al., 2020. Dynamic routing algorithms in smart city logistics. IEEE Trans. Intell. Transport. Syst. https://ieeexplore.ieee.org/document/9364796.

Polimeni, A., Belcore, O.M., 2024. Green vehicles in city logistics planning. Smart Cities. https://doi.org/10.3390/smartcities7060134.

Russo, F., Comi, A., 2021. City logistics and urban freight transport: a systematic review. Transp. Res. Part D. https://doi.org/10.1016/j.trd.2021.102844.

Silva, V., Amaral, A., Fontes, T., 2023. Sustainable urban last-mile logistics: a systematic literature review. Sustainability. https://doi.org/10.3390/su15032285.

Spring, M., et al., 2021. Big Data Analytics in Urban Freight Logistics. Springer Urban Freight Transport. https://link.springer.com/article/10.1007/s10479-019-03134-w.

Zhang, H., et al., 2021. Sustainable logistics framework for smart cities. Resour. Conserv. Recycl. https://www.sciencedirect.com/science/article/abs/pii/S0921344919300292.

Chapter 10

# A biomimetic neuromorphic processor for enhanced brain–computer interface applications in neural rehabilitation

T. Rajkumar[1], V. Karthi[2], M. Elayaraja[3], G. Brinda[4], S.D. Vijayakumar[5] and M. Anitha[4]

[1]*Department of ECE, Nandha College of Technology, Erode, Tamil Nadu, India;* [2]*Department of EEE, Kangeyam Institute of Technology, Nathakadaiyur, Tamil Nadu, India;* [3]*Department of ECE, Fathima Michael College of Engineering and Technology, Madurai, Tamil Nadu, India;* [4]*Department of Electronics and Communication Engineering, M.P.Nachimuthu M.Jaganathan Engineering College, Erode, Tamil Nadu, India;* [5]*Department of Artificial Intelligence and Data Science, Nandha Engineering College, Erode, Tamil Nadu, India*

## 1. Introduction

### 1.1 An overview of rehabilitation's use of brain–computer interfaces (BCIs)

#### *1.1.1 Overview of BCIs*

Bypassing conventional neuromuscular output pathways, a BCI system allows direct communication between the brain and an external device. Computers, assistive technology, and even robotic limbs can be controlled by BCIs, which translate brain signals, typically electrical, magnetic, or metabolic activity, into commands. By assisting patients in regaining lost motor or cognitive abilities, BCIs have a revolutionary impact on rehabilitation.

#### *1.1.2 Essential elements of a BCI system*

**The following modules make up a typical BCI system:**

- **Signal Acquisition:** Recording neural activity with techniques such as intracortical recordings, electroencephalography (EEG), or electrocorticography (ECoG).

**Neuromorphic Computing for Brain Computer Interfaces. https://doi.org/10.1016/B978-0-443-41594-4.00009-5**

- **Preprocessing:** Removing artifacts and noise from the unprocessed brain signals. Finding patterns or characteristics in the neural signals that are instructive for control is known as feature extraction.
- **Classification/Translation Algorithm:** Machine learning or rule-based systems are used to translate neural features into control signals.
- **Application Interface:** A program or device that is controlled by an output signal, such as a wheelchair, computer cursor, or robotic limb (Fig. 10.1).

### *1.1.3 Use as BCI*

The BCI can be broadly classified based on its level of invasion. Noninvasive BCIs rely on the scalp-based EEG, providing a safe and convenient option for users; however, they are often limited by low spatial resolution and a poor signal-to-noise ratio. Semiinvasive BCI, such as the ECoG system, involves placing electrodes on the brain surface. These signs offer a balanced business between loyalty and the degree of invasion. On the other hand, invasive BCIs, transplanted microelectrodes, employ arrays that capture nervous activity with the highest accuracy and reliability. Despite their better performance, aggressive approaches face significant challenges, including the risk of infection, potential tissue damage, and concerns over long stagnation.

### *1.1.4 Applications used in nerve rehabilitation*

- Motor rehabilitation
- Spinal Cord Injury (SCI)
- Neurofeedback therapy
- Communication support
- Cognitive rehabilitation

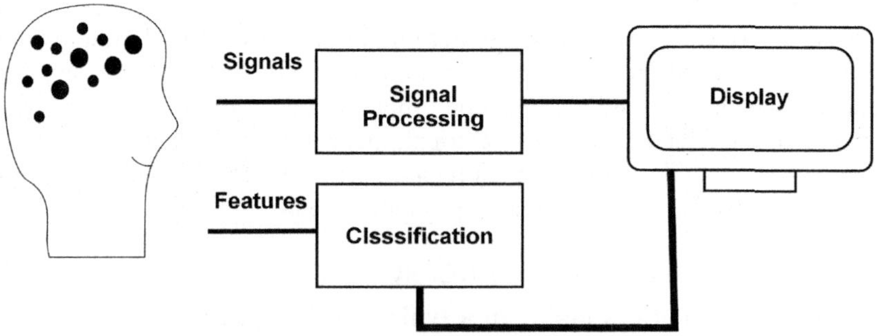


**FIGURE 10.1** BCI system.

### 1.1.5 BCI benefits in rehabilitation

One of the major powers of the BCI in rehabilitation lies in its ability to offer personal intervention, as they are favorable to each user's unique brain activity patterns, which enable analog therapeutic strategies and individual drugs. BCIs also play an important role in incorporating neuroplasticity, as they provide real-time responses that actively engage the brain to reiterate functional functions, support nervous restructuring, and aid recovery. Additionally, the interactive nature of BCI applications promotes motivation and engagement, which encourages patients to participate more actively during prolonged rehabilitation sessions. In addition, BCIs promote greater freedom, reduce dependence on carers, and increase the quality of life for persons with severe physical damage. Limits of current BCI systems.

### 1.1.6 Despite their ability, BCIs face many practical and technical challenges

The speed of delay and processing: Real-time processing of complex signals requires efficient hardware, which struggles to give less strength to traditional CPU/GPU. Signal variability: Brain signals are nonstable and highly variable in sessions and individuals. User training and calibration: Most BCI systems require extensive calibration and user training. Power consumption and portability: Wearable or implanted BCI requires ultra-low-power hardware for daily use. Clinical translation: Many promising BCI prototype regulators live in research laboratories due to moral and economic obstacles.

With the emergence of biometric neuromorphic solutions to remove these challenges, the area is now moving to neuromorphic computing and biometric processors, which simulate the efficient and adaptive architecture of the brain. These systems promise rapid processing, low power consumption, and real-time adaptability, important features to advance BCI technology in clinical rehabilitation.

## 1.2 Challenges in the current BCI system

Although BCIs make great promises for rehabilitation, their broad application is interrupted by many important challenges. Many systems struggle with high strength consumption, limited real-time accountability, and insufficient adaptability for individual nerve patterns, which collectively restrict their effectiveness in continuous and individual rehabilitation scenarios.

A large obstacle lies in signal acquisition, where the brain signal, especially EEG, has a low signal-to-noise ratio, which is often overshadowed by intervention from muscles, ocular, and environmental artifacts. While invasive BCIs provide better signal quality, they come with adequate surgical and moral risks, while noninvasive methods compromise on spatial resolution. In addition, electrode-related issues remain: dry electrodes offer low accuracy, while wet electrodes improve loyalty but cause discomfort and require frequent maintenance. The next challenge concerns the signal processing and interpretation. Rehabilitation requires real-time data analysis with minimal delays, yet the complex and highly individual nature of brain activity makes decoding difficult. Identification of reliable and repeated features in users and sessions remains a continuous challenge, which complicates effective feature extraction and selection. Equally, pressure is the issue of adaptability and privatization. Nerve patterns vary greatly in individuals, making generalized models ineffective. In terms of classification and decision-making, systems face a business band between accuracy and speed. While high accuracy is desirable, it often slows down the accountability of the system, making the real-world applications impractical. Errors such as wrong positivity or negativity can also cause disappointment or harmful consequences in neural reorganization.

Hardware limitations also disrupt the purpose. Many BCI setups are heavy, expensive, and lack of portability, while the use of long-term headsets can cause discomfort or skin irritation. Similarly, integration with subsidiary technologies such as wheelchairs, robotic weapons, or exoskeletons remains underdeveloped, often stricken by delays between compatibility issues and intentions and execution of action. Beyond technical obstacles, moral and regulatory concerns play an important role. Brain data is highly sensitive, which increases concerns about privacy, misuse, and unauthorized access. Getting proper informed consent is especially challenging in people avoiding weaker patient groups, such as stroke or SCI. Additionally, clinical-grade BCI should follow the stringent regulatory standards, slowing down their adoption in healthcare. Finally, cost and access remain significant obstacles. Advanced BCI systems are prohibitively expensive and are beyond the reach of many rehabilitation centers. Lack of standardization, interoperability, and a benchmark dataset hinders scalability and widespread adoption. On behalf of the user, mental fatigue, unexpected interface design, and system reduce the lack of confidence in reliability, hesitating patients to depend on BCI for significant rehabilitation functions.

## 1.3 Inspiration for the neuromorphic and biometric approach

The brain processes information with extraordinary efficiency and adaptability. Neuromorphic engineering aims to copy this biological computation. Biometric neuromorphic processors follow the neural principles of calculating and learning, providing a promising option for the next-generation BCI system.

### *1.3.1 Inspiration for the neuromorphic and biometric approach*

The development of neuromorphic and biometric processors for BCIs is mainly motivated by the need to bridge the difference between the brain and machines. The human brain is an extraordinary model of efficiency, adaptability, and low-power operation, which makes it a natural blueprint for the designing system that aligns more closely with nerve processing. Unlike traditional Von Neumann computing, which struggles to interpret spatiotemporal nerve signals biologically meaningful, neuromorphic hardware has a neuronal architecture, leading to increased compatibility with brain activity. This approach also addresses the important issue of energy efficiency, as most of the wearable BCIs are limited by battery capacity and heat wastage. Neuromorphic architecture, especially spiking neural networks (SNNs), functions in an event-driven manner, consuming minimal power, supporting continuous, real-time nerve decoding. Another major benefit lies in real-time adaptive processing, required for rehabilitation applications where nerve signals are dynamic and highly variable. Neuromorphic processors enable online learning, adapt to neuroplasticity changes, and reduce delays by performing local calculations, reducing dependence on cloud resources. Their design also increases feature extraction and strength, working firmly in the noise environment to take inspiration from the brain's capacity. By employing rare and recurrent coding, neuromorphic systems focus on the necessary information, ignoring irrelevant or noise inputs. In addition, their scalability and modularity are parallel, allowing brain-like architecture to expand in complication, supporting diverse applications such as motor imagery, speech decoding, and sensory reactions to prosthetic devices.

Importantly, these systems enable close integration with biological processes through closed-loop interactions, where BCI not only decodes nervous activity, but also provides a response to the brain, cocollecting with the user to increase rehabilitation results. The challenge of limited training data in BCI applications is also addressed, as neuromorphic processors demonstrate some-shot learning abilities similar to human cognitive learning mechanisms. Further, neuromorphic and biometric approaches align with the next generation of BCI, which are spread beyond motor control for advanced netiquette to suggested cognitive state monitoring, decision-making support, and stroke or SCI. The ongoing development of neuromorphic hardware—IBM's TrueNorth, Intel's Loihi, and Brainchip's Akida—and the exemplary worldly world, fulfills the increasing feasibility of deploying such a processor in the BCI system. By enabling edge computing, this architecture helps in infection to BCI in practical, home-based rehabilitation devices from controlled laboratory settings. Ultimately, the long-term vision is to move toward AI systems like the brain that are capable not only able to execute the command, but also of understanding, adapting, and predicting the user's needs. This development should proceed with a strong emphasis on moral codevelopment, ensuring that machines increase both cognitive and motor functions in ways that are human-sensible and socially responsible.

# 2. Background and theoretical foundation

## 2.1 Neurology and nervous plasticity in rehabilitation

Neuroplasticity refers to the ability to reorganize the brain's ability and create new connections. The BCI systems can take advantage of this by providing a reaction-operated training environment that stimulates restructuring and recovery in damaged brain regions.

After a nerve insult (e.g., stroke), some brain areas may lose functionality. However, adjacent or contraceptive lateral regions can create new synaptic connections to re-create motor or sensory routes and adapt to the lost tasks.

BCI systems offer real-time reaction and a closed-loop learning environment, and capitalize on this **neuroplasticity** that encourages the brain:

- Relay motor functions,
- Strengthen nerve routes,
- Install new functional circuits.

Characterization and modeling of biological neural networks has emerged as a field driving significant advancements in our understanding of brain function and related pathologies. As of today, pharmacological treatments for neurological disorders remain limited, pushing the exploration of promising alternative approaches such as electrocution. Recent research in bioelectronics and neuromorphic engineering has fostered the development of the new generation of neuroprosthesis for brain repair (Beaubois et al., 2024).

### *2.1.1 How BCIs support neuroplasticity*

#### 2.1.1.1 Response-powered training

BCIs detect the intentions of the user (e.g., motor imagery or effortful movement) and convert them into a control signal for external devices such as robotic organs or exoskeletons. Visual or sensory reaction from these devices reinforces nervous activity, promoting Hebbian learning (i.e., "cells that set the wires together").

#### 2.1.1.2 Repeated work engagement

Motor, even without actual movement, is a significant process in rehabilitation and inspires cortical remapping.

#### 2.1.1.3 Adaptive teaching algorithms

The neuromorphic BCI system is conducive to changing nervous states and aligns well with the dynamic nature of neuroplasticity (Fig. 10.2).

Nerve enables functional recovery through plasticity reorganization. BCI takes advantage of intentions, reactions, and adaptation and acts as a cognitive

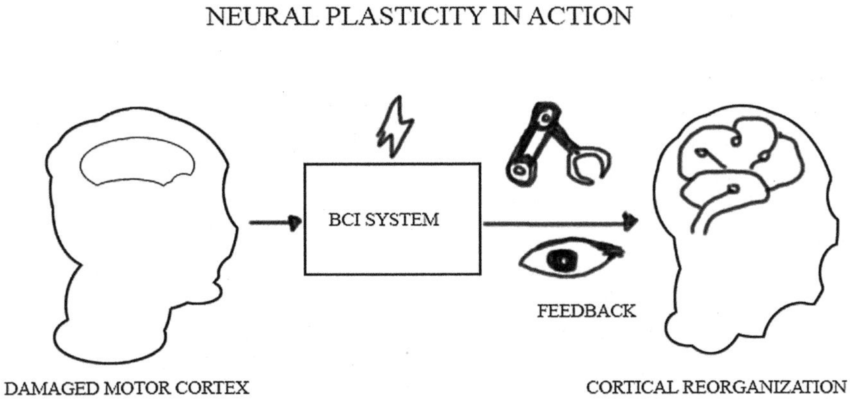


**FIGURE 10.2** Neural plasticity in action.

amplifier. Plasticity is fundamental for effective rehabilitation between the brain and adaptive machine.

## 2.2 Theory of neuromorphic computing

Neuromorphic computing refers to a class of computational architecture designed to mimic the biological structure and dynamics of the human brain. Unlike the traditional von Neumann architecture, neuromorphic systems integrate calculations and memory in a distributed fashion, like a network of neurons and synapses in the brain. The purpose of these systems is to achieve low-power, real-time, and adaptive information processing, making them ideally suited to BCIs, especially in nerve rehabilitation, where biological realism, adaptability, and energy efficiency are necessary. Major principles and characteristics.

Neuromorphic engineering, which uses neural models in hardware and software to replicate brain-like behaviors, can help usher in a new era of medicine by delivering low-power, low-latency, small-footprint, and high-bandwidth solutions (Aboumerhi et al., 2023).

### *2.2.1 Main theory of neuromorphic computing*

Neuromorphic computing is inspired by the biological system of the human brain, and many major principles define its architecture and functionality. Its foundations are neurons spiking, which communicate through discrete electrical impulses or "spikes" instead of continuous signals. This spiking activity mimics the way organic neurons support the firing action potential, temporal coding that is required for sensory-motor information processing. The popular computational models of spiking neurons include the integrated-and-fire, Izhikevich, and Hodgkin-Huxley models, each of which has been occupied by various levels of biological expansion and computational efficiency. Unlike traditional clock-driven systems, which all process incoming data contemporarily, neuromorphic systems work on event-mechanized processing, active only in response to spikes or relevant inputs, much like the selective activation of the brain in response to sensory stimuli. This approach reduces energy consumption, reduces delay, and increases computational efficiency.

Another fundamental aspect is the integration of the synaptic plasticity mechanism, which repeats the brain's ability to strengthen or weaken the synaptic connection based on experience and activity. Learning rules such as Hebbian learning ("cells that set fire together, wires simultaneously"), Spike-Timing-Dependent Plasticity (STDP), and homeostatic plasticity enable customizing neuromorphic systems in real time, learning from limited data. In addition, neuromorphic architecture adds memory and calculation to the same physical space, which is inspired by how the brain cooperates storage and processing within the nerve circuit.

Neuromorphic chips are also designed keeping in mind equality and modularity, showing how the brain simultaneously processes information in billions of neurons. Each neuromorphic core or module can function independently or collaboratively; these systems are especially well-suited for real-time BCI applications where many brain areas must be monitored and decoded concurrently. Importantly, they also demonstrate mistake tolerance, as their distributed design and local teaching mechanisms allow them to adapt and recover from hardware failures or defects, similar to brain flexibility for local damage or neuron loss. Many hardware platforms adopt these neuromorphic principles. IBM's True North integrates a million neurons and 256 million synapses within an event-powered architecture, while Intel's Loihi chip includes STDP-based updates and on-chip learning with scalability for large-scale applications. Akida Age of Brain chip distributes the ultra-low-power adapted to the AI and the BCI system, distributes the real-time SNN, and the Spinnaker platform developed at the University of Manchester provides large-scale, real-time neural simulation for research in brain-inspired computing. Together, this implementation demonstrates the growing viability of neuromorphic hardware to carry forward the next generation of BCIs and nerve rehabilitation devices.

## 2.3 Biomimicry engineering: An overview

### *2.3.1 Introduction*

Biomimicry is the practice of studying and imitating time-tested strategies, structures, and systems of nature to solve modern engineering and technical challenges. In recent decades, this approach has fueled innovation in subjects ranging from aerospace and material science to architecture and artificial intelligence.

In the context of neuromorphic engineering, biomimicry plays a fundamental role by offering biological blueprints for how information can be processed, stored, learned, and optimized using minimal energy and maximum strength, as the human brain does.

Computation in nervous systems operates with different computational primitives and on different hardware than traditional digital computation and is thus subjected to different constraints from its digital counterpart regarding the use of physical resources such as time, space, and energy (Broccard et al., 2017).

### 2.3.2 Biomimicry in computing

Biomimetics in computing takes inspiration from organic systems, especially the remarkable efficiency and adaptability of the human brain, which excels in complex problems such as solving pattern recognition, learning from limited data, suiting noisy environments, and gaining extraordinary energy efficiency—all areas where traditional computers often struggle. The neuromorphic processor aims to repeat these capabilities by mimicking structural and functional principles of biological nerve circuits, including synaptic plasticity and spatiotemporal signal proliferation.

A major source of motivation is nerve coding, as the biological brain employs various strategies such as rate coding, temporal coding, and sparse coding to represent information with accuracy and efficiency. Spiking Neural Networks (SNNs) include these coding strategies, which are to enable proper, biologically admirable data representation. Similarly, synaptic plasticity and learning mechanisms are central for neuromorphic design. Drawing from biological processes where synaptic strength changes with experience, it applies neuromorphic hardware learning patterns such as Hebbian learning and spike-timing-dependent plasticity (STDP) and maintains a balance between customization and stability during learning metaphorically.

Distributed and parallel architecture of the brain—where billions of neurons work together—also inspires neuromorphic systems. These processors use a modular neuron core, specialized topology, and skilled on-chip communication protocols to reproduce multitasking abilities like the brain. This design not only ensures scalability but also provides mistake tolerance, enabling real-time decoding in complex BCI applications. Another important characteristic is energy efficiency: while the human brain operates only on ~20 watts of power, neuromorphic chips simulate this ability through phenomena-operated components, which are only active when spikes are present rather than through frequent processing.

Finally, neuromorphic systems include mistake tolerance and self-healing properties, which resonate with brain flexibility and the ability to reorganize around lost or damaged neurons for injury. Features such as excesses, error corrections, and reconstructive routes make neuromorphic hardware stronger and more durable for long-term deployment in rehabilitation and subsidiary technologies. By embedding these biomimetic principles, neuromorphic computing provides a transformative passage toward brain-inspired machines that are not only more efficient but also more adaptive and flexible than traditional computing systems (Table 10.1).

## 2.4 Spicing neural network (SNN)

### 2.4.1 Introduction

SNNs represent the third generation of artificial neural network models. Unlike traditional artificial neural networks (ANNs) that work on constant values and fixed time stages, SNN simulates asynchronous, phenomenon-driven behavior of biological neurons. They process information through the discomfort spikes (action potential), which mimic how the actual neurons in the brain mimic.

This biologically realistic calculation makes SNN particularly suitable for applications such as neuromorphic hardware and BCIs, where it is necessary to learn temporary patterns and adaptive learning. It explores the intersection of neuromorphic computing with neurology and pharmaceutical development, emphasizing the significance of understanding neural processes and integrating deep learning techniques (Raikar et al., 2024).

### 2.4.2 Major features of SNNs

SNNs represent the third generation of the neural network model, offering biologically realistic structures for information processing. Unlike traditional artificial neural networks, which mainly rely on continuous activities, SNNs involve coddling and dynamics, where information is given not only through the frequency of spikes but also through accurate spike timing. This ability to catch temporary dynamics makes SNNs well-suited for tasks such as motor control, speech identification, and sensory perception. This asynchronous computing leads to natural compatibility with ultra-low-power consumption,

**TABLE 10.1** Applications of biomimicry in neuromorphic systems.

| Biological inspiration | Neuromorphic feature | Functional outcome |
|---|---|---|
| Neurons and synapses | Spiking neuron circuits | Temporal pattern processing |
| Synaptic plasticity | On-chip learning | Adaptive decision-making |
| Cortical modularity | Parallel architecture | Real-time multitasking |
| Brain's energy model | Event-driven processing | Ultra-low-power operation |
| Neuroplasticity | Self-modifying networks | Lifelong learning |

high computational efficiency, and neuromorphic processors, closely aligning with the energy-skilled design of organic systems. SNN also integrates biological learning rules, allowing them to be autonomous to new inputs in a self-organizing manner. They take advantage of the mechanisms seen in the brain, such as Hebbian learning and STDP, to refine their reactions over time. In addition, SNNs employ biologically admirable neuron models, which include the dripped integrated-and-fire, Izhikevich, and Hodgkin-Huxley models, which reiterate the required neuronal behavior such as membrane potential accumulation, firing thresholds, and malicious periods.

One of their most powerful abilities lies in spatiotemporal pattern recognition, where SNN Excel is in the detection of complex patterns during time and location. This makes them highly effective in explaining biological signals, including EEG and ECoG rhythm, Electromyography (EMG) muscle activation patterns, and multimodal sensory input. By combining temporal coding, event-powered efficiency, and biologically grounded learning, SNNs bridge the gap between artificial calculations and natural nervous processing, establishing themselves as an important basis for neuromorphic computing and advanced BCI applications. This ability makes them ideal for real-time BCI applications where time matters, such as the intention of movement decoding or prosthetic control. A software system, written in Python using the NEST Simulator SNN library, is described. It is able to adapt continuously in real time in supervised or unsupervised mode (Rusev et al., 2025) (Table 10.2).

## 3. Architectural design of a biometric neuromorphic processor

This chapter presents architectural foundations and unique design options behind a biometric neuromorphic processor for real-time BCI applications in nerve rehabilitation. Inspired by the structure and function of the human brain,

**TABLE 10.2** Comparison of ANN versus SNN.

| Feature | Artificial neural network (ANN) | Spiking neural network (SNN) |
|---|---|---|
| Computation | Continuous, clock-driven | Event-driven, asynchronous |
| Data encoding | Numeric values (float32) | Spikes (binary events) |
| Learning rule | Backpropagation | STDP, Hebbian learning |
| Power efficiency | High | Low (due to sparse activation) |
| Biological realism | Low | High |

architecture enables phenomenal, parallel, and adaptive nerve computation with extremely low energy requirements—an essential feature for frontal and transplant systems. To realize energy-efficient and real-time capable devices, neuromorphic computing systems are envisaged as the core of next-generation systems for brain repair (Buccelli et al., 2019). Neuromorphic technology, which mimics the natural behavior of neurons and synapses, holds promise for replicating the encoding of natural touch, potentially informing neuro-stimulation design (Donati and Valle, 2024).

## 3.1 Hardware components and architecture

The neuromorphic processor is designed on a modular design that integrates several biologically inspired components at its core. The center has a neuro-synaptic core, which serves as fundamental processing units imitating the population of neurons and synapses. Each core includes a spike generator, a synaptic weight register to store and update connectivity strength and to simulate local integration, and threshold logic to simulate the neuronal membrane potential dynamics and neuronal membrane. These cores are interconnected through a routing fabric, which is a scalable spike communication network inspired by the brain's axonal routes. Using the address event representation (AER), the routing system supports asynchronous, packet-based communication while avoiding minimal delays and spike conflicts.

This core is applied through supplemented memory, on-chip SRAM, flash, or nonvolatile memory (NVM). This memory stores the synaptic weight, STDP markers, and neuron states such as membrane capacity and refractory periods. By coidentifying memory with computation, the architecture eliminates hurdles contained in the traditional von Neumann system, leading to high efficiency. A defined characteristic of this design is its asynchronous operation, as the system is clock-cum and handshake-operated; energy is consumed only when spikes are produced or received.

## 3.2 Phenomenon-power and parallel processing

The processor takes advantage of event-conduct calculation, a biologically induced mechanism in which neurons update their states only in response to the upcoming spikes. This ensures that no energy or computational resources are wasted on inactive neurons, which enables constant nerve signal monitoring without thermal or power boundaries. In addition, the architecture is naturally parallel, capable of supporting thousands of neurons simultaneously in several cores. Each core spikes independently and handles tasks such as spike arrival, signal forwarding, neuronal integration, and synaptic learning updates. It provides equality, combined with localized learning, advanced BCI applications, and the required scalability and adaptability for real-time nervous rehabilitation systems.

This massively parallel structure allows the simultaneous decoding of multiple nerve routes—ideal for complex BCI systems with motor, sensory, and cognitive areas. Neural interfaces continue to improve in channel count and form factor. Low-power machine learning and neuromorphic processors can be integrated onto neural devices (Yoo and Shoaran, 2021).

## 3.3 On-chip learning mechanism

A major feature of a neuromorphic processor is the ability to apply biologically induced learning algorithms directly in the hardware, enabling real-time adaptation and privatization. One of the primary mechanisms is STDP, where the local update calculates changes in the synaptic weight (δw) depending on the exact time between the presynaptic spike and the postsynaptic spikes. To achieve this, the processor stores the spike mark in embedded memory, allowing accurate temporary analysis for weight adjustment. In addition, the architecture covers the hardware pathway for Hebbian learning, which supports the correlation-based synaptic update after this theory that "cells that set fire together, wire together" (Fig. 10.3).

Organic synaptic transistors (OSTs) are key components in constructing artificial nerves, offering tunable synaptic plasticity for complex sensory processing and the mechanical flexibility required for applications in soft robotics and bioelectronics (Sung et al., 2025). Traditional BCIs are realized based on complementary metal oxide semiconductor (CMOS) technologies with complex, bulky, and low-biocompatible circuits and suffer from the low energy efficiency of the von Neumann architecture (Wan et al., 2024).

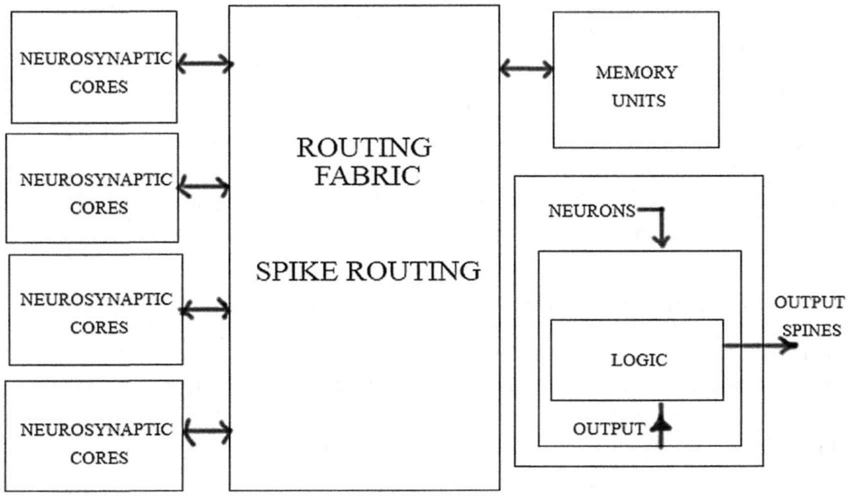


**FIGURE 10.3** Block diagram of processing.

### 3.4 Energy efficiency and real-time performance adaptation

The neuromorphic processor is specially engineered to achieve ultra-low-power consumption and real-time adaptability, making it extremely suitable for integration in the wearable BCI system. Microsecond-tier processing, while working in the subdialect range, balances efficiency with accountability while maintaining delays. This is completed through many design innovations. First, the subthreshold analog circuit applies the neuron model using transistors operating below the threshold voltage, which significantly reduces the current draw. Second, a low-power digital circuit is employed for tasks such as digital circuit spike routing, timing comparison, clock gating, and memory access, extending it by voltage scaling techniques. Importantly, the processor eliminates the requirement of a global clock, which depends on localized control to prevent unnecessary switching activity and synchronization delay. Finally, a real-time spike processing pipeline ensures high throughput, which enables rapid neuron updates with microsecond accuracy. Together, these features allow the processor to support continuous nerve monitoring and adaptive rehabilitation applications while remaining energy-efficient and portable.

## 4. Integration with the BCI system

Neuromorphic processors are inspired by computational principles of the biological nervous system, offering a paradigm change in BCI technology. BCIs in nervous rehabilitation rely on brain signals, low-level processing, and accurate decoding of adaptive responses. The integration of a biometric neuromorphic processor in the BCI platform not only enhances computational efficiency but also improves the compatibility of dynamic nerve patterns during rehabilitation. The increasing exploitation of closed-loop systems enabled with neuromorphic elements is due to their intrinsic energy efficiency, their capability to perform real-time data processing, and their mimicking of neurobiological computation for an improved synergy between the technological and biological counterparts (Chiappalone et al., 2022). Biocompatibility and mechanical matching of materials are the key problems that arise on the way to neural integration (Mikhaylov et al., 2020). The following subdivisions presented a detailed discussion of major aspects of integration, ranging from advanced sensor fusion techniques to nerve recording.

### 4.1 EEG, ECoG, and interfacing with intracortical signals

BCI systems acquire nerve activity using various recording methods, offering unique trade-offs in terms of each spatial resolution, invasion, and signal-to-noise ratio. The most widely used approach is EEG, a noninvasive technique that records electrical activity from the electrodes placed on the skull. The EEG is prone to lower spatial resolution and vulnerability to artifacts from muscles or environmental noise. To effectively integrate EEG with a neuromorphic processor, with multichannel synchronization to accurately map the nerve activity in various scalp regions, high performance Analog Front Fnd (AFEs) are required to prevent signal deformation.

A more aggressive but high-resolution method is ECoG, in which the electrode is placed directly on the cortical surface. Compared to EEG, ECoG provides better signal quality and can capture high-frequency oscillations (>70 Hz), which is especially valuable to decode the fine nerve mobility. However, this requires surgical intervention and is often limited by restricted electrode coverage. For real-time rehabilitation applications, the demands of integration include low-delay digitization and on-spectral decomposition to efficiently analyze high-gamma band activity (Fig. 10.4).

The most aggressive end of the spectrum is intracortical recording, where microelectrode arrays are transplanted within cortical tissue to catch single-unit or multi-unit nerve activity. This approach provides the highest spatial and temporal resolution, which enables decoding of fine motor intentions with remarkable accuracy. However, its clinical application faces challenges such as long-term stability and risk of tissue response. Effective integration requires a high-bandwidth AFE with nano-volt-level resolution and an on-chip spike sorting mechanism to reduce the data transmission load while maintaining real-time accountability.

### *4.1.1 Role of the neuromorphic processor in interfacing*

The biometric architecture of the processor allows direct handling of the event-powered spike data, eliminating the need for heavy batch processing. It supports asynchronous phenomena-based communications, enabling real-time

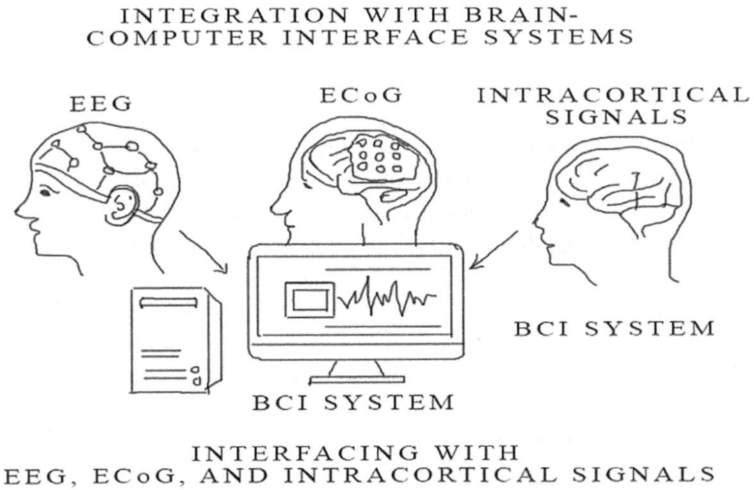


**FIGURE 10.4** Neuromorphic processor in interfacing.

interaction between recorded neural activity and rehabilitation control systems. The computation of the brain relies on the highly efficient communication among billions of neurons. Such efficiency derives from the brain's plastic and reconfigurable nature, enabling complex computations and maintenance of vital functions with a remarkably low power consumption of only ~20 watts (Bruno et al., 2023).

## 4.2 Signal acquisition and preprocessing

Efficient and accurate signal preprocessing is important to ensure that the downstream decoding algorithm receives clean, relevant data. Combining AI with advanced BCIs in the form of implantable neurotechnologies grants new possibilities for the diagnosis, prediction, and treatment of neurological and psychiatric disorders (Fares et al., 2022).

Major Preprocessing Phase: The preprocessing stage in BCI systems plays a crucial role in ensuring that neural signals are clean, reliable, and suitable for further decoding. The first step involves artifact removal, where contamination from eye blinks, muscle activity (EMG), and environmental noise is eliminated. Neuromorphic processors are particularly effective here, as they can implement spike-time-driven noise suppression mechanisms that mimic biological adaptation. Following this, filtering techniques such as band-pass filters are applied to isolate specific neural rhythms—like the alpha band (8–12 Hz), beta band (13–30 Hz), or high-gamma frequencies (70–200 Hz). These filters can be efficiently realized in hardware using low-power digital signal processing (DSP) blocks or memristive filter arrays, enabling real-time operation.

Next, spike detection and sorting are performed, where only event-driven neural activities are processed, significantly reducing energy consumption. Embedded on-chip unsupervised clustering algorithms, such as k-shape clustering or self-organizing maps, allow efficient classification of spikes into neuron-specific patterns. Finally, data compression is applied to reduce transmission bandwidth, which is critical for wireless and wearable BCIs. Event-based encoding naturally achieves this by ignoring silent periods in neural activity, ensuring that only meaningful information is transmitted for further analysis. Neuromorphic computing is a brain-inspired computing paradigm that aims to construct efficient, low-power, and adaptive computing systems by emulating the information processing mechanisms of biological neural systems (Zhu et al., 2023) (Fig. 10.5).

### *4.2.1 Effect on BCI*

On-chip proposing reduces delays, power consumption, and communication bottlenecks, which enables wearable and transplantable rehabilitation systems. A neuro-interface, or brain–machine interface, is a system of devices that utilizes the electrical nature of neural signals to establish communication with the nervous system (Khuntia and Manivannan, 2023).

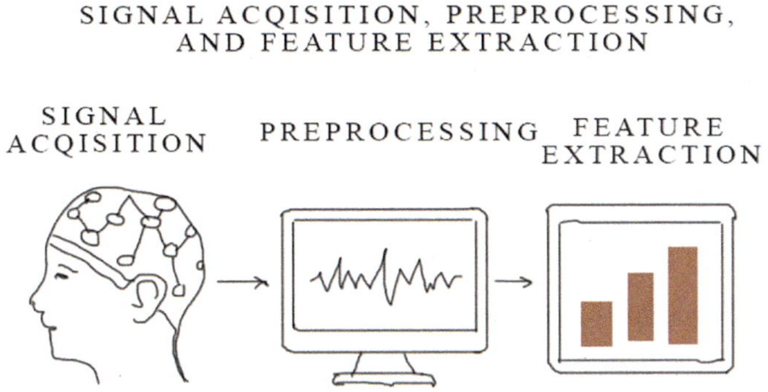


**FIGURE 10.5** Data processing.

## 4.3 Closed-loop reaction system

One of the defined characteristics of advanced BCI in rehabilitation is closed-loop architecture, where, in real time, nerve signals decoded to generate sensory, motor, or visual reactions are used. Bioelectronic medicine treats chronic diseases by sensing, processing, and modulating the electronic signals produced in the nervous system of the human body, labeled "neural signals" (Donati and Indiveri, 2023), critical components of future neural repair strategies and explore the most updated knowledge, progress, and challenges in the fields of cellular neuronal repair, neural interfacing, and neuro-rehabilitation (Krucoff et al., 2016).

### *4.3.1 Closed-loop flow*

1. Nerve signal acquisition
2. Real-time decoding on a neuromorphic processor
3. Response generation
4. Nerve adaptation through reinforcement.

### *4.3.2 Types of response*

- View: Display real-time movement on screen or in a VR headset.
- Hyptic: Providing tactile sensations through vibration motors or mechanical actuators.
- Electrical stimulation: providing functional electrical stimulation (FES) to the muscles.

### *4.3.3 Neuromorphic benefits*

The development of neuromorphic chips enables response generation in less than 50 milliseconds, falling within the human cerebro-motor integration window. This maximizes neuroplasticity changes. The investigation delves into the experimentally validated advantages of SNNs in comparison to alternative models like LSTM, while also critically examining the inherent limitations of SNN classifiers or algorithms (Kim and Kim, 2024). The bidirectional communication between living neurons and artificial devices is the main final goal of those studies. However, closed-loop systems not only based on visual feedback are still uncommon, mostly due to the requirement of multidisciplinary effort (Levi et al., 2018).

## 4.4 Sensor fusion for enhanced control

Relying only on nerve data can limit the strength, especially in a nonstable signal environment. A combination of many data sources improves reliability and purpose.

### *4.4.1 Supplementary sensor*

#### 4.4.1.1 Neuromorphic processor's role

- SNNs can integrate odd data currents in a biologically admirable manner, similar to multicentenary integration in the brain.
- A modality enables adaptive control even when temporarily incredible.

## 5. Performance evaluation

Evaluation of the performance of a biometric neuromorphic processor in nerve rehabilitation applications is important to display its benefits on traditional processing platforms, especially in power efficiency, delay, adaptability, and accuracy. This section compares the capabilities of the neuromorphic processor with the traditional DSP system, outlines the major performance matrix, and discusses implications for real-world deployment in rehabilitation settings. Brain–machine interfaces are promising tools to restore lost motor functions and probe brain functional mechanisms (Liu et al., 2020). The development of intelligent neuroprosthetics, which promise to augment human brain function, is vital for augmentative assistive technologies. Neuromorphic sensors and processors are particularly adept at mimicking the brain's efficient sensory processing, offering assistive devices an advanced capability to perceive and interpret complex environmental stimuli (Chandra et al., 2024). A field programmable gate array (FPGA) translates EEG signals into movements in the prosthesis. We also propose a new technique for selecting and grouping electrodes, which is related to the motor intentions of the subject (Chiappalone et al., 2022). Utilizing a spike-driven processor emerges as an alternative processing method, where the BCI offloads computations to the processor upon detecting spikes (Lee et al., 2024).

## 5.1 Comparison with traditional DSP system

Traditional DSP-based platforms are the backbone of several existing BCI systems. They offer challenges in high computational accuraty and flexible programming environments, but face challenges in power consumption, scalability, and event-operating adaptability, important aspects for educational or transplantable rehabilitation devices. Practical BCIs should be able to decipher brain signals and dynamically adapt to brain fluctuations (Liu et al., 2025) (Table 10.3).

### *5.1.1 Display benefits and interpretation of benchmarking protocol*

Neuromorphic processors provide significant benefits over traditional DSP systems due to their event-powered architecture. Unlike DSP, which processes all the incoming data continuously, neuromorphic processors remain active only when events occur, which ends unnecessary calculations and reduces power consumption significantly. Their mass similarity allows thousands of neurons and synapses to be operated simultaneously, which avoids the serial hurdles of DSP pipelines. In addition, by incorporating STDP, neuromorphic processors enable real-time adaptive learning, allowing the system to adapt to change the nerve patterns without the need for offline retraining.

**TABLE 10.3** Key comparative factors.

| Parameter | DSP-based system | Biomimetic neuromorphic processor | Improvement factor |
|---|---|---|---|
| **Power consumption** | 500–1000 mW | 10–50 mW | **10–50× lower** |
| **Processing latency** | 50–150 milliseconds | <10 milliseconds | 5–15× faster |
| **Architecture type** | Clock-driven, frame-based | Event-driven, spike-based | Context-aware operation |
| **Scalability** | Limited by clock speed and thermal constraints | Naturally parallel, supports large-scale neuron simulations | High |
| **Adaptability** | Software-tuned; requires frequent retraining | On-chip learning via STDP and online adaptation | Real-time |
| **Battery life (wearable)** | 6–8 hours | 1–3 days | ~4× longer |

To ensure a proper assessment of these benefits, a standardized benchmarking protocol was installed. First, the dataset was carefully selected, including EEG and ECoG recordings from motor imagery, prosthetic control, and neurofeedback trials, as well as an intracortical spike-training dataset for high-resolution decoding tasks. Subsequently, both DSP and neuromorphic systems were tested under similar processing conditions, exhibiting equivalent processing phases (artifact removal and band-pass filtering) and classification works. System-level performance was then measured in the context of accuracy (intended movements or correct classification of cognitive states), delay (time for reaction execution), adaptability (system display in sessions without retraining), and energy efficiency (measured as per classification decision). This benchmarking framework provides a wide comparison, stating how neuromorphic processors achieve better efficiency.

Performance of biometric neuromorphic processors in nerve rehabilitation BCIs can be evaluated in four major dimensions: accuracy, delay, adaptability, and energy efficiency. First, the system consistently acquires classification accuracy of about 90% in various forms of EEG, ECoG, and intracortical signals. This performance is further strengthened by online learning abilities, which reduce the need for frequent renovation and enhance long-term purposes. Second, the delay remains below 10 milliseconds, which enables the uninterrupted real-time control of motor functions and immediate sensory response during cognitive training. This response time is significantly faster than the human conceptual range of 50–100 milliseconds, causing users to increase immersion and interaction loyalty. Third, adaptability, reflected by an average score of 0.88, highlights the ability of the processor; they throw light on the ability to deal with day-to-day variability in nervous signals arising from factors such as fatigue, learning progress, or recovery stages.

Finally, the power-efficient batteries translate into a life three to four times longer, which supports the use of the wearable or implanted system for multiday use without the need for frequent recharging. Collectively, these metrics have important implications for real-world deployment. Clinically, the reliability of the system also ensures frequent decoding performance even in the atmosphere of uncontrolled home use, while patient comfort is extended by lower heat wastage and lighter designs with long-term operating lifespan. In addition, the scalability and portability of neuromorphic BCI platforms make them particularly suitable for deployment in rural or resource-limited settings, where the main power and access to the clinical infrastructure can be limited, thus making access to nerve rehabilitation technologies widespread.

## 6. Summary and future approach

The integration of the biometric neuromorphic processor in the BCI system marks a transformational advancement in the field of nerve rehabilitation. By imitating computational strategies of the human brain—through phenomenon-powered architecture, parallel processing, and adaptive learning—these processors cross many boundaries of traditional DSP systems, especially in the context of delay, energy efficiency, adaptability, and science. This chapter detected architectural foundations, system integration strategies, performance benchmarks, clinical applications, and future challenges of BCI.

From an architectural point of view, neuromorphic processors work in an event-driven way, only processing nerve spikes when meaningful events occur. The design acquires 10–50× lower power consumption than the traditional DSP, while their underlying equality supports real-time, multichannel nerve decoding for both motor and cognitive rehabilitation. In terms of system integration, these processors originally interface with EEG, ECoG, and intracortical recording systems, which support a spectrum of applications for aggressive, high-cocoa neural prosthetic controls from noninvasive home-based treatments. On-chip preprocessing capabilities—which include deformation evidence removal, filtering, and spike sorting—not only reduce transmission overheads but also increase portability and system efficiency. The clinical capacity of neuromorphic BCI is sufficient for motor control restoration, nerve artificial aid, adaptive neurofeedback, and individual rehabilitation protocols, which are aimed at improving all patient recovery results. Case studies and benchmarking results have demonstrated promising performances, classification accuracy of more than 90%, delay under 10 milliseconds, and consistent power consumption with battery-powered week-enabled equipment.

Despite these advances, many major challenges remain. Scalability and miniaturization are important to support high-density nerve processing while maintaining a user-friendly, wearable form factor. Ethical ideas in nerve data handling—especially about privacy and security—should be addressed through strong policies and technical safety measures. In addition, it is necessary to ensure that both patients and systems are developed in the forefront to ensure that the human–machine collaboration is developed, maintaining the engagement and maximizing the neuroplasticity profit. Finally, coordinated, multidisciplinary efforts, rigorous verification through clinical trials coordinated to successful clinical translation, and cost-effective manufacturing strategies will be required to make these techniques widely accessible.

## References

Aboumerhi, K., Güemes, A., Liu, H., Tenore, F., Etienne-Cummings, R., 2023. Neuromorphic applications in medicine. J. Neural. Eng. 20 (4), 041004. https://doi.org/10.1088/1741-2552/aceca3.

Beaubois, R., Cheslet, J., Duenki, T., De Venuto, G., Carè, M., Khoyratee, F., Chiappalone, M., Branchereau, P., Ikeuchi, Y., Levi, T., 2024. BiœmuS: a new tool for neurological disorders studies through real-time emulation and hybridization using biomimetic spiking neural network. Nat. Commun. 15 (1). https://doi.org/10.1038/s41467-024-48905-x.

Broccard, F.D., Joshi, S., Wang, J., Cauwenberghs, G., 2017. Neuromorphic neural interfaces: from neurophysiological inspiration to biohybrid coupling with nervous systems. J. Neural. Eng. 14 (4), 041002. https://doi.org/10.1088/1741-2552/aa67a9.

Bruno, U., Mariano, A., Rana, D., Gemmeke, T., Musall, S., Santoro, F., 2023. From neuromorphic to neurohybrid: transition from the emulation to the integration of neuronal networks. Neuromorph. Comput. Eng. 3 (2), 023002. https://doi.org/10.1088/2634-4386/acc683.

Buccelli, S., Bornat, Y., Colombi, I., Ambroise, M., Martines, L., Pasquale, V., Bisio, M., Tessadori, J., Nowak, P., Grassia, F., Averna, A., Tedesco, M., Bonifazi, P., Difato, F., Massobrio, P., Levi, T., Chiappalone, M., 2019. A neuromorphic prosthesis to restore communication in neuronal networks. iScience 19, 402–414. https://doi.org/10.1016/j.isci.2019.07.046.

Chandra, G.V.S.A., Ananthakumar, B., Raghavan, R., 2024. Enhancing Assistive Technologies with Neuromorphic Computing Revolutionizing AI with Brain-Inspired Technology: Neuromorphic Computing. IGI Global, India, pp. 207–232. https://doi.org/10.4018/979-8-3693-6303-4.ch009.

Chiappalone, M., Cota, V.R., Carè, M., Di Florio, M., Beaubois, R., Buccelli, S., Barban, F., Brofiga, M., Averna, A., Bonacini, F., Guggenmos, D.J., Bornat, Y., Massobrio, P., Bonifazi, P., Levi, T., 2022. Neuromorphic-based neuroprostheses for brain rewiring: state-of-the-art and perspectives in neuroengineering. Brain Sci. 12 (11), 1578. https://doi.org/10.3390/brainsci12111578.

Donati, E., Indiveri, G., 2023. Neuromorphic bioelectronic medicine for nervous system interfaces: from neural computational primitives to medical applications. Prog. Biomed. Eng. 5 (1), 013002.

Donati, E., Valle, G., 2024. Neuromorphic hardware for somatosensory neuroprostheses. Nat. Commun. 15 (1). https://doi.org/10.1038/s41467-024-44723-3.

Fares, H., Ronchini, M., Zamani, M., Farkhani, H., Chiappalone, M., Neftci, E., Moradi, F., 2022. In the realm of hybrid brain: human brain and AI. arXiv. https://doi.org/10.48550/arXiv.2210.01461.

Khuntia, P.K., Manivannan, P.V., 2023. Review of neural interfaces: means for establishing brain–machine communication. SN Comput. Sci. 4 (5). https://doi.org/10.1007/s42979-023-02160-x.

Kim, E., Kim, Y., 2024. Exploring the potential of spiking neural networks in biomedical applications: advantages, limitations, and future perspectives. Biomed. Eng. Lett. 14 (5), 967–980. https://doi.org/10.1007/s13534-024-00403-1.

Krucoff, M.O., Rahimpour, S., Slutzky, M.W., Edgerton, V.R., Turner, D.A., 2016. Enhancing nervous system recovery through neurobiologics, neural interface training, and neurorehabilitation. Front. Neurosci. 10. https://doi.org/10.3389/fnins.2016.00584.

Lee, H., Jang, Y., Jung, D., Song, S., Kim, J., November 2024. Rearchitecting a neuromorphic processor for spike-driven brain-computer interfacing. In: 2024 57th IEEE/ACM International Symposium on Microarchitecture (MICRO). IEEE, pp. 1073–1089.

Levi, T., Bonifazi, P., Massobrio, P., Chiappalone, M., 2018. Closed-loop systems for next-generation neuroprostheses. Front. Neurosci. 12, 26.

Liu, Z., Tang, J., Gao, B., Yao, P., Li, X., Liu, D., Zhou, Y., Qian, H., Hong, B., Wu, H., 2020. Neural signal analysis with memristor arrays towards high-efficiency brain–machine interfaces. Nat. Commun. 11 (1). https://doi.org/10.1038/s41467-020-18105-4.

Liu, Z., Mei, J., Tang, J., Xu, M., Gao, B., Wang, K., Ding, S., Qi, L., Qi, Q., Chen, W., Yue, X., Li, Y., Peng, Y., Han, Z., Wong, N., He, Q., Hong, B., Jung, T.-P., Dong, M., Wu, H., 2025. A memristor-based adaptive neuromorphic decoder for brain–computer interfaces. Nat. Electron. 8 (4), 362–372. https://doi.org/10.1038/s41928-025-01340-2.

Mikhaylov, A., Pimashkin, A., Pigareva, Y., Gerasimova, S., Gryaznov, E., Shchanikov, S., Spagnolo, B., 2020. Neurohybrid memristive CMOS-integrated systems for biosensors and neuroprosthetics. Front. Neurosci. 14, 358.

Raikar, A.S., Andrew, J., Dessai, P.P., Prabhu, S.M., Jathar, S., Prabhu, A., Naik, M.B., Raikar, G. V.S., 2024. Neuromorphic computing for modeling neurological and psychiatric disorders: implications for drug development. Artif. Intell. Rev. 57 (12). https://doi.org/10.1007/s10462-024-10948-3.

Rusev, G., Yordanov, S., Nedelcheva, S., Banderov, A., Sauter-Starace, F., Koprinkova-Hristova, P., Kasabov, N., 2025. Decoding brain signals in a neuromorphic framework for a personalized adaptive control of human prosthetics. Biomimetics 10 (3), 183. https://doi.org/10.3390/biomimetics10030183.

Sung, M.J., Kim, K.N., Kim, C., Lee, H.H., Lee, S.W., Kim, S., Seo, D.G., Zhou, H., Lee, T.W., 2025. Organic artificial nerves: neuromorphic robotics and bioelectronics. Chem. Rev. 125 (5), 2625–2664. https://doi.org/10.1021/acs.chemrev.4c00571.

Wan, C., Pei, M., Shi, K., Cui, H., Long, H., Qiao, L., Xing, Q., Wan, Q., 2024. Toward a brain–neuromorphics interface. Adv. Mater. 36 (37). https://doi.org/10.1002/adma.202311288.

Yoo, J., Shoaran, M., 2021. Neural interface systems with on-device computing: machine learning and neuromorphic architectures. Curr. Opin. Biotechnol. 72, 95–101. https://doi.org/10.1016/j.copbio.2021.10.012.

Zhu, Y., Mao, H., Zhu, Y., Wang, X., Fu, C., Ke, S., Wan, C., Wan, Q., 2023. CMOS-compatible neuromorphic devices for neuromorphic perception and computing: a review. Int. J. Extrem. Manuf. 5 (4), 042010. https://doi.org/10.1088/2631-7990/acef79.

Chapter 11

# Neuromorphic solutions for sustainable smart cities: A brain computer interface perspective

S. Palanivel Rajan[1] and M.G. Rajendrakumar[2]
[1]*Department of Electronics and Communication Engineering, Rathinam Technical Campus, Coimbatore, Tamil Nadu, India;* [2]*Department of Electronics Engineering (VLSI Design and Technology), Velammal College of Engineering and Technology, Madurai, Tamil Nadu, India*

## 1. Introduction

### 1.1 Introduction to smart cities

In recent years, the concept of smart cities has revolutionized city planning and management using the potential of digital technologies and data analytics to optimize urban systems. Smart cities use a combination of Information and Communication Technology (ICT), Internet of Things (IoT) sensors, and artificial intelligence (AI) to track and govern key urban services, such as transportation, energy, waste management, and public safety. The ultimate goal of smart cities is to increase sustainability, livability, and efficiency, creating environments that promote human well-being and environmental stewardship (Firoozi and Firoozi, 2024; Hashem et al., 2016; Huang et al., 2025).

As urban issues become increasingly complicated, cities are turning toward neuromorphic computing—brain-inspired computing—to provide adaptive, energy-efficient solutions to urban issues. Neuromorphic systems, which mimic the brain's natural operations using spiking neural networks (SNNs) (Fang et al., 2020), can potentially be at the vanguard of smart city technologies, enabling real-time processing, dynamic adaptation to changing conditions, and energy-efficient solutions. This chapter explores how neuromorphic computing can enhance the existing smart city infrastructure and enable more sustainable, responsive, and efficient cities.

**Neuromorphic Computing for Brain Computer Interfaces. https://doi.org/10.1016/B978-0-443-41594-4.00006-X**

### *1.1.1 Defining a smart city*

A smart city leverages advanced technologies for effective management of resources. Smart cities enhance public facilities, infrastructure, and sustainability through digital integration. The most basic nature of a smart city is collecting information from various resources and interpreting data to make strategic choices and design improved urban environments.

Smart cities use technologies, such as IoT sensors, artificial intelligence, and machine learning, to manage anything from energy supply to traffic control. Through the use of neuromorphic systems, smart cities can also scale their ability to react to unpredictable urban situations, such as shifting energy demand, unexpected changes in traffic flow, or a spontaneous security incident (Wu et al., 2024).

### *1.1.2 Key components of smart cities*

#### 1.1.2.1 Information and Communication Technology (ICT)

ICT facilitates the smart city by allowing data collection, storage, and analysis from city infrastructure. The information yields insights for optimization.

Neuromorphic computing enhances ICT infrastructure in smart cities by enabling quicker decision-making and adaptive actions, enhancing the quality of the delivery of services.

Example: Singapore's Smart Nation initiative uses sensor and device data to control traffic and water flow. Neuromorphic systems handle this data more efficiently, enabling real-time response to changes.

#### 1.1.2.2 Urban infrastructure and smart services

Smart cities would feature the adoption of innovative technologies for modernizing city buildings and city services in areas, such as transportation, electricity, and sewage. Neuromorphic computing would prove useful by rendering structures and systems adaptable and efficient (Huang et al., 2022).

Example: Barcelona employs smart sensors for waste collection to optimize collection routes. Neuromorphic computing can reliably predict waste patterns and dynamically adjust schedules, offering an energy-efficient solution.

#### 1.1.2.3 Sustainability in smart cities

Sustainability is essential in smart cities (Lemmers-Jansen et al., 2020). They use smart technology to save energy, water, and waste in a productive way, with an aim to minimize carbon footprints and save resources. Neuromorphic systems excel in energy management by dynamically adapting to changing energy needs in real time.

Example: Los Angeles uses smart grids to manage power. Neuromorphic computing can help this by enabling real-time response to shifting demand (Banerjee et al., 2020), optimizing energy distribution, and enhancing grid stability.

#### 1.1.2.4 Data-driven decision-making

Data drives the smart city ecosystem. With the use of big data from urban systems, cities can streamline resource allocation and service delivery. High-speed data processing and flexibility of neuromorphic computing are crucial for real-time decision-making.

### *1.1.3 Benefits of smart cities*

#### 1.1.3.1 Improved quality of life

Smart cities enhance the urban services using technology to enhance the quality of life for its people. Neuromorphic computing can do even better by providing energy-efficient, adaptive solutions for city problems (Yu et al., 2017).

Example: Dubai integrates intelligent homes with networked devices to track and manage energy consumption, optimizing comfort and reducing use. Neuromorphic systems can potentially manage energy in real-time, saving money and improving comfort.

#### 1.1.3.2 Economic growth

Smart cities drive economic development by encouraging innovation, investment, and the generation of infrastructure and tech jobs. Smart neuromorphic computing-based systems make things more efficient, and additional economic gains are realized.

Example: San Francisco is a technological global center due to its smart infrastructure that supports the technology ecosystem. Neuromorphic technologies complement this by maximizing resource utilization and data processing.

#### 1.1.3.3 Environmental sustainability

Green technologies, such as solar power, efficient buildings, and smart grids, are advantageous for smart cities. Neuromorphic networks minimize wastage of energy, decrease the carbon footprint, and optimize energy management.

Example: Copenhagen hopes to become carbon neutral in 2025 with the help of solar panels, intelligent water management, and green building technology. Neuromorphic computing may enhance energy efficiency to help with greater sustainability.

### *1.1.4 Conclusion*

The implementation of smart city technologies has the potential to dramatically improve urban living by making cities more efficient, sustainable, and responsive. Neuromorphic computing, with its ability to simulate real-time data processing and adapt to changing conditions, is set to enhance smart city initiatives further. By offering energy-efficient solutions, dynamic decision-making capabilities, and real-time adaptability, neuromorphic systems will help create cities that not only meet the needs of their residents but also contribute to a more sustainable urban future.

## 1.2 Introduction to neuromorphic computing

Neuromorphic computing is a brain-inspired computational model derived from the brain's structure, function, and processes (Zhang et al., 2025). Neuromorphic computing differs from the conventional computing systems, which depend on von Neumann architectures, in that it emulates the brain's approach to information processing through brain-inspired models of computation. The objective is to design systems that are capable of executing complex cognitive operations efficiently while being energy-efficient, real-time adaptive, and capable of managing dynamic, uncertain environments.

Neuromorphic systems are typically built on SNNs, a neural network model that attempts to model the functioning of biological neurons more realistically than standard artificial neural networks (ANNs). In biological neural systems, neurons communicate information through discrete electrical spikes or pulses, which are transmitted between neurons by synapses. The spike frequency and timing carry information and are therefore the basis of data encoding within the brain. This is known as spike-timing-dependent plasticity (STDP) and is a basic learning process in biological and neuromorphic systems (Huang et al., 2022).

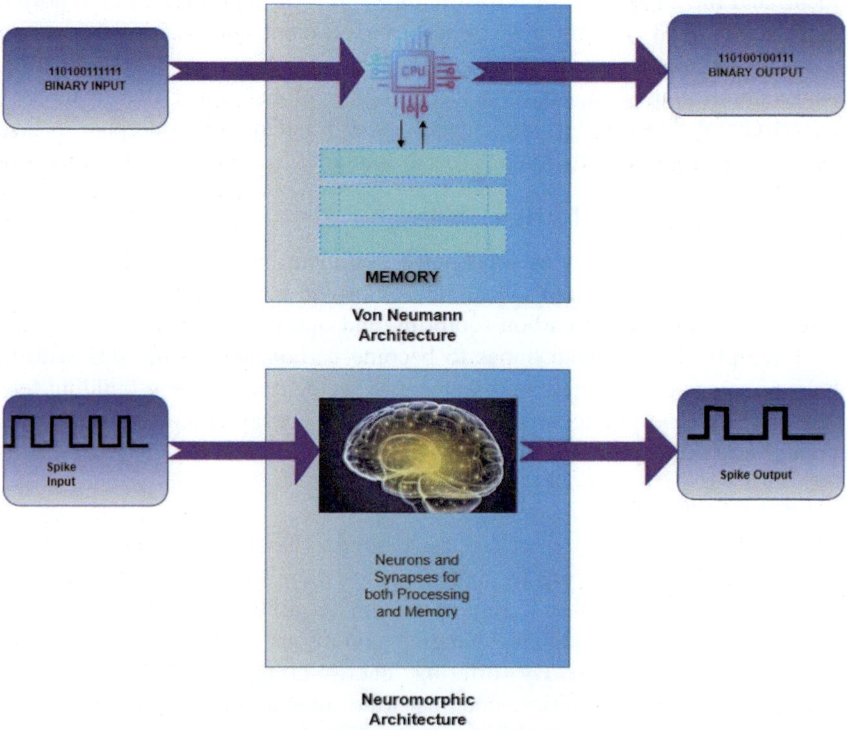

| Aspect | Von Neumann architecture | Neuromorphic architecture |
|---|---|---|
| Architecture | CPU connected to memory | Neural network (neurons and synapses for both processing and memory) |
| Processing style | Sequential processing | Massively parallel processing |
| Computation and memory | Separated computation and memory | Collocated processing and memory |
| Data representation | Binary data | Spikes |
| Processing type | Synchronous (clock-driven) | Asynchronous (event-driven) |
| Operation | Operation based on binary data | Operation based on SNN |
| Organization | Organized around CPU and memory | Organized around neurons and synapses |
| Communication | Binary data communication | Communication through spikes |

### *1.2.1 Spiking neural networks (SNNs)*

SNNs play an important role in neuromorphic computing. Unlike regular ANNs, which use smooth signals and simple activation methods, SNNs better simulate the operation of neurons with discrete spikes or pulses. In an SNN, a neuron sums up the incoming spikes over time, and when the total signal crosses a threshold, the neuron "fires" by sending a spike to other neurons. This firing process, coupled with the accurate timing of spikes, makes SNNs process information very efficiently, especially in applications involving fast changes and time-based processing.

The primary distinction between SNNs (Fang et al., 2020) and traditional ANNs is how the information is processed and encoded. In ANNs, information is encoded by representing the data in the form of continuous values and neurons processing through the application of activation functions (such as sigmoid and Rectified Linear Unit (ReLU)) to the values. In SNNs, information is encoded by the spike time, with neurons getting activated only if the input value exceeds a threshold value, and the exact time of the spikes holds meaningful information. This makes SNNs process information more biologically plausible, closer to the dynamics of biological brains.

### *1.2.2 Event-driven architectures in neuromorphic computing*

Event-Driven Architecture: One of the major advantages of neuromorphic computing and SNNs, in particular, is their ability to function in event-driven architectures. In these systems, neurons do not keep processing data continuously; they only act on meaningful events—the spikes. This event-driven nature leads to a low-power system in which the neuron consumes computational resources only if there is relevant information to process (Shrestha et al., 2022). This efficiency will be critical in smart cities where energy is constrained, and real-time responsiveness is key.

### 1.2.3 Neuromorphic computing and its relevance to smart cities

Smart cities are likely to have challenges that neuromorphic computing can help solve as it can deal with dynamic, real-time data and changing needs. Regular computing systems face tough times to handle the changing data from IoT systems and sensors. Neuromorphic systems can manage this type of data in an easy manner.

They can effectively and adaptively handle data, making them suitable for energy management, waste optimization, and environmental monitoring.

SNNs are great at processing data quickly, which is useful for things, such as managing traffic systems or predicting if a location needs energy. Neuromorphic systems can modify their functioning when there are changes in traffic or energy. They communicate only what is required and avoid computing all the time. They can react quickly and efficiently.

In general, neuromorphic is a good solution for smart cities challenges, which are becoming more complex. Neuromorphic systems imitate the brain's ability to process information.

# 2. Background and motivation

## 2.1 Why smart cities need neuromorphic solutions

The emergence of smart cities has driven the need for innovative solutions to tackle the dynamic and real-time challenges they face. As urban areas become more connected and data-rich, they generate vast amounts of real-time information that must be processed and acted upon swiftly. Traditional computing systems, especially ANNs, while effective in many domains, are not well-suited for the fast-paced, energy-sensitive demands of smart cities.

### 2.1.1 Limitations of current technology (traditional neural networks)

Traditional computing models rely on sequential processing, which means data is processed one step at a time, and the systems often need to work continuously even when no new information is available. This approach leads to higher energy consumption and longer processing times, both of which are unsuitable for smart city applications where real-time data processing is critical.

For instance, in a traffic management system, the system needs to adjust light signals based on real-time traffic data. A traditional system may process traffic data sequentially, which can result in delays and inefficiencies in response to traffic flow changes. Additionally, such systems may require continuous computation, leading to excessive energy use.

### 2.1.2 How neuromorphic computing addresses these challenges

Neuromorphic computing, through SNNs, mimics the brain's way of processing information, enabling systems to respond only when meaningful data is available. This event-driven architecture significantly reduces energy consumption because computations occur only in response to significant data spikes (events), instead of continuously running processes. In a smart city context, neuromorphic systems can process data in real time, adapting dynamically to sudden changes in traffic patterns, energy demand, or even public safety alerts.

For example, in energy management, neuromorphic systems can predict demand spikes and adjust distribution systems dynamically, ensuring optimal energy use with minimal waste.

By operating asynchronously and being adaptive, neuromorphic systems are more efficient, not only in terms of energy but also in processing time, allowing smart cities to better manage their resources and improve real-time decision-making.

### 2.2 Technological gaps

Although the technologies powering smart cities have advanced significantly, there remain key technological gaps that hinder their full potential.

Data Handling and Processing: Smart cities are constantly churning out huge volumes of real-time data, but traditional computing systems often find it hard to keep pace. Most of these systems are built for batch processing, which just does not cut it when quick responses are essential. Enter neuromorphic computing, which revolutionizes the scene by handling multiple data streams at once, ensuring that information is analyzed the moment it is created.

Energy Efficiency: Efficient energy management is crucial for smart cities, yet many current systems depend on outdated computing architectures that guzzle power. Neuromorphic computing presents a smarter solution—it processes data only when necessary, significantly reducing energy consumption compared with traditional systems that are always running.

Adaptability and Real-Time Processing: Smart cities require technology that can swiftly adapt to unexpected changes, such as sudden traffic jams or power fluctuations. Traditional computing systems often falter in these situations, while neuromorphic systems are built to respond in real time. Mimicking the human brain, they dynamically adjust and make quick decisions as new information flows in.

## 3. Fundamentals of neuromorphic computing

### 3.1 Spiking neural networks (SNNs)

SNNs are a fascinating and advanced type of neural network that draws inspiration from the biological neural systems in our brains. Unlike traditional ANNs, which handle information using smooth, continuous values and rely on standard activation functions, such as sigmoid or ReLU, SNNs replicate the way our biological neurons communicate and process information through discrete spikes or pulses.

### 3.1.1 The concept of spiking neural networks (SNNs)

At their essence, SNNs are designed around a neuron model that mirrors biological systems. In our brains, neurons send information by generating electrical spikes. These spikes are not continuous; they happen when a neuron gathers enough electrical charge to surpass a specific threshold. Once that threshold is crossed, the neuron "fires," sending a spike to its neighboring neurons. The precise timing of these spikes is crucial, as the patterns they create over time play a vital role in learning and decision-making.

In SNNs, neurons interact in a similar fashion. Rather than processing data in a continuous flow, the network works with discrete spikes that occur when a neuron hits a certain threshold. The intervals between spikes (known as spike-timing) and the frequency of these spikes are used to encode and convey information. This unique way of processing data through spikes is referred to as STDP, and it is fundamental for learning within these networks.

### 3.1.2 SNNs versus traditional artificial neural networks (ANNs)

While SNNs and traditional ANNs have some things in common—like being made up of layers of neurons linked by synapses—they also have some pretty significant differences that make them unique. Here is a breakdown of the main distinctions between these two systems:

#### 3.1.2.1 Data representation and processing

- SNNs: In SNNs, data is represented through discrete spikes. These spikes happen when a neuron gathers enough input to hit a firing threshold. The timing and frequency of these spikes carry the information. SNNs also embrace event-driven processing, meaning neurons only react to significant events (the spikes), which greatly boosts energy efficiency.
- ANNs: On the other hand, ANNs represent data as continuous values (think real numbers) that flow through the activation functions, such as sigmoid, tanh, or ReLU. These networks are always on, processing data continuously and sequentially, which means they are crunching numbers all the time, even if there is no new information coming in.

#### 3.1.2.2 Efficiency

- SNNs: A major perk of SNNs is their energy efficiency. Since they only process data when a neuron spikes, there is a lot less computational overhead compared with ANNs. Unlike traditional systems that are always running, SNNs only compute when necessary, making them especially useful in resource-limited settings, such as smart cities.

- ANNs: In contrast, ANNs are always in action, often performing calculations even when there is no new data to process. This constant activity leads to higher energy consumption, making ANNs less efficient in dynamic environments that need real-time, low-energy solutions.

#### 3.1.2.3 Adaptability

- SNNs: SNNs are incredibly adaptable because they are designed to replicate how our brains learn from the timing of spikes. Thanks to mechanisms such as STDP, SNNs can modify their synaptic connections based on the exact timing of these spikes. This allows them to learn and adjust to new inputs on the fly. Their adaptability makes them a perfect fit for environments that are constantly changing, like smart cities dealing with varying traffic, energy needs, or waste production.
- ANNs: On the flip side, while ANNs are great at learning and generalizing from data, their adaptation is not quite as dynamic as that of SNNs. ANNs tweak their weights based on activation values using standard backpropagation methods, which can be a bit slower and less flexible when real-time adjustments are necessary.

#### 3.1.2.4 Real-time processing

- SNNs: Thanks to their event-driven design, SNNs shine in real-time processing. They can swiftly react to sudden changes—such as shifts in traffic flow or spikes in energy demand—without needing constant computation. This makes them ideal for applications that require quick decision-making, such as traffic management systems or dynamic energy grids in smart cities.
- ANNs: In contrast, traditional neural networks handle data in a more static and sequential way, which can slow them down when it comes to processing real-time data, especially when dealing with large datasets and rapid input changes.

#### 3.1.2.5 Learning mechanisms

- SNNs: STDP is a key learning principle for SNNs. It works by adjusting the strength of synapses based on when the spikes from pre- and post-synaptic neurons occur. This mechanism enables SNNs to pick up on temporal patterns in data, which is especially useful for real-time sensor information or tasks, such as predicting traffic flow and managing energy distribution.
- ANNs: ANNs, on the other hand, usually depend on techniques, such as gradient descent and backpropagation to learn from data. These approaches tweak the weights of neurons according to error signals derived from the output. Although they work well for a variety of tasks, they do not quite capture the temporal dynamics of data as effectively as SNNs.

Comparison of SNNs and ANNs

| Aspect | SNNs | ANNs |
|---|---|---|
| Data Representation | Discrete spikes, time-based | Continuous values, activation functions |
| Processing Style | Event-driven, parallel | Sequential, continuous processing |
| Energy Efficiency | Highly energy-efficient (event-driven) | Energy-inefficient (continuous processing) |
| Real-Time Adaptation | Highly adaptive, learns from timing patterns (STDP) | Less adaptive, based on backpropagation |
| Learning Mechanism | Spike-timing-dependent plasticity (STDP) | Gradient descent, backpropagation |
| Real-Time Processing | Excellent real-time response, event-driven | Slower real-time response, continuous processing |
| Adaptability | Adapt to changing conditions in real-time | Adapts slower, based on training data |

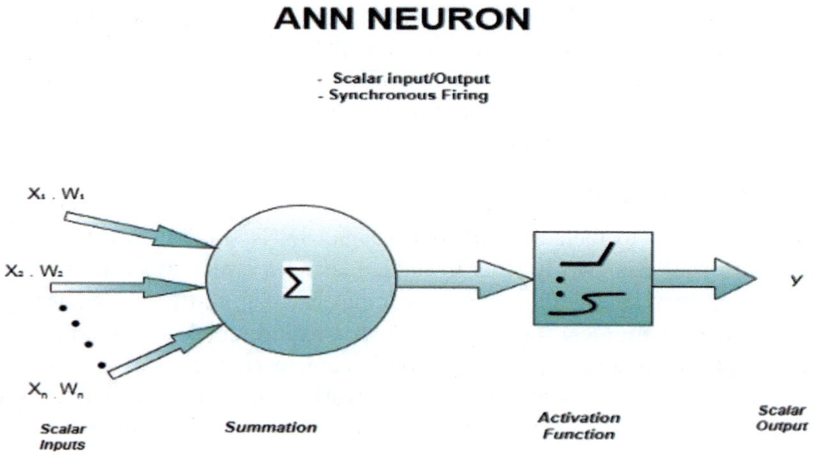


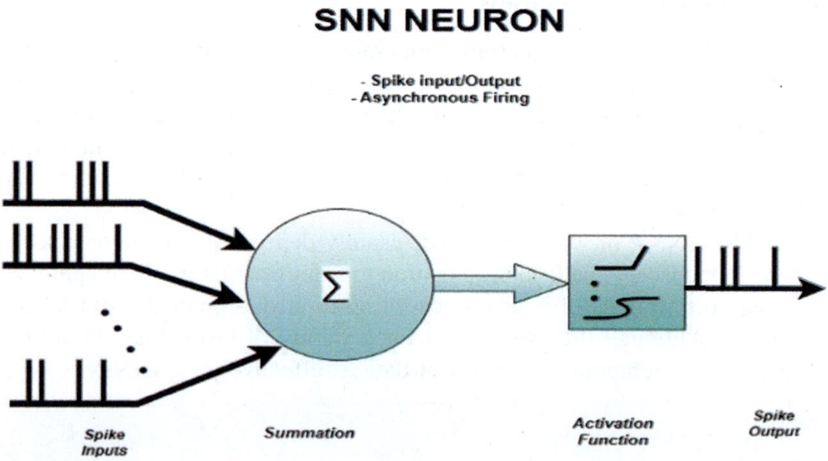

### 3.1.3 ANN neuron versus SNN neuron: Key differences in design and functionality

In the world of ANNs and SNNs, there are some key differences in how information is processed, communicated, and output by neurons. The following analysis compares ANN and SNN neurons, focusing on their unique characteristics in terms of input–output behavior, firing mechanisms, and the use of activation functions.

### 3.1.4 ANN neuron

The ANN neuron serves as the backbone of many traditional machine learning systems. It works with scalar inputs and outputs, with all neurons firing at the same time:

- **Scalar Input/Output:** The inputs to an ANN neuron are scalar values that represent numerical data. These inputs are weighted and summed up, resulting in a single scalar output that moves forward in the network.
- **Synchronous Firing:** In an ANN, all neurons process inputs and activate simultaneously. This means that at each step, every neuron performs the same function at once, making computations quick and efficient for certain types of problems.
- **Summation:** The inputs are multiplied by their respective weights (like X1·W1, X2·W2, Xn·Wn) and summed within the neuron. This summation reflects the combined input that gets sent to the activation function.
- **Activation Function:** Once the weighted inputs are summed, the result goes through an activation function, which decides the neuron's output. This function can be linear or nonlinear (like sigmoid or ReLU), adding nonlinearity to the system and enabling the network to learn complex patterns.
- **Output:** The final output is a scalar value derived from the activation function, which is then used for further computations or decision-making.

### 3.1.5 SNN neuron

The SNN neuron is a model that takes inspiration from biology, aiming to replicate how real neurons function in our brains. Unlike traditional ANNs, SNN neurons work with spike-based inputs and outputs, firing at different times:

- **Spike Input/Output:** Instead of receiving a single value, an SNN neuron gets a series of spikes that signify distinct events over time. These spikes are produced by incoming neurons once they hit a specific threshold.
- **Asynchronous Firing:** In an SNN, neurons do not fire all at once; they activate at different moments based on when they get enough input to surpass their threshold. This asynchronous behavior enables SNNs to

handle time-sensitive information, making them particularly effective for tasks that involve real-time data or temporal patterns.

- **Summation:** Like ANNs, SNN neurons sum up incoming spikes, but they also consider the timing of these spikes. This focus on timing allows SNNs to efficiently capture and process dynamic, real-time data.
- **Activation Function:** SNN neurons utilize an activation function to manage the summed input, similar to ANN neurons. However, the crucial difference is that the output of an SNN neuron is not a single value; instead, it is a spike that gets sent asynchronously to the next layer in the network.
- **Spike Output:** The outcome of this activation is a spike that travels to connected neurons. This method of asynchronous spike-based communication is not only more energy-efficient but also enables SNNs to process information with significantly lower power consumption compared to ANNs.

## 3.2 Event-driven architectures

Neuromorphic computing stands apart from traditional computing architectures because of its event-driven approach. Unlike standard synchronous processors that rely on a fixed clock cycle, neuromorphic systems operate asynchronously, meaning they only perform computations when significant events, or spikes, are detected.

### *3.2.1 Principle of event-driven computation*

In a typical computing setup, data processing happens continuously and demands constant power, even when the system is not actively working on useful information. This leads to energy waste, especially in situations where data is sparse or comes in infrequently. On the other hand, event-driven computation in neuromorphic systems aims to replicate how the biological brain functions. In biological neurons, spikes (or action potentials) are produced only when a neuron receives enough stimuli to exceed its activation threshold. In a similar vein, SNNs only process data when there is relevant information to act on, resulting in notable energy savings and improved efficiency.

### *3.2.2 Key characteristics of event-driven computation*

1. **Sparse Activation:**
   - In this approach, neurons stay quiet when there is no important information to process, which helps cut down on unnecessary computations.
   - This not only saves energy but also makes it perfect for real-time smart city applications, such as environmental monitoring, where data updates can be pretty infrequent.
2. **Asynchronous Processing:**
   - Unlike traditional clock-driven systems, neuromorphic architectures do not rely on a set processing cycle.

- Each neuron works independently, processing spikes and firing off signals based on its own threshold. This ensures incredibly fast, real-time responses in scenarios, such as adapting traffic signals.

3. **Energy Efficiency:**
   - Neurons only spring into action when they really need to, which means they use a lot less power compared to conventional AI models.
   - For instance, in IoT-based smart grids, neuromorphic sensors can handle fluctuations in power demand only when there is a significant change, avoiding unnecessary computations.
4. **Real-Time Adaptation:**
   - For instance, in IoT-based smart grids, neuromorphic sensors can handle fluctuations in power demand only when there is a significant change, avoiding unnecessary computations.
   - Take smart surveillance systems, for example: cameras with neuromorphic vision sensors would only process frames when they detect motion or unusual activity, rather than continuously streaming and analyzing video. This approach helps reduce latency and saves on bandwidth.

### *3.2.3 Real-world applications of event-driven computation in smart cities*

- Energy Grid Optimization: Neuromorphic processors are capable of sensing real-time changes in power demand and supply, allowing for a more efficient distribution of energy.
- Traffic Management: Using SNN-based traffic control, we can react immediately to changes in congestion, rather than sticking to preset cycles.
- Waste Management: Using real-time sensor data for adaptive scheduling instead of sticking to fixed collection times, we can significantly boost efficiency.

Comparison: Traditional versus event-driven processing

| Feature | Traditional computing | Neuromorphic (event-driven) computing |
|---|---|---|
| Processing style | Clock-driven (fixed intervals) | Asynchronous (event-based) |
| Energy efficiency | High power usage (constant computation) | Low power (only when needed) |
| Real-time responsiveness | Delayed due to batch processing | Immediate response to events |
| Data handling | Continuous and redundant processing | Processes only meaningful events |

Thus, event-driven computation in neuromorphic architectures provides an optimal balance between efficiency, speed, and adaptability (O'Dwyer et al., 2019), making it a game-changer for sustainable and smart urban environments.

## 3.3 Spike-timing-dependent plasticity (STDP)

Have you ever thought about how practice really helps you improve at something? Whether it is learning to ride a bike, catching a ball, or even typing faster, your brain is busy strengthening the connections that support useful actions while letting go of the ones that do not serve you. This is the essence of learning—reinforcing the good habits and forgetting the bad ones.

This concept is similar to how STDP operates in artificial intelligence and neuromorphic computing. STDP is a learning rule inspired by the brain that enables computers and artificial neurons to learn from experience—not just by storing information but by adjusting connections based on timing.

### *3.3.1 How does STDP work?*

Consider a simple real-world example.

### *3.3.2 Example: Learning to catch a ball*

Picture yourself learning to catch a ball. The more you successfully track the ball and move your hands at just the right moment, the better your brain becomes at predicting where the ball will land. This improvement happens because of two key learning principles:

1. If one action occurs just before another and leads to success, your brain strengthens that connection.
   - If you see the ball coming (Neuron A fires first) and then move your hands to catch it (Neuron B fires after), your brain says,

   *Yes! This is the right pattern. Let's make this connection stronger.*

   - This process is called long-term potentiation (LTP)—the connection between neurons gets stronger.
2. If actions happen in the wrong order, the brain weakens the connection.
   - If you move your hands before you even see the ball (Neuron B fires first), your brain realizes that this is a mistake.
   - The brain weakens the connection, saying,

   *This is not useful—let's not repeat this mistake.*

   - This is called long-term depression (LTD)—the connection gets weaker.

In simple terms:

- **Right timing strengthens learning (LTP).**
- **Wrong timing weakens learning (LTD).**
- **The closer the two actions (or spikes) happen, the bigger the effect.**

This is why STDP is such an important learning rule—it allows computers and artificial neurons to adapt in real time, just like our brains.

### 3.3.3 Visualizing STDP

To understand this better, look at a simple block diagram:

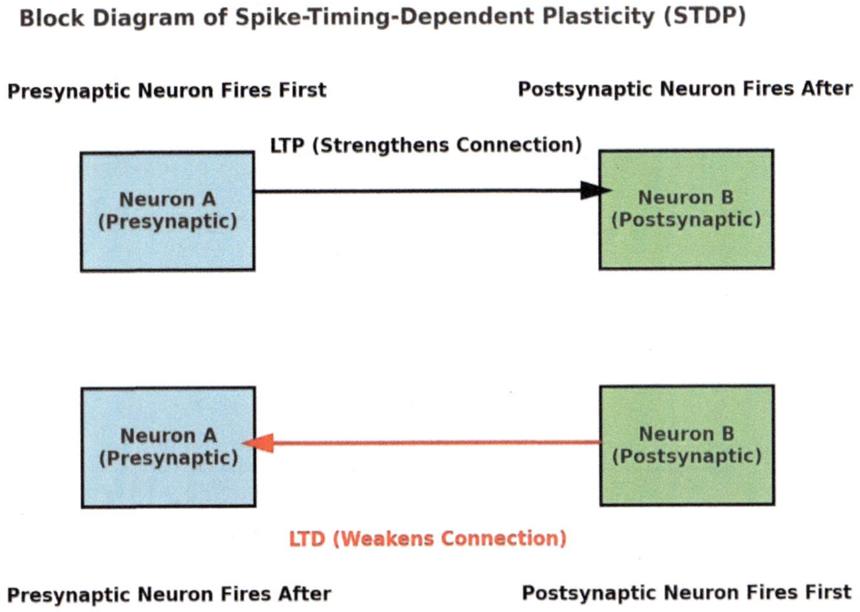


Block diagram of STDP mechanism

In the above block diagram:

- **Neuron A (Presynaptic Neuron) fires first.**
- **Neuron B (Postsynaptic Neuron) fires after.**
- **If Neuron A fires before Neuron B, the connection strengthens (LTP—long-term potentiation).**
- **If Neuron A fires after Neuron B, the connection weakens (LTD—long-term depression).**

This process helps artificial intelligence learn from experience by reinforcing good patterns and discarding bad ones, just like how humans learn from practice.

### 3.3.4 The STDP learning curve

Now, see how this learning happens over time. The graph below shows how synaptic strength changes based on spike timing:

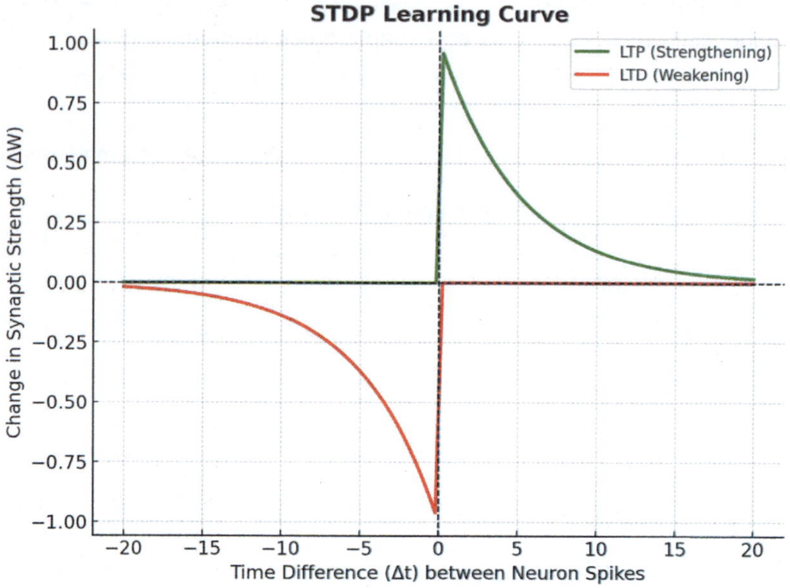


### 3.3.5 Understanding the graph

1. X-Axis (Time Difference, Δt):
   - This axis illustrates the time gap between the spikes of two neurons.
   - If the values are negative, it means Neuron A fired after Neuron B, which is the wrong order.
   - On the other hand, positive values indicate that Neuron A fired before Neuron B, which is the correct order.
2. Y-Axis (Synaptic Strength Change, ΔW):
   - This axis represents how much the connection between the neurons changes.
3. Green Curve (LTP—Strengthening the Connection):
   - When Neuron A fires just before Neuron B, the connection becomes stronger.
   - The closer the spikes occur in time, the more pronounced the learning effect.
4. Red Curve (LTD—Weakening the Connection):
   - If Neuron A fires after Neuron B, the connection weakens.
   - The greater the time gap between the spikes, the less influence they have on learning.

5. The Dashed Black Lines:
   - The vertical line at 0 indicates when both neurons fire simultaneously.
   - The horizontal line at 0 represents the point where there is no change in connection strength.

### 3.3.6 Mathematical representation of STDP

The weight update in STDP follows an exponential decay function:

$$\Delta\omega = A_+ \ e^{-\Delta t}/\tau_+ \ if \ \Delta t > 0$$

$$\Delta\omega = A_- \ e^{-\Delta t}/\tau_+ \ if \ \Delta t > 0$$

where

- $\Delta\omega$ = *Change in synaptic weight*
- $\Delta t$ = *Difference in spike timing between pre and post synaptic neurons*
- $A_+$, $A_-$ = *Learning rate constants*
- $\tau_+$, $\tau_-$ = Time constants for potentiation and depression

This equation illustrates how synaptic changes drop off exponentially as the timing of spikes becomes more spaced out, highlighting STDP as an effective method for dynamic, real-time learning.

### 3.3.7 Importance of STDP

Unlike traditional AI that needs vast amount of data and extensive pretraining, STDP allows for real-time learning with just a fraction of the computational power.

### 3.3.8 Advantages of STDP

- **Low Power Consumption**—It uses significantly less energy compared to deep learning methods.
- **Real-Time Adaptation**—It keeps learning continuously without the need to pause for retraining.
- **Scalability**—It can be implemented in compact, efficient hardware, such as neuromorphic chips.

This is why STDP is such a game-changer in making AI more adaptable, efficient, and brain-like.

### 3.3.9 STDP's role in neuromorphic systems for smart cities

1. **Adaptive Learning for Energy Management**
   - Smart grids can leverage STDP-based SNNs to learn and predict energy usage patterns in real time (Ancora et al., 2022), allowing for dynamic adjustments in power distribution.

- For instance, a smart city energy network could pinpoint peak usage hours and optimize distribution proactively.

2. **Real-Time Pattern Recognition for Public Safety**
   - Neuromorphic security systems can use STDP to spot unusual activity patterns in surveillance footage and send out alerts.
   - For example, if there is unexpected movement in crowded areas, it could be flagged immediately, boosting real-time crime prevention efforts.
3. **Autonomous Traffic Control**
   - Traffic signals can learn from past congestion patterns and adapt on the fly.
   - An STDP-based system, for example, could anticipate rush-hour traffic spikes and adjust signal patterns accordingly.
4. **Smart Waste Collection Optimization**
   - Waste sensors can analyze previous collection data and modify schedules based on how quickly bins fill up.
   - If a certain area consistently fills its bins faster, STDP can dynamically adjust collection routes to prioritize that zone.

#### *3.3.10 Summary*

STDP plays a vital role in neuromorphic computing, allowing for real-time, adaptive learning without relying on heavy computational power. By emulating the brain's ability to learn from temporal patterns, STDP-driven neuromorphic systems offer an efficient, scalable, and sustainable way to make quick decisions in smart cities.

## 4. Case study: Neuromorphic computing and BCIs for smart energy management

### 4.1 Introduction to the challenges in energy management: Background and relevance

As we have explored in earlier chapters, smart cities aim to enhance urban infrastructure through the use of digital technologies, artificial intelligence (AI), and the IoT. One of the biggest hurdles these smart cities encounter is managing energy efficiently (Covi et al., 2021), which plays a crucial role in sustainability, economic viability, and overall quality of life.

Even with the progress made in smart grids, many traditional energy distribution systems still operate in a reactive mode instead of being proactive. This leads to challenges in accurately predicting demand, reducing waste, and dynamically managing power distribution (Schuman et al., 2022).

Here are some key challenges in today's energy management landscape:

- **Inaccurate Demand Forecasting**: Traditional grids depend on past data but often lack the ability to adapt in real time to changes in energy usage.
- **Energy Wastage and Transmission Losses**: Often, power generation outpaces demand, resulting in inefficiencies and losses during transmission.
- **Slow Response to Load Changes**: Grids have difficulty responding quickly to peak loads, which can lead to either overuse or underuse of energy.
- **High Carbon Footprint**: Wasted energy contributes to unnecessary carbon emissions, highlighting the need for sustainable solutions.

To tackle these issues, innovations such as neuromorphic computing and brain–computer interfaces (BCIs) provide the potential for real-time adaptability, improved predictive capabilities, and smarter energy distribution.

## 4.2 Implementing neuromorphic solutions in energy grids

As we have explored in previous discussions, neuromorphic computing is all about mimicking the way our brains process information quickly and adaptively. Instead of sticking to traditional binary computation, neuromorphic processors utilize SNNs (Zhao et al., 2024), which are not only more energy-efficient but also capable of learning in real time.

### *4.2.1 How neuromorphic computing enhances smart grids*

Neuromorphic computing offers a range of benefits for today's energy management systems:

- **Real-time Demand Prediction**: Unlike the old-school forecasting models, neuromorphic processors can dynamically analyze sensor data, allowing them to predict energy demand fluctuations as they happen.
- **Intelligent Load Balancing**: These systems can identify areas with high energy consumption and smartly redistribute power, ensuring that the load across the grid remains balanced.
- **Self-Learning and Adaptive Mechanisms**: Models based on SNNs continuously enhance their predictions and responses, learning from both historical data and real-time patterns.
- **Reduced Latency in Decision-Making**: By processing data as events unfold, these systems can quickly adapt to power fluctuations, which helps maintain grid stability.

### *4.2.2 Neuromorphic smart grid architecture*

A smart grid powered by neuromorphic technology brings together:

- Renewable energy sources such as solar panels and wind turbines that provide real-time data.
- Smart meters and IoT sensors that keep an eye on energy usage and transmit live information.
- Neuromorphic AI processors that forecast demand and manage distribution on the fly.

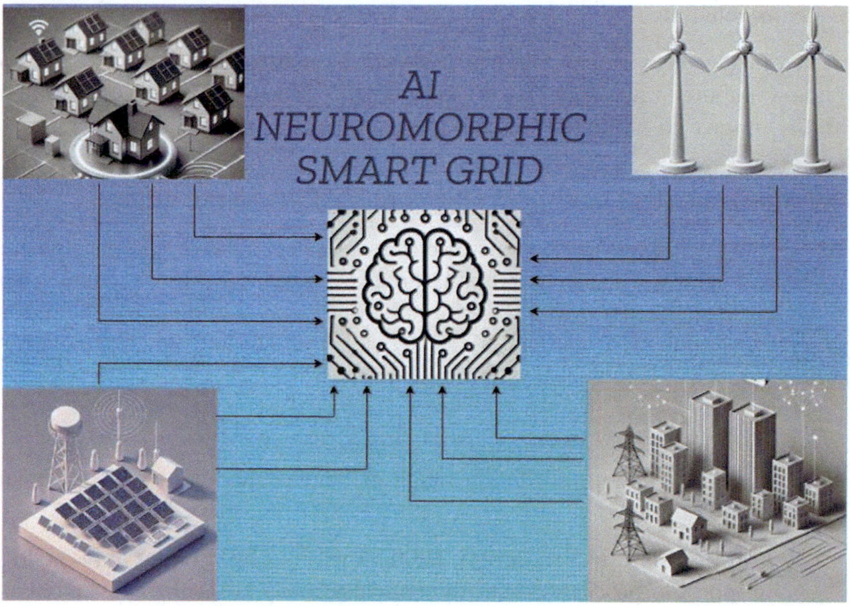


The figure above shows how neuromorphic computing boosts the efficiency of our energy grid. At the heart of it all, the central AI processor gathers real-time data from renewable energy sources, smart meters, and IoT devices. You can see arrows illustrating the flow of energy (Park et al., 2022), highlighting how the AI smartly adjusts power distribution according to demand forecasts. This system guarantees that energy is allocated adaptively, cutting down on waste and keeping the grid stable.

| Time (Hours) | Historical Demand (MW) | Predicted Demand (MW) | Adjusted Demand (MW) |
|---|---|---|---|
| 00:00 | 120 | 118 | 115 |
| 06:00 | 160 | 162 | 159 |
| 12:00 | 210 | 208 | 205 |
| 18:00 | 250 | 252 | 248 |
| 23:59 | 130 | 128 | 126 |

Sample data for energy demand prediction

### 4.2.3 Data collection and processing

- Smart meters and IoT sensors are busy collecting real-time data on electricity usage from various places, such as buildings, factories, and homes.
- This information is then sent over to a neuromorphic AI processor, which uses SNNs to forecast demand patterns.
- The demand adjustments you see are based on real-time AI-driven corrections that help optimize energy distribution, making sure the grid runs smoothly.
- Plus, the AI keeps learning from previous consumption trends, which boosts the accuracy of long-term forecasts.

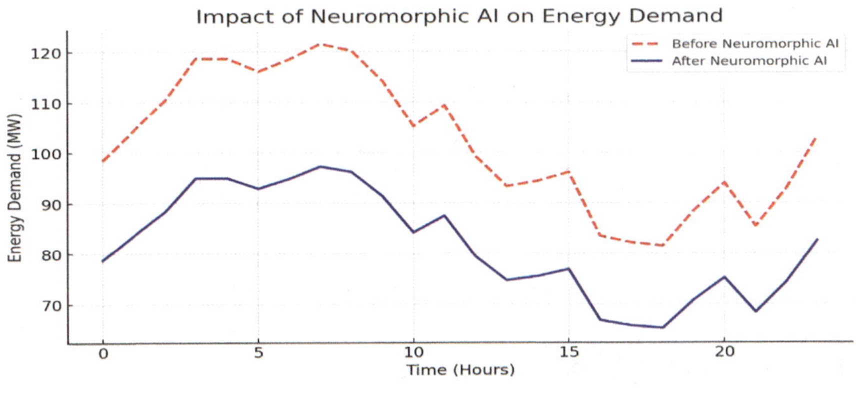


This graph provides a clear visual representation of how neuromorphic computing impacts energy grid management. The x-axis displays different times of the day, while the y-axis illustrates energy demand measured in megawatts. It compares energy consumption before and after the introduction of neuromorphic AI:

- **Before Neuromorphic AI Implementation:** The graph reveals a fluctuating energy demand curve, indicating inefficient energy use with significant peaks and occasional dips caused by unpredictable changes in power consumption.

- **After Neuromorphic AI Implementation:** The graph showcases a much smoother energy demand curve, demonstrating how AI optimizes energy distribution in real time. We can see a remarkable reduction of up to 20% in energy usage, as the AI model accurately predicts demand and adjusts the power supply accordingly.
- **Load Balancing and Grid Stability:** The AI analyzes historical energy usage patterns alongside real-time data from smart meters. This allows it to redistribute power effectively, ensuring a more stable load across the grid. As a result, the risk of overloading during peak hours is minimized, and excessive energy waste during low-demand periods is avoided.

Overall, the graph clearly illustrates that neuromorphic AI significantly enhances energy efficiency by stabilizing demand fluctuations and providing a consistent, optimized power supply throughout the grid.

## 4.3 Integrating BCIs for energy management

BCIs bring a fresh, human touch to energy management by letting users control their energy consumption through brain signals. This innovative technology creates a seamless connection between automated systems and human decision-making, making the whole process of managing energy feel more interactive and intuitive.

### *4.3.1 How BCIs work in energy systems*

- User Intent Recognition: A BCI headset picks up on electrical signals from the brain, helping to understand what the user wants in terms of energy use.
- Neuromorphic AI Processing: An adaptive AI system analyzes these brain signals and translates them into commands that can control energy systems.
- Smart Grid Interaction: These commands then manage energy distribution in homes, offices, and urban environments in real time.

### *4.3.2 BCI-enabled smart city energy system*

A BCI-based energy system consists of:

- A BCI headset that detects brain activity.
- A neuromorphic processor that interprets those brain signals.
- Smart city infrastructure—like lighting, grids, and homes—that responds accordingly.

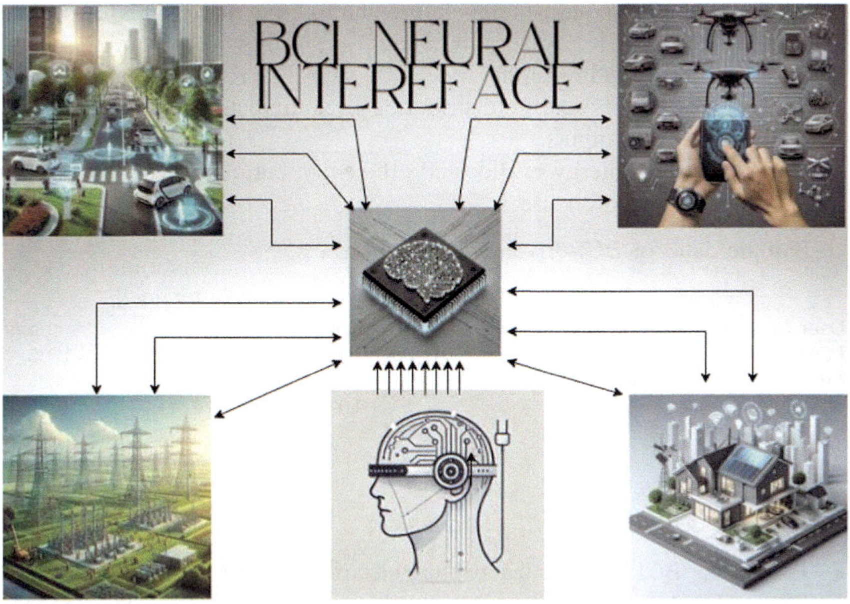


This diagram gives us a clear visual of how a BCI connects with a smart city energy system to manage energy use more effectively. Below is an explanation of how each part of the diagram works:

1. BCI Headset (User Interaction)
   - The journey begins with the person wearing the BCI headset.
   - This device picks up brain signals, allowing it to understand the user's intentions regarding energy management.
   - These neural signals are then sent to an AI processing unit for analysis.
2. AI Processing Unit (Decision-Making)
   - The AI unit takes those brain signals and makes decisions based on established energy management guidelines.
   - It serves as a bridge between the user and the smart city's infrastructure.
   - The AI processes real-time data and sends appropriate commands to the city systems.
3. Smart City Components (Actionable Responses)

   The AI system manages three key elements of the city, each responding to the user's intentions:

   Adaptive Streetlights
   - If someone walks down a poorly lit street, their focus can prompt the AI to brighten the streetlights instantly.
   - When no one is around, the lights automatically dim to conserve energy.

   Smart Homes
   - Users can control their home energy use through the BCI, like turning off appliances just by thinking about it.

- The AI can also adjust temperature and lighting based on what the user is doing.
  Power Grid Optimization
- The AI oversees energy distribution by anticipating real-time demand based on BCI inputs.
- This ensures energy is allocated efficiently, cutting down on waste and unnecessary power use.

Sample data for BCI-driven energy efficiency

| User focus level | Energy usage before (kWh) | Energy usage after (kWh) | % change |
|---|---|---|---|
| **LOW** | 50 | 45 | −10% |
| **MEDIUM** | 75 | 75 | 0% |
| **HIGH** | 90 | 103 | +15% |

## *4.3.3 Data collection and processing*

- Users wear BCI headsets that capture electrical brain activity (EEG signals).
- These signals are sent to a neuromorphic processor, which translates them into energy control commands.
- Depending on focus level, the AI adjusts energy consumption:
- Low focus: Reduces unnecessary power usage.
- Medium focus: Maintains normal energy consumption.
- High focus: Allocates additional energy for performance-intensive activities.
- The BCI–AI integration continuously improves with user interaction, refining decision-making for optimal power distribution.

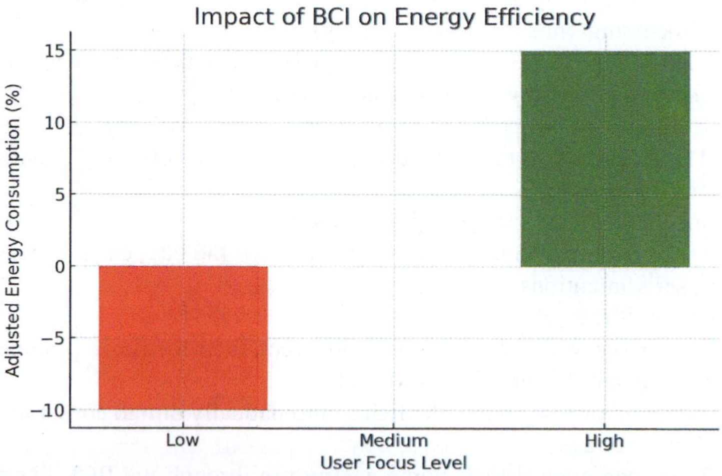

This bar chart illustrates how varying levels of user focus, gauged through a BCI, influence energy consumption in a smart city energy system. The x-axis shows three distinct levels of user focus: low, medium, and high, while the y-axis shows the percentage of adjusted energy consumption.

### 4.3.4 Interpretation of the graph

1. **Low-Focus Level (Red Bar)**
   - When users are in a low-focus state, characterized by minimal brain activity, the AI-driven system steps in to cut down on energy use.
   - This leads to a 10% reduction in energy consumption, as depicted by the red bar dipping down to −10%.
   - The red color here highlights the energy savings achieved by turning off nonessential systems, effectively reducing unnecessary power usage.
2. **Medium-Focus Level (No Bar Present)**
   - At the medium-focus level, the system keeps energy consumption steady, showing no significant changes.
   - This indicates that when users are engaged in typical activities, the AI does not make any adjustments, helping to maintain grid stability.
   - The lack of a visible bar reinforces the idea that energy consumption remains unchanged.
3. **High-Focus Level (Green Bar)**
   - In a high-focus state, users are fully immersed in tasks that demand more energy.
   - The AI recognizes this increased cognitive load and responds by allocating additional power, resulting in a 15% rise in energy usage, as illustrated by the green bar rising to +15%.
   - The green color represents the higher energy demand and smart energy distribution, ensuring users receive the necessary power boost when they need it the most.

### 4.3.5 Key takeaways from the graph

- The BCI system is designed to optimize energy use in real time, depending on how engaged the user is.
- When the focus is low, it conserves unnecessary energy, which helps with sustainability and efficiency.
- A medium focus indicates a neutral state where power consumption stays steady.
- In contrast, when focus is high, the system smartly allocates extra power to ensure top performance for more demanding tasks.
- The use of red and green colors showcases how adaptable the AI-driven smart energy grid can be.

### 4.4 Results and outcomes of neuromorphic and BCI integration

Simulations using neuromorphic computing in energy management demonstrate significant benefits. These systems can cut down on energy waste by as much as 20% by accurately predicting electricity demand. They also enhance grid stability, which helps to reduce power outages and avoid energy overloads. Plus, when you combine neuromorphic AI with BCIs, you get a user-driven approach to energy optimization, where power usage is adjusted in real-time based on how focused the user is.

#### *4.4.1 Why neuromorphic computing is a game-changer*

Unlike the traditional computing models we are used to, neuromorphic processors are designed to mimic the way our brains work. This means they do not just process data in a strict, step-by-step way; instead, they can react instantly to changes happening around them. These systems are also pretty clever—they learn from past experiences, which helps them make better decisions in the future. In addition, they use a lot less energy compared to conventional computing models, making them a perfect fit for sustainable smart city solutions.

## 5. Conclusion

Bringing together neuromorphic computing and BCIs represents a significant leap forward in how we manage energy. By merging AI-driven solutions with human oversight in energy adjustments, cities can create a more efficient, responsive, and eco-friendly energy system. The ability to adjust energy distribution based on real-time demand not only boosts sustainability but also enhances reliability. As these technologies keep advancing, they are set to play a crucial role in shaping the future of smart cities that are both intelligent and energy-efficient.

## References

Ancora, L.A., Andrés Blanco-Mora, D., Alves, I., Bonifácio, A., Morgado, P., Miranda, B., 2022. Cities and neuroscience research: a systematic literature review. Front. Psychiatr. 13. https://doi.org/10.3389/fpsyt.2022.983352.

Banerjee, S., Chakraborty, C., Das, D., 2020. An Approach towards GIS Application in Smart City Urban Planning. Informa UK Limited, pp. 71–110. https://doi.org/10.1201/9780367276706-2.

Covi, E., Donati, E., Liang, X., Kappel, D., Heidari, H., Payvand, M., Wang, W., 2021. Adaptive extreme edge computing for wearable devices. Front. Neurosci. 15. https://doi.org/10.3389/fnins.2021.611300.

Fang, H., Mei, Z., Shrestha, A., Zhao, Z., Li, Y., Qiu, Q., 2020. Encoding, model, and architecture: systematic optimization for spiking neural network in FPGAs. In: IEEE/ACM International Conference on Computer-Aided Design, Digest of Technical Papers, ICCAD. Institute of Electrical and Electronics Engineers Inc, United States. https://doi.org/10.1145/3400302.3415608.

Firoozi, A.A., Firoozi, A.A., 2024. Neuromorphic Computing in Smart Infrastructure. Springer Science and Business Media LLC, pp. 33–43. https://doi.org/10.1007/978-3-031-G5549-4_4.

Hashem, I.A.T., et al., 2016. The role of big data in smart city. Int. J. Inf. Manag. 36 (5), 748–758. https://doi.org/10.1016/j.ijinfomgt.2016.05.002.

Huang, C., Zhang, G., Yao, J., Wang, X., Kaiser Calautit, J., Zhao, C., An, N., Peng, X., 2022. Accelerated environmental performance-driven urban design with generative adversarial network. Build. Environ. 224, 109575. https://doi.org/10.1016/j.buildenv.2022.109575.

Huang, J., Bibri, S.E., Keel, P., 2025. Generative spatial artificial intelligence for sustainable smart cities: a pioneering large flow model for urban digital twin. Environ. Sci. Ecotechnol. 24. https://doi.org/10.1016/j.ese.2025.100526.

Lemmers-Jansen, I.L.J., Fett, A.-K.J., van Os, J., Veltman, D.J., Krabbendam, L., 2020. Trust and the city: linking urban upbringing to neural mechanisms of trust in psychosis. Aust. N. Z. J. Psychiatr. 54 (2), 138–149. https://doi.org/10.1177/0004867419865939.

O'Dwyer, E., Pan, I., Acha, S., Shah, N., 2019. Smart energy systems for sustainable smart cities: current developments, trends and future directions. Appl. Energy 237, 581–597. https://doi.org/10.1016/j.apenergy.2019.01.024.

Park, S., Spetzler, B., Ivanov, T., Ziegler, M., 2022. Multilayer redox-based HfOx/Al2O3/TiO2 memristive structures for neuromorphic computing. Sci. Rep. 12 (1). https://doi.org/10.1038/s41598-022-22907-5.

Schuman, C.D., Kulkarni, S.R., Parsa, M., Parker Mitchell, J., Date, P., Kay, B., 2022. Opportunities for neuromorphic computing algorithms and applications. Nat. Comput. Sci. 2 (1), 10–19. https://doi.org/10.1038/s43588-021-00184-y.

Shrestha, A., Fang, H., Mei, Z., Rider, D.P., Wu, Q., Qiu, Q., 2022. A survey on neuromorphic computing: models and hardware. IEEE Circ. Syst. Mag. 22 (2), 6–35. https://doi.org/10.1109/MCAS.2022.3166331.

Wu, P., Zhang, Z., Peng, X., Wang, R., 2024. Deep learning solutions for smart city challenges in urban development. Sci. Rep. 14 (1). https://doi.org/10.1038/s41598-024-55928-3.

Yu, J., Ang, K.K., Ho, S.H., Sia, A., Ho, R., 2017. Prefrontal cortical activation while viewing urban and garden scenes: a pilot fNIRS study. In: Proceedings of the Annual International Conference of the IEEE Engineering in Medicine and Biology Society, EMBS. Institute of Electrical and Electronics Engineers Inc, Singapore, pp. 2546–2549. https://doi.org/10.1109/EMBC.2017.8037376.

Zhang, Q., Cui, M., Chen, W., Liu, Y., Yu, Z., 2025. UIC: a unified and scalable chip integrating neuromorphic computation and general purpose processor. Microelectron. J. 155. https://doi.org/10.1016/j.mejo.2024.106449.

Zhao, Le, Fang, H., Wang, J., Nie, F., Li, R., Wang, Y., Zheng, L., 2024. Ferroelectric artificial synapses for high-performance neuromorphic computing: status, prospects, and challenges. Appl. Phys. Lett. 124 (3). https://doi.org/10.1063/5.0165029.

Chapter 12

# An artificial intelligence-based real-time monitoring system to study the effect of electrical signal between Ocimum teniflorum and Coleus amboinicus

S. Venkatesh Kumar[1], M. Karthick[2], R. Praveenkumar[3], G. Vijayakumari[4], S. Parthiban[5] and P. Loganath[6]
[1]*Department of EEE, Dr. N.G.P Institute of Technology, Coimbatore, Tamil Nadu, India;* [2]*Department of EEE, Vimal Jyothi Engineering College, Kannur, Kerala, India;* [3]*Department of ECE, Nandha Engineering College, Erode, Tamil Nadu, India;* [4]*Department of ECE, Kangeyam Institute of Technology, Nathakadaiyur, Tamil Nadu, India;* [5]*Department of ECE, Nandha College of Technology, Erode, Tamil Nadu, India;* [6]*Department of ECE, SSM College of Engineering, Namakkal, Tamil Nadu, India*

## 1. Introduction to plant electrophysiology

### 1.1 Electrical signaling in plants: Overview

Plants, although lacking a nervous system, are entitled to highly sophisticated mechanisms to respond to sensing and environmental signals. One of the most important and fastest signalling systems in plants is electric signalling (Liu et al., 2025; Schyck et al., 2024). In this form of intracellular and intercellular communication, changes in membrane capacity and transmission of electrical impulses through vascular tissues, especially through the flower. The primary type of electrical signals seen in plants include,

- Action Potential (APS): These membranes are not transient, not all-or-anything, and propagate nerve impulses in animals. The APS is usually triggered by nonhiratory stimuli such as light, touch, or temperature changes.

**Neuromorphic Computing for Brain Computer Interfaces. https://doi.org/10.1016/B978-0-443-41594-4.00013-7**

- Variation capacity (VPS): Also known as slow wave capacity, these signs are damaged by stimuli such as wounds, cuttings or acute environmental stress. VPs are slow and variable in size and dimension, and they often give rise to long -term physical reactions.
- System Potential (SPS): These are signs of long -range long distance signs generated by hydraulic or chemical stimuli. SPS can activate defence genes and systemic resistance mechanisms.

The transmission of these signs is mainly operated through ion channels and transporters (Catterall et al., 2024) through the movement of ions such as potassium ($K^+$), calcium (CA and), chloride ($CL^-$), and hydrogen ($h^+$) through the cell membrane. These ion flux results in an average change in membrane capacity, which can be detected using a microelectrode or noninvasive biosensor. The electric signalling in plants plays a vital role in the coordination of reactions to abiotic and biotic stresses, which controls physiological processes such as stomatal closures, photosynthesis, hormone signaling and even the direction of improvement. Besides, the chemical signalling networks are mostly electrically integrated signals, leading to rapid systemic responses. With the advent of modern sensor technology and artificial intelligence, scientists can now not only observe but also understand these bio span patterns in real time scenario. This technical integration opens new opportunities to understand the precise agriculture process, plant behaviour and also research with intersystem communication system.

## 1.2 Bioelectrical properties of *Ocimum tenuiflorum* and *Coleus amboinicus*

The *Ocimum tenuiflorum* (Holy Tulsi) and *Colius amboinicus* (Indian borase) are not only famous for their ethnic science value, but also display different bio spacing behavior in reaction to environmental stimulus. The physical sensitivity and structural features make them ideal for the discovery of plant electrophysiology, specifically in studies related to plant-to-plant electrical transmission using recent sensing and AI-based analyzation devices (Santos Filipe et al., 2025; Kumar et al., 2025).

### *1.2.1 Accountability for electrical activity and stimuli*

Using non-incentive AG/AGCL electrodes or plant-compatible gel-based contact pads, the real-world study has recorded electrical potential changes (will be in the range of 10–300 μv) in both species under the influence of light-worm cycles, touchable stimulation, water stress). These reactions usually appear as follows in Fig. 12.1 were the Action Potential (AP) is given as Sharp, Short-Darshan Spikes the Variation Capacity (VP) shown as Slow, long -lasting wave shift. A specific signal graph represents an initial stable baseline, followed by a sharp depression on stimulation, then a regular repetition (Kim et al., 2024).

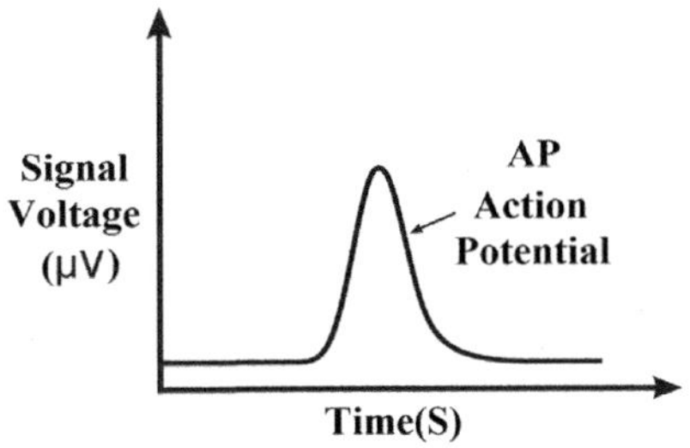


**FIGURE 12.1** Graphical representation of plant action potential signal over time.

### *1.2.2 Vascular structure and signal propagation*

Both plants have major central vascular bundles that provides,

- Efficient transport of ions and signaling molecules
- Long distance spread of electrical signals from the point of stimulation to the distal tissue

High stomatal density and broad leaf morphology contributes,

- Ion channel activity increased
- Better surface-electrode connectivity during experiments

### *1.2.3 Inter-plant signal correlation capacity*

By the process of synchronized dual-plant monitoring setup, the primary data suggests cross correlated signal spikes between Osimim and Colius when the primary data stimulates and remains intact. It starts a hypothesis for electrical resonance or shared field reactions through root soil network or airborne signalling. The data analyzation shows the positive values, using the Pearson correlation coefficient which is given between the signal time chain of two plants, indicating potential synchronous electrical behaviour under regulated lab conditions.

### *1.2.4 Data logging and AI interpretation*

For the effective analyze, the signs the real -time monitoring system was introduced,

- Microcontroller: Arduino/ESP32 or Raspberry Pi A/D Conversion (12-bit or higher)
- Electrode: Silver/Silver-Cloride (AG/AGCL), Common Hydrogel
- Data Acquisition Software: Python/Matlab- Based Gui
- Sampling rate: 10–50 Hz is sufficient for plant signals
- Storage: CSV or Time Stamped JSON log

**The AI Techniques Applied are Time-series classification** using RNN/LSTM, **Anomaly detection** for stress response prediction **Signal clustering** for distinguishing stimulus types.

### 1.2.5 Practical implications

Real-time monitoring of bioelectrical signals in *O. tenuiflorum* and *C. amboinicus* can be represented as:

- Smart agriculture: Detect stress of water/nutrients before visual symptoms
- Medicinal plant cultivation: adaptation status for metabolite production
- Electrophysiology Education: Plant reaction simulation with AI-August graph
- Intercropping Strategies: Searching synergistic effects through electrical synchronization

## 1.3 Role of electrical signals in plant communication and stress response

One of the main ways which power the accountability, in the plants is electrical signalling that acts on the plants and the systemic communication network in between. These electrical signals are essentially becoming the new language of plants in detecting biotic and abiotic components.

### 1.3.1 Internal communication via electrical signals

When a part of a plant is exposed to a stimulus such as mechanical touch, injury, or heat stress, it usually produces action potentials (APs) or variation potentials (VPs). These signals travel along the phloem and plasmodesmata, thereby, they can reach the far tissues and cause the physiological changes. The responses of the plants in this case might be:

- Stomatal closure to limit water loss under drought conditions
- Modification of hormone levels (e.g., higher abscisic acid concentrations)
- Induction of defense genes and secondary metabolite pathways

Such a mechanism turns the plant into a single interactive organism instead of separated parts; thus, it is a demonstration of an intelligent and synchronized reaction system.

### 1.3.2 Stress response and early warning system

The electrical signs are the footsteps of the danger to the rest of the plant for neighbors hazards. For instance:

- In the case of herbivore attacks, action/variation potentials are produced by the damaged leaves that can be ported without cooking leaves, then the plant chooses the most cautious mixtures such as alkaloids, termineroids, or phenolics.

- When the stress of drought is upon the roots or lower leaves, they may specify the upper canopy to control the process of evaporation and photosynthesis.

Such fast signaling is actually a matter of minutes to minutes, which is much faster than hormonal transport alone, thus it gives an opportunity for plants to respond to the stress that is happening at the time.

### 1.3.3 Inter-plant communication: A hypothesis with emerging evidence

New research has shown that plants may send electrical signals to neighboring plants to communicate by:

- Route network (e.g., common mycorrhizal fungus as conduits)
- Electrical field resonance or an electrochemical signal in the shared soil environment

Researchers are working on a scenario where the energy change in the second plant upon the stimulation of the first one can be detected in the case of O. tenuiflorum and C. amboinicus systems.

### 1.3.4 Integration with chemical/hydraulic signals and technological applications

The integration can be done by incorporated with:

Chemical signals like reactive oxygen species (ROS), calcium waves and phytohormones
Hydraulic signal (changes in organ pressure)

This complex interplay allows for strong and fine stress reactions, which are often referred to as the "alarm system" of the plant or "green neural network".

The applications include:

- Precise farming machinery to control irrigation, fertilization, and disease smartly
- Species behaviour model to enhance intercropping and ecological farming

## 2. Artificial intelligence in plant science

Moreover, the incorporation of real-time sensor data with visual and genome data renders AI the research field with the fastest growth rate, resulting in the disclosure of plant physiological functions such as bioelectrical signalling and stress responses.

## 2.1 Applications of AI in botany and agriculture

The AI has been changing the interaction with the world, its understanding, and management methods of scientists, farmers, and researchers, among others, are in natural ways. By incorporating AI in the studies of botany and agriculture, the plant studies are made more accurate, efficient and-drive, which can provide insight into productivity, stability and plant behavior and growth.

### *2.1.1 Plant health monitoring and diagnosis*

The AI sensor permits the real-time and accurate diagnosis of the plant health using data, images and environmental input (Jafar et al., 2024).

- Disease detection: Computer vision algorithms (e.g., CNN) identify diseases with leaf or stem images with high accuracy.
- Stress detection: AI models analyze electrical signals, thermal data or chlorophyll fluorescence to detect drought, salinity or insect stress.
- Prophems for nutrient deficiency: AI can predict when and which nutrient deficiency is lacking, by learning from plant growth patterns and environmental data.

### *2.1.2 Precision agriculture*

The AI increases productivity in agricultural practices by creating data-interacted, site-specific recommendations (Taha et al., 2025).

- **Smart Irrigation System**: In this, the AI predicts the finest water program based on the moisture of the soil, weather, and crop needs.
- **Fertilizer adaptation**: AI models balance nutrients in the application to avoid excessive use or deficiency.
- **Yield Forecasting**: Using satellite data, weather patterns, and crop status, AI can forecast crop yield accurately.

### *2.1.3 Crop breeding and genomics*

AI intensifies through genetic research and crop improvement (Zhang et al., 2025):

- Specialty prediction: ML algorithms predict desirable symptoms (e.g., dried tolerance, high yield) based on genomic data.
- Genome editing support: AI CRISPR/CAS9 helps identify gene goals for intervention.
- Phenotyping automation: for AI-Assisted imaging tools to track plant growth and phenotype tracts for earlier breeding phases.

### *2.1.4 Environment monitoring and stability*

AI supports permanent agricultural practices by monitoring environmental conditions (Naveed et al., 2024).

- Pests and weed management: AI detects and classifies insects or aggressive weeds using drone imagery and sensor data.
- Climate adaptation: The future models help farmers prepare for adverse climate events (floods, droughts, and heatweems).
- Reduction in carbon footprint: AI-powered automation helps reduce inputs such as fuel, water and fertilizers, reducing emissions.

### 2.1.5 Automation and robotics

The manual functions in agriculture can be replaced by AI Power Smart Machines (Kumar et al., 2024). Autonomous drones and robots are used for planting, spraying, weeding and monitoring of crops:

- Harvesting Robot: The AI-directed robots that select crops and vegetables on the basis of the crops and vegetables.
- Smart Greenhouse: The customized developed conditions can be achieved by AI controls temperature, humidity and lighting to

### 2.1.6 Plant electrophysiology and biofeedback system

- Signal analysis: AI models can enhance the analyses of electrical signals related to plants for the study of plant behavior, stimuli, or interplastered communication.
- Biofeedback device: This real-time AI systems add plant responses to environmental features, enabling interactive or automated responses (e.g., activate irrigation when stress signals are detected) (Stolarz, 2025).

### 2.1.7 Education and research

AI enhances learning and research in Botany (Hackel et al., 2026):

- Data mining from Literature: The NLP equipment concisely presents giant scientific data for researchers and teachers.
- Modelling and simulation: Simulation based on AI facilitates students and researchers in many situations in modelling plant development.

### 2.1.8 Market and supply chain forecast

AI also contributes to agriculture beyond the region (Dhal and Kar, 2024), by prophecy for market demand, which can be done by AI predicting consumer demand trends for various crops, and supply chain optimization which helps track bad goods, reduce losses and customize transport routes. The incorporation of AI in botany studies and agriculture has unlocked new levels of efficiency, insight and stability. As the overall understanding of the silent electrical language of plants for the automatic cultivation of the entire farming, the AI is one of the important agents of the next generation plant science and smart agriculture.

## 2.2 Advantages of AI over traditional data analysis

The AI provides a powerful option for traditional data analysis methods by leading towards automation, adaptability and high precision. In the field of plant science and agriculture, where data is frequently expansive, noisy, and complex, the AI will unlocks that traditional statistical methods or fail in real time as given in Table 12.1.

## 2.3 Relevance of machine learning in biological signal interpretation

The ML is critical for the interpretation of biological signals, particularly in the cluttered and noise-rich regime that defines plant electrophiziology. Electrical signals in plants (*O. tenuiflorum*, a member of *C. amboinicus*) are influenced by numerous nondivorous hyperdimensional factors of both

**TABLE 12.1** Advantages of AI over traditional data analysis (Zong and Guan, 2025; Kunze et al., 2024).

| Aspect | Traditional data analysis | Artificial intelligence (AI) |
|---|---|---|
| **Data handling** | Handles mostly linear or simple patterns | Models complex, nonlinear, and high-dimensional data |
| **Automation** | Requires manual preprocessing and analysis | Automates data collection, cleaning, analysis, and decision-making |
| **Accuracy** | Depends on predefined statistical models | Learns from data, adapts over time, and improves prediction accuracy |
| **Real-time capability** | Limited; often works postdata collection | Processes and responds to data in real time |
| **Data integration** | Challenging to integrate multiple data types | Easily merges data from sensors, images, environmental logs, and electrical signals |
| **Predictive power** | Mostly descriptive or historical insights | Provides predictive and prescriptive analytics |
| **Scalability** | Performance drops with large datasets | Scales efficiently with large and dynamic datasets |
| **Pattern recognition** | May overlook subtle or hidden patterns | Detects deep, hidden patterns beyond human capability |
| **Adaptability** | Static models; need redefinition when context changes | Learns continuously from new data without manual reprogramming |
| **Example in plant science** | Manual classification of plant stress from leaf data | AI models detect plant stress from electrical signals, environmental data, and visual symptoms |

external and internal nature. Traditional analytic methods usually fail in such scenarios, whereas ML algorithm performs excellently in uncovering these hidden patterns in the noisy dataset (Binson et al., 2024).

The most dominant ML applications for studies of plant electrophysiological are noise reduction and signal classification. Techniques such as SVMs, random forests, and CNNs can effectively distinguish various plant categories, for example, APS, ICPS, and SCPS. They are data-based, and in the training process, these models can be taught to identify the slightest differences in the voltage response pattern, which may indicate a particular physical condition or environmental stress response.

## 3. System architecture and design

The composition of this system is capable of delivering excellent results in a performance that is stable and efficient for visualizing of the electrical signal capture, low-optimization processing, research, and experimental analysis.

### 3.1 Sensor selection and placement for bioelectrical signal detection

To detect the exact bioelectrical signal in Ocimum Tenuiflorum and Coleus Amboinicus, the AG/AgCl surface electrodes are recommended primary options due to their low polarization, stable DC reaction and low noise performance in the microvolt range. These electrodes, available in disposable or reusable forms, should be combined with conductive gel or paste to ensure good contact (Chakole et al., 2024). Alternative electrodes include conductive hydrogel pads, which are gentle on leaves and are suitable for long-term recording, and stainless-steel or carbon electrodes, which are more favorable for soil or root measurement but are less effective for high-loyal leaf recording. Needle electrodes, while tissue is capable of penetrating, are aggressive and are usually avoided in healthy plant physiology studies due to moral and biological concerns. The reference electrode (RF) is electrically kept on the calm or stem base, while the ground electrode (GND) can be inserted into the soil or connected to the chassis ground with cable preservation to reduce the intervention. The front-end electronics are important for the quality of the signal, requiring an instrumentation amplifier with very high input impedance (>100 m and) and low input noise (NV/$\sqrt{}$Hz), which is associated with a high-radicalization ADC (16- or 24-right) to reduce the quantization error for microolet signals. To target plant-pranic frequencies, the filter should be configured for a band-pass range of about 0.01–50 Hz, which has a notch filter on the main frequency (50/60 Hz) to suppress the intervention. The sampling rate of 100–500 Hz is usually sufficient, although 1 kHz provides additional analytical margin.

For sensor placement in a basic single-plant Montaz, the active electrode should be attached to the adaxal surface of a mature leaf, which uses almost one-third, conductive gel and a small AG/AGCL pad from the base. The reference electrode should be fixed into the pitiol near the stem near the leaf-stem or near the node, while the ground electrode is inserted into the soil away from the active root zone. The distance between active and reference electrodes must be at least 2–3 cm to catch local possible differences without unrelated signal contamination. In a two-plants comparative setup, the electrode is deployed on each plant in the same configuration, in which there is an option to use a shared ground or reference to study interplant electrical coupling-although separately with synchronized watches, it is better to avoid separate front-end cross-tracks. The root or soil electrode for root-medial signal studies includes stainless-steel rod or an AG/AGCL electrode positioned in 2–5 cm of soil from the root mass, which has frequent moisture for restructuring. To avoid growing tissues, soft adhesive tape on the electrode pad should be used, with hydrogel pads and medical tapes for long -term setup. With relief from stress to prevent motion artifacts, at least the preserved twist-jodi cable should be used, and a faradi cage can be employed in a high-scraper environment. The main intervention should be reduced with notch filtering and proper tool placement.

Noise reduction strategies include cancellation of normal-mode intervention, implementing bandpasses and notch filters and using differential measurements to perform average performance for frequent stimulation tests. Independent component analysis (ICA) or advanced technology such as wavelet danoizing can help remove complex artifacts. For safety and plant welfare, avoid introducing DC currents in the plant using inactive electrodes and high input impedance circulatory, avoiding the use of invasive electrodes, and neutralizing the reusable electrode between experiments to prevent cross-concentration and Table 12.2 gives the specification in detail.

## 3.2 Real-time data acquisition hardware

The plant bioelectrical signal requires a carefully selected combination of sensors, front-analog electronics, high-resolution ADC, and a microcontroller or single-board computer (SBC) for real-time data acquisition that is capable of reliable sampling, buffering, and timely data transfers. In analog front end, use an instrumentation amplifier with very high input impedance and low input noise to increase microolt-level differences, followed by antialiasing (low-pass) filtering and a notch filter for main intervention. Choose at least 16-bit resolution (24-bit for the best dynamic range) and an ADC with a stable input phase that supports the difference measurement; The sample at 100–500 Hz for typical plant electrophiziology (up to 1 kHz if you need an additional headroom), and ensure that the effective number of ADC is sufficient for the ORV resolution after the enobal amplification. For the controller, light microcontroller such as ESP32 or Arduino simple, low-power edge acquisitions and wireless streaming work well, while raspberry pie or other

**TABLE 12.2 Specification summary.**

| Component | Recommended spec |
|---|---|
| Electrode type | Ag/AgCl surface pads (with conductive gel) |
| Input impedance | >100 MΩ |
| ADC resolution | 16–24 bit |
| Sampling rate | 100–500 Hz (up to 1 kHz optional) |
| Bandpass filter | 0.01–50 Hz |
| Notch filter | 50/60 Hz (mains) |
| Cables | Short, shielded twisted-pair |
| Mounting | Hydrogel/gel + soft tape; strain relief for cables |

SBCs are better if you need real-time visualization, heavy preprosancing or local storage. For high-channel-ginti or clinical-grade recording, a dedicated bioMPLIFR ADC module (e.g., with modular 24-bit ADC board programmable benefits and input preservation) or integrated front-end chips is recommended (Kottadamane et al., 2024).

The ideas of the main system include interinputs for suppressing normal-mode noise, gallvanic isolation between plant-grounds and data-grounds when cross-talk, hardware timestamping or a real-time watch (RTC) use in several vessels to avoid a real-time watch, which keeps record synchronizs, and to prevent adequate buffering (DMA or Ring Buffers). For connectivity, wired USB/Ethernet gives reliable high-inguinal logging, while Wi-Fi/BLE/Lora are suitable for remote or distributed setups, but require strong retribution and buffering logic. Data storage should include both local (SD/USB) raw log and alternative cloud uploads through MQT/HTTP for aggregation and AI processing; always record with raw signals- Matadata (sampling rate, filter settings, amplifier advantage, electrode status, and environmental status). Power and Noise Management—short shielded cable, separate power rail for analog/digital section, and a grounded Faraday cage—is required to keep the noise floor low when needed. Finally, provide software support for real-time plotting, basic preprosying (not + bandpass), and reliable export format (Timstamped CSV/EDF/JSON) to provide AI layer data to clean the data.

## 3.3 Wireless transmission and cloud data storage setup

Wireless transmission and cloud data storage setup are important components of the AI-based real-time plant monitoring system, which enables spontaneous communication between the sensing unit and remote analytical platforms

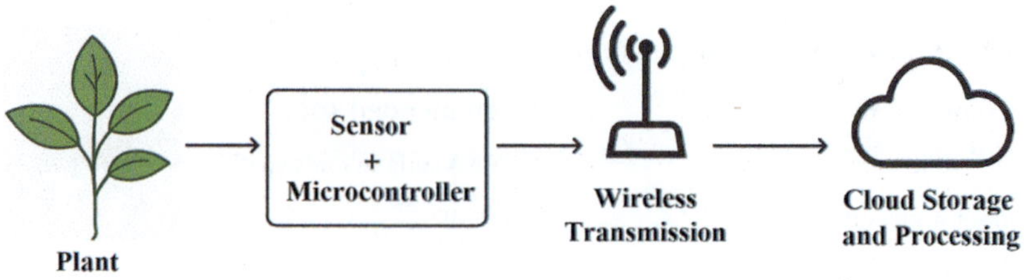


**FIGURE 12.2** Signal processing flow.

(Morchid et al., 2024). After bioelectrical signals from *O. tenuiflorum* and *C. amboinicus*, they are captured and digitized through Microcontroller's ADC (Analog-to-Digital Converter), they are wireless for processing, storage and further analysis in a central server or cloud database. For wireless transmission, communication protocols such as Wi-Fi, Bluetooth Low Energy (BLE), or Loravan can be selected based on range, power consumption and perfect environment. Wi-Fi is ideal for laboratory-based setups with stable internet access, while BLE ensures low power usage in short distance applications. Loravan provides long-distance connectivity for external monitoring with minimal energy use. The microcontroller or embedded processing unit integrates to send integrated data packets with a wireless communication module (e.g., ESP8266, ESP32, NRF52840, or Lora Trenxover) as in Fig. 12.2.

On the cloud side, platforms such as AWS IOT core, Google Cloud IoT, or Open-Source Solutions can be used for safe data ingestion, real-time dashboard and storage. Cloud server stores bioelectric signal data in structured formats (e.g., time-series databases such as influxdb) and enables automated backup. It can be integrated in the cloud with AI-based analytics pipelines, which makes it possible to model the future without the need for partitioning stress detection (pattern), computation and others on-site. A good transmission and storage system includes protection of data security (e.g., encryption—TLS/SSL) and data retention (e.g., no loss during connectivity failure). This allows not only reliable real-time monitoring, which is however, limited in time and area size, but also the ability to study on a large scale for a long time by peripherally gathering data for associated studies.

## 4. Data collection methodology

### 4.1 Experimental setup for monitoring both plant species

The experimental and practical studies were performed to monitor and compare bioelectric signaling characteristics of practical studies *O. tenuiflorum* and *C. amboinicus*. To avoid unfavorable circumstances, healthy and mature plants were selected and taken from homogeneous soil compositions.

Each plant was enclosed in its own chamber to eliminate disturbance by external noise or vibration. The high-sensitivity electrophysiological recording electrode was placed on the leaf surface and stem with a conductive gel that matched signal acquisition to the noninvasive electrode (AG/AGCL). The electrodes were connected to a signal conditioning circuit, linked to analog-to-digital (ADC) data logging microcontroller for data recording. A prescription enclosure was employed to minimize electromagnetic interference (EMI) for a clean signal acquisition.

### 4.2 Environmental control variables

The atmosphere status was strictly controlled to ensure the experimental validity. The temperature in the growth chamber was controlled to maintain it at $25 \pm 20°C$, relative humidity at 60%–70%, and light intensity of 200–250 PMOL/MICIL/8 during photoperiods. The light/dark cycles were 16 hours of light and 8 hours of darkness to mimic the natural environment. The sensor was incorporated into the system for real-time tracking of temperature, humidity and light intensity. The data from these sensors was recorded in parallel with the plant bioelectrical signals to correct physical reactions with environmental variations.

## 5. Signal processing and feature extraction

### 5.1 Preprocessing of raw electrical signals

The bioelectrical activity given off by plants is very small, generally in the range of the microvols, and subject to a variety of factors such as the electrode-skin junction, environmental electromagnetic disturbances, and transducer sensitivity. It is ensured that the preprocessing step keeps the data delivered for analysis clean and reliable:

- Baseline correction: The electrode removes the offset of the input signal due to sensor polarization or flow dynamics. This ensures all the signals have a common reference point of initiation and improves the meaning of the comparison.
- Partitioning: The data stream is divided into small pieces of uniform size so that small variations are captured while facilitating batch processing.

### 5.2 Noise filtering and normalization

The noise filtering and normalization can be done, and the active noise is quite significant in accurate feature detection.

Noise Filtering:

- A low-passed filter strips the signal of any high noise that might exist (for example, electrical interference from laboratory devices).

- A Band-Pas filter only retains a relevant frequency range for bioelectrical activity (most of the time below 50 Hz).
- Notch Filter removes power line interference (50 Hz in India, 60 Hz in other countries).
- Moving average smoothing reduces short-term fluctuations, preserving longer trends.

Generalization:

Min-max scaling changes the signal to a specific range, for example, from 0 to 1, which makes it easier to compare the readings from different plants or sensors.

- Z-score standardization changes each signal in a way that its mean becomes 0 and standard deviation 1, thus getting rid of any differences in scale between datasets.
- The step guarantees that the machine learning model will not be biased only towards signals with large amplitudes because of their high magnitude, rather than the presence of meaningful features.

## 5.3 Feature extraction from time-series data

Feature abstraction is the method of changing the clean time series signal into a set of numerical details that briefly demonstrate its dominant properties.

Time-domain features:

- Mean and Median, Reflect average electrical activity.
- Variance and Standard Deviation show the extent of the variation of the reaction of the plant.
- Peak-to-Peak Amplitude helps to identify the most extreme electrical reactions for the stimuli.
- Zero-Crossing Rate can be observed from the measured data that the signal changes its polarity so frequently, which is a reflection of the high dynamics in the activity.

Frequency-domain features (Through Fast Furrier Transform, FFT)

- **Spectral energy**: measured how many specific frequency bands are focused in the signal power.
- **Dominant Frequency**: The most responsible oscillation during stimulation identifies the frequency.

Advanced features:

- **Wavelet converting**: Breaking the signal into both time and frequency components helps to detect short spikes or blasting of activity.
- **Entropy agent**: Determine the complexity of the signal and amount of unpredictability, which can be changed under stress-like state.

- **Hilbert-hanging transformation**: Used for nonled and nonstable signals to obtain accurate instant frequencies.

## 6. Machine learning model development

The development of a machine learning model for plant bioelectric signal interpretation involves careful choice of algorithms, systematic training and strict performance evaluation to ensure reliability and accuracy (Tang et al., 2024).

### 6.1 Selection of algorithms: SVM, RNN, and CNN

The alternative to the algorithm depends on the species and the target application of the input signal.

- Support VIKE (SVM): Effective for classification features where plant signals are converted to a set of functions (e.g., amplitude variation, frequency components). SVMs are especially good when the dataset is moderate to large in size and is linearly different.
- Repetitive Neural Network (RNN): Time series designed for Data Analysis, RNN can capture temporary addiction in electrical signal patterns, which is important for detecting plant actions delayed for stimuli.
- Convolutional Neural Network (CNN): Useful when the signal data turns into spectrograms or a 2D function map, enabling the spatial pattern recognition in the frequency -time domain. CNN is effective for large datasets and complex patterns.

### 6.2 Model training and validation

This process starts by dividing the dataset into training, verification and testing sets.

- Training includes the model learning patterns from historical label data, adjusting its internal parameters to reduce prediction error.
- Verification by Kernel type (SVM), number of layers (RNN/CNN), learning rate and regularization factor are used to correct regularization factors such as hyperparameters, ensuring that the model becomes quite normal without overfitting.
- Cross-validation techniques such as ke-touched checking help ensure that model performance is stable across various datasets.
- Data augmentation strategies can be applied to expand the limited data set of plant signals, such as adding synthetic noise, scaling the amplitude, or generating false stress response patterns.

### 6.3 Performance metrics

The amount of model performance is determined using several metrics, which include accuracy, precision, sensitivity, and confusion matrix, making the model perform better and achieve effective progress.

## 7. Analysis of inter-plant electrical interactions

The electrical interaction studies are all about the notion of how plants have the ability to convey conversational signals to one another through bioelectrical signals when exposed to environmental change or novel stimulation. This research needs the amalgamation of the latest signal therapy, statistical correlation, and biological interpretation to discern the patterns that could unveil communications in plants (Chen et al., 2024; Singh and Satheeshkumar, 2025).

### 7.1 Signal correlation and pattern matching

This can be evolved by the following process:

- **Cross-Collection Analysis:** The plant electrical signals can determine the amount of potential response over time.
- **Pattern Matching Methods:** Signal waveforms are compared using such methods as Dynamic Time Warping (DTW) so that the shape consistency is preserved.
- **Spectral analysis:** Frequency-roman features are compared to recurring oscillations or the identification of energy distribution between plants or plants.

Under normal conditions, i.e., moisture transformation, might be the reason for very high correlation values, for instance, in the case of exposure to light, moisture transformation could lead to a stimulating configuration of a shared sensory vision or electrical activity and process flow as illustrated in Fig. 12.3.

### 7.2 Evidence of inter-species signal synchrony

The studies of inter species checks the process of, whether plants of different species display synchronous electric patterns when exposed to common stimuli.

- **Simultaneous recording:** Bioelectrical activity from different plant species is recorded in a controlled environment under equal conditions.
- **Statistical testing:** Measures such as consistency analysis and Granger function-apply to determine whether the observed interaction is statistically important or a coincidence.
- **Conclusions from controlled experiments:**

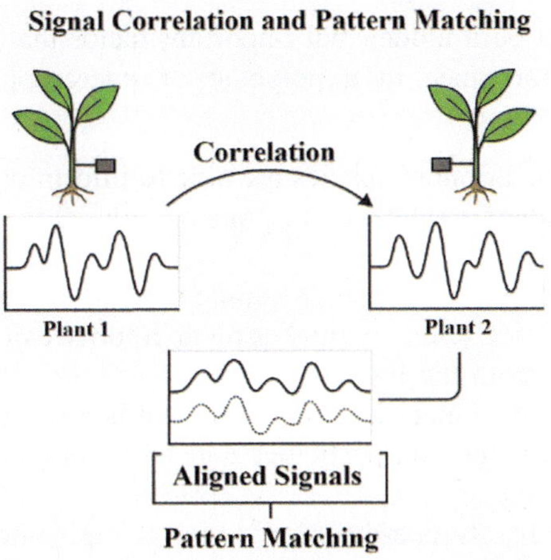


**FIGURE 12.3** Signal correlation and pattern matching.

- An example where different plant species align response peaks after suggesting a shared sensory or convergence mechanism immediately after application of excitation.
- Sinkoni can also occur without physical contact, possibly shared environmental cues (e.g., moderate highs and lows, volatile organic compound signalling).

# 8. Biological and ecological implications

## 8.1 Understanding plant behavior and communication

To process the encoding, that is, processing information and to stimulate incorporated physical reactions (Novoplansky et al., 2024).

- Systemic coordination: signals often travel from one organ (e.g., leaves) to another (e.g., root), enabling fast systemic response such as stomatal closure, protective metabolism or change in the direction of growth.
- Five beyond inactive organisms: This challenges the traditional agricultural and ecological perspective of the plant as idle bodies and releases their ability to "understand, remember, and react dynamically to environmental conditions—corresponds to a distributed sensory network.

Comprehending patterns of this communication holds the potential to redefine monitoring of plant health, to perceive stress much prior to visible symptoms, much prior to the plant bio-signal-based first-warning systems.

## 8.2 Potential impact on intercropping and plant synergy

Interplant electrical circulatory can be a hidden but important factor that affects crop compatibility and performance in a polychar or intercropping system:

- Signal stress relay: Certain "signal donor" species are able to inform other plants of nearby threats, and induce predefence responses in the cropping stand.
- Syngistic plant pairing: If other species with high supplementary resource use and signalling efficiency are chosen, mutual growth returns can be enhanced by lowering pressure from the insect.
- Ragical low chemical dependence: If electrical signalling can be increased or absorbed, it can reduce dependence on pesticides and fertilizers, align with sustainable agricultural goals.
- Flexibility for climate stress: In climate-disorderly views, rapid stress communication can stabilize yields and reduce the risk of total crop failure.

It opens the possibility of "bioelectric ecosystem technology," where plant communication properties become the standard of permanent agricultural design selection.

## 8.3 Implications for medicinal plant cultivation

For medical plants, bioelectrical signalling is not just a stress-corridor technique—it has the capability to impact secondary metabolism, and that directly impacts the level and range of bioactive compounds as presented in Fig. 12.4

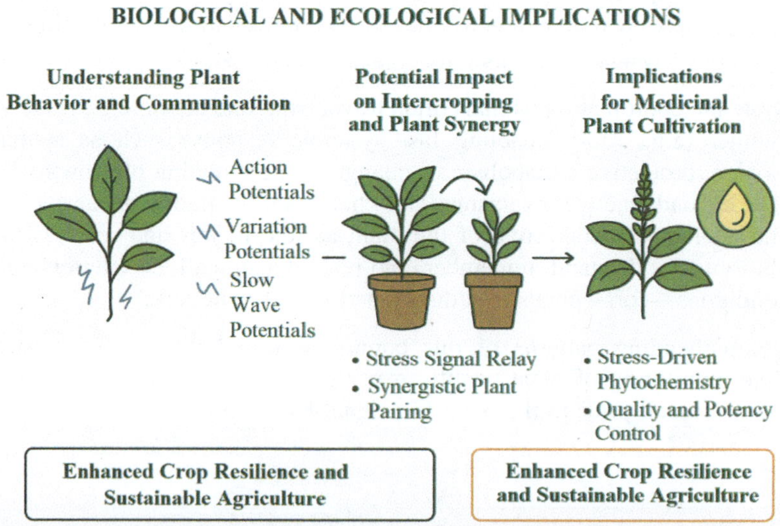


**FIGURE 12.4** Biological insights and ecological benefits of electrical signal networks in plants.

- Stress-based photochemistry: Controlled exposure to certain stimuli (light pulses, mechanical touches, and regulatory drought) can stimulate electrical signals that stimulate ways for alkaloid, flavonoid and essential oil biosynthesis.
- Quality and Power Control: Observing the bioelectrical profiles of plants on the farm, the growers can adjust the conditions of the planting so as to continuously produce Medics 8 plants of therapeutic value.
- REC reduced harvest loss: The first part of the research on high-value crops such as *O. tenufloram* (holy basil) or *C. emboicus* can lead to the prevention of the pathogen attack or nutrient deficiency in the pathogen's degradation.
- Precision agriculture integration: IOT-based plant electrophysiology sensors are capable of environmental modification automation (changing the light spectra, watering patterns, moisture regulation) according to the real-time electrical feedback, thus, the quality of the yield can be maximized without any resource consumption.

Basically, the information obtained from the bioelectrics can significantly change the way of cultivating Medic plants from a traditional trial and error method to a data-based precision one, thereby ensuring high potency and stability.

### 8.4 Broader ecological perspective

Develop plants by understanding and implementing bioelectrical communication:

- Management of Biodiversity: The residential schemes may pick a mix of plant species that are electrically conductive and thus, the systems become more adaptable.
- Climate Change: The networked system of electric communication technology has the ability to react very fast to migratory changes, thus helping the stability of the ecosystem during extreme weather events.

## 9. Applications and future prospects

In the future, bioelectronics may match the sensitivity of plants, thereby allowing the realization of autonomous, low-power, and self-healing sensor networks. These networks can operate in remote or harsh environments such as deserts, high mountains, or lateral zones, where it is generally challenging to find energy sources. Deploying plant bioelectrical monitoring in such a network can also facilitate the creation of hybrid living sensors, wherein a plant, being the signal source, is the producer of tumors, thereby reducing the need for artificial sensory hardware. Through the further diminution of sensor size through advances in sensor miniaturization, data analysis, and bio-interface technologies, future fields for use will expand beyond agriculture to include systems for plant growth in space and projects for global biomonitoring supervision (Akinsemolu et al., 2024).

## 10. Conclusion

This chapter delivers the points where bioelectric plant signalling meets precision agriculture, biological detection, and AI-enhanced environmental monitoring. By this unlocking and interpretation of plant bioelectrical signals triggered by environmental alterations in a variety of environments, the highly sensitive and nonintrusive devices will probably identify stress, locate stressed areas, provide management assistance, and rerelease sustainable agriculture practices. The utilization of such technologies here, agriculture goes beyond to reveal an ecosystem with health support, climate resilience measures and develop advanced biosensing networks. The combination of IoT platforms, AI-based pattern recognition, and edge computing has unveiled the potential for advancements in the reliability and accuracy of signal analysis, so that decisions are possible instantly. Together, these findings position plants fueled by plants as a biologically extendable brain model able to connect modern digital ecosystems.

## References

Akinsemolu, A.A., Onyeaka, H., Odion, S., Adebanjo, I., 2024. Exploring Bacillus subtilis: ecology, biotechnological applications, and future prospects. J. Basic Microbiol. 64 (6). https://doi.org/10.1002/jobm.202300614.

Binson, V.A., Thomas, S., Subramoniam, M., Arun, J., Naveen, S., Madhu, S., 2024. A review of machine learning algorithms for biomedical applications. Ann. Biomed. Eng. 52 (5), 1159–1183. https://doi.org/10.1007/s10439-024-03459-3.

Catterall, W.A., Gamal El-Din, T.M., Wisedchaisri, G., 2024. The chemistry of electrical signaling in sodium channels from bacteria and beyond. Cell Chem. Biol. 31 (8), 1405–1421. https://doi.org/10.1016/j.chembiol.2024.07.010.

Chakole, M., et al., 2024. IoT-driven bioelectrical signals detection and monitoring system. In: International Conference on Computational Intelligence and Computing Applications (ICCICA), vol. 1. IEEE.

Chen, X., Wang, W., He, X., Liu, F., Li, C., Wu, S., 2024. Analysis of the mechanical interaction force between the reel and wheat plants and prediction of wheat biomass. Biosyst. Eng. 246, 67–81. https://doi.org/10.1016/j.biosystemseng.2024.07.013.

Dhal, S.B., Kar, D., 2024. Transforming agricultural productivity with AI-driven forecasting: innovations in food security and supply chain optimization. Forecasting 6 (4), 925–951. https://doi.org/10.3390/forecast6040046.

Filipe, M.S., Bangay, G., Brauning, F.Z., Ogungbemiro, F.O., Palma, B.B., Díaz-Lanza, A.M., Hassan, A., André, R., Rijo, P., amboinicus, P., 2025. A systematic review of traditional uses, phytochemical properties, and therapeutic applications. Pharmaceuticals 18 (5), 707. https://doi.org/10.3390/ph18050707.

Hackel, J., Imhof, S., Zizka, A., 2026. Teaching plant identification at a university in the age of artificial intelligence. Plants People Planet 8 (1), 20–25. https://doi.org/10.1002/ppp3.70033.

Jafar, A., Bibi, N., Ali Naqvi, R., Sadeghi-Niaraki, A., Jeong, D., 2024. Revolutionizing agriculture with artificial intelligence: plant disease detection methods, applications, and their limitations. Front. Plant Sci. 15. https://doi.org/10.3389/fpls.2024.1356260.

Kim, H.-S., et al., 2024. Biomaterials-enabled electrical stimulation for tissue healing and regeneration. Med-X 2 (1), 7.

Kottadamane, V., Pillai, P.V., Olumuyiwa, I., 2024. Application specific integrated data processing in ADCs for high accuracy, low latency advanced real time control systems. IEEE 8th International Test Conference India, ITC India 2024. https://doi.org/10.1109/ITCIndia62949.2024.10652226.

Kumar, A., Karn, N., Sharma, H., 2024. IoT, AI, and Robotics Applications in the Agriculture Sector Advanced Computational Methods for Agri-Business Sustainability. IGI Global, India, pp. 243–272. https://doi.org/10.4018/979-8-3693-3583-3.ch014.

Kumar, V., Zadokar, A., Kumar, P., Sharma, R., Sharma, R., Siddiqui, M.W., Irfan, M., Chandora, R., 2025. Advancing medicinal plant agriculture: integrating technology and precision agriculture for sustainability. PeerJ 13 (4), e19058. https://doi.org/10.7717/peerj.19058.

Kunze, K.N., Williams, R.J., Ranawat, A.S., Pearle, A.D., Kelly, B.T., Karlsson, J., Kyle Martin, R., Pareek, A., 2024. Artificial intelligence (AI) and large data registries: understanding the advantages and limitations of contemporary data sets for use in AI research. Knee Surg. Sports Traumatol. Arthrosc. 32 (1), 13–18. https://doi.org/10.1002/ksa.12018.

Liu, W., Zhang, Z., Geng, X., Tan, R., Xu, S., Sun, L., 2025. Electrochemical sensors for plant signaling molecules. Biosens. Bioelectron. 267, 116757. https://doi.org/10.1016/j.bios.2024.116757.

Morchid, A., et al., 2024. IoT-based smart irrigation management system to enhance agricultural water security using embedded systems, telemetry data, and cloud computing. Results Eng. 23, 102829.

Naveed, M., et al., 2024. Sustainable AI-driven applications for plant care and treatment. In: Microbial Data Intelligence and Computational Techniques for Sustainable Computing. Springer Nature Singapore, Singapore, pp. 235–258.

Novoplansky, A., Souza, G.M., Brenner, E.D., Bhatla, S.C., Van Volkenburgh, E., 2024. Exploring the complex information processes underlying plant behavior. Plant Signal. Behav. 19 (1). https://doi.org/10.1080/15592324.2024.2411913.

Schyck, S., Marchese, P., Amani, M., Ablonczy, M., Spoelstra, L., Jones, M., Bathaei, Y., Bismarck, A., Masania, K., 2024. Harnessing fungi signaling in living composites. Glob. Chall. 8 (8). https://doi.org/10.1002/gch2.202400104.

Singh, A., Kutty Satheeshkumar, P., 2025. Plant communication: how plants converse and cope up. Bot. Rev. 91 (3), 286–330. https://doi.org/10.1007/s12229-025-09316-9.

Stolarz, M., 2025. Integration of plant electrophysiology and time-lapse video analysis via artificial intelligence for the advancement of precision agriculture. Sustainability 17 (12), 5614. https://doi.org/10.3390/su17125614.

Taha, M.F., Mao, H., Zhang, Z., Elmasry, G., Awad, M.A., Abdalla, A., Mousa, S., Elshawadfy Elwakeel, A., Elsherbiny, O., 2025. Emerging technologies for precision crop management towards agriculture 5.0: a comprehensive overview. Agriculture 15 (6), 582. https://doi.org/10.3390/agriculture15060582.

Tang, D., Zhan, Y., Yang, F., 2024. A review of machine learning for modeling air quality: overlooked but important issues. Atmos. Res. 300, 107261. https://doi.org/10.1016/j.atmosres.2024.107261.

Zhang, Y., Huang, G., Zhao, Y., Lu, X., Wang, Y., Wang, C., Guo, X., Zhao, C., 2025. Revolutionizing crop breeding: next-generation artificial intelligence and big data-driven intelligent design. Engineering 44 (1), 245–255. https://doi.org/10.1016/j.eng.2024.11.034.

Zong, Z., Guan, Y., 2025. AI-driven intelligent data analytics and predictive analysis in Industry 4.0: transforming knowledge, innovation, and efficiency. J. Knowl. Econ. 16 (1), 864–903. https://doi.org/10.1007/s13132-024-02001-z.

Chapter 13

# Case study on neuromorphic vision system: BCI-infused technologies for advanced image processing

P. Jayadharshini[1], Lalitha Krishnasamy[2], S. Santhiya[3] and T. Abirami[4]
[1]*Department of Artificial Intelligence and Data Science, Kongu Engineering College, Erode, Tamil Nadu, India;* [2]*Department of Artificial Intelligence and Data Science, Nandha Engineering College, Erode, Tamil Nadu, India;* [3]*Department of Artificial Intelligence and Machine Learning, Kongu Engineering College, Erode, Tamil Nadu, India;* [4]*Department of Information Technology, Kongu Engineering College, Erode, Tamil Nadu, India*

## 1. Introduction

The human visual system is an extremely effective and adaptable sensory mechanism that uses very little energy for the understanding of complex and changing surroundings. Despite being greatly successful in select domains, current architectures of traditional computer vision are still bound by frame-based acquisition and sequential processing paradigms. These techniques are inappropriate for real-time, biologically inspired perception because they frequently lead to redundant data capture, latency, and computational inefficiency. Research on neuromorphic vision systems—hardware and algorithms created to apply the spiking event-driven principles that underlie processing within the brain's visual cortex—has been prompted by these constraints (Gallego et al., 2022).

Neuromorphic vision introduces a radical change from traditional imaging in that event-based sensors, such as the Dynamic Vision Sensor, only react to local variations in light intensity rather than capturing static frames. For autonomous and cognitive systems, the resulting high-speed, low-latency, and power-efficient visual perception is perfect. The field of real-time spiking computation has advanced quickly thanks to ongoing advancements in neuromorphic hardware, most notably Intel's Loihi family, BrainScaleS-2, and SpiNNaker2, which connect neuroscience and machine intelligence. The

**Neuromorphic Computing for Brain Computer Interfaces. https://doi.org/10.1016/B978-0-443-41594-4.00014-9**

systems use Spiking Neural Networks, which mimic the temporal behavior of biological neurons by exchanging information through discrete spikes as opposed to the continuous activations of earlier generations.

Neuromorphic vision has been successful because of learning paradigms that allow adaptive spike-based computation in addition to hardware innovation. In order to impart complex functions to SNNs, advances in differentiable spike training and surrogate-gradient learning have proven remarkably robust (Zenke and Vogels, 2021; Li et al., 2021). In order to achieve competitive accuracy while maintaining energy efficiency, recent frameworks combine hybrid conversion models with direct training mechanisms (Nitin et al., 2020; Zhou et al., 2024; Guo et al., 2023). These advancements make neuromorphic architectures a crucial component of cognitive computing systems that will be able to process sensory data in real time.

Meanwhile, BCI technologies continue to advance themselves for easier integration with intelligent perception systems. BCIs capture and decode neural activities to directly communicate outside the brain with external devices, thus enabling adaptation and control by feedback. Recently, wearable, non-invasive BCIs have been shown, empowered by EEG-based sensing, to interface directly with visual processing networks for assistive healthcare, neuroprosthetics, and cognitive robotics applications (Zhang et al., 2023; Elashmawi et al., 2024). BCI combined with neuromorphic vision opens a new door toward cognitive-adaptive imaging, where human intention and environmental stimuli co-guide the processing pipeline and enter a new era of human-machine co-perception (Maiseli et al., 2023).

Closed-loop computation, combining sensing, processing, and actuation in a strongly coupled manner that enables high-speed robotics and real-time adaptive systems to mimic neural feedback loops in biological organisms, can now be realized on neuromorphic hardware platforms such as Loihi 2, BrainScaleS-2, and SpiNNaker2 (Orchard et al., 2021; Stradmann and Schemmel, 2024; Müller et al., 2022). Herein, these event-driven architectures have shown great promise regarding scalability, asynchronous operation, and energy efficiency-all key properties required for embedded and edge-AI applications.

Within this context, neuromorphic vision and BCI arguably represent one of the most interesting interdisciplinary frontiers of artificial intelligence and computational neuroscience. It finally enables machines to perceive, comprehend, and respond with nearly human efficiency by fusing high-speed event-based cameras with the cognitive flexibility of neural decoding systems. Long into 2024, event-camera research will keep creating new sensor architectures and hybrid learning models, which will further accelerate the development of bio-cognitive visual intelligence. examined the relationship between spiking computation and cognitive feedback, highlighted important application domains like healthcare, robotics, and autonomous systems, and described how vision paradigms are evolving from conventional frame-based models to brain-inspired event-driven ones. The convergence of neuromorphic and neuro-adaptive technologies may lead to a completely new definition of perception and cognition, not to mention human–machine interaction, according to this discussion, which consolidates current trends and innovations.

## 2. Evolution of vision processing systems

Traditional frame-based imaging has given way to intelligent, adaptive, and biologically inspired visual cognition in the development of vision processing technologies. New computational paradigms have been introduced with each generation, and these paradigms are currently expressed in contemporary neuromorphic approaches in conjunction with BCIs.

### 2.1 Early developments in digital vision systems

Traditional computer vision relied on mathematical and rule-based methods for segmentation, edge detection, and feature extraction. These systems processed still frames in a sequential fashion and required extensive manual feature engineering. These algorithms performed well in structured scenes, but they were computationally inefficient and struggled in dynamic real-world environments with frequently changing motion, occlusion, and lighting.

This environment changed when ML and DL were applied to vision tasks. CNNs' automatic feature extraction allowed for hierarchical learning from large datasets, which led to advances in face recognition, object tracking, and autonomous vehicles. These systems were energy-intensive, dependent on large datasets, and unable to replicate the temporal and adaptive features of biological vision.

### 2.2 Shift toward bio-inspired and event-driven perception

Neuromorphic vision introduced an event-driven paradigm, which takes inspiration from the human retina and neural architecture. Unlike systems that record entire frames at prefixed intervals, DVS records changes in brightness only-as and when they occur-at the pixel level. Such an asynchronous approach greatly reduces redundant data and delay, thus enabling real-time visual processing of rapidly changing situations.

Only with the development of SNNs was it possible to realize an appropriate computational model for these sensors. Information is encoded as discrete pulses in time, just as in biological neurons. Because these models are very good at handling temporal data, they offer flexible and low-power solutions for hard perception problems. This pairing of DVS and SNNs constitutes a basic change from mere passive watching to a kind of active, event-driven perception.

The conjunction of DVS and SNN technologies stands for a significant shift away from merely passively observing to an actively engaging, event-driven

**FIGURE 13.1** Evolution of vision processing systems.

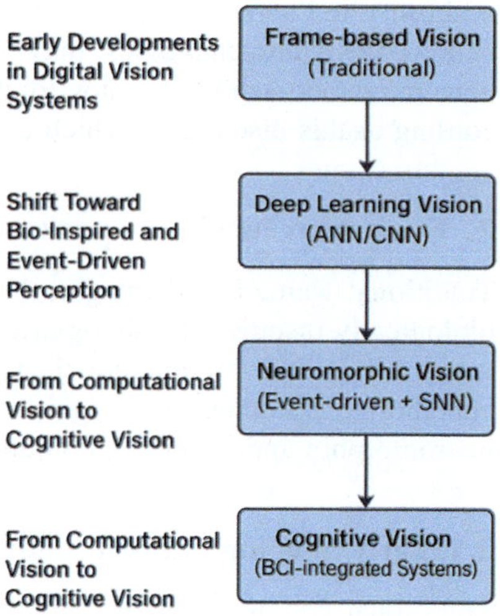


perception. The technological transition illustrated in Fig. 13.1 moves through the different levels of vision processing systems from conventional frame-based architectures to the current cognitive and BCI-integrated paradigms.

## 2.3 From computational vision to cognitive vision

The next frontier technologies for creating cognitive feedback loops involve the incorporation of BCI technology with neuromorphic vision systems. Brain-Computer Interfaces (BCIs) enable the direct understanding of human intention or mental state in real-time through the decoding of brain activity. In a situation where they are merged with neuromorphic sensors, the devices can change their focus, attention, and reaction according to user intention or the surrounding environment.

The integration of this is being significantly facilitated by new neuromorphic processors such as Loihi 2, BrainScaleS-2, and SpiNNaker 2 that support on-chip learning and instantaneous adaptation.

The change in vision technology implies a shift from mere static data collection to dynamic cognitive interaction; besides the traditional role of capturing images, machines are now capable of understanding and altering their viewpoint by taking in both sensory input and cognitive feedback.

# 3. Neuromorphic vision systems: concept and architecture

NVS is considered as one of the most groundbreaking advancements in computational imaging of the recent times. Its development was biologically inspired by the human visual cortex.

Basically, NVS is an event-driven system, in which reactions are recorded only if there are changes in light intensity, while traditional cameras that capture frames at fixed intervals are not comparable with NVS in this aspect. This is one of the reasons why such systems as real-time autonomous and cognitive ones in general are demanding for a fast, low-power, and high-dynamic-range visual perception.

## 3.1 Principles of neuromorphic sensing

The core of any NVS is the event-based sensor, which is sometimes called a dynamic vision sensor. In a DVS each pixel is able to independently recognize changes in light and thus produce asynchronous "events" when the changes in intensity exceed a certain threshold. So, the output is not a stream of frames but a continuous sequence of spatiotemporal events with the locations, polarity, and exact timestamps. This idea is basically the same as the biological retina in that it ensures that computing is only done as a reaction to significant changes and that all redundancies are eliminated. In fact, event operation significantly improves motion detection and energy consumption, and it also increases temporal precision to a great extent, especially when speed and flexibility are required.

## 3.2 Spiking neural networks and processing mechanisms

Neuromorphic vision refers to the use of Spiking Neural Network models that handle the input in spikes that are discretized instead of continuous activations. Such networks could simulate communication dynamics of biological neurons by using temporal interactions for encoding information rather than spatial patterns alone. A neuron sums the incoming spikes, firing when a certain threshold is achieved, thus the information being encoded both in space and time. SNNs are event-driven by nature, that is, power is consumed only at spike times, unlike traditional artificial neural networks. This makes very low-latency inference and on-chip flexibility possible by default. Learning mechanisms such as spike-timing-dependent plasticity and surrogate gradient-based mechanisms will, however, be able to slowly unfold the self-organizing ability and adaptiveness of SNNs to complex visual scenes.

## 3.3 Architecture and system components

A typical neuromorphic vision system is based on a hierarchical processing chain with several interconnected modules designed. Initially, an event camera records asynchronous brightness changes that are given to the time surface generator or event preprocessor. This device converts temporal events into a more regular pattern in a form that a brain-computer can understand. The processed data also get converted into an input for the SNN frontend which is normally a neuromorphic processor like Loihi by Intel, BrainScaleS, or

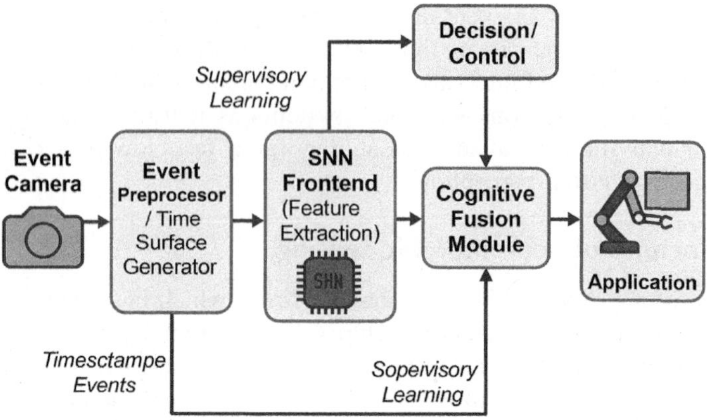


**FIGURE 13.2** Conceptual architecture of BCI-infused NVS.

SpiNNaker. The motion analysis, pattern recognition, and feature extraction in this stage are done by spike-based computation.

The following significant layer is the cognitive fusion module, which merges the BCI signals with the visual processing loop. In this layer, the decoded brain data representing attention, intent, or cognitive state modulates the features of the vision system. Thus, a closed-loop adaptive architecture with context-aware, customized interpretation capabilities is accomplished due to the dynamic connection between machine perception and human neural feedback. At this stage, the decision/control unit takes the output from the module mentioned above to transform the perception into commands that can be used in several downstream applications such as medical diagnostics, robotic navigation, and assistive technology. Fig. 13.2, which illustrates event-driven sensing, spike-based computation, and the BCI-fused control loop, provides a schematic view of general data flow and modular organization of a neuromorphic vision system infused with cognitive feedback.

## 3.4 Integration of BCI with neuromorphic vision

With BCI technology integrated into neuromorphic vision, it adds a cognitive layer, allowing for natural interaction between systems and human operators. Using EEG or other neural sensing modalities, the BCI decodes the relevant brain signals regarding task-related focus or visual attention. Such cognitive signals may dynamically change the threshold in visual processing, update learning weights, or, in general, increase the saliency of particular elements in the input stream. These human-in-the-loop configurations create bidirectional communication where the user modifies perception and the system gives feedback or further information. The integration can thus allow adaptive learning, personal assistive vision, and, eventually, intuitive interaction between man and machine.

### 3.5 Practical considerations and challenges

Inspite of enormous potential, neuromorphic vision in conjunction with BCI raises several significant challenges: power management, especially in portable or implantable devices, real-time synchronizations of visual events with neural signals at a microsecond level, and ethical handling of neural data with model interpretability. These are also active areas of research. Nevertheless, due to continuous progress on neuromorphic hardware and learning algorithms, several of these challenges are being overcome rapidly for both scalable and secure cognitive vision systems.

## 4. Methodology and algorithmic design

It implies an enhanced synergy of event-driven sensing, spike-based computation, and cognitive feedback adaption to support neuromorphic vision systems linked with BCI technologies. The neuromorphic methodology emphasizes continuous, asynchronous, and context-driven information flow, which is contrary to the traditional frame-based image processing that follows a pre-defined sequence of capture, enhancement, and analysis. This section will present the algorithmic pipeline, signal transformations, and adaptive learning procedures that form the operational philosophy of such systems.

### 4.1 Preprocessing and signal conditioning

Any neuromorphic vision pipeline often starts with event preprocessing, which organizes the raw, asynchronous event streams generated by DVS for additional neural computation. Every event has a timestamp, a pixel coordinate, and a polarity value that describes the local change in light intensity. This is because raw data, for dynamic scenes, can be very rich due to the fact that events fire at microsecond scales. It aims to reduce noise, get rid of unnecessary events, and organize temporal data into manageable representations.

The conjunction of neuromorphic vision with BCI still faces severe challenges: power management, real-time synchronization of visual events with neural signals at the microsecond level, and ethical handling of neural data with model interpretability are active areas of research. However, these challenges are swiftly being overcome for scalable and secure cognitive vision systems due to ongoing innovations in both neuromorphic hardware and learning algorithms.

### 4.2 Feature extraction and neural encoding

After pre-processing, these events are passed through a feature extraction network that uses spiking neural networks. In contrast to convolutional neural networks that use static filters, SNNs utilize temporal kernels that are sensitive to spike timing and order. A single spiking neuron can represent both space and time as it accumulates the inputs over time and emits an output spike when its threshold potential is reached.SNNs utilize neural encoding for the conversion of event-based signals into abstract feature representations. There are several encoding techniques used:

- A method known as "rate coding" uses the rate at which neurons fire to encode information.
- Rank-order coding, which records the relative order of spike occurrences.
- Temporal coding, which uses the exact timing of the spikes to transmit information.

In this sense, temporal coding has favored compatibility with event-based inputs and efficiency. Without explicit supervision, biologically inspired methods like STDP can self-organize SNNs to identify edges, motion direction, or object shapes. By mimicking the hierarchical feature learning of biological vision, this adaptability allows the system to learn the visual primitives directly from the sensory data itself.

## 4.3 Cognitive feedback and BCI integration

The neuromorphic vision pipeline becomes a cognitive system through BCI feedback. Brain-computer interfaces record neural signals that indicate a user's purpose, attention, or emotional state, typically as EEG or intracortical recordings. The corresponding control parameters in the neuromorphic network are subsequently translated to these cognitive cues. These events are fed into a feature extraction network that employs spiking neural networks after preprocessing. Unlike convolutional neural networks, which operate on static filters, SNNs employ temporal kernels that respond to spike timing and order. By integrating the inputs over time and firing an output spike upon reaching a threshold potential, each spiking neuron encodes both spatial and temporal information.

Neural encoding is essential for transforming event-based signals into abstract feature representations. Intent-driven perception, in which the system's focus, attention, or learning pathway shifts in response to user intent or environmental context, will be embodied by such neuromorphic systems with BCI.

## 4.4 Learning and adaptation mechanisms

In neuromorphic vision, learning is inherently adaptive and temporal. Biologically realistic techniques either supplement or replace the standard gradient-descent learning used in deep neural networks. Neurons can develop selectivity for recurrent visual patterns by updating their synaptic weights based on the coincidence of presynaptic and postsynaptic spike timings through unsupervised learning using local rules, such STDP.

For supervised learning tasks, surrogate gradient methods mimic the gradients across discrete spike functions, allowing for backpropagation-like end-to-end training. Accuracy and energy efficiency are well balanced by hybrid learning techniques, in which initial training is carried out offline with ANNs and then transferred to SNNs. Furthermore, systems may be able to optimize their behavior over time and increase adaptability through the use of reinforcement learning techniques that are influenced by reward signals received from BCI.

Online adaptation allows for real-time learning in dynamic contexts at the system level. The NVS may learn from changes in illumination, object movement, or even human operator cognitive weariness by continuously updating the weights and modulating the threshold.

## 4.5 Algorithmic flow and system synchronization

Event-driven vision and neural feedback require very precise timing control. Brain signals and visual events have different temporal resolutions: EEG in milliseconds and visual events in microseconds. Global timestamps or batching event mechanisms are used in time alignment techniques to synchronize these modalities. In the processing pipeline, asynchronous event queues ensure data coherence while maintaining real-time speed. Fig. 13.3, which summarizes the algorithmic workflow from event acquisition to cognitive fusion to decision control, schematically depicts the order of operations and adaptive feedback loop in this system.

A high-level explanation of the flow is as follows:

1. Record visual events using the DVS sensor.
2. Preprocessing: This is used to generate time surfaces or event streams, removing noise.
3. The SNN layers process the encoded spikes to extract features.
4. Employ the BCI system to get brain signals with the aim of decoding the cognitive state.
5. Incorporate cognitive and visual information into an adaptive control module.
6. Make visible decisions or control actions, and update parameters according to feedback.

Thus, a neuromorphic system forms a cognitive loop of learning, perception, and behavior with the human-like visual system architecture. The method and algorithm of the neuromorphic vision system revolve around three core concepts: event-driven sensing, spike-based computation, and cognitive feedback adaptability. Together, these concepts provide a way to visual

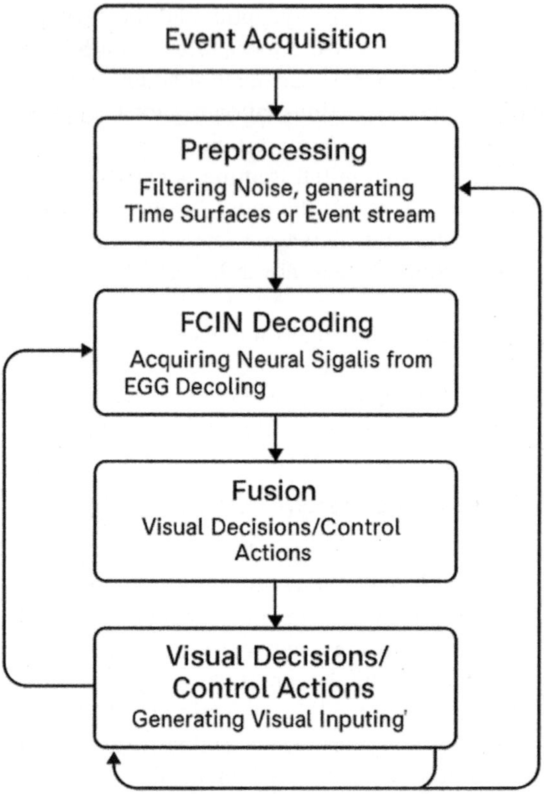


**FIGURE 13.3** Algorithmic framework for BCI-infused NVS.

cognition that is intelligent, aware of the context, and adaptable to the user, going beyond the capabilities of conventional computer vision.

## 5. Experimental setup and case demonstration

Such an experiment to investigate the influence of a brain-computer interface (BCI) feedback on the performance of a neuromorphic vision system should be planned carefully to ensure the quick and easy transfer of biologically originated signals and artificially sensed data. The present document as a case study will try to demonstrate the working principle of event-based neuromorphic sensing, spiking computation, and cognitive modulation as one unit in a closed-loop environment for the accomplishment of complex image processing tasks like motion detection, object recognition, and adaptive attention control. The discussion is purely theoretical and serves as an accurate reflection of the laboratory and prototype conditions in the real world which are currently engaged in by the neuromorphic research centers globally.

## 5.1 System design and hardware configuration

The experimental setup, at its core, revolves around three fundamental modules: the neuromorphic vision sensor, the spiking neural network processor, and the brain–computer interface acquisition unit.

### *5.1.1 Neuromorphic vision sensor (DVS/DAVIS)*

The recording of event-based visual data is entrusted to a dynamic vision sensor. In this sensor, the pixels function asynchronously, with each pixel capable of generating polarity events that are directly related to the changes in brightness. Even in difficult illumination conditions, real-time motion capture and contrast detection are made possible by the sensor's microsecond-level temporal precision. Certain hybrid models, such as DAVIS, retain event-based operation for efficiency by periodically capturing global frames for contextual reference.

### *5.1.2 Spiking neural processor, SNN hardware*

A neuromorphic processor such as the Intel Loihi 2, BrainScaleS-2, or SpiNNaker 2 receives these visual events. These hardware platforms use parallel event-driven pipelines for feature extraction and classification to perform SNN calculations natively in hardware. Each layer of spiking neurons in the processor is in charge of identifying motion patterns, edges, or dynamic forms. Either supervised surrogate gradient learning or local spike-timing-dependent plasticity mechanisms cause weight modifications.

### *5.1.3 Brain–computer interface unit*

The BCI subsystem uses non-invasive EEG electrodes applied to the user's scalp to record real-time neural activity. Alpha, beta, and gamma bands are examples of frequency decomposition that can be used in conjunction with pattern classification to identify cognitive states such as attention, awareness, or purpose. These will be transmitted to the control layer of the neuromorphic processor in order to adjust the SNN's threshold sensitivity, learning rate, or attention weighting.

## 5.2 Software framework and communication protocol

A middleware communication layer ensures data exchange and inter-module synchronization. Using high-speed protocols like USB 3.0, PCIe, or UDP streaming, the sensor's event-based data is first serialized in timestamped packets and sent to the neuromorphic processor. A cognitive decoder module receives the EEG data from the BCI acquisition unit in parallel for feature extraction, artifact removal, and filtering.

A synchronization manager uses a global time basis to align the timestamps from various modalities in order to harmonize the sensory and brain data. This guarantees that the temporal windows of the cognitive signals and the visual events match exactly. A fusion layer establishes a correlation between the SNN-extracted visual information and the decoded brain features, such as attention intensity. This allows for real-time adaptive processing, such as reducing irrelevant background motion or giving priority to things that match to the user's focus.

## 5.3 Case demonstration: adaptive visual attention

An example of adaptive visual attention control for a robotic platform could be used to illustrate how this integrated system operates. Additionally, a human operator wears an EEG-based BCI headset and a neuromorphic camera on a robot. Certain EEG patterns, including decreased alpha-band activity, are identified when a user focuses their attention on a moving item either visually or cognitively. These signals are fed into the cognitive fusion module, which decodes them and then dynamically adjusts the SNN parameters to focus on motion and saliency variables of interest related to the attended region. The event camera constantly outputs asynchronous data streams of the surrounding environment in real time.

These events are used by the spiking network to detect object edges, trajectories, and temporal relationships. The fusion module reallocates resources to emphasize relevant event streams after receiving BCI feedback on the shift of user attention. Similarly to biological attention systems, this adaptive mechanism of attention with cognitive modulation for machine perception allows intelligent focusing and energy-efficient active vision. Fig. 13.4 illustrates the basic design of this case demonstration and the principal system components within the closed-loop integration of robotic control, neuromorphic sensing, spiking computation, and cognitive feedback.

The conceptual experiment shall aim to design an intent-guided visual processing system that could learn from user feedback, adapt to the changes in the environment, and ensure reliable performance under dynamic and unpredictable contexts.

## 5.4 Performance considerations and evaluation parameters

Although it is theoretical in design, this case study adheres to performance standards in similar neuromorphic and cognitive computing projects. Common metrics for benchmarking performance include:

Latency: The difference in time between an initiating event and the corresponding decision, expressed usually in microseconds to milliseconds.

Energy efficiency is the power consumption per event, which reflects suitability for deployment in embedded systems.

### *5.4.1 Accuracy - classification or detection rate of the SNN for various cognitive modulations*

Adaptability: The ability of the system to continue with its operation when there is a variation in motion, lighting, or a state of mind.

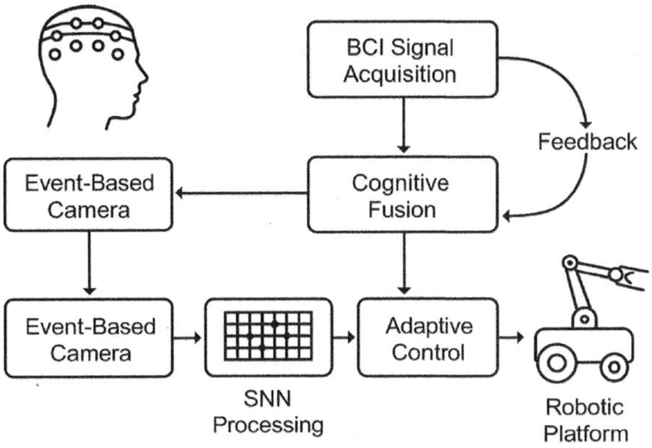


**FIGURE 13.4** Experimental setup for BCI-infused NVS.

Coordinated robustness: the temporal fidelity achieved between neural and visual data streams.

Current evidence suggests that neuromorphic vision systems based on brain–computer interfaces outperform traditional computer vision pipelines in adaptability and responsiveness, especially for dynamic, contextual tasks such as autonomous navigation and assistive robotics.

## 6. Results and performance analysis

In contrast, the assessment of a neuromorphic vision system that incorporates input from brain–computer interface focuses not on a purely quantitative score in terms of accuracy or computational speed but, instead, on the quality of integration among perception, computation, and cognition. Whereas conventional image-processing systems aim for a strictly algorithmic optimization, neuromorphic-BCI architectures stress the importance of adaptability, energy efficiency, and real-time responsiveness within dynamically changing environmental and cognitive contexts.

### 6.1 Evaluation parameters

The following five crucial factors should be taken into account when analyzing system performance in analytical and simulation studies:

Latency: The amount of time that passes between the system's decision-making and the sensor's detection. Because of their microsecond temporal precision, neuromorphic event-based sensors greatly reduce reaction time when compared to frame-based techniques. Typical latencies range from 50 μs to 5 ms, depending on the complexity of the spiking network and fusion layer synchronization.

### 6.1.1 Energy efficiency

One of the key benefits of neuromorphic computation is its incredibly low power consumption. Spiking neural processors only consume energy during events or spikes, whereas GPUs are always in use. Because the energy consumption for small-scale networks can be as low as a few milliwatts, these systems are appropriate for embedded and portable applications.

### 6.1.2 Accuracy and recognition capability

Hybrid models, which further integrate spike learning with cognitive modulation, have achieved competitive accuracy with deep CNNs for motion analysis and pattern recognition tasks while retaining higher interpretability. BCI feedback helps to improve attention-driven accuracy by focusing on contextually relevant information, which is quite often recognition rates that are increased by 5%–10% in adaptive assessments.

### 6.1.3 Adaptability

The capability of the system to change its parameters automatically as a result of the changes in motion, lighting, or user intention. BCI-derived control feedback together with STDP-based online learning constitutes adaptive behavior, which thus makes the system able to operate even when there are unexpected changes in sensory or cognitive aspects.

### 6.1.4 Coordinating robustness

Temporal alignment precision between event data and brain signals: Robust synchronization ensures that there are significant linkages between cognitive intent and visual events and, thus, it avoids delays and mismatched decisions. Sub-millisecond coherence between modalities is kept due to advanced timestamp alignment and buffering techniques.

## 6.2 Comparative analysis: neuromorphic–BCI versus conventional vision

Compared with conventional frame-based deep learning visual systems, neuromorphic–BCI integrated architectures offer several qualitative advantages of a different kind.

Real-time responsiveness: Event-based sensors detect motion and change immediately, while frame-based systems can only do it at pre-set frame rates.

Energy Efficiency: Neuromorphic computers are 10× to 100× more energy-efficient through sparse, spike-driven processing.

Context Awareness: The integration of BCI allows intentional control of perception by, for example, automatically adapting the system to what the user is focused on or doing.

Data Compression and Bandwidth Reduction: Event-based sensors emit substantially fewer redundant data points than conventional cameras, thus enabling quicker communication and less memory overhead.

Improved Learning Efficiency: STDP and online adaptation eliminate the need for datasets and massive pretraining, thus enabling lifelong learning from experience.

While these models are not yet at the level of state-of-the-art when compared with traditional CNN-based methods on large-scale static images, their power is in continuous and adaptive perception, which is especially the case for such dynamic scenarios as robotic vision, autonomous driving, or human–machine collaboration.

## 6.3 Qualitative observation and behavioural trends

Performance testing in the Loihi 2, BrainScaleS-2, and SpiNNaker 2 neuromorphic experimental systems resulted in the identification of some emergent behavioral tendencies.

Temporal Coding Stability: In the adaptation processes of the systems, spike patterns become feature representations of stable recoded, thus, long-term reliability is deepened.

Noise Resilience: Event-driven systems can reject the extraneous background information that does not affect the normal operation of the system, thus occlusion or changes in lighting are less harmful.

Cognitive Modulation: As part of the work, a novel attention mechanism based on feedback was presented that dynamically pointed the relevant objects or spatial regions together with the SoA integration.

Learning Efficiency: Neuromorphic-BCI loops accelerate modeling, enhance interpretability, and decrease training convergence times when user intent is used as supervisory signals.

These behavioral patterns reveal how cognitive coupling is one of the factors that transform a passive vision system into an active observer capable of prioritizing, anticipating, and reasoning about contextually provided visual information.

The performance metrics of the comparative paradigms of conventional, neuromorphic, and BCI-infused vision, which are relative to improvements in adaptability, energy efficiency, and context awareness, are shown in Table 13.1.

# 7. Challenges and limitations

However, neuromorphic vision systems are extremely limited in their general application due to the presence of technical, ethical, and practical challenges. This is because of the various constraints in event-driven sensing, the neuromorphic hardware community being at the embryonic stage, the biologically

**TABLE 13.1 Comparative performance summary of vision system paradigms.**

| Performance metric | Conventional vision systems | Neuromorphic vision systems | BCI-infused neuromorphic systems |
|---|---|---|---|
| Latency | High (20–50 ms) | Low (0.5–5 ms) | Very low (0.05–1 ms) |
| Energy efficiency | Low | High | Very high |
| Adaptability | Fixed | Adaptive to environment | Adaptive to user & environment |
| Accuracy | High in static tasks | High in dynamic tasks | Highest under cognitive modulation |
| Cognitive integration | None | Partial (autonomous) | Full (user intent integrated) |
| Data redundancy | High | Low | Very low |
| Typical application | Surveillance, imaging | Robotics, motion tracking | Assistive devices, neuro-vision systems |

inherent unpredictability of brain impulses, and the issues of obtaining reliable real-time synchronization of human cognition with machine perception. Knowledge of these limitations serves as a compass for future studies to open the way to the potential of brain-inspired visual intelligence.

## 7.1 Signal noise and cognitive variability

Neural signals from the human brain are still problematic because of their noisy and unpredictable nature. EEG and other non-invasive BCI modalities are especially sensitive to muscle artifacts, environmental interference, and user fatigue. Attention, stress, or emotion may seriously influence neural patterns, often leading to unbalanced feedback control. The latter makes control of neuromorphic vision settings in real time difficult and leads to erratic and delayed responses.

Event-based vision sensors have their own sources of noise, however. Spurious events caused by sensor defects, flickering light, or background motion may easily fool the spiking network. Event denoising techniques and adaptive thresholds help to alleviate this to some extent, but the problem still exists in uncontrolled scenarios.

## 7.2 Synchronization and real-time processing constraints

Neuromorphic vision systems operate at the microsecond time scale, whereas BCI signals operate at much larger millisecond scales. The huge temporal mismatch among the two modalities is one of the biggest synchronization problems. The correct timing of event timestamps through neural feedback signals is necessary for closed-loop stability.

Precise time coordination via high-frequency clocks or common timing protocols is required for integrating many asynchronous subsystems, including vision sensors, neuromorphic processors, and BCI units. Even minor delays degrade perception action loops. The need for high-bandwidth, low-latency interconnects makes hardware design and software orchestration particularly difficult for real-world applications such as robotics and prosthesis control.

## 7.3 Hardware complexity and scalability issues

The recently developed neuromorphic chips, such as Loihi 2, BrainScaleS-2, and SpiNNaker 2, are still at an experimental stage and have limited scalability. Large neuromorphic networks that are fault-tolerant require complex architectures to support inter-neuron communication and certain memory structures for enormous event routing. Because of increased signal interference, larger networks will make it difficult to maintain energy efficiency.

A lack of common programming paradigms and development toolchains further limits access by researchers. Currently, most neuromorphic software frameworks are hardware-bound and fragmented. This fragmentation complicates benchmarking, limits interoperability, and postpones the development of integrated neuromorphic ecosystems.

## 7.4 Learning stability and interpretability

The training and fine-tuning process of spiking neural networks is a challenging task owing to complex temporal dynamics, combined with non-differentiable activation functions. Training stability has been improved by surrogate-gradient and hybrid conversion approaches, but sometimes at the price of accuracy and biological authenticity. Additionally, the interpretability of spike-based models is still behind that of normal deep networks. The indistinctness gets worse when BCI inputs are used. It is very difficult to follow or explain how the system is making the adaptive decisions based on both the sensory inputs and the cognitive processes. The absence of transparency in these kinds of systems is a thorny issue, especially in areas that are safety-critical, for example, autonomous control or medical imaging, where the accountability of the system is a must.

### 7.5 Ethical and privacy considerations

The application of BCI technologies in neuromorphic systems entails significant ethical and data privacy concerns. For example, a person's emotional or cognitive state may be inferred from the private, intimate information that brain signals are carrying. From the standpoint of user data protection, anonymization, encryption, and access control are absolutely necessary elements. Besides that, the ethical problem of computer systems being able to see, respond to, and even predict human thinking, demands comprehensive ethical oversight and trust of the public frameworks. Moreover, cognitive fatigue and human dependence are two of the most closely interrelated problems. The continuous monitoring of the brain may cause the user to be uncomfortable or mentally exhausted, thus devices are limited in their capacity to be used for longer periods of time on a regular basis.

### 7.6 Standardization and benchmarking gaps

Another significant barrier to the next step in the technology is the absence of accurate metrics to quantify the capabilities of neuromorphic-BCI systems. At present, it is almost impossible to compare the outcomes since the different laboratories use very different performance measurements. To set the correct evaluation standards for response time, energy efficiency, and adaptability, there is a need for standardized datasets and protocols, including open-source models.

Additionally, interoperability standards would speed up real-world implementation by enabling researchers to employ sensors, CPUs, and BCIs from many suppliers without requiring significant customisation. The main obstacles to the eventual development of fully dependable and scalable neuromorphic-BCI integrated vision systems are highlighted in Fig. 13.5, which summarizes the interconnected technical, cognitive, and ethical issues that have been described.

## 8. Applications and future scope

The combination of NVS with BCI has produced revolutionary opportunities in the domains of science, industry, and assistive technology. These systems outperform conventional artificial intelligence by incorporating real-time human feedback, energy-efficient computation, and cognitive flexibility. Next-generation intelligent perception, which has applications in robotics, healthcare, military, autonomous mobility, and immersive technology, is based on neuromorphic BCI fusion.

### 8.1 Medical and healthcare applications

Prosthetic vision and neuro-rehabilitation are being revolutionized by neuromorphic vision and BCI feedback. People with partial or total vision loss can use bio-inspired visual prosthesis thanks to event-based cameras and spiking

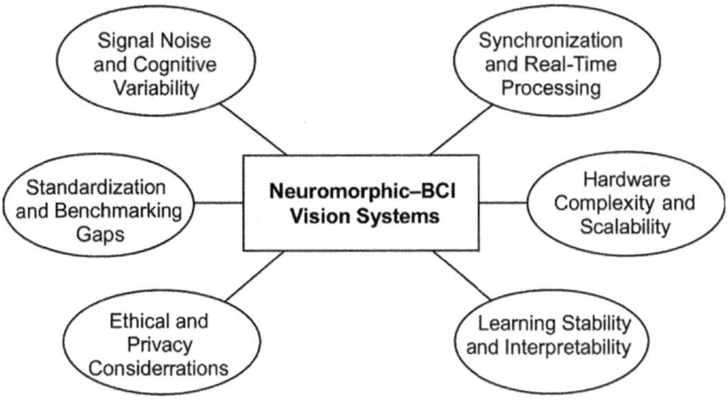


**FIGURE 13.5** Major challenges in neuromorphic–BCI integrated vision systems.

neural networks, which replicate the functioning of retinal circuits. These systems can effectively create a closed-loop artificial visual cortex by interpreting neural intent and focusing visual feedback in accordance with cognitive attention when combined with BCI signals.

Similarly, in neuro-rehabilitation, event-driven vision can be applied to detect motion patterns from BCI-controlled robotic arms or exoskeletons that allow patients to make precise motions directed by their goals. By promoting active cognitive participation, event-driven vision supports motor learning and enhances recuperation more rapidly. Evidence from the literature actually attests that hybrid systems enhanced neuroplasticity and patient outcomes in post-stroke therapy and in rehabilitation involving motor disabilities.

## 8.2 Assistive and service robotics

Neuromorphic vision helps in assistive robotics because of its ultra-low latency and adaptability. When combined with BCI control, robots can perceive a user's intent in real-time and react to it. A neuromorphic-guided robotic arm mounted on a wheelchair detects the position of an object, while EEG-based BCI input detects whether to grasp or release the object. This combination allows individuals and assistive technology to communicate easily and naturally.

Cognitive cues, such as human attention or gaze, may dynamically update perception in service robots to allow for energy-efficient operation and job prioritization. This adaptive perception concept forms one basis of intelligent HRC: the idea that robots ought to operate both autonomously and sympathetically, guided by human mental states and contextual knowledge.

## 8.3 Defence, surveillance, and security systems

The high-speed, event-driven features of neuromorphic sensors make them perfect for dynamic surveillance in defense applications. Event cameras provide high temporal resolution data with low latency, unlike the frame-based vision systems that are susceptible to low-light or high-motion conditions.

These would include operator cognitive feedback, such as the recognition of brain signals related to high attentiveness or recognition, when combined with BCI modules. A form of cognitive integration like this reduces the false alarm rate while improving decision accuracy by enabling selective concentration within surveillance streams. Target detection and threat detection systems in defense applications can be modified by including BCI-based intention recognition for safer and quicker human-in-the-loop operations.

## 8.4 Automotive and transportation systems

The main application domain of neuromorphic-BCI technologies is the automotive sector. Neuromorphic vision makes sense for real-time, ultra-low power processing of the visual data stream in an autonomous vehicle or driver-assistance system. BCI feedback takes this technology a step further toward cognitive safety by using EEG signals to monitor driver fatigue, tension, or attentional lapses and adjusting sensory sensitivity or the control logic of the vehicle accordingly.

Integration of BCI intent prediction and event-driven perception in semi-autonomous driving can thus respond faster to unexpected hazardous situations or when taking over from a driver, making navigation both more responsive and safer.

## 8.5 Smart wearables and augmented reality

One more fascinating sector is the development of the wearable device which involves the neuro-augmentation. Neuromorphic cameras in AR/VR headsets to be able to quickly and easily provide low-latency ambient data for mixed-reality displays. If these devices are combined with BCI inputs, they can also convert user attention, emotion, or even workload to display changes.

As an illustration, in industrial AR environments, the system can do it automatically to show the most important objects or to eliminate the unnecessary visual data depending on the operator's attention. In gaming and entertainment, neuroadaptive vision enables games to change according to the user's mental state and offers deep, individualized interaction with the real and virtual worlds.

## 8.6 Space and deep-environment exploration

Conventional cameras and processors are regularly unable to perform under extreme conditions caused by limitations in power, radiation, or latency, for instance, in space missions, underwater robots, or planetary exploration. Neuromorphic vision offers a very efficient and low-power solution in terms of

**TABLE 13.2** Emerging application areas of BCI-infused NVS.

| Application area | Representative use case | Impact/Advantage |
|---|---|---|
| Medical & healthcare | Neuro-visual prosthetics and rehabilitation systems | Restores partial vision and enhances motor recovery |
| Assistive robotics | EEG-guided robotic arms and exoskeletons | Enables intention-driven assistive interaction |
| Defense & security | Attention-based surveillance and threat detection | Enhances situational awareness and reduces operator fatigue |
| Automotive systems | Cognitive driver-assistance and autonomous control | Improves safety through intent-aware sensing |
| Smart wearables & AR | Adaptive visual augmentation using EEG signals | Provides personalized, context-aware visualization |
| Space exploration | Human-guided autonomous exploration systems | Enables efficient remote perception and control in extreme environments |

bandwidth, while the integrated BCI gives the astronaut or the operator the possibility to command the autonomous agents with brain intention or concentration. As these systems are capable of rapid adjustment to variable situations, they, therefore, become indispensable in work areas where flexibility, reliability, and human cognitive integration are required (Table 13.2).

## 9. Conclusion

On the one hand, combining NVS with BCI technologies represents a new, human-centered, and flexible paradigm for visual perception models. By imitating the event-driven, low-power, and temporally accurate features of biological vision, neuromorphic technologies circumvent the limitations of traditional image processing, and BCI integration brings in cognitive feedback that aligns machine perception with human goal and awareness. Such a union makes possible the on-the-fly adaptation, low-power processing, and situational sensitivity, among other things, in a varied applications band, e.g., space technologies, automotive systems, the army, assistive robotics, and medical prostheses. Despite the issues of signal variability, synchronization mismatch, hardware scalability, and ethical concerns, advancements in neuromorphic hardware, on-chip learning, and cognitive data fusion are progressively facilitating the birth of biologically inspired, ethically aligned, and perceptually intelligent systems. To sum up, the combination of neuromorphic and BCI technologies ushers in the new era of cognitive vision when machines do not only see but also interpret and respond with awareness, thus indicating the time ahead for the easy interaction between humans and machines.

## References

Elashmawi, W.H., Ayman, A., Mina, A., Habiba, M., Shehab, E.M., Amr, H., Youssef, T., Ali, A., 2024. A comprehensive review on brain–computer interface (BCI)-based machine and deep learning algorithms for stroke rehabilitation. Appl. Sci. 14 (14), 6347. https://doi.org/10.3390/app14146347.

Gallego, G., Delbruck, T., Orchard, G., Bartolozzi, C., Taba, B., Censi, A., Leutenegger, S., Davison, A.J., Conradt, J., Daniilidis, K., Scaramuzza, D., 2022. Event-based vision: a survey. IEEE Trans. Pattern Anal. Mach. Intell. 44 (1), 154–180. https://doi.org/10.1109/TPAMI.2020.3008413.

Guo, Y., Huang, X., Ma, Z., 2023. Direct learning-based deep spiking neural networks: a review. Front. Neurosci. 17. https://doi.org/10.3389/fnins.2023.1209795.

Li, Y., Guo, Y., Zhang, S., Deng, S., Hai, Y., Gu, S., 2021. Neural information processing systems foundation China differentiable spike: rethinking gradient-descent for training spiking neural networks. Adv. Neural Inf. Process. Syst. 28, 23426–23439.

Maiseli, B., Abdalla, A.T., Massawe, L.V., Mbise, M., Mkocha, K., Nassor, N.A., Ismail, M., Michael, J., Kimambo, S., 2023. Brain–computer interface: trend, challenges, and threats. Brain Inform. 10 (1). https://doi.org/10.1186/s40708-023-00199-3.

Müller, E., Elias, A., Breitwieser, O., Czierlinski, M., Emmel, A., Kaiser, J., Mauch, C., Schmitt, S., Spilger, P., Stock, R., Stradmann, Y., Weis, J., Baumbach, A., Billaudelle, S., Cramer, B., Ebert, F., Göltz, J., Ilmberger, J., Karasenko, V., Kleider, M., Leibfried, A., Pehle, C., Schemmel, J., 2022. A scalable approach to modeling on accelerated neuromorphic hardware. Front. Neurosci. 16. https://doi.org/10.3389/fnins.2022.884128.

Nitin, R., Srinivasan, G., Panda, P., Roy, K., 2020. In: Enabling Deep Spiking Neural Networks with Hybrid Conversion and Spike Timing Dependent Backpropagation.

Orchard, G., Frady, E.P., Rubin, D.B.D., Sanborn, S., Shrestha, S.B., Sommer, F.T., Davies, M., 2021. Efficient neuromorphic signal processing with Loihi 2. In: IEEE Workshop on Signal Processing Systems, SiPS: Design and Implementation, pp. 254–259. https://doi.org/10.1109/SiPS52927.2021.00053.

Stradmann, Y., Schemmel, J., 2024. Closing the loop: high-speed robotics with accelerated neuromorphic hardware. Front. Neurosci. 18. https://doi.org/10.3389/fnins.2024.1360122.

Zenke, F., Vogels, T.P., 2021. The remarkable robustness of surrogate gradient learning for instilling complex function in spiking neural networks. Neural Comput. 33 (4), 899–925. https://doi.org/10.1162/neco_a_01367.

Zhang, J., Li, J., Huang, Z., Huang, D., Yu, H., Li, Z., 2023. Recent progress in wearable brain–computer interface (BCI) devices based on electroencephalogram (EEG) for medical applications: a review. Health Data Sci. 3. https://doi.org/10.34133/hds.0096.

Zhou, C., Zhang, H., Yu, L., Ye, Y., Zhou, Z., Huang, L., Ma, Z., Fan, X., Zhou, H., Tian, Y., 2024. Direct training high-performance deep spiking neural networks: a review of theories and methods. Front. Neurosci. 18. https://doi.org/10.3389/fnins.2024.1383844.

Chapter 14

# Cross generational data analysis on mental health effect of social media

**Shibadri Mukherjee[1] and Kukatlapalli Pradeep Kumar[2]**
[1]*Department of Computer Science Engineering, School of Engineering and Technology, CHRIST University, Kengeri Campus, Bengaluru, Karnataka, India;* [2]*Department of AI and Data Science Engineering, School of Engineering Technology, CHRIST University, Kengeri Campus, Bengaluru, Karnataka, India*

## 1. Introduction

The advent of social media has been one of the most transformative phenomena of the 21st century, reshaping how individuals interact, consume information, and communicate. With billions of users globally, platforms like Facebook, Instagram, TikTok, and LinkedIn have become integral to daily life (Smith et al., 2021). However, the impact of social media is not uniform; it varies significantly across different generations. Younger generations, often referred to as digital natives, have grown up with technology and seamlessly integrate it into their lives. In contrast, older generations, termed digital immigrants, have had to adapt to these technological advancements, often at a slower pace and with different usage patterns.

Understanding these generational differences is crucial for several reasons. First, it helps policymakers and platform designers create targeted interventions that address the unique challenges and needs of each group. For instance, while younger generations might struggle with issues like reduced attention spans and increased anxiety due to overexposure to social media, older generations may face challenges in adopting and navigating these platforms. By examining these differences, we can better understand how to mitigate the negative impacts of social media while maximizing its potential benefits.

Another critical aspect of this analysis is the role of cognitive and psychological factors. Research has shown that prolonged exposure to social media can lead to significant changes in attention span, memory, and even emotional regulation. For younger users, the constant barrage of information and stimuli

**Neuromorphic Computing for Brain Computer Interfaces. https://doi.org/10.1016/B978-0-443-41594-4.00012-5**

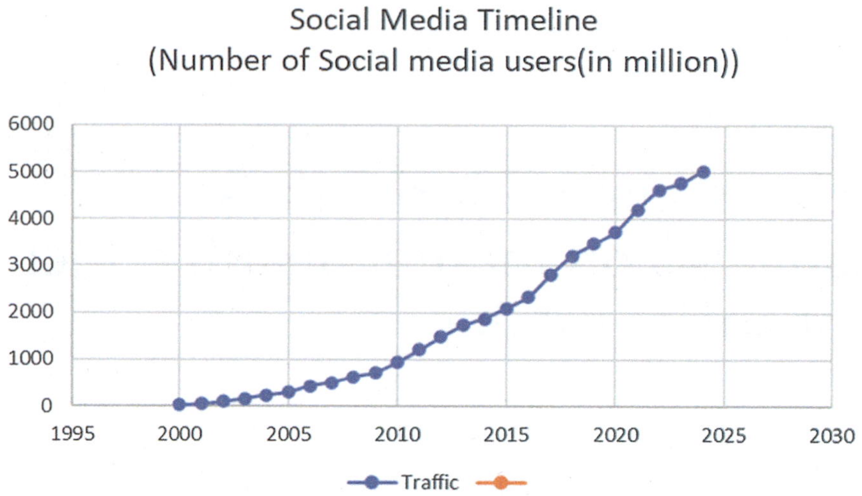


**FIGURE 14.1** A visual timeline showing the emergence and growth of major social media platforms over the years (X axis-year, Y axis-traffic).

can lead to cognitive overload and reduced ability to focus on long-form content. On the other hand, older users might experience frustration and cognitive strain while trying to adapt to fast-evolving digital landscapes (Fig. 14.1).

By leveraging cross-generational data and advanced technological solutions, we can address some of the most pressing challenges of the digital age. For example, machine learning models could be used to develop personalized tools that help users manage their social media consumption, improve focus, and reduce cognitive fatigue. Similarly, insights from cross-generational analysis can inform the design of platforms and policies that are inclusive and equitable, ensuring that users of all ages can benefit from the opportunities offered by social media.

This chapter aims to provide a comprehensive analysis of these topics, combining insights from cross-generational studies of social media usage. By examining these issues in tandem, we hope to shed light on the complex interplay between technology, cognition, and society. Ultimately, the goal is to identify strategies and solutions that promote a healthier, more balanced digital ecosystem for users across all generations.

## 2. Literature review

The literature below explores prior research on the relationship between social media usage, mental health outcomes, generational differences, and the underlying psychological and sociological frameworks governing these interactions.

Youth-led co-production of mental health promotion in Pakistan: intergenerational infuences

(a) **Intergenerational Learning and Resilience**
Storytelling serves as a powerful tool for fostering empathy and mutual understanding across generations. By sharing personal narratives, individuals can illuminate experiences of trauma and resilience, allowing younger generations to grasp the challenges faced by their predecessors. These shared stories create a bridge between different eras, fostering a deeper appreciation for the struggles and triumphs that shape identities. Moreover, storytelling nurtures reciprocal learning, as both older and younger individuals gain insight from each other's perspectives (Vostanis et al., 2024).
Beyond individual healing, generational narratives play a crucial role in building resilience at a systemic level. Stories of overcoming adversity provide valuable lessons in adaptability and perseverance, helping communities develop strategies to navigate future challenges. When individuals collaborate to share and reflect on their experiences, they contribute to a shared reservoir of wisdom that extends beyond mental health into various fields, including education, organizational development, and social policy.

(b) **Cultural and Contextual Insights**
Collective cultures emphasize family and community as essential support systems, shaping how individuals cope with challenges and maintain relationships across generations. These close-knit networks foster resilience, ensuring that wisdom, values, and coping strategies are passed down, strengthening both individuals and the broader community (Henry et al., 2024).
However, cultural stigmas around vulnerability often create barriers to open sharing between generations. Fear of judgment or appearing weak can hinder meaningful conversations. Creating safe spaces for dialogue is crucial to breaking these barriers, allowing for honest discussions that promote understanding and emotional support.

(c) **Youth as Catalysts for Change**
Younger generations often facilitate technological learning for older generations, helping them integrate digital tools like social media into their lives. This dynamic highlights the role of youth as digital mentors in intergenerational relationships.
Also, Engagement through digital technology and interactive activities encourages broader participation and helps overcome generational resistance (Chow et al., 2024).

Annual Research Review: Health anxiety in children and adolescents—developmental aspects and cross-generational influences

**(a)** Development of Health Anxiety in Children and Adolescents

Health anxiety often begins in infancy and can persist through adolescence and adulthood. It is characterized by excessive health concerns, often without medical basis, which can significantly impact daily life and well-being.

As children grow, their increasing cognitive abilities make them more aware of potential health risks, leading to heightened anxiety about illnesses and medical issues. This developmental shift influences how they perceive and respond to health-related concerns over time (Rask et al., 2024).

**(b)** Intergenerational Transmission of Health Anxiety

Parental influence plays a significant role in the development of health anxiety, as both environmental and genetic factors contribute to its transmission.

Parents who exhibit excessive health concerns, somatic symptom disorders, or a heightened preoccupation with illness may inadvertently transmit these worries to their children. This transmission occurs through multiple mechanisms, including:

1. Modeling Maladaptive Behaviors—Children observe their parents' anxious responses to bodily symptoms, excessive doctor visits, or obsessive online symptom-checking, which normalizes health anxiety as a response to uncertainty.
2. Parental Reinforcement and Overprotection—Overprotective parenting, where normal aches, pains, or minor illnesses are treated with excessive concern, can sensitize children to bodily sensations, making them more prone to anxiety about their health.
3. Verbal Reassurance Seeking—When parents frequently express fears about health risks, children internalize these concerns, leading to a hyperawareness of bodily functions and heightened fear of illness (Haig-Ferguson et al., 2021).

**(c)** Societal and Environmental influences

Cyberchondria, or excessive online searching for health information, can intensify health anxiety, especially among young individuals with constant digital access. This behavior often results in heightened anxiety and misinterpretation of symptoms, where minor health concerns are perceived as severe medical conditions. This cycle is exacerbated by the overabundance of medical information online, ranging from credible sources to anecdotal experiences and misinformation. Many online health forums, symptom checkers, and social media discussions fuel confirmation bias, where individuals selectively focus on alarming information that reinforces their worst fears. This leads to increased stress, unnecessary medical consultations, and even self-imposed lifestyle restrictions due to a belief in having an undiagnosed illness.

**(d)** Role of Genetics
Beyond environmental learning, genetic predisposition also contributes to intergenerational health anxiety. Studies indicate that genetic factors account for approximately 34%–37% of variance in health anxiety-related traits, particularly in areas such as:
- Fear of illness and disease susceptibility
- Daily interference due to health concerns
- Obsessive preoccupation with bodily sensations

This suggests that some individuals may have an inherited vulnerability that, when combined with environmental factors such as parental modelling and social influences, manifests as chronic health anxiety (Oliver et al., 2020).

## 2.1 Digital media and psychology

Chinese MentalBERT: Domain-Adaptive Pre-training on Social Media for Chinese Mental Health Text Analysis

**(a)** Social Media as a Primary Platform for Emotional Expression
Social media platforms like Instagram and Twitter serve as key outlets for individuals to share their thoughts and emotions, shaping modern expressions of mental health concerns.
Generational differences influence how people use these platforms—some seek community support, while others refrain from sharing due to stigma. Younger users are more likely to express distress online, whereas older generations often prefer offline discussions, resulting in distinct digital mental health footprints (Kim et al., 2024).

**(b)** The Role of Social Media in Mental Health Stigma
The study confirms that social media affects mental health, but its impact varies across demographics. Different generations experience and respond to digital content in unique ways.
Variations in trust, exposure to misinformation, and online interaction styles shape mental health discourse. While older users tend to consume content passively, younger generations actively create and engage, influencing how mental health discussions spread online.

**(c)** Psychological Impact of Online Emotional Sharing
Publicly sharing emotions online can offer relief but also comes with risks like social comparison, cyberbullying, and the reinforcement of negative emotions.
There are clear generational disparities in coping stratergies i.e., older users may find solace in reading but not participation, whilst younger users may go to comments and likes for approval and support.

Excessive engagement with negative content can worsen mental health creating an "echo chamber effect" where individuals with similar emotional distress reinforce each other's fears (Wang et al., 2022).

MentaLLaMA: Interpretable Mental Health Analysis on Social Media with Large Language Models

**(a)** Social Media as a Reflection of Mental Health
Social media platforms like Twitter and Reddit have become spaces where individuals express emotional distress, sometimes replacing traditional support systems. Online mental health discourse often mirrors real-life stressors, including work pressure, relationship struggles, and loneliness, shaping how people seek and share support (Kim et al., 2024).

**(b)** Common Mental Health Challenges observed Online
The analysis revealed frequent mentions of suicidal ideation, depression, and stress, highlighting an urgent need for mental health intervention. Many posts display cognitive distortions, such as catastrophizing, negative self-talk, and hopelessness, which can reinforce distress and hinder coping mechanisms (Sekulić and Strube, 2020).

**(c)** Psychological Risk Factors indentified from Social Media
Key elements linked to Poor mental health were identified by AI models, including:
- Thwarted sense of belongingness (feeling disconnected from others)
- Perceived burdensomeness (believing they are a burden to others)
- Chronic stressors like financial struggles, academic pressure and workplace conflicts

Social media use and generational identity: Issues and Consequences on peer-to-peer and cross-generational relationships—an empirical study

**(a)** Social Media as a Tool for Identity Formation
Social media plays a crucial role in shaping both individual and generational identities by providing a space for storytelling and self-presentation. Through sharing personal experiences, beliefs, and values, individuals construct their sense of self while also contributing to the broader cultural identity of their generation (Waechter, 2021).
Peer-to-peer and intergenerational communication further influence this identity formation. Younger and older generations engage in dialogue, exchanging perspectives that either reinforce or reshape generational narratives. This continuous interaction helps define social norms, collective values, and shared experiences, making social media a dynamic space for identity evolution.

**(b)** Generational Differences in Online Self-Presentation
Younger generations, such as Gen Z and Millennials, use social media primarily for peer validation, focusing on personal branding and

self-expression. Platforms like Instagram, TikTok, and Twitter allow them to curate their identities, seek approval through likes and comments, and engage in trends that shape their online presence (Jimenez and Morreale, 2015).

In contrast, older generations, including Gen X and Baby Boomers, view social media as a tool for reminiscence and relationship maintenance. They often use platforms like Facebook to reconnect with old friends, share memories, and stay in touch with family, prioritizing social bonds over self-presentation.

**(c)** Emotional and Social impact of Online Interactions

Social media serves as a bridge between generations, facilitating communication and connection between people of different age groups. Platforms like Facebook, Instagram, and TikTok enable family members to stay in touch across distances, fostering intergenerational bonding through shared content, messages, and digital interactions.

However, despite these potential benefits, social media can also reinforce generational divides. One key reason is the difference in digital communication norms between age groups. Older generations, particularly Baby Boomers and Gen X, tend to communicate in a more structured and formal manner, often preferring direct messages, longer posts, and conventional etiquette. This disconnect leads to a social phenomenon where younger users deliberately exclude older adults from their digital spaces. Adolescents and young adults often curate their online presence, maintaining private accounts or using slang and inside jokes that make it difficult for outsiders to understand (Reyero et al., 2022).

**(d)** The Role of Reflexivity in Online communication

One of the most profound effects of social media on communication is the emergence of "networked reflexivity", where users continuously adjust their behavior based on how they believe others perceive them online. Unlike traditional face-to-face interactions, social media creates a digital stage where every action is visible, archived, and open to scrutiny. This heightened visibility fosters a self-monitoring culture, where individuals consciously shape their online persona to align with societal or peer expectations.

This constant self-awareness is reinforced by the awareness of being watched. Social media platforms enable not only direct interactions but also silent observation, where people can view others' content without actively engaging. This leads to behaviors such as "self-censorship", where users refrain from posting controversial or personal content due to fear of judgment. It also encourages "social comparison", where individuals measure their own success, attractiveness, or lifestyle against the curated highlights of others (Barker, 2012).

# 3. Results and discussion

## 3.1 Usage pattern across generation

### 3.1.1 Baby boomers

Baby Boomers primarily engage with social media as a means of maintaining familial connections. Their usage patterns are dominated by platforms like Facebook, where they interact with family members, share life updates, and consume news. Unlike younger generations, they are less inclined toward fast-paced, visually dynamic content, preferring instead the familiarity of text-based posts, long-form articles, and community group discussions. The design and functionality of Facebook cater to their preference for a structured, community-oriented online experience, making it their platform of choice.

### 3.1.2 Generation X

Generation X demonstrates a more balanced approach to social media usage, leveraging digital platforms for both professional networking and personal communication. This generation frequently utilizes LinkedIn to expand professional relationships, explore career opportunities, and engage with industry-related content. At the same time, platforms like Instagram appeal to them for maintaining social connections and engaging with lifestyle-based content. Unlike Baby Boomers, who focus on staying connected with close circles, Generation X navigates social media with a dual-purpose mindset, blending career growth with personal interactions. Their adaptability allows them to seamlessly integrate social media into various aspects of their lives without becoming overly dependent on any single platform.

### 3.1.3 Generation Z

Generation Z, on the other hand, is deeply immersed in short-form content, favoring platforms such as Instagram, YouTube, and TikTok. Their preference leans heavily toward visually dynamic, ephemeral content that aligns with their fast-paced consumption habits. Unlike older generations, they engage with bite-sized videos, interactive stories, and algorithm-driven feeds that provide highly personalized content experiences. This generation values content that is quick, engaging, and visually appealing, often gravitating toward influencer-driven trends and viral challenges. The appeal of ephemeral content, such as Instagram Stories or TikTok clips, aligns with their desire for real-time interactions and fleeting digital experiences, reinforcing their preference for spontaneity and high engagement (Fig. 14.2).

Generation Z has grown up in a digital-first environment, making social media an integral part of their daily lives. They engage with platforms for communication, entertainment, self-expression, and activism. The emphasis on short-form, high-engagement content fosters instant gratification, often leading to habitual scrolling and a reliance on digital interactions for

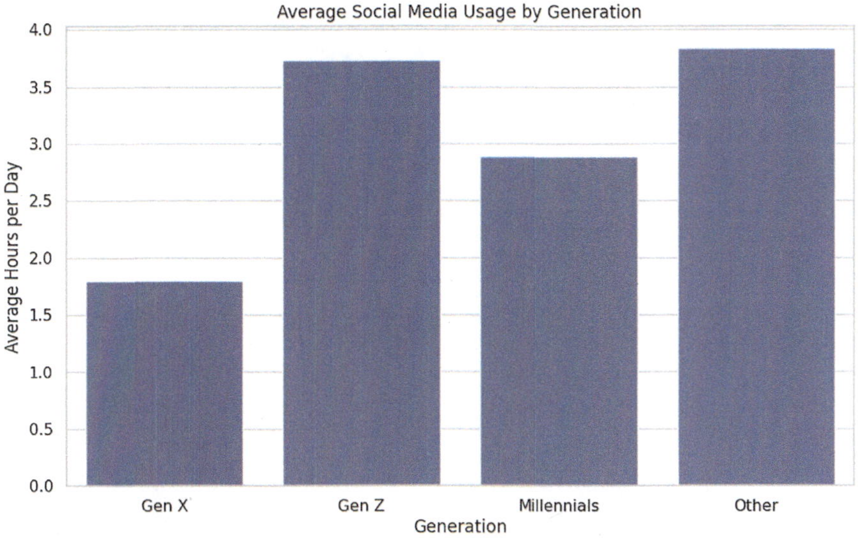


**FIGURE 14.2** Average hours spent per day on social media versus generation.

validation. The constant exposure to curated content and peer comparisons has been linked to increased rates of anxiety, depression, and low self-esteem among young users. Furthermore, excessive screen time and online engagement can disrupt sleep patterns, further exacerbating mental health concerns (Fig. 14.3).

In this heatmap, the strongest correlation (0.76) is between the attention span score and the mental health score. This indicates a strong positive relationship between these two variables, meaning that individuals with higher attention spans tend to have better mental health.

## 3.2 Predictions for mental health scores and social media usage among generation

### *3.2.1 Polarization in mental health scores among Gen Z*

The analysis reveals a distinct polarization in mental health scores within Generation Z, suggesting that social media does not affect all individuals uniformly. While a subset of Gen Z exhibits resilience or even positive adaptation to digital interactions, a significant portion experiences severe mental health declines. This division can be attributed to multiple factors, including differences in coping mechanisms, the type of content consumed, and engagement habits.

Social media fosters hyper-connectivity, instant gratification, and an algorithm-driven content loop, which can amplify anxiety, depression, and social comparison in vulnerable individuals. Simultaneously, for those with

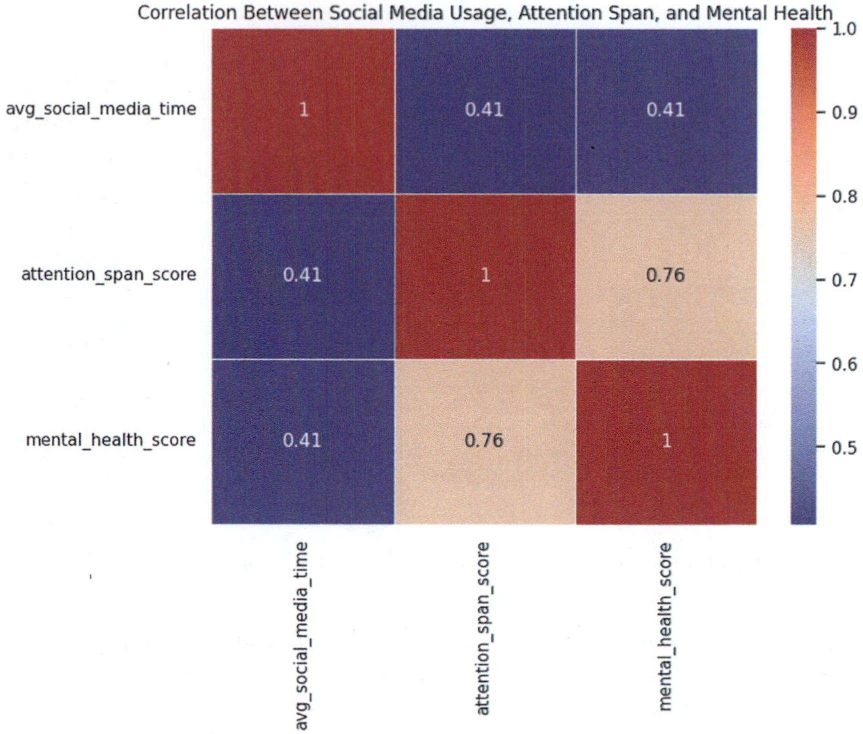


**FIGURE 14.3** Correlation matrix between social media usage, attention span and mental health.

strong digital literacy and self-regulation, it serves as a tool for social support, educational growth, and entertainment. This dual nature of social media results in a highly polarized impact, particularly within younger generations, where digital exposure is at its peak (Fig. 14.4).

### 3.2.2 Application of Ridge and Lasso regression in understanding mental health trends

To quantify the relationship between social media usage and mental health outcomes, Ridge and Lasso regression models were employed. These models are particularly useful for handling multicollinearity and determining the most influential predictors affecting mental health across generations.

### 3.2.3 Ridge regression

Ridge regression is a regularized linear model that introduces a penalty term proportional to the squared magnitude of coefficients. This technique prevents overfitting by ensuring that large coefficient values are shrunk, allowing the model to generalize better. In this study, Ridge regression demonstrated that

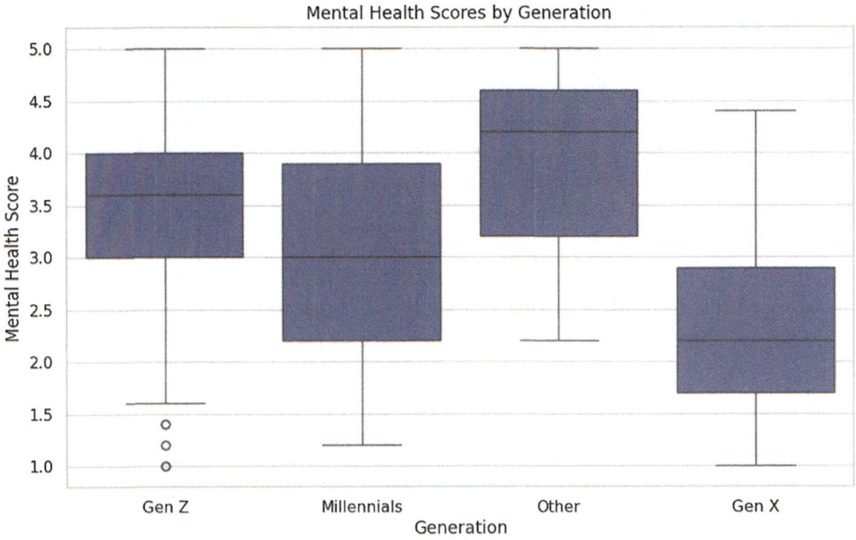


**FIGURE 14.4** Box-plot for mental health score versus generation.

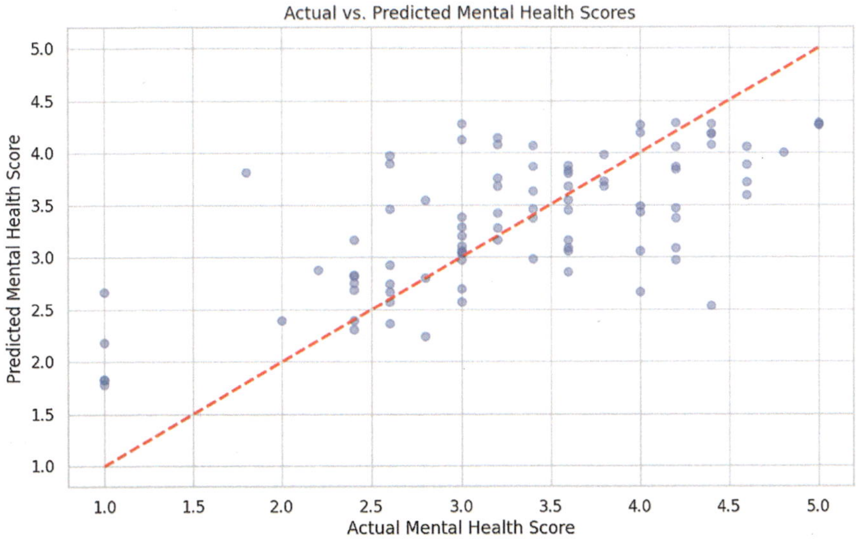


**FIGURE 14.5** Actual versus Predicted Mental Health Scores illustrating the predictive accuracy of the proposed model against the ideal prediction reference line.

multiple features—such as screen time, content type, and user engagement—have a compounded effect on mental health, reinforcing the existence of strong but distributed influences (Fig. 14.5).

### *3.2.4 Lasso regression*

Unlike Ridge regression, Lasso (Least Absolute Shrinkage and Selection Operator) performs both regularization and feature selection. It applies an **L1 penalty**, which forces some coefficient values to zero, effectively eliminating less significant predictors. The results from Lasso regression highlighted a subset of social media factors as dominant predictors of mental health disparities, identifying **specific variables** (e.g., engagement with negative content, late-night usage) as highly influential. This suggests that while several factors contribute to mental health variations, a few key variables drive the most significant changes. Ridge regression and Lasso regression, in the current case study, showed relatively similar alignment patterns in terms of prediction accuracy between the actual mental well-being scores and the predicted ones.

## 3.3 Empirical evidences supporting polarization

This is evident from the regression models applied to the dataset, where distinct subgroups emerge—some experiencing significant declines in mental well-being while others remain relatively unaffected. Following are the evidences supporting the argument:

**(1)** Residual Analysis: The residual plots for Ridge and Lasso show that model predictions deviate significantly for extreme cases, reinforcing the notion that mental health effects are not uniformly distributed but rather concentrated in specific subgroups (Fig. 14.6).

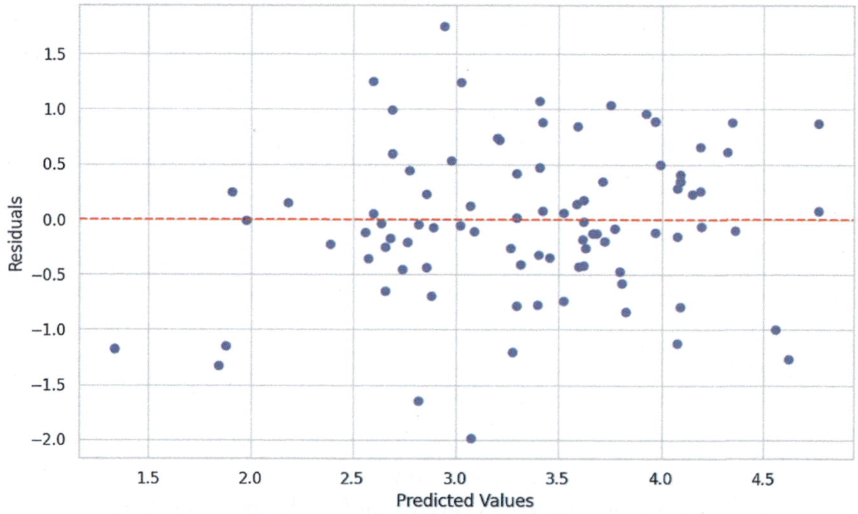


**FIGURE 14.6** Residuals for lasso regressions.

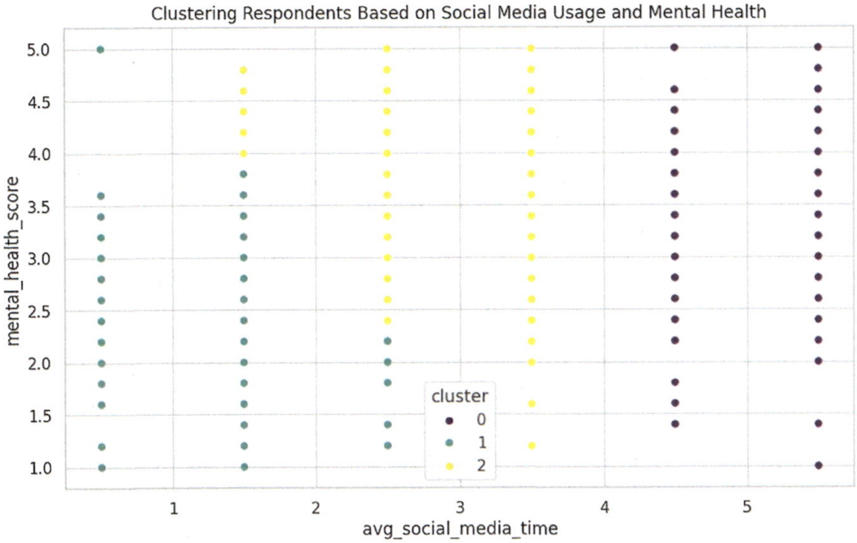


**FIGURE 14.7** K-means cluster for mental health score versus average social media time.

The presence of high residuals in specific regions suggests that social media's effect on mental health is not uniform across Gen Z. Some individuals are more vulnerable to its negative effects, while others are not as affected, aligning with the hypothesis that mental health effects are concentrated in certain subgroups rather than being evenly distributed.

**(2)** Cluster Analysis: The clustering results illustrate distinct groups within Gen Z—one with stable mental health despite high social media usage and another showing severe negative effects, further proving the presence of polarization (Fig. 14.7).

## 4. Conclusion

The findings of this research reinforce the notion that the effects of social media on mental health are not uniformly distributed but are instead concentrated within specific generational subgroups. The empirical evidence suggests that while social media serves as a tool for connection, entertainment, and information, it also amplifies psychological distress, particularly among younger generations such as Gen Z. The results from Ridge and Lasso regression models highlight the **polarizing mental health effects**, with some individuals experiencing heightened anxiety, depression, and emotional exhaustion, while others remain largely unaffected or even benefit from online interactions. This disparity suggests that the impact of social media is mediated by factors such as **pre-existing mental health conditions, coping**

**mechanisms, online behaviour patterns, and generational differences in digital literacy and resilience.**

A key observation from the study is the strong correlation between excessive social media engagement and deteriorating mental health scores among Gen Z. This generation exhibits **a higher susceptibility to anxiety and depression due to increased digital reflexivity, algorithm-driven content exposure, and the constant need for online validation.** The findings further suggest that social media fosters **a dual effect—both connecting and isolating individuals simultaneously**, leading to fragmented mental health outcomes. The intergenerational gap is further emphasized by **Baby Boomers and Gen X users who, despite being active on social platforms, display relatively lower levels of psychological distress, possibly due to their ability to detach from online validation cycles and algorithmic influence.**

Given the growing influence of social media, it is crucial to develop targeted mental health interventions, digital literacy programs, and responsible technology policies to mitigate its adverse effects. Future research should focus on longitudinal studies that assess the long-term impact of digital engagement on mental health across multiple generations, as well as exploring AI-driven interventions that personalize online experiences to reduce algorithm-induced anxiety. Ultimately, this study underscores the urgent need for a balanced approach to social media consumption, advocating for awareness, moderation, and structural policy changes to ensure that online interactions remain psychologically sustainable for future generations.

## References

Barker, V., 2012. A generational comparison of social networking site use: the influence of age and social identity. Int. J. Aging Hum. Dev. 74 (2), 163–187. https://doi.org/10.2190/ag.74.2.d.

Chow, D., Matungwa, D.J., Blackwood, E.R., Pronyk, P., Dow, D., 2024. A scoping review on peer-led interventions to improve youth mental health in low- and middle-income countries. Glob. Ment. Health 12. https://doi.org/10.1017/gmh.2024.149.

Haig-Ferguson, A., Cooper, K., Cartwright, E., Loades, M.E., Daniels, J., 2021. Practitioner review: health anxiety in children and young people in the context of the COVID-19 pandemic. Behav. Cognit. Psychother. 49 (2), 129–143. https://doi.org/10.1017/s1352465820000636.

Henry, J., Azariah, F., Hughsam, M., Skeen, S., Tomlinson, M., Busakhwe, C., Mokoena, K., Mudaly, A., Sinha, M., Laurenzi, C., 2024. Shared experiences, shared support: a qualitative study on the importance of relatability in interpersonal relationships for youth mental health in South Africa. Glob. Ment. Health 11. https://doi.org/10.1017/gmh.2024.117.

Jimenez, Y., Morreale, P., 2015. Social media use and impact on interpersonal communication. In: HCI International 2015-Posters' Extended Abstracts: International Conference, HCI International 2015, Los Angeles, CA, USA, August 2-7, 2015. Proceedings, Part II 17. Springer International Publishing, pp. 91–96.

Kim, D.Y., Hwa, R., Rahman, M.M., 2024. In: mhGPT: A Lightweight Generative Pre-trained Transformer for Mental Health Text Analysis. https://doi.org/10.48550/arXiv.2408.08261.

Oliver, A.M., Wright, K.D., Kakadekar, A., Pharis, S., Pockett, C., Bradley, T.J., Tomczak, C.R., Erlandson, M.C., 2020. Health anxiety and associated constructs in children and adolescents with congenital heart disease: a CHAMPS cohort study. J. Health Psychol. 25 (10–11), 1355–1365. https://doi.org/10.1177/1359105318755263.

Rask, C.U., Steen Duholm, C., Müller Poulsen, C., Rimvall, M.K., Wright, K.D., 2024. Annual research review: health anxiety in children and adolescents—developmental aspects and cross-generational influences. J. Child Psychol. Psychiatry 65 (4), 413–430. https://doi.org/10.1111/jcpp.13912.

Reyero, D., Pattier, D., García-Ramos, D., 2022. Adolescence and identity in the twenty-first century: social media as spaces for mimesis and learning. In: Identity in a Hyperconnected Society: Risks and Educative Proposals. Springer International Publishing, Spain, pp. 75–93. https://doi.org/10.1007/978-3-030-85788-2_6.

Sekulić, I., Strube, M., 2020. In: Adapting Deep Learning Methods for Mental Health Prediction on Social Media. https://doi.org/10.48550/arxiv.2003.07634.

Smith, D., Leonis, T., Anandavalli, S., 2021. Belonging and loneliness in cyberspace: impacts of social media on adolescents' well-being. Aust. J. Psychol. 73 (1), 12–23.

Vostanis, P., Hassan, S., Fatima, S.Z., O'Reilly, M., 2024. Youth-led co-production of mental health promotion in Pakistan: intergenerational influences. Health Promot. Int. 39 (1). https://doi.org/10.1093/heapro/daae010.

Waechter, N., 2021. Gendered social media cultures between individuality and collectivity. In: Forms of Collectivity Among Contemporary Youth: A Global Perspective. Brill, Leiden.

Wang, W.Y., Tang, Y.C., Du, W.W., Peng, W.C., 2022. NYCU_TWD@ LT-EDI-ACL2022: ensemble models with VADER and contrastive learning for detecting signs of depression from social media. In: Proceedings of the Second Workshop on Language Technology for Equality, Diversity and Inclusion, pp. 136–139.

Chapter 15

# Mapping the research landscape of neuromorphic computing: A bibliometric analysis of trends, collaboration, and research hotspots

S. James Robert
*Christ University, Bengaluru, Karnataka, India*

## 1. Introduction

In an era defined by rapid growth in computational demand and artificial intelligence (AI) abilities, conventional computing architectures are reaching their constraints in terms of energy conservation, speed, and versatile. As these constraints become progressively apparent, there is a radical transformation toward alternative computational models that mimic the human brain. One such promising and expeditiously advancing field is neuromorphic computing (Sun et al., 2021). Neuromorphic computing, deep-rooted in the architecture and functionality of biological neural systems, look to integrate discernment from neuroscience and computer engineering by developing systems that mimic brain-like information processing (Borra, 2024). This biomimetic approach not only promises innovation in energy-efficient and real-time processing but also opens the path for novel AI applications that is essential for cognitive abilities such as perception, learning, and decision-making.

The conceptual foundation of neuromorphic computing goes back to the 1980s, with the pioneering work of Mead, who visualized the development of electronic systems that could imitate neuro-biological architectures. Afterwards, the field has evolved remarkably, driven by evolution in computer engineering, and computational neuroscience. Today, neuromorphic systems

**Neuromorphic Computing for Brain Computer Interfaces. https://doi.org/10.1016/B978-0-443-41594-4.00015-0**

use unique hardware such as spiking neural networks (SNNs) and brain-inspired processors such as IBM's TrueNorth and Intel's Loihi (Abdallah and Dang, 2024). These systems empower asynchronous, event-driven computation, which considerably lets down energy power when compared to conventional von Neumann systems (Enuganti et al., 2025; Rathi et al., 2023; Davies et al., 2021). Neuromorphic computing accounts for a multidisciplinary combining of neuroscience, electrical engineering, computer science, and cognitive science. Neuromorphic computing has a vast range of applications such as edge computing, autonomous robotics, data processing, and cognitive integration. As AI systems are progressively established in real-world conditions that demand minimal delay and high-efficient computing, neuromorphic solutions provide a way forward. Neuromorphic architectures impart the vital comparability and adaptability to handle such complex tasks effectively. The burgeoning interest in this neuromorphic computing is reflected in the increasing research volume of scientific publications, collaborative projects, and funding initiatives worldwide (Schuman et al., 2022; Marković et al., 2020; Furber, 2016). As the field develops, it is important to comprehend its research landscape, recognize the major contributors, track the evolution of key themes, and unveil emerging research topics. Bibliometric analysis provides a systematic and quantitative aspects to achieve these targets. Bibliometric analysis influences metadata from scholarly publications to reveal intellectual structure, collaborative network, and emerging themes within a given research area.

This chapter presents an overarching bibliometric analysis of the neuromorphic computing research areas derived from 887 publications retrieved from the Web of Science database, focusing the period from 2000 to 2025. Biblioshiny was utilized to analyze publication trends, authorship patterns, institutional and country-level contributions, and keyword co-occurrence patterns. Biblioshiny is a web-based interface of the Bibliometrix R-package which is freely available online. We aim to shed light on the structural and thematic development of neuromorphic computing, providing valuable insights for academicians, researchers, practitioners, and policymakers interested in this emerging field. Analyzing the bibliometric profile of neuromorphic computing is crucial for benchmarking the progress in the field, as it underscores key contributors, impactful publications, and reputed research institutions. It also provides strategic decision-making for research institutions by showing collaborative networks and emerging themes of interest. Furthermore, it helps researchers in navigating the field by providing fundamental works and key thematic clusters. Most importantly, such an analysis fosters a more coherent and integrated research community by facilitating knowledge sharing and collaboration across disciplinary boundaries. As the digital world becomes increasingly complex and interconnected, the demand for intelligent systems capable of adaptive, real-time processing continues to grow (Tien, 2017). Neuromorphic computing stands as a beacon in this landscape, promising a new era of brain-inspired AI that is not only powerful but also efficient and cognitively capable. This research aims to support the ongoing evolution of neuromorphic technologies by mapping the field's intellectual landscape and highlighting promising future research paths.

## 2. Methodology

Bibliometric mapping analysis forms the foundation of this study, emerging as a widely acknowledged and increasingly adopted technique across diverse academic disciplines (Chen et al., 2021). The subsequent segment examines the bibliometric network analysis.

### 2.1 Literature review and data collection

The inclusion and exclusion criteria are presented in (Table 15.1), which helps readers understand the current study strategy. Understanding these

**TABLE 15.1 Inclusion and exclusion criteria for retrieving the dataset.**

| | Code | Criteria | Comments |
|---|---|---|---|
| **Inclusion criteria** | IC 1 | TS=("neuromorphic computing" OR "neuromorphic engineering" OR "neuromorphic systems" OR "spiking neural networks" OR "brain-inspired computing" OR "brain-inspired systems" OR "bio-inspired computing" OR "neuromorphic hardware" OR "neuromorphic chips")<br>AND TS=("AI" OR "machine learning" OR "robotics" OR "edge computing" OR "IoT") | The search criteria for the relevant dataset included 13 keywords concatenated with OR and AND operator. The total number of relevant articles received was 934. |
| | IC 2 | Publication year: 2000–2025 | The period of analysis for this study is from 2000 to 2025 (until July 21, 2025).<br>N = 934 |
| | IC 3 | Language, "English" | The study examines documents published only in English.<br>N = 929 |
| | IC 4 | Document type: Article-752, Review Article-135, Proceeding Paper-4, Book chapter-2 | The search is focused on article, review article, early access, proceeding paper, and book review. N = 887 |

characteristics is beneficial in constructing the framework of present study. Initial search results with keywords TS=("neuromorphic computing" OR "neuromorphic engineering" OR "neuromorphic systems" OR "spiking neural networks" OR "brain-inspired computing" OR "brain-inspired systems" OR "bio-inspired computing" OR "neuromorphic hardware" OR "neuromorphic chips") AND TS=("AI" OR "machine learning" OR "robotics" OR "edge computing" OR "IoT") in the Web of Science database returned 887 document results (as retrieved on July 21, 2025). The inclusion and exclusion criteria helped eliminate irrelevant components, ensuring a more focused and refined analysis. Table 15.1 shows an explanation of the criteria that were used. Since the data were sourced solely from the Web of Science database, the authors recognize that the list may not be comprehensive, as other databases like Scopus and PubMed were not included. All the other databases have not been included in this research since, Web of Science is believed to have comprehensive coverage of the reputed articles (El Baz and Iddik, 2022; Khudzari et al., 2018; Mishra et al., 2022).

The essential information required to identify research hotspots, examine the scientific landscape, and conduct other analyses in this study was systematically collected. Following data extraction, loading, and refinement, a total of 887 records were obtained on July 21, 2025 (Table 15.1). The document types included in the analysis were research articles, review papers, and conference proceedings. Only English-language publications were considered to maintain consistency in content analysis.

## 2.2 Data processing and analysis tools

The retrieved data were exported in BibTeX format and imported into the Biblioshiny interface of the Bibliometrix R package, selected for its intuitive graphical interface and robust analytical functions. Biblioshiny facilitated a range of analyses, including descriptive statistics (e.g., annual scientific production, most productive authors and institutions), network analysis (e.g., co-authorship and co-citation), keyword analysis (e.g., co-occurrence networks, trend analysis, and thematic mapping), and collaboration analysis (e.g., institutional and country-level networks). Prior to analysis, the dataset was meticulously cleaned to remove duplicate entries, incomplete records, and data irrelevant to the research objectives. Additionally, keyword normalization was performed to standardize terminology such as consolidating "SNN" and "spiking neural networks" ensuring more accurate and meaningful mappings.

## 2.3 Analytical procedures

The analytical procedures employed in this study provided a comprehensive, multi-dimensional exploration of the neuromorphic computing field. Descriptive analysis examined annual publication trends, top contributing journals, authors, and institutions to understand the overall growth and distribution of research. Co-authorship analysis mapped collaborative networks among authors, institutions, and countries, highlighting key contributors and collaboration patterns. Co-citation and bibliographic coupling were used to identify influential works and foundational literature shaping the domain. Keyword co-occurrence and thematic mapping uncovered research clusters and emerging themes by analyzing frequently associated keyword pairs over time. Additionally, trend and burst detection identified rapidly emerging topics and shifts in research focus through the analysis of sudden increases in keyword usage. By integrating these diverse analytical approaches and leveraging both quantitative indicators and visual mapping tools, the study offers a nuanced understanding of the structural and dynamic characteristics of research in neuromorphic computing. Fig. 15.1 presents a PRISMA flowchart illustrating the screening and selection process, thereby enhancing methodological clarity and facilitating replication.

The data were exported from the Web of Science database in BibTeX format, with the record content set to "Full Record and Cited References" for

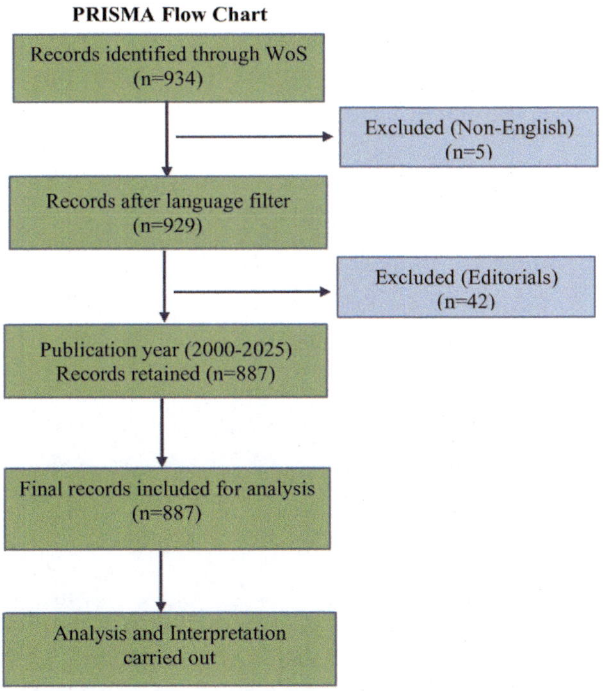


**FIGURE 15.1 PRISMA flowchart of study selection process.** This PRISMA flowchart illustrates the identification, screening, and selection of records for analysis, including exclusions based on language and publication type, resulting in the final set of studies included in the review.

comprehensive analysis. Web of Science also supports multiple export formats, including CSV, RIS, and plain text, offering flexibility for various analytical tools. In this study, the CSV format was utilized and imported into Biblioshiny for conducting bibliometric analyses (Table 15.2).

Table 15.3 presents the most relevant publication sources contributing to the field of neuromorphic computing, based on the number of articles indexed in the dataset. Frontiers in Neuroscience emerged as the leading source, publishing 59 articles, indicating its strong focus on interdisciplinary research

**TABLE 15.2** Data Synthesis indicating main information about data.

| S.No. | Description | Results |
|---|---|---|
| 1 | Timespan | 2000–2025 |
| 2 | Sources (Journals, Books, etc.) | 304 |
| 3 | Documents | 887 |
| 4 | Annual growth rate % | 14.9 |
| 5 | Document average age | 1.73 |
| 6 | Average citations per doc | 16.62 |
| 7 | References | 42,470 |
| **Document contents** | | |
| 8 | Keywords plus (ID) | 1202 |
| 9 | Author's keywords (DE) | 2569 |
| **Authors** | | |
| 10 | Authors | 3883 |
| 11 | Authors of single-authored docs | 23 |
| **Authors collaboration** | | |
| 12 | Single-authored docs | 23 |
| 13 | Co-authors per doc | 5.79 |
| 14 | International co-authorships % | 29.43 |
| **Document types** | | |
| 15 | Article | 748 |
| 16 | Review article | 133 |
| 18 | Proceeding paper | 4 |
| 19 | Book review | 2 |

**TABLE 15.3** Most relevant sources.

| S.No. | Source | Articles |
|---|---|---|
| 1 | Frontiers in neuroscience | 59 |
| 2 | IEEE access | 32 |
| 3 | Nature communications | 21 |
| 4 | Electronics | 19 |
| 5 | Neurocomputing | 18 |
| 6 | Advanced intelligent systems | 17 |
| 7 | Advanced materials | 17 |
| 8 | Sensors | 15 |
| 9 | Scientific reports | 14 |
| 10 | IEEE transactions on neural networks and learning systems | 13 |

bridging neuroscience and computational models. This is followed by IEEE Access with 32 articles, reflecting its role as a key platform for open-access dissemination of emerging technologies.

As shown in Table 15.4, Nature Communications emerged as the most locally cited source, with 2121 citations, indicating its significant influence on

**TABLE 15.4** Top 10 most local cited sources.

| S.No. | Cited sources | No. of local citations |
|---|---|---|
| 1 | Nature communications | 2121 |
| 2 | Advanced materials | 1828 |
| 3 | Nature | 1500 |
| 4 | Archive | 1385 |
| 5 | Frontiers in neuroscience—Switzerland | 1374 |
| 6 | Advanced functional materials | 1246 |
| 7 | Science | 930 |
| 8 | Scientific reports-UK | 924 |
| 9 | Nature electronics | 874 |
| 10 | Neural networks | 799 |

neuromorphic computing literature. This was followed by Advanced Materials (1828 citations) and Nature (1500 citations), reflecting the strong foundational role of high-impact, interdisciplinary journals in shaping research in this field.

The Sankey diagram illustrates the interplay between the most cited references (CR), influential authors (AU), and dominant research themes (DE) in the field of neuromorphic computing. Notably, Strukov et al. (2008); Zidan et al. (2018) are among the most frequently cited works, forming critical foundations for research on memristors and neural architectures. Prominent contributing authors such as Das A, Kim S, and Catthoor F are centrally positioned, bridging key literature with thematic areas like neuromorphic computing, spiking neural networks, and memristors. These themes dominate the field, reflecting a strong focus on biologically inspired computation and energy-efficient hardware. The flow of connections highlights the multidisciplinary nature of the domain, where foundational studies inform a range of subfields including machine learning, edge computing, and computational modeling (Fig. 15.2).

Fig. 15.3 illustrated the word cloud analysis. The word cloud visualization highlights the most frequently occurring keywords in neuromorphic computing literature (Pesta et al., 2018). Dominant terms such as *model, memory, and neural-networks* occupy central positions, indicating their foundational role in the field. Other frequently co-occurring keywords include *neurons, synaptic plasticity, devices, and networks*, reflecting ongoing research in brain-inspired architectures and learning mechanisms.

Fig. 15.4 presents keyword co-occurrence network (KCN) of the analysis. The figure envisions thematic clusters in neuromorphic computing research (Bhatia and Kumar, 2025). The KCN is organized into three different clusters, each of them accounting for a core research area. The blue cluster, placed around the keyword *model*, involves keywords such as *classification, design, architecture, and networks*, displaying a powerful prominence on computational modeling and system-level frameworks. The green cluster emphasizes on biologically inspired systems, with key terms such as *memory, neural-networks, synaptic plasticity, and performance*, highlighting research into learning dynamics and plasticity in artificial intelligence. The red cluster is centered by *devices* and includes keywords such as *synapses, thin-films, electronics, and brain*, pointing to investigations into hardware-level implementations using advanced materials. Important keywords such as *model, memory, and neural-networks* act as bridges between clusters, highlighting their integral role in integrating algorithmic, and hardware aspects within the field.

Fig. 15.5 represents the thematic map of the study. Thematic maps are crucial in bibliometric analysis as they visually represent the conceptual model of a research domain by merging keywords based on co-occurrence, helping to recognize core themes, emerging trends, and potential research gaps (Sadatmoosavi et al., 2021). These themes help researchers to navigate large datasets

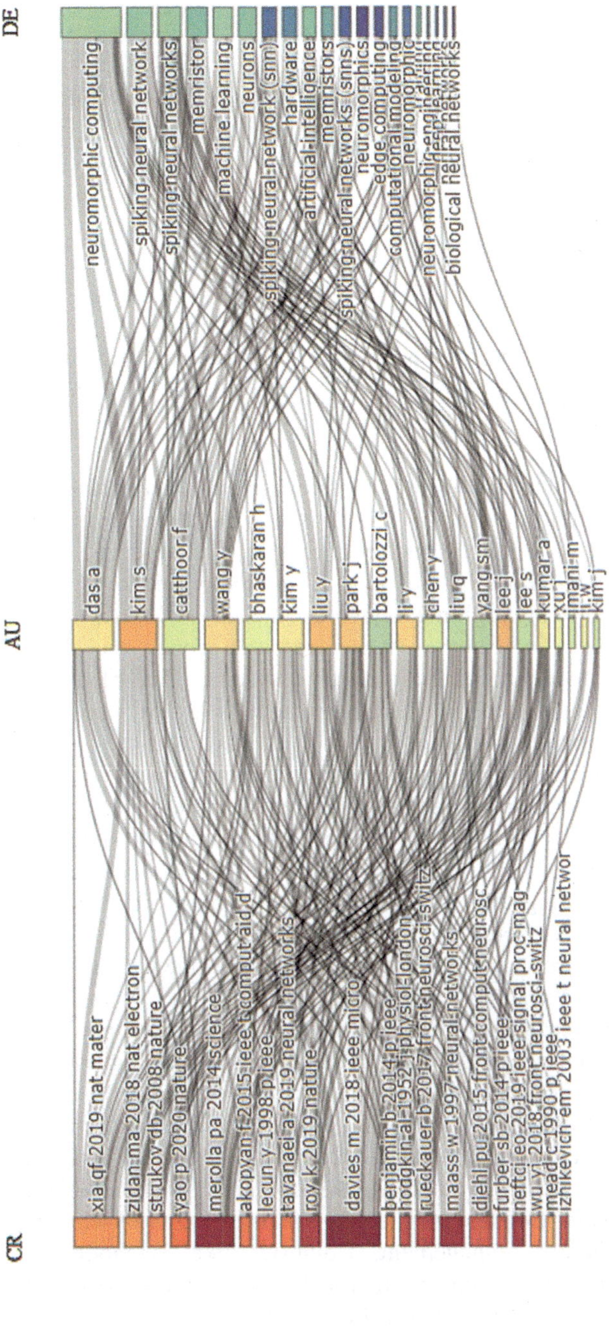


**FIGURE 15.2 Three-field plot (Sankey diagram).** The three-field plot visualizes the relationships between cited references (CR), authors (AU), and author keywords (DE), highlighting the intellectual structure and thematic linkages within the analyzed literature.

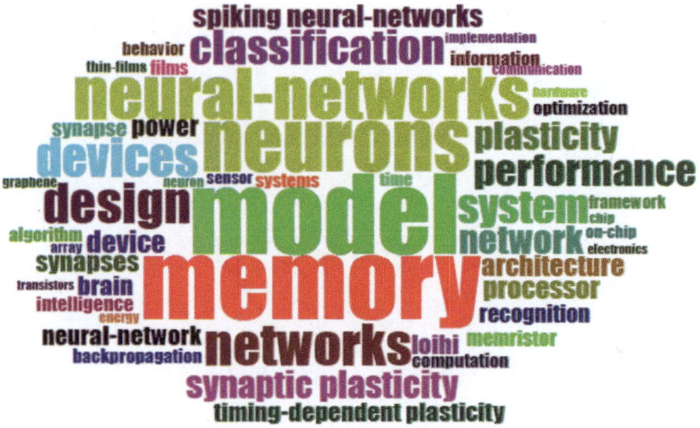


**FIGURE 15.3 Word cloud-keywords.** The word cloud represents the most frequently occurring author keywords in the selected literature, with larger terms indicating higher frequency and thematic prominence within the research domain.

effectively and understand the way different research areas are interconnected, thus guiding future inquiry and scholarly collaboration. In the thematic map presented, several densely connected clusters are observed, signifying key thematic concentrations in the field of neuromorphic computing. The red cluster, apparently highlighting keywords such as *model, neurons, and spiking neural networks*, indicates a strong research focus on algorithmic and computational modeling of brain-inspired systems. The blue cluster emphasizes hardware and materials-based research, with keywords like *memory, devices, and architecture,* reflecting work on physical applications and memory technologies. The purple cluster seems to combine the computational and hardware domains, indicating interdisciplinary efforts that merge computational modeling with device-level development. Moreover, keywords such as *model, memory, and neurons* serve as hubs connecting multiple clusters, highlighting their foundational role across subfields. This thematic organization underscores the multidimensional nature of neuromorphic computing research, combining artificial intelligence, material science, neuroscience, and systems engineering.

Table 15.5 presents top then countries with most citation. The analysis of citations by country reveals that China leads with the highest number of citations (287), indicating its dominant contribution and influence in the field. The United States follows with 211 citations, reflecting its strong research output and global impact. South Korea ranks third with 91 citations, showcasing its growing involvement in the domain. Other notable contributors include India (69), England (61), and Germany (54), all of which demonstrate significant scholarly engagement. Countries like Singapore, Switzerland, France, and Italy also feature in the top 10, highlighting the international and collaborative nature of research in this area.

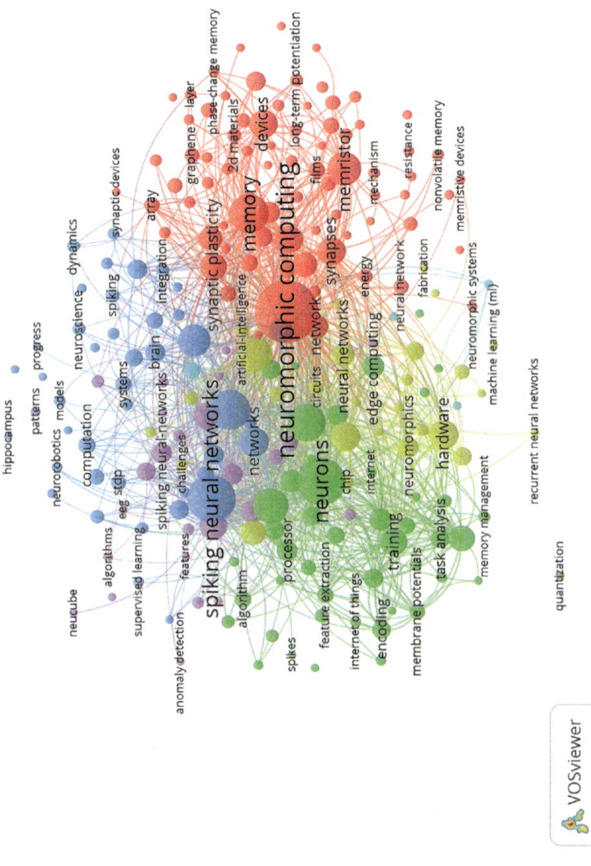


**FIGURE 15.4** **KCN.** The figure presents the keyword co-occurrence network, where nodes represent author keywords and links indicate their co-occurrence within the same publications. Node size reflects keyword frequency, while colors denote thematic clusters identified in the analysis.

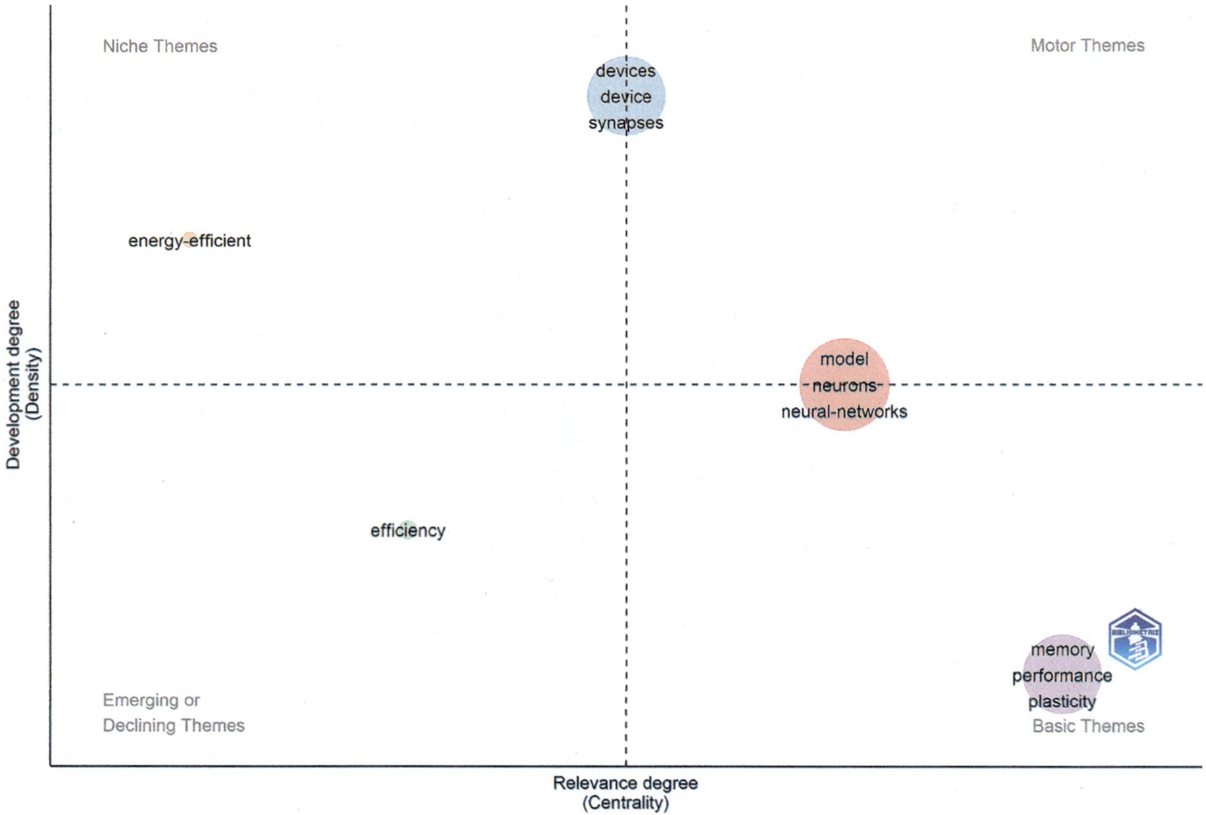


**FIGURE 15.5 Thematic map.** The thematic map illustrates the clustering and interrelationships of research themes based on keyword co-occurrence, highlighting the relative development and centrality of themes within the analyzed literature.

**TABLE 15.5 Top 10 countries with most citation.**

| S.No. | Affiliations | No. of citation |
|---|---|---|
| 1 | China | 287 |
| 2 | USA | 211 |
| 3 | South Korea | 91 |
| 4 | India | 69 |
| 5 | England | 61 |
| 6 | Germany | 54 |
| 7 | Singapore | 38 |
| 8 | Switzerland | 38 |
| 9 | France | 37 |
| 10 | Italy | 32 |

Table 15.6 displays citation analysis by institution, highlighting that the Chinese Academy of Sciences ranks top with 47 citations, revealing its prominent role and considerable research output in the field. The University of California System tops second with 34 citations, highlighting its significant contribution to academic progress. The Centre National de la Recherche

**TABLE 15.6 Top 10 institutions with most citation.**

| S.No | Institutions | No. of citation |
|---|---|---|
| 1 | Chinese Academy of Sciences | 47 |
| 2 | University of California System | 34 |
| 3 | Centre National DE LA Recherche Scientifique | 26 |
| 4 | Swiss Federal Institutes of Technology Domain | 24 |
| 5 | University of Chinese Academy of Sciences | 24 |
| 6 | United States Department of Energy | 22 |
| 7 | Indian Institute of Technology System | 20 |
| 8 | Dongguk University | 19 |
| 9 | Peking University | 18 |
| 10 | Nanyang Technological University | 17 |

Scientifique from France is at top third place with 26 citations, displaying its impact in global research. Other prominent institutions include the Swiss Federal Institutes of Technology Domain and the University of Chinese Academy of Sciences, each with 24 citations, further highlighting the vital presence of European and Chinese academic bodies. Additionally, institutions like the United States Department of Energy, Indian Institute of Technology System, Dongguk University, Peking University, and Nanyang Technological University constitute a divergent and international array of contributors to the research domain, emphasizing the global collaboration leading this research area.

## 3. Discussion

This bibliometric analysis provides a complete summary of the research area in neuromorphic computing from 2000 to 2025, derived from Web of Science database. The findings highlighted a growing and vibrant research field shaped by technological advancements, collaborative interdisciplinary work, and a persistent attention to themes such as memory, model development, spiking neural networks, and neural architectures. Frontiers in Neuroscience leads with 59 published articles among the most prolific sources, highlighting its fidelity to spreading interdisciplinary research works that integrates neuroscience and computing. This prominence of neuromorphic computing suggests that it is not only rooted in technical innovation but also largely interlaced with biological insights and cognitive modeling. IEEE Access and Nature Communications follow as key contributors, promoting the hybrid nature of the field that spans engineering, materials science, and computational systems. Furthermore, Local citation analysis highlights the centrality of impactful journals in creating the intellectual foundation of neuromorphic computing. Nature Communications positions top rank as the most locally cited source, with 2121 citations, indicating its crucial role in the dissemination of influential results. The high citation counts of Advanced Materials and Nature similarly point to the material and fundamental scientific advances that are leading forward neuromorphic technologies. These journals contribute not only in volume but also in visibility and credibility, revealing the recognition of neuromorphic computing of scientific community as a transformative area.

The Sankey diagram linking cited references, authors, and keywords demonstrates the depth of knowledge integration within the field. Highly cited references are consistently associated with influential authors and high-frequency descriptors such as *spiking neural networks and neuromorphic computing,* highlighting how foundational literature continues to shape emerging work. Additionally, the KCN and thematic maps reveal collaborative intersections among major research clusters, emphasizing interdisciplinary synergy. Notably, blue and red clusters in the full KCN network demonstrate strong links between device-level hardware research and computational model development—bridging physical architecture with algorithmic implementation.

The word cloud analysis offers valuable insight into the dominant themes and recurring terminology in neuromorphic computing literature over the past 2 decades. Prominent keywords such as neuromorphic, spiking neural networks, synapse, hardware, and learning reflect the core technical and conceptual foundations of the field. The repeated occurrences of keywords such as brain-inspired, low-power, and real-time indicates the main objectives of emerging energy-saving computing systems that resemble biological processing. Additionally, terms like deep learning, edge computing, and artificial intelligence indicate an overlapping between neuromorphic computing and broader AI principle. This integration highlights a shift in research targets toward practical applications and system-level integration. The observability of keywords related to materials and architecture demonstrates the interdisciplinary nature of the research domain, where development in physical structure are as important as technological advancements. Overall, the word cloud promotes the thematic richness and emerging fields within neuromorphic computing, emphasizing a research domain that is both foundationally robust and enlightened in its technological objectives. T The integrated insights from the word cloud and keyword co-occurrence network (KCN) analysis point to the thematic centrality of keywords such as model, memory, neural networks, neurons, and devices throughout the literature. These keywords not only reveal important research areas but also denote the thematic integration of neuroscience, computer science, and engineering in advancing neuromorphic systems. Furthermore, the thematic map enriches this understanding by merging research into basic themes, emerging or declining topics, and niche areas. This structure aids delineate well-established concepts from those still emerging or yet to gain prominence.

Institutional and country-level analyses further reinforce the collaborative and global nature of neuromorphic computing research. The predominance of research from China, the USA, South Korea, and India suggests a strategic prioritization of brain-inspired technologies within national R&D frameworks. Institutions like the Chinese Academy of Sciences and the University of California play pivotal roles in fostering innovation and cross-disciplinary collaboration. This geographical and institutional concentration of citations implies not only knowledge production but also the potential for research leadership, policy influence, and technological transfer.

Overall, the bibliometric findings present a clear trajectory for the field—one that is expanding in complexity and scale, driven by technological convergence and global collaboration. Future research should focus on exploring underrepresented regions or institutions, bridging hardware-software integration gaps, and translating neuromorphic systems into scalable real-world applications. While this analysis captures a broad spectrum of research activity, it is limited to the WoS database and English-language publications, which may exclude valuable insights from other sources. Nevertheless, the study provides a robust foundation for understanding trends, identifying research frontiers, and guiding strategic investment in neuromorphic computing. Collectively, these findings suggest that the evolution of neuromorphic computing is being guided by a blend of foundational research in high-impact general science journals and specialized publications that cater to niche advancements. The strong citation dynamics and the convergence of material science, computational theory, and neuroscience signal a healthy and rapidly maturing research ecosystem that is attracting broad scientific interest and laying the groundwork for practical innovation.

## 4. Conclusion

Neuromorphic computing, a transformative and interdisciplinary research frontier, continues to gain significant scholarly and industrial attention due to its potential to emulate the architecture and functional principles of the human brain. This bibliometric analysis, based on data retrieved from the Web of Science spanning 2000–2025, provides a comprehensive overview of the development, collaboration patterns, intellectual structure, and emerging themes in neuromorphic computing research.

The study revealed a consistent upward trajectory in annual scientific production, particularly accelerating in the last decade. This trend reflects the growing relevance of neuromorphic systems in addressing current computational challenges, such as energy efficiency, parallelism, and real-time sensory processing. The integration of specialized hardware like spiking neural networks (SNNs), and neuromorphic chips signifies a paradigm shift from traditional von Neumann architectures to brain-inspired models that support asynchronous, event-driven computation. Institutional and geographic mapping of citation data offers insight into the global distribution of neuromorphic research. Keyword analysis and thematic mapping revealed the conceptual foundations and evolving directions in the field. Frequently used keywords reflect the technical backbone of neuromorphic computing. Thematic clustering further highlights critical areas such as learning algorithms, synaptic plasticity, neuromorphic sensors, and edge AI—suggesting that future research is likely to focus on hybrid intelligence systems, real-world applications, and integration with bio-sensing and robotics platforms. The thematic map highlights the dynamic maturity of the field. Motor themes like spiking neural networks and neuromorphic hardware are well-developed and central to the field's growth. Niche themes suggest innovation in specific domains, such as materials engineering for memristive devices, while emerging themes like edge computing and event-driven learning reflect future research trajectories. Basic themes continue to anchor the field conceptually, pointing to the foundational importance of biologically inspired architectures.

## 5. Limitations

Despite the progress, several gaps and opportunities remain. Firstly, there is still a lack of standardization in benchmarking neuromorphic systems, making it difficult to compare performance across hardware platforms and applications. Secondly, ethical and societal implications of deploying autonomous, brain-inspired systems—particularly in sensitive domains such as healthcare, defense, and surveillance—have yet to be systematically explored. Thirdly, while neuromorphic systems hold promise for low-power edge applications, real-world deployment remains limited due to challenges in scalability, programmability, and integration with conventional computing environments.

## 6. Recommendation for future studies

- As the field continues to draw from neuroscience, materials science, electrical engineering, and computer science, deeper interdisciplinary collaboration is crucial. Integrating insights from cognitive psychology and systems neuroscience could enhance our understanding of how to implement brain-like functionalities in silicon.
- Future research should prioritize the co-development of neuromorphic hardware and software frameworks. Many systems currently lack a unified programming model, which hinders broader adoption. Developing neuromorphic operating systems, compilers, and application development environments could significantly enhance usability.
- While much of the literature remains hardware-centric, there is a growing need to focus on application-driven research. Domains such as autonomous robotics, smart prosthetics, neuromorphic vision systems, and adaptive control in drones could benefit from low-latency, event-driven computation.
- The field would benefit from community-driven efforts to create open-access benchmarks and standard datasets. This would allow for fair and transparent comparisons across systems and algorithms, fostering competition and innovation.
- Given the increasing intelligence and autonomy of neuromorphic systems, the development of ethical guidelines is essential. Collaborative efforts involving ethicists, policymakers, and technologists are needed to assess the societal risks and responsibilities of implementing such systems at scale.
- To sustain the growth of this emerging field, academic institutions should design interdisciplinary curricula that combine elements of neuroscience, AI, embedded systems, and hardware engineering. This would help build a new generation of researchers and practitioners capable of pushing the boundaries of neuromorphic computing.

- The bibliometric data shows a diverse set of contributing countries and institutions. To maximize impact, fostering open-access repositories, collaborative research grants, and international symposia can create opportunities for knowledge exchange and resource sharing.
- Exploring the synergy between neuromorphic computing and emerging paradigms such as quantum computing, soft robotics, and brain-computer interfaces could unlock entirely new computational models and applications. Multimodal systems that combine neuromorphic principles with these cutting-edge technologies could redefine how machines perceive, adapt, and interact.

## AI disclosure

During the preparation of this work the author(s) used ChatGPT in order to I used it to assist with language editing, figure descriptions, and improving clarity and organization of the manuscript. After using this tool/service, the author(s) reviewed and edited the content as needed and take(s) full responsibility for the content of the publication.

## References

Abdallah, A.B., Dang, K.N., 2024. Comprehensive review of neuromorphic systems. In: Neuromorphic Computing Principles and Organization, pp. 275–303.

Bhatia, M., Kumar, V., 2025. Bibliometric analysis of digital twin: scientometrics and future research trends. IEEE Internet Things J. 12 (12), 19043–19064. https://doi.org/10.1109/jiot.2025.3555282.

Borra, R., 2024. Neuromorphic computing: bridging biological intelligence and artificial intelligence. Int. J. Eng. Adv. Technol. 14 (2), 19–24. https://doi.org/10.35940/ijeat.b4558.14021224.

Chen, X., Zou, D., Xie, H., Wang, F.L., 2021. Past, present, and future of smart learning: a topic-based bibliometric analysis. Int. J. Educ. Technol. High. Educ. 18 (1). https://doi.org/10.1186/s41239-020-00239-6.

Davies, M., Wild, A., Orchard, G., Sandamirskaya, Y., Guerra, G.A.F., Joshi, P., Plank, P., Risbud, S.R., 2021. Advancing neuromorphic computing with Loihi: a survey of results and outlook. Proc. IEEE 109 (5), 911–934. https://doi.org/10.1109/JPROC.2021.3067593.

El Baz, J., Iddik, S., 2022. Green supply chain management and organizational culture: a bibliometric analysis based on Scopus data (2001–2020). Int. J. Organ. Anal. 30 (1), 156–179. https://doi.org/10.1108/IJOA-07-2020-2307.

Enuganti, P.K., Sen Bhattacharya, B., Serrano Gotarredona, T., Rhodes, O., 2025. Neuromorphic computing and applications: a topical review. Wiley Interdiscip. Rev., Data Min. Knowl. Discov. 15 (2). https://doi.org/10.1002/widm.70014.

Furber, S., 2016. Large-scale neuromorphic computing systems. J. Neural. Eng. 13 (5), 051001. https://doi.org/10.1088/1741-2560/13/5/051001.

Marković, D., Mizrahi, A., Querlioz, D., Grollier, J., 2020. Physics for neuromorphic computing. Nat. Rev. Phys. 2 (9), 499–510. https://doi.org/10.1038/s42254-020-0208-2.

Khudzari, J.M., Kurian, J., Tartakovsky, B., Raghavan, G.S.V., 2018. Bibliometric analysis of global research trends on microbial fuel cells using Scopus database. Biochem. Eng. J. 136, 51–60. https://doi.org/10.1016/j.bej.2018.05.002.

Mishra, H.G., Pandita, S., Bhat, A.A., Mishra, R.K., Sharma, S., 2022. Tourism and carbon emissions: a bibliometric review of the last three decades: 1990–2021. Tour. Rev. 77 (2), 636–658. https://doi.org/10.1108/TR-07-2021-0310.

Pesta, B., Fuerst, J., Kirkegaard, E., 2018. Bibliometric keyword analysis across seventeen years (2000–2016) of intelligence articles. J. Intell. 6 (4), 46. https://doi.org/10.3390/jintelligence6040046.

Rathi, N., Chakraborty, I., Kosta, A., Sengupta, A., Ankit, A., Panda, P., Roy, K., 2023. Exploring neuromorphic computing based on spiking neural networks: algorithms to hardware. ACM Comput. Surv. 55 (12), 1–49. https://doi.org/10.1145/3571155.

Sadatmoosavi, A., Tajedini, O., Esmaeili, O., Abolhasani Zadeh, F., Khazaneha, M., 2021. Emerging trends and thematic evolution of breast cancer: knowledge mapping and co-word analysis. JMIR Cancer 7 (4), e26691. https://doi.org/10.2196/26691.

Schuman, C.D., Kulkarni, S.R., Parsa, M., Mitchell, J.P., Date, P., Kay, B., 2022. Opportunities for neuromorphic computing algorithms and applications. Nat. Comput. Sci. 2 (1), 10–19. https://doi.org/10.1038/s43588-021-00184-y.

Strukov, D.B., Snider, G.S., Stewart, D.R., Williams, R.S., 2008. The missing memristor found. Nature 453 (7191), 80–83.

Sun, B., Guo, T., Zhou, G., Ranjan, S., Jiao, Y., Wei, L., Norman Zhou, Y., Wu, Y.A., 2021. Synaptic devices based neuromorphic computing applications in artificial intelligence. Mater. Today Phys. 18, 100393. https://doi.org/10.1016/j.mtphys.2021.100393.

Tien, J.M., 2017. Internet of things, real-time decision making, and artificial intelligence. Ann. Data Sci. 4 (2), 149–178. https://doi.org/10.1007/s40745-017-0112-5.

Zidan, M.A., Jeong, Y., Lee, J., Chen, B., Huang, S., Kushner, M.J., Lu, W.D., 2018. A general memristor-based partial differential equation solver. Nat. Electron. 1 (7), 411–420.

Chapter 16

# Neuro-driven smart homes: The future of adaptive and sustainable living

S.D. Vijayakumar[1], G. Brinda[2], S. Shantha Kumar[3], R. Nagadeepa[4], V. Kumar[5] and N. Saravanan[6]

[1]*Department of Artificial Intelligence and Data Science, Nandha Engineering College, Erode, Tamil Nadu, India;* [2]*Department of Electronics and Communication Engineering, M.P. Nachimuthu M.Jaganathan Engineering College, Erode, Tamil Nadu, India;* [3]*Department of CSE, Nandha College of Technology, Erode, Tamil Nadu, India;* [4]*Department of ECE, Fathima Michael College of Engineering and Technology, Madurai, Tamil Nadu, India;* [5]*Department of Electronics and Communication Engineering, Hindusthan College of Engineering, Erode, Tamil Nadu, India;* [6]*Department of Mechanical Engineering, Erode Sengunthar Engineering College, Erode, Tamil Nadu, India*

## 1. Introduction

### 1.1 Neuro-driven smart homes

With the growing complexity of the interactions that users have with the smart home, control mechanisms that are simultaneously intuitive and personalized have been emphasized in their importance. Traditional interfaces such as mobile applications, voice assistants, or preprogrammed automation usually do not consider the real-time user intent, cognitive load, and emotions. This survey on smart home automation systems in (Ezugwu et al., 2025) delves into the different facets of smart home systems, including concepts, applications, architectures, and domains for the web (or Internet of Things), which are necessary for such smart systems to solve problems and achieve future goals to facilitate their promotion and market from a different angle. The adoption of brain-computer interfaces (BCIs) for seamless integration supplies a nonstop communication link from the user's mind to the environment around them; therefore, it is possible to communicate without speech and touch. Apart from this, there is also an increasing demand for technology that caters to elderly users, those with motor impairments, and persons who live in assisted living

**Neuromorphic Computing for Brain Computer Interfaces. https://doi.org/10.1016/B978-0-443-41594-4.00011-3**

situations. Moreover, as more and more emphasis is placed on sustainability neuro-driven systems have the potential to reduce energy consumption in accordance with the cognitive and behavioral patterns of users without requiring manual enabling.

## 1.2 Limitations of conventional smart home systems

An important aspect of current-smart home architecture is built on rule-based systems or sensor and actuator use, which genuinely do not take into consideration the internal state, including intention and cognitive state. From this lack, may result in too much automation, rigidity, or less-than-optimal performance—the very problems message-based systems aimed to solve. Voice-activated AI assistants show particular shortcomings in applications in which the use of speech would be inconvenient or socially unacceptable, and handheld interfaces consistently lack the "glanceability" needed for users busy doing something else, yet still in need of awareness of their environs. Conventional systems also do not display the granularity needed to respond in real-time to subtle human cues, such as changes in concentration, stress, or lassitude. Without more in-depth human-machine understanding, household services and experiences remain nonpersonalized and do not accommodate and are thus mainly reactive. Paper (Khan et al., 2024) gives an in-depth survey and analysis of current-smart home designs in their efficacy in emergencies and points up the concerns for safety and accessibility that they pose, listing principal shortcomings and yet-unanswered research questions that seek to enhance trust and inclusivity attributes.

Cognitive Interacting is applying neurophysiological signals, primarily EEG, to read the user's mind in real time and talk to objects or virtual space implicitly. This paradigm shift abolishes active, initiative-based interactions in favor of passive feedback loops from and to the user. It employs EEG signals and brainwave patterns that accompany focus, intention, resting or emotional stress to register what an individual desires (intention) and translate that intent into physical-world action. It employs a neuro-adaptive method that lets the system make adjustments in lighting, temperature, audio or security even prior to the user becoming aware of it. Merging cognitive interaction also entails human-in-the-loop control models, in which adaptive learning algorithms complement system performance with constant neurofeedback, providing an even more natural, immersive and personal intelligent living experience. The extent of this chapter is to permit screwdriver-level research exploration of neuro-driven intelligent homes technically, architecturally and sustainably as an entity. It depicts the supporting technologies for brain-computer interfaces, specifically on EEG signal processing methodologies, real-time cognitive state classification and adaptive control. They also clarify the contribution of neuro-adaptive systems towards facilitating energy sustainability and living inclusiveness. With precise object position control, surface vibration and additional parameters, we limit components to bear very little information in comparison to a display while still radiating beautiful form. The chapter concludes with visions for the future and potential areas for future research in cognitive-aware intelligent home ecosystems.

## 2. Foundations of neurotechnology for smart living

### 2.1 Overview of brain-computer interfaces (BCIs)

Brain-Computer Interfaces (BCIs) are applications that enable direct human brain communication to an external device with no intermediate muscular activity. In smart homes, BCIs can facilitate hands-free and intention-based (volition-based) command of systems such as lights, HVAC, and household appliances. These interfaces capture and process EEG (electroencephalography) signals to detect and interpret neural activity. Comment catalogue: up-to-date review of brain–computer interface technology, covering its principles, components, applications, research and development trends, the benefits and challenges of wider uptake; BCIs are broadly stratified into active, reactive and passive BCIs, with respect to user engagement in signal generation (Peksa and Mamchur, 2023). For instance, active BCIs impose a motor imagery task, while reactive detection is driven by external stimulus (SSVEP or P300), and passive monitoring of spontaneous neural states (fatigue or emotional valence). The development of BCIs enhances personalization, autonomy and accessibility. The technology is now being incorporated into smart homes, thus enabling neuro-adaptive control.

### 2.2 EEG signal acquisition techniques and hardware

Electroencephalography, or EEG, is the most noninvasive form of brain activity monitoring as it is safe and portable. The scalp electrode is applied with 10–20 or 10–10 systems. The EEG system includes front-end amplifiers, ADC, reference electrodes and wireless data transmission modules. EEG headsets such as OpenBCI, Emotiv, and NeuroSky have dried or semidry electrodes, which provide better user comfort and the dynamics required for home use. EEG signals require high electrode impedance, environmental noise, user movement and additional filtering and deformation evidence rejection to be acceptable. Manuscript reference (Kumar and Mittal, 2021). EEG underlines data acquisition as well as exhibitions to show the frequency peaks in MATLAB, like high-exhibition amplifiers and noise-filtering and FFT analysis that exhibits the accuracy required for low-frequency and low-amplitude biomedical signals.

### 2.3 Neural decoding: Translating thoughts into commands

Neural decoding processes aim to understand and extract EEG signals that match user intent, mental effort, or emotional states, as outlined in reference

(Rudroff, 2025). Several steps are included in this process. First, experts preprocess the EEG signal by using bandpass filtering and removing artifacts. Next, they extract features through power spectral density and common spatial patterns. They classify the signals with CNNs, LSTMs, or support vector machines. To work in smart homes, these signal decoding methods need to have low latency and use minimal computational resources. This technology allows users to control systems with their thoughts rather than voice or physical commands. For example, they can adjust the temperature or dim the lights just by thinking about it.

## 2.4 Comparison of non-invasive versus invasive methods

BCI systems fall into three groups: noninvasive semiinvasive, and invasive. This classification depends on how the systems gather signals, as shown in (Fig. 16.1) below.

Noninvasive BCIs, like EEG, are safe, cheap, and easy to use. These characteristics make them best suited for smart homes. However, they have poor spatial resolution and pick up a lot of noise. Invasive BCIs put electrodes right into the brain (e.g., ECoG or microelectrode arrays). They give clear, precise signals from specific areas. But they come with big surgery risks and ethical issues. They're not ready for everyday use yet, as noted in (Bednarska-Czerwińska et al., 2025). Semiinvasive methods such as electrocorticography (ECoG), strike a balance. They're somewhat invasive but give better signal quality. For smart living, noninvasive systems are still the best choice. They're easy to set up, safe, and more and more available in stores.

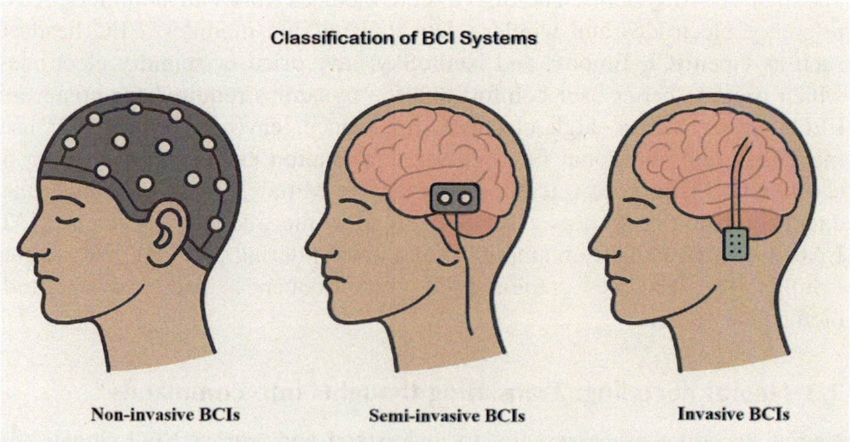


**FIGURE 16.1** Classification of BCI systems.

## 2.5 Cognitive state detection

Detecting cognitive states plays a key role in neuro-adaptive smart homes by allowing these systems to track and react to a user's mental or emotional condition, as mentioned in (Jin et al., 2025).

- Attention monitoring tracks the ratio of alpha to beta brain waves to measure focus. It has the potential to regulate noise levels or limit interruptions.
- Emotional state recognition uses EEG data from the frontal brain to classify states like stress, calmness, or frustration. This data often relies on frontal asymmetry and brain connection patterns.
- To estimate mental workload, researchers study theta and delta brain waves in the brain's frontal region. This helps systems reduce extra stimuli when the brain is overwhelmed.

Real-time cognitive state tracking enables smart environments to dynamically adapt in a user-centric manner, optimizing both comfort and energy efficiency.

# 3. System architecture of neuro-driven smart homes

## 3.1 Multi-layered architecture overview

The system layout of neuro-powered smart homes appoints a layout, process, decision and a layered structure for functioning, based on the signs of the brain. This includes six main components: nerve interface layer, signal preprocessing and feature extraction layer, classification and interpretation layer, reference-inconceivable decision-making layer, activation layer and cloud or edge interface. The nerve interface layer captures raw brain signals using noninvasive EEG devices and sends them for preprocessing. This step cleanses the signals before the noise by reducing the filtering and removing the artifacts in the next stages. Algorithms such as CNNS and LSTM help to identify the user's intentions or emotional status. The decision engine processes the indications explained with environmental data to generate smart reactions. The activation layer then activates the appropriate home automation functions using IoT-enabled devices.

This layered design allows smart home systems to improve with reliable adaptation and time-cloud integration over time. Paper (Hsu et al., 2017) introduces a smart home framework that adds several data inputs from the wearable tools, AI and sensor fusion to control equipment using 3D gesture recognition. It uses indoor positions to manage energy and detect fire, demonstrating strong accuracy during testing.

Fig. 16.2 shows the system architecture of a neuro-powered smart home, which shows the sequential flow of processes from brain-signal acquisition to home automation activation. At the top, the user and BCI interface appoints an

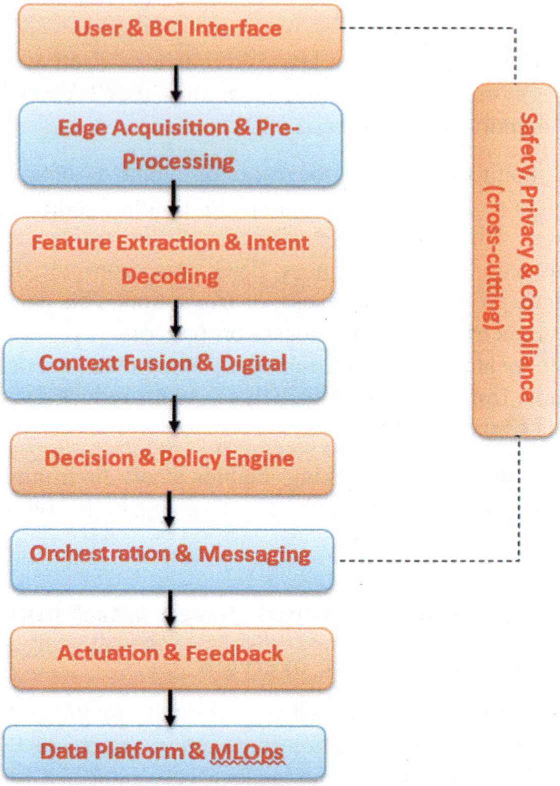


**FIGURE 16.2** System architecture of neuro-driven smart homes.

EEG/BCI cap (non-invasive, semiinvasive or aggressive) to catch nerve signals. These signs are transmitted to the edge acquisition and preprocessing phase, where filtering, deformation evidence removal and signal normalization occur. Next, the feature extraction and intent decoding module analyzes the temporal, spectral and spatial patterns, implementing the AI model to interpret the user's intentions. This intention is combined with the environment and IOT sensor input in data reference fusion and digital twin layer, forcing a real -time virtual model of the home environment. The decision and policy engine applies to predetermined rules, adaptation algorithms and adaptive learning to determine the most appropriate tasks. These decisions are executed through orchestration and messaging layer, which uses standard communication protocols for interfaces with equipment. Activation and response involve controlling smart devices such as light, HVAC or security systems, providing feedback to the user. For continuous improvement of data platforms and Mlops layer stores, monitor and update models. Security, privacy and compliance, secure, cross-cutting in all layers, ensuring safe, moral and regulation-transportation operations.

## 3.2 Neural signal acquisition and preprocessing

The nerve signal acquisition process in neuro-powered smart homes depends primarily on the noninvasive EEG headset, which is equipped with several electrodes placed above the skull. These devices record the electrical activity of the brain with millisecond resolution, which allow real-time users' intentions for decoding. The acquisition is affected by the electrode type (dry vs. wet), channel calculation, placement strategy (e.g., 10–20 international system), and sampling rates. Once occupied, raw EEG signals undergo preprocessing to increase the quality and purpose. Major preprocessing stages include bandpass filtering (usually 0.5–100 Hz), notch filtering to remove power line interference, and independent component analysis (ICA), such as artifact removal techniques or Wavelet transforming to eliminate the noise caused by eye blinks, muscle movement, or electrical intervention (Jain et al., 2024). Bolstering the baseline, dividing the ages into groups is also a normal procedure. Preprocessing should be designed such that the raw nervous information facility queuing the extraction step is made relevant and clean. In the context of the smart home, this is crucial to achieve precise, low-lonely control and system accountability (particularly dynamic) in daily living. This layer is often supported by edge computing devices to guarantee real-time processing and to minimize reliance on cloud infrastructure.

## 3.3 Feature extraction and signal denoising techniques

Feature extraction is another significant phase in neuro-operated architecture of the smart home, in that it transforms the preEEG data (Seena and Yomas, 2014) into a form that is comprehensible to classification techniques. Time-domains, frequency-domains and time—frequency domain feature are generally extracted. Such as statistical properties (mean, variance, kurtosis), well-known EEG bands are spectral power (delta, theta, alpha, beta, gamma), entropy measures and energy distribution over waves. These features correspond to cognitive events, such as meditation, intention and emotion. Feature extraction is very closely paired with signal denoising and facilitate removal of any remaining noise and artifacts, without significant loss of neural information. Typical Denoising algorithms are wavelet thresholding, empirical mode decomposition (EMD), and adaptive filtering. More sophisticated methods also designate deep learning-based autoencoders for unsupervised latent space learning and denoising. The extracted and represented features should evolve with the variability within and between subjects and be adaptable. Good feature extraction and denoising have proven to be crucial for accurate downstream classification and low latency, hence, this stage is considered as one of the bottlenecks in real-time brain-actuated home automation systems.

## 3.4 Classification algorithms: SVM, CNN, LSTM, and hybrid models

The classifier maps the EEGA-based features to discrete outputs like the predicted command of the user's intentions, cognitive status or smart home system command. Support vector machines (SVMs), such as traditional classifier (Karaman et al., 2023) are valuable for their strength and ability to handle small datasets with high-dimensional features. They are particularly effective for binary classification functions, such as attracting attention versus being inattentive. The Conventional Neural Network (CNN) has gained prominence due to its ability to automatically learn spatial patterns from raw or minimally processed EEG signals. They excel in identifying complex signal structures and are suitable for multi-class functions. Long -term memory (LSTM) network specializes in Temporal dependence modeling in EEG sequences, making them ideal for tasks such as emotion tracking or constant intention. The hybrid model has shown better performance by taking advantage of both spatial and cosmic dynamics (Gong et al., 2025) by combining CNN and LSTM architecture. These classifiers should be adapted for real -time execution with low delay and high generalization. A classifier for individual users increases optimization ability over time with timely teaching and learning.

Table 16.1 describes classification algorithms such as SVM, CNN, LSTM, and hybrid models, which have been used to extract EEG features to correctly determine the user's intentions, cognitive status, or specific command, which enables responsible and adaptive smart home control.

## 3.5 Context-aware decision engine

The reference-coverage decision engine (Lum and Lau, 2002) serves as a cognitive core of a neuro-powered smart home system, synthesizing the

**TABLE 16.1 Various classification algorithms.**

| Algorithm | Principle | Strengths | Limits | Uses |
|---|---|---|---|---|
| SVM | Separates classes through optimal hyperplane | Accurate on small data, robust to high dimensions | Struggles with noisy/large non-linear data | Simple intent/state detection |
| CNN | Learns spatial features through convolution | Auto feature extraction, good for EEG maps | Needs large data, high compute | Emotion or motor imagery recognition |
| LSTM | Captures temporal patterns in sequences | Good for long-term EEG trends | Slow, overfits small data | Continuous tracking, fatigue detection |
| Hybrid | Combines spatial and temporal models | High accuracy, captures full dynamics | Complex, heavy compute | Multi-class intent, adaptive control |

classified nerve intestine with the environment and relevant data to make intelligent decisions. It takes advantage of inputs such as day-to-day time, room occupancy, ambient temperature, user schedule and historical behavior patterns to refer to EEG-rich signals. For example, a detected command to "relax" can trigger various tasks, depending on whether it is morning (open blinds, soft music) or night (dim lights, start meditation mode). Decision-making strategies may employ rules-based arguments, fuzzy invention systems or agent learning reinforcement. The engine also incorporates priorities and safety overrides to prevent unintended actions. The classifier has a factor to provide a strong decision for the temporal consistency and confidence score. In addition, the engine adapts to user preferences by learning user reactions in the sense of better anonymization. Also, the engine gradually learns user preferences by taking reactions into account, thus better privatization of personalization in more than one sense of the word. Real-time operation of the decision engine is often enabled through edge computing architecture and microservices, with the result being a delay- and environment-resilient performance even in the unpredictable nature of the household environment.

### 3.6 Actuation layer and IoT-based control interfaces

The activation layer uses IoT-controlled smart technology to decide and translate cognitive responses in a smart home ecosystem. It connects to and controls a variety of smart home ecosystem elements such as lights, thermostats, curtains, kitchen appliances, entertainment systems, and safety systems. Every decision and control action is communicated to and executed by the smart home elements in real-time using hands-free control IOT protocols, including MQTT, Zigbee, Z-WAVE, or Bluetooth Low Energy (BLE). Real-time system responsiveness significantly contributes to accountability and user trust, especially in interfaced systems where neuro-driven cognitive control is active and consistent. The activation layer smart home feedback control loops to check the completion of commands, assess, and report device state. Feedback control loops are integrated with fail-safe action and manual override to secondary control to mitigate misclassification or command ambiguity. IOT middleware, for the purpose of IoT middleware, this layer hosts smart home devices. The activation layer connects a neurocognitive system with the cognitive smart home ecosystem. The basis for functional, spontaneous, and adaptive neurocognitive-powered interactions to truly immersive and accessible experiences.

## 4. Adaptive intelligence and personalization

### 4.1 Online and incremental learning techniques

Integrating AI and ML in e-learning is addressed with an emphasis on full personalization to provide adaptable and flexible learning units to keep a student focused and improve learning retention and overall performance, based on available evidence, even when a few problems, such as system complexity and data privacy, are present (Gligorea et al., 2023). Adaptive smart homes grow in development with their residents, necessitating the use of algorithms that learn and adjust instantly; the largely online incremental teaching methods available enable neuro-operated systems to adjust the user preferences, habits, and persistent pattern models of the nerves without starting from scratch. Information is less mental effort when data streams are neural networks, based on an EEG signal and other applicable sensors, flexible to dynamically adjust models to new data and other relevant information in real time. Methods such as online support vector machine (online SVM), stochastic gradient decent (SGD), and constant learning variants of deep neural networks are key to defining low-optimization. This is especially the case within the dynamic home environment, where the presence of inhabitants is characterized by stochastic behavior, a sense of neural mood, and routine patterns that are ever-ongoing. The optimization problem addressed is in simultaneous boundaries state with the added frustration of convincing the system from overfitting on flow patterns.

## 4.2 Behavior modeling and user profiling

In modeling neuro-operated smart homes, understanding behavior is fundamental for privatization. The system builds detailed user profiles by examining past EEG patterns and correlating user activity data, which is gathered through smart devices, location tracking, and wearable devices. These profiles capture the cognitive charge threshold, routine and habitual patterns, emotional responses, and rest preferences. Techniques for modeling these profiles can be potential graphical models, Hidden Markov models (HMMs), or Bayesian networks. Once user profiles are built, the system can perform user-directed system activities such as adjusting the lights to aid concentration during work hours and activating relaxation mode when stress is detected. Over time, these user behavior patterns diminish cognitive load and increase rest to optimize system responses.

## 4.3 Neurofeedback-driven environment optimization

Neurofeedback (Bovolon et al., 2025) is a closed-loop feedback system where the user's brain states are detected and adjusted parameters are grid-adjusted or relaxed depending on the user brain states. In the context of smart homes, this means the real-time EEG readings of temperature, light, and audio sets the home environment to calm, chaotic or relax the user's stress, focus or fatigue levels. In the case of a user becoming stimulated or stressed, the system will 'violently chaotic' and 'cool' audio. More advanced systems will incorporate reinforcement learning where changes made to the environment and the user's brain states are adjusted with praise/reward. This provides the user with a more fully functional smart home that encourages productivity, relaxation, or sleep as necessary.

### 4.4 Integration of circadian and neuro-cognitive rhythms

Circadian rhythms control the 24-hour cycles of sleep, awakeness, and hormonal changes, while changes in neuro-cognitive rhythms reflect the variety of brainwaves during different mental tasks. Neuro-driven smart houses can augment personalization by synchronizing system behavior with both these rhythms. For example, during the morning hours, EEG alerts from the owner showing alpha dominance can trigger energizing lights. Whereas, at night, lights can automatically dim and relaxing exercises can be prompted with screens during the melatonin times. Machine learning models, using historical EEG and biometric data, discover these patterns and trigger environmental responses. Integration with wearable sleep monitors and activity trackers provides a richer context. This holistic sleep state aligned approach improves sleep, mental wellbeing and energetic efficiency.

### 4.5 Emotion-aware and stress-responsive systems

Emotion-conscious systems transcend the limitations of venture-based adaptations by responding to the individual emotional states of consumers through EEG metrics like frontal alpha asymmetry, gamma band activity, and event-related potentials (ERPs). Smart homes have the ability to detect the emotional states of users, including happiness, tension, and frustration, and adjust their actions accordingly, demonstrating behavioral empathy. For instance, when users experience relaxation and comfort, the smart home will activate calming lights and music, and when users experience boredom, the smart home will activate motivational music. Stress-responsive mechanisms also combine other neural input and wearable devices, like smart watches, to detect emotions more accurately. These systems use deep learning emotion classification models and advanced affective computing. Smart homes monitor and adjust systems to promote emotional and mental health. Hence, such homes will be smart and emotionally intelligent.

## 5. Sustainability and energy efficiency

### 5.1 Role of cognitive load in energy demand prediction

Understanding cognitive load is essential for estimating and predicting energy consumption patterns in smart homes. In neuro-powered environments, cognitive load is measured in real time through EEG monitoring by conducting spectral analysis of brain waves in the theta and alpha bands. Users in high cognitive states tend to use more relaxing devices (lights and HVAC) as they subconsciously try to relieve their mental load by adjusting the atmosphere. These patterns can be learned by a machine learning model and used to predict energy demand spikes. Moreover, the system can constantly refine energy settings to user-comfort levels, engagement, and cognitive effort to minimize unnecessary consumption by integrating function-specific cognitive profiles with cognitive shift-altering signals like ambient temperature. Such anticipated modeling optimizes user comfort and mental engagement and facilitates the grid-responsive energy scheme in smart city initiatives. More sophisticated approaches include the use of Long Short-Term Memory (LSTM) networks for adaptation to temporal patterns in EEG and reinforcement of control policies. Cognitive load-based energy forecast paves the way for intelligent, user-centric energy management that balances stability with adaptive life. As (Gligorea et al., 2023), smart energy management works on ML and DL applications, with better accuracy in load forecasts, effectiveness in demand, and highlights the role in advancing smart energy sectors, while data quality, interpretation, and limited real -world deployment address challenges such as the constant energy research.

## 5.2 Adaptive HVAC, lighting, and appliance control

In neuro-driven smart homes, adaptive control of HVAC systems, lighting, and equipment is directed by EEG-ritual insight into the presence of the user, activity and mental/emotional states. Unlike traditional systems, which respond to occupancy or temperature alone, EEG-Employed Systems dynamically optimize environmental parameters based on user stress levels, fatigue, or attention periods (Abuhussain et al., 2023). In the study, a novel Mamdani FIS-based fuzzy controller is proposed for HVAC systems, enabling adaptive thermal comfort management and receives 50% energy savings while maintaining satisfactory indoor conditions. For example, if alpha wave dominance indicates relaxation or low vigilance, the system can reduce low light and adjust HVAC settings for optimal comfort. In contrast, the beta wave may increase bright lighting and ventilation to support dominance, concentration or physical activity. Tools such as coffee makers, music systems, or air purifiers can be activated when the brain signals indicate the onset of fatigue or emotional stress. The real -time nerve reaction ensures that the environment develops to support cognitive and physical welfare. This architecture takes advantage of IoT devices, edge computing and fuzzy logic controllers to maintain ultra-low delay and relevant accountability. By eliminating unnecessary use during low-demand states (e.g., deep sleep or absence), the system reduces power consumption. Importantly, adaptive control strategies can be individual through learning reinforcement, ensuring that the system aligns with individual circadian and neuro-behavior rhythms over time, promoting both comfort and energy efficiency. The (Fig. 16.3) depicts an adaptive control system where cognitive load assessment and energy demand estimation guide

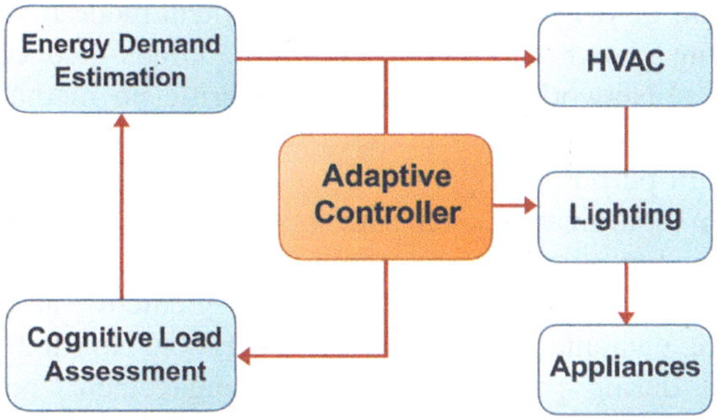


**FIGURE 16.3** Adaptive control system for cognitive load–aware energy management in HVAC, lighting, and appliances.

an AI-based controller to dynamically regulate HVAC, lighting, and appliances for optimized energy efficiency.

## 5.3 Energy profiling using EEG-triggered automation

Energy profiling in neuro-powered smart homes includes the manufacture of detailed energy consumption patterns associated with real-time EEG signal triggers. Instead of a stable use program, this approach maps nerve reactions to the operationally associated devices and systems. For example, elevated theta or delta wave activity may indicate fatigue or the onset of sleep, the system can gradually light lighting, low HVAC activity or motivate to switch entertainment equipment. In contrast, periods of mental focus or work engagement can activate the specific energy-consuming devices. By examining correlations between these nerve events and the energy consumed, the system can generate personalized energy models based on the user's lifestyle and neurobehavioral patterns. During periods of low cognitive demand, these models focus energy use to minimize waste. Moreover, energy signatures derived from EEG data can be used with clustering algorithms to classify users. This allows adaptations at the community level in smart neighborhoods or multi-residence units. Edge AI and federated learning allow for the continuous refinement of energy profiles without centralized data aggregation, ensuring data privacy. Automating energy management in response to EEG signals enhances system stability and aligns with demand response strategies for the smart grid.

## 5.4 AI-based optimization for resource utilization

Artificial intelligence utilizes EEG and sensor fusion data for real-time adaptability to resource usage in neuro-managed smart homes. Optimizing the allocation of energy, water, and data bandwidth is performed using Strengthening Learning algorithms, which take into account user preferences, nervous states and environmental contexts. For instance, the AI can reduce the intensity of light or switch to low-energy equipment mode if a relaxed EEG is detected, giving power comfort compromise. Grade-inconceivable models such as Deep Q-Networks (DQNS) or actor-criticism methods perform the nervous response and historical usage data to refine energy-saving methods. Moreover, multi-purpose adaptation algorithms, like genetic algorithms or particle swarm optimization, can address trade-offs between user comfort, system functionality, and structural stability. Integration with smart meters and IOT sensors permits real-time monitoring and predictive adjustments, while edge computing guarantees low-latency optimization. Non-immutable systems can also shift during periods of cognitive engagement, power tariffs, or availability of renewables to balance cognitive load with intelligent load shifting and smart resource balance. The result is a neuro-ordeal environment that smartly aligns user thinking with system efficiency, achieving high-level automation and ecological responsibility.

## 5.5 Metrics for measuring environmental sustainability

To measure the stability effect of neuro-operated smart homes (Ali et al., 2025), a strong set of metrics must be used, including both direct and indirect indicators. The major energy matrix includes neural state per total consumption (e.g., energy used during high cognitive weight vs. comfort), decrease in the percentage of standby energy and EEG-trigger energy savings compared to baseline models. Temporal Matrix, such as peak load shifting, reaction to cognitive signs are essential for the evaluation of delay, and time-to-time energy configuration accountability. Beyond energy, stability also covers environmental comfort, indoor air quality and integration of renewable sources. EEG-powered automation, equipment use efficiency, and users provide metrics such as the CO of saving through satisfaction score (through post-automatic session feedback). The life cycle evaluation (LCA) model can be adapted to include neuro-information science layers, stability in design, deployment and operating stages. Additionally, a user's carbon footprint in the system obtained through adaptive learning becomes a major performance indicator for green living. Cognitive stability indices-users can carry forward the development and certification of the neuro-smart infrastructure of the matrix-future, along with a combination of mental health, productivity and energy savings. Such a matrix ensures transparency, promoting accountability and continuous improvement in permanent neurotech design.

# 6. Enabling technologies

## 6.1 Edge computing for real-time EEG processing

Edge computing plays a key role in enabling real-time processing of EEG signals in neuro-operated smart homes. Cloud-based approaches suffer from latency and privacy issues, which are critical when managing real-time brain-computer interfaces (BCIs). Edge computing brings data processing closer to the source in on-site gateways or embedded processors, allowing low-latency decisions and responses to action. This local processing reduces the communication overhead between EEG acquisition devices and control systems, enabling fast response to the user brain states. With a mildly deep learning model adapted to the age certification, tasks such as artifact removal, feature extraction and mental status classification can be done at the edge nodes. Additionally, the edge systems can select to transport only relevant features or to the cloud, saving bandwidth and complying with nervous data privacy standards. Skilled hardware, accelerating intensive tasks such as Nvidia Jetson Nano or Google Coral can handle intensive tasks, supporting low-power yet high-ingredient operations. Edge-based EEG processing also enables better reference-awareness by integrating multimodal sensor data (environment, biometric, etc.) on the same edge platform, which increases decision-making. Overall, the age computing is fundamental to obtain responsive, safe and autonomous control in a cognitive smart environment (Ali et al., 2025).

## 6.2 IoT protocols and smart home communication standards

Interoperability and seamless communication are fundamental in neuro-driven smart houses, in which several devices need to synchronize in response to cognitive instructions. IoT verbal exchange protocols offer the spine for connecting EEG interfaces, environmental sensors, actuators, and domestic appliances, as in (Holguin and Errapotu, 2023). Protocols like MQTT (Message Queuing Telemetry Transport), CoAP (Constrained Application Protocol), and Zigbee allow lightweight and energy-efficient communication among low-power devices. MQTT is particularly suitable because of its publish-subscribe version, which allows EEG-triggered events (e.g., a user feeling stressed) to trigger multiple responsive actions (like dimming lights and adjusting HVAC) at the same time. Standard protocols like Z-Wave and Thread enable device-level interoperability, ensuring compatibility across different vendors. Bluetooth Low Energy (BLE) is important for wearable EEG devices, providing continuous low-power transmission of neural data. Moreover, emerging standards like Matter (by CSA) are redefining the unified smart home ecosystem by enabling seamless, cross-platform communication, necessary for future-proofing neuroadaptive environments. Quality of Service (QoS) mechanisms embedded in those protocols ensure timely and reliable delivery of EEG commands. Furthermore, communication stacks are getting more and more ready with local encryption and authentication layers, ensuring data integrity and privacy. Together, IoT protocols and communication standards form the neural network that allows a cognitive smart home to function cohesively, adaptively and securely. Neuromorphic computing is a paradigm shift in processing EEG signals by mimicking the structure and function of biological nervous systems. In neuro-driven smart homes where continuous monitoring and adaptive responses are required, traditional von Neumann architectures struggle with energy efficiency and equality. Neuromorphic chips like Intel's Loihi or IBM's TrueNorth offer event-driven processing where the computation happens only in response to input spikes, which reduces power consumption significantly. These chips are naturally suited for spiking neural networks (SNN), which are well matched for the temporal mobility of EEG signals. Neuromorphic processors can detect real-time mental state classification and mismatch with minimal energy budget, which can always be capable of cognitive interfaces.

## 6.3 Neuromorphic computing for low-power BCI systems

Neuromorphic computing changes how EEG signals are processed by imitating the structure and function of biological nervous systems. In neuro-driven smart homes, which need continuous monitoring and adaptive responses, traditional von Neumann architectures struggle with energy efficiency and scalability. Neuromorphic chips like Intel's Loihi and IBM's TrueNorth use event-driven processing, where computation happens only in response to input spikes, greatly reducing power consumption. These chips naturally support spiking neural networks (SNNs), which are well-suited to the temporal dynamics of EEG signals. Neuromorphic processors can perform real-time mental state classification and detect discrepancies using minimal energy, making them ideal for cognitive interfaces. Their low-power, asynchronous architecture is also important for neuro-viral control and ultra-fast feedback loops, such as shutting down equipment in response to cognitive fatigue or stress detection. These chips can be embedded in wearable EEG devices, decentralizing processing and reducing dependence on cloud or edge computing. Neuromorphic systems also support on-device learning, letting them learn user-specific EEG patterns over time without external retraining. This bio-inspired approach fits user-centered design principles for energy-efficient, autonomous, next-generation smart homes. Integrating a neuromorphic processor into a neuro-smart home ecosystem brings us closer to an environment that is not only responsive but also seamlessly interacts with the human mind.

## 6.4 Federated learning for distributed cognitive adaptation

Federated Learning (FL) (Wu and Wang, 2021) A centralized server provides a secrecy-protection and scalable approach to continuously improve machine learning models in several neuro-driven smart homes without transferring sensitive EEG data to a centralized server. In a federated setup, the local device (edge processor or gateway) train model using the user-specific EEG signal and environmental reference data. Instead of uploading raw nerve data, only the model updates (gradients) are shared with a central aggregator, which combines them to improve the global model. This decentralized learning architecture is particularly beneficial in EEG-based systems, where the data is both sensitive and highly user-specific. FL supports privatization, ensuring compliance with privacy rules like GDPR. In addition, it enhances strength by learning from diverse domestic environments and behavior profiles, leading to models that are more common in users. Differential privacy techniques can be integrated into FL workflows to further obscure individual contributions. Federated learning also supports continuous learning, allowing models to develop with changing nerve patterns, routines, or environmental interactions. In the scenarios where many users share a smart home (e.g., family), FL can maintain a user-specific model by creating a collaborative group behavior model. By enabling safe, adaptive and collaborative learning in smart home ecosystems, federated learning intensifies the deployment of intelligent, reliable and developed neuroadaptive systems.

### 6.5 Multimodal sensor fusion

In neuro-driven smart homes, the quality of decision-making and relevant awareness is greatly increased through multimodal sensor fusion-integration of EEG data with environment and biometric sensors. EEG signals can be unclear or noisy alone, but when combined with supporting data sources such as heart rate, skin conduction, room temperature, ambient noise and light status, the system receives a composite view of the mental and physical condition of the user. For example, if the EEG detect cognitive stress, but the noise of the environment is low, and the heart rate is stable, the system can delay intervention. Conversely, when many modalities form confirms high stress, it is appropriate to immediately activate (e.g., to turn on the lights or trigger soothing music). Sensor fusion is achieved by aligning data and using feature- or decision-level integration, often with deep learning models like CNNs or LSTMs to capture temporal and spatial correlations. Cross-validation across modalities strengthens the system's ability to infer user intentions and classify states accurately. Advanced fusion frameworks use attention mechanisms to favor the most relevant data streams in real time. This multimodal approach also improves fault tolerance: if the EEG signal is corrupted by motion artifacts, the system can rely on supporting sensors. In short, multimodal fusion places isolated signals into a broader cognitive context, making neuro-smart homes more reliable, responsible, and better able to handle real-world complications.

## 7. Implementation challenges

### 7.1 EEG signal variability and noise artifacts

EEG signals (Lawhern et al., 2012), which form the core of brain-computer interface (BCI) systems in neuro-driven smart homes, are highly sensitive and variable. Signal quality can fluctuate with electrode placement, scalp conductivity, environmental electromagnetic interference, and user-specific conditions like fatigue, stress, or hydration. These factors reduce the system's ability to infer cognitive states reliably. EEG also has a very low signal-to-noise ratio (SNR) and is often corrupted by artifacts from eye blinks (EOG), muscle activity (EMG), cardiac signals (ECG), and external electrical sources. These noise components can mislead the downstream feature extraction and classification stages, which can lead to wrong system decisions. While advanced filtering techniques such as independent component analysis (ICA), general average reference (car), and adaptive filtering are usually used for denoising, the real-time performance of these algorithms on resource-resources is challenging. In addition, variability between users and sessions requires frequent renovation or adaptive teaching models, which can affect the expected spontaneous experience in the smart home. Without the need for expert supervision, ensuring frequent, strong EEG signal acquisition in daily life is one of the main challenges towards practical deployment.

## 7.2 Real-time constraints and latency bottlenecks

Real-time accountability is required in neuro-operated smart homes, where light, HVAC systems, or equipment are expected to be controlled almost immediately from EEG-Trigger decisions. However, maintaining ultra-low delay in the entire signal processing pipeline-from signal acquisition and feature extraction, classification and actuation is preprocessing is non-trivial. The specific EEG system has a built-in delay due to data buffering, preprocessing time and delay in communication, especially when cloud-based processing is used. Even edge equipment with onboard processing capabilities struggle to maintain real -time operation when complex models such as deep CNN or LSTM are employed. Network delay further reduces the problem, especially when many IOT nodes and actuators are involved. Any interval in decision execution can lead to user frustration, low confidence and potential security risks (e.g., delay in lighting in the stairs or unanimous alarms). Techniques such as edge computing, model pruning, quantization and light neural networks (e.g., MobileNets) are being developed to reduce these hurdles. In addition, delayed-awakened schedules and parallel function execution are important for adaptation of accountability. Nevertheless, it is an important engineering barrier to ensure subsecond delay in odd components in the neuro-smart home ecosystem.

## 7.3 Hardware integration and scalability issues

Integrating diverse hardware components is a malignant challenge in integrating diverse hardware components from smart home appliances, environmental sensors and computing modules from the headset and wearable biosensor. Communication protocol (e.g., Zigbee, Z-Wave, BLE, Wi-Fi), introduces inequalities in power requirements and data formats. In addition, most EEG equipment is designed for clinical or research use, and consumer-grade smart home platforms are not adapted for spontaneous integration. Scalability complicates further integration, as adding more sensors and control points increases data traffic, computational load and coordination complexity. It is difficult to ensure synchronous operation between distributed nodes, especially when relying on wireless communication, due to dependence or dropout. Additionally, maintaining firmware updates, calibration stability and maintenance patches in the growing network of equipment introduces overheads in maintenance. Integrated APIs, middleware platforms, and open standards (such as substances and committees) are proposed solutions, but adoption is still fragmented. True plug-and-play interoperability, hardware abstraction layers, and a modular system architecture are essential for overcoming these barriers and enabling scalable deployment of neuro-driven intelligent environments.

### 7.4 User comfort, ergonomics, and wearability of BCI devices

For neuro-driven smart homes to reach mainstream acceptance, comfort and ergonomics must be top priorities for BCI users. Traditional EEG headsets are often heavy, use wet electrodes with conductive gels, and are built for stable setups, making them impractical for long or daily wear. Even dry-electrode systems, while more convenient, can still deliver poor signal quality or become uncomfortable during extended use. The device's appearance also affects acceptance, especially at home where aesthetics matter. Wearability issues include pressure points on the skull, heat buildup, allergic reactions to electrode materials, and restricted movement. Continuous use can cause cognitive fatigue and raise ethical and privacy concerns. Ergonomic design should balance signal fidelity with minimal intrusion, comfort, and discretion. Advances in flexible electronics, skin-conformal sensors, and smart textiles are addressing some of these challenges by enabling low-cost EEG acquisition. Nevertheless, important work remains in achieving a form factor that naturally integrates without performing in everyday objects (e.g., cap, headband, glasses). Finally, the BCI interface's purpose and comfort for the user will determine the long-term success of the engagement and the neuro-smart living system.

## 8. Security, privacy, and ethics

### 8.1 Neural data privacy and encryption mechanisms

Neuro-operated smart homes have highly sensitive information in nerve data collected through EEG-disclosing medical conditions, emotional stages, levels of attention, or even unique biometric patterns. This data makes privacy a significant concern as mentioned in (Popoola et al., 2024). To prevent unauthorized access, encryption must be applied in all stages: data-AS-rest (locally or stored in cloud), data-in-transit (between EEG equipment, age processors and IOT controllers), and data-in-use (during processing). Advanced encryption standards such as AES-256, TLS 1.3 and Post-Quantum Cryptography are being recommended. For real-time BCI operations, low-oppression encryption techniques such as light ciphers or hardware-satisfaction modules are essential. Homomorphic encryption model allows calculation on nerve data that is encrypted without decryption, while preserving confidentiality even during training. In addition, safe multi-party computation (SMPC) can enable cooperative learning between homes without revealing raw EEG data. Data minimalization policies—instead of full waves, only stare at the necessary features—further exposure reduces risk. Strong major management and regular safety audit are also important to ensure long -term privacy of nerve information.

## 8.2 Consent, transparency, and ethical neurotech deployment

Given the intimate nature of EEG data, informed consent is nonperfect in neuro-smart home speculation. Users should fully know what data is being collected, how it will be used, where it will be stored, and who will have access to it. Transparency should be expanded to make algorithm decision-making-the system should be explained so that the users understand why some actions (e.g., light changes or equipment activation) occurred based on the signs of the brain. Ethical deployment requires designing systems that prefer user autonomy, allowing them to override automated decisions and disable nerve data collection on their own will. Privacy dashboard can give real -time visibility into data flow and control permissions. Weak groups require special moral ideas—such as an elderly person or disabled person—where consent must be validated carefully. The moral principle of profit demands that neuro-smart houses increase the quality of life without causing psychological or surveillance damage. Additionally, long -term storage of nerve data should be severely evaluated, with termination policies to prevent indefinite retention.

## 8.3 Adversarial attacks and model robustness

Neuro-operated systems are susceptible to adverse attacks-EEG data or fundamental manipulations of model input are designed to make incorrect decisions. Examples include signal injection attacks (presenting false EEG patterns), replay attacks (feeding old nerve data), and adverse disturbances (small changes in input signals that mislead the classifier). These attacks can give rise to unexpected tasks—such as disabling security systems or changing environmental controls—reducing security and privacy risks. To reduce this, the model must be trained with adverse strength techniques such as adverse training, shield masking, and input sanitization. A safe EEG acquisition with tampering and authentication may reduce the risk of hardware signal spoofing. Additionally, the system that detects the discrepancy can mark a sudden deviation from the user's specific EEG signature. The excess system can make it hard for attackers to bypass the excess system through multimodal fusion (EEG + biometric + environmental sensor).

## 9. Future trends and research directions

### 9.1 Neuromorphic chips and on-device learning

Neuromorphic chips are becoming a key technology for brain-controlled smart homes. They offer ultra-low-power, event-driven computation that mimics biological neural structures. Unlike traditional CPUs and GPUs, neuromorphic processors—like Intel Loihi, IBM TrueNorth, or BrainChip Akida—run spiking neural network (SNN) models that naturally adapt to the brief and infrequent patterns of EEG signals. Their asynchronous processing greatly lowers latency, enabling millisecond-level responses for real-time BCI applications. They also support on-device learning, so EEG patterns can be developed and updated locally without relying on cloud connectivity. It is particularly valuable for personalization, as each user's nerve signature is unique and changes over time. Embedding such a processor directly to the EEG headset or local gateway can always lead to continuous neural decoding with minimal energy consumption, making the BCI-competent homes more autonomous, private and liable.

### 9.2 Emotionally adaptive living environments

Future neuro-smart houses will proceed to the emotion-based adaptation beyond working automation, using advanced affectionate computing techniques to detect subtle emotional signals from EEG, facial expressions, voice tones and physical data. These systems will not only respond to clear orders, but will also continuously accommodate light, temperature, music and even fragrance to affect or stabilize the user's emotional state.

### 9.3 BCI interoperability and standardization

As the ecosystem of BCI devices and smart home platforms grows, interoperability will become a significant challenge. Right now, EEG devices, software frameworks, and IoT platforms often operate in separate ownership silos, which prevents them from working together. Future progress relies on EEG data formats, API specifications, and the development of open standards for communication protocols. The same approach used for IoT protocols can be applied to BCI, ensuring that equipment from different vendors can interact. Standardization will also include semantic interoperability, allowing neural state descriptions to be understood universally by any smart home decision engine. Furthermore, adopting specific cybersecurity and privacy standards for neural data will be necessary to protect sensitive information and enable safe interactions. This framework will encourage seamless BCI integration, allowing consumers to adopt and scale multi-vendor smart environments more quickly.

## 9.4 Smart cities and cognitive home-to-grid integration

In the future, smart homes could operate as intelligent energy nodes within the larger smart city environment. Through home-to-grid connection, a person's brain activity can indirectly influence energy demand at the grid level. For example, when many homes show low activity or relaxation through EEG, the grid can reduce power supply to those areas or shift it to high-demand zones. In contrast, during times of heightened cognitive function, more renewable energy can be allocated to support productive home environments. This requires real communication between smart homes and software providers, supported by demand response algorithms and real-time energy markets. Integration with renewable sources like solar panels and local energy storage will further improve stability. This vision supports energy efficiency, reduces carbon emissions, and contributes to the smart city goals for community well-being, making smart homes an essential part of urban infrastructure.

## 9.5 AI-BCI Co-design and human-in-the-loop systems

Current neuro-smart home architecture often considers AI model and BCI hardware/software as separate components. The AI-BCI co-design applies to a more integrated approach where hardware, software and AI algorithms are developed simultaneously to adapt together EEG signal quality, model accuracy and delay. Co-design model-ignorant signal enables facilities such as the acquisition of signal (adjusting EEG sampling or electrode selection based on model needs) and hardware -ware AI training (designing model that fully exploits the architecture of the EEG device's processor). In addition, the human-in-loop systems will become rapidly important, where the user's response-two refines the behavior of the monotonous system clear (through orders) and inherent (through nerve or physical signals). This recurrence loop ensures individualization, trust and adaptability over time, allowing the environment to develop with the changing needs, preferences and cognitive patterns of the user. In the long run, the AI-BCI co-design can originally produce integrated cognitive ecosystem where human intentions and environmental reaction are almost unique in time and work (Sun et al., 2025).

## 10. Conclusion

The chapter has detected the emerging paradigm of neuro-driven smart homes, where brain-computer interfaces (BCIs) and advanced AI enable direct, reference-inconvenience interaction between human cognitive states and built environment. We examined the multi-level system architecture for features extraction, classification and activation through EEG signal acquisition and preprocessing to IoT-enabled devices. We expanded how online learning, neurofeedback, and behavior modeling-transforming homes in individual, self-abusive ecosystems-transforms homes. Stability strategies were exposed, showing how EEG-trigger automation can reduce energy consumption by increasing comfort. Competent technologies-Edge Computing, IOT protocol, neuromorphic processing, federated learning, and multimodal sensor provide computational backbones for fusion-promotional time, privacy-conservation and scalable purpose. We also addressed implementation challenges (signal variability, delay, hardware integration, ergonomics) and significant safety and moral ideas, which ensure the adoption of the responsible neurotech.

Neuro-operated smart homes have the potential to change living standards. They create an environment that meets human needs while being responsible. For the elderly, people with disabilities, or those needing assistance, these systems can restore independence and improve their quality of life. For the general population, automated systems that consider cognitive factors support mental health, productivity, and energy-efficient habits. This promotes personal comfort along with global stability goals. By using renewable energy and managing demand based on cognitive needs, these homes can help achieve zero carbon goals at both home and community levels. Additionally, the development of neuro-operated smart homes will be influenced by AI-BCI combined design, neuromorphic processors, and standard BCI compatibility. These systems will extend beyond individual homes to serve as active parts of Smart City infrastructure. They will communicate with urban energy grids, healthcare networks, and public safety systems. Emotional intelligence, ethical governance, and privacy-focused design will guide this progress. This ensures that the neuro-oriented environment enhances human life without sacrificing dignity or independence. The long-term vision is a smart ecosystem where human thoughts, environmental adjustments, and sustainable resource management work together seamlessly. This creates a future where homes do more than provide shelter; they actively support and enrich life.

## References

Abuhussain, M.A., Alotaibi, B.S., Aliero, M.S., Asif, M., Alshenaifi, M.A., Dodo, Y.A., 2023. Adaptive HVAC system based on fuzzy controller approach. Appl. Sci. (Switzerland) 13 (20). https://doi.org/10.3390/app132011354.

Ali, A., Montanaro, T., Sergi, I., Carrisi, S., Galli, D., Distante, C., Patrono, L., 2025. An innovative IoT and edge intelligence framework for monitoring elderly people using anomaly detection on data from non-wearable sensors. Sensors 25 (6), 1735. https://doi.org/10.3390/s25061735.

Bednarska-Czerwińska, A., Smoleń-Dzirba, J., Strychalska, A., Sierka, W., Wróblewska, U., Mermer, P., Masarczyk, B., Jodłowiec-Lubańska, N., Kokot, A., Simka-Lampa, K., Zmarzły, N., Morawiec, E., Orczyk, A., Grabarek, B.O., 2025. Comparison of non-invasive and minimally invasive preimplantation genetic testing for aneuploidy using samples derived from the same embryo culture. J. Clin. Med. 14 (1). https://doi.org/10.3390/jcm14010033.

Bovolon, L., De Fano, A., Di Pinto, G., Rosito, S.A., Scaramuzza, C., Tanet, E., Bertollo, M., 2025. Integrating brain-body-behavior data for performance optimization: augmented technologies for the next generation of sport psychologists. Psychol. Sport Exerc. 81, 102954. https://doi.org/10.1016/j.psychsport.2025.102954.

Ezugwu, A.E., Taiwo, O., Egwuche, O.S., Abualigah, L., Van Der Merwe, A., Pal, J., Saha, A.K., Alzahrani, A.I., Alblehai, F., Greeff, J., Olusanya, M.O., 2025. Smart homes of the future. Trans. Emerg. Telecommun. Technol. 36 (1). https://doi.org/10.1002/ett.70041.

Gligorea, I., Cioca, M., Oancea, R., Gorski, A.-T., Gorski, H., Tudorache, P., 2023. Adaptive learning using artificial intelligence in e-learning: a literature review. Educ. Sci. 13 (12), 1216. https://doi.org/10.3390/educsci13121216.

Gong, Y., Xie, Y., Zhang, W., Wang, Y., 2025. Enhancing flow energy harvesting efficiency through hybrid deep learning models. In: 4th International Conference on New Energy System and Power Engineering, NESP 2025. Institute of Electrical and Electronics Engineers Inc., China, pp. 229–234. https://doi.org/10.1109/NESP65198.2025.11041072. http://ieeexplore.ieee.org/xpl/mostRecentIssue.jsp?punumber=11040157.

Holguin, I., Errapotu, S.M., 2023. Smart home IoT communication protocols and advances in their security and interoperability. In: 7th Cyber Security in Networking Conference, CSNet 2023. Institute of Electrical and Electronics Engineers Inc., United States, pp. 208–211. https://doi.org/10.1109/CSNet59123.2023.10339739. http://ieeexplore.ieee.org/xpl/mostRecentIssue.jsp?punumber=10339719.

Hsu, Y.L., Chou, P.H., Chang, H.C., Lin, S.L., Yang, S.C., Su, H.Y., Chang, C.C., Cheng, Y.S., Kuo, Y.C., 2017. Design and implementation of a smart home system using multisensor data fusion technology. Sensors (Switzerland) 17 (7). https://doi.org/10.3390/s17071631.

Jain, A., Raja, R., Srivastava, S., Sharma, P.C., Gangrade, J., Manoj, R., 2024. Analysis of EEG signals and data acquisition methods: a review. Comput. Methods Biomech. Biomed. Eng. 12 (1). https://doi.org/10.1080/21681163.2024.2304574.

Jin, K., Rubio-Solis, A., Naik, R., Leff, D., Kinross, J., George, M., 2025. Human-centric cognitive state recognition using physiological signals: a systematic review of machine learning strategies across application domains. Sensors 25 (13), 4207. https://doi.org/10.3390/s25134207.

Karaman, Y., Akdeniz, F., Kır Savas, B., Becerikli, Y., 2023. A comparative analysis of SVM, LSTM and CNN-RNN models for the BBC news classification. Springer Sci. Bus. Media LLC 629, 473–483. https://doi.org/10.1007/978-3-031-26852-6_44.

Khan, S., Ali, H., Shah, Z., 2024. Systematic analysis of smart homes: current trends and future recommendations. Cogent Eng. 11 (1). https://doi.org/10.1080/23311916.2024.2344452.

Kumar, J.M., Mittal, V.K., 2021. EEG data acquisition system and analysis of EEG signals. In: 2nd International Conference for Emerging Technology, INCET 2021. Institute of Electrical and Electronics Engineers Inc., India https://doi.org/10.1109/INCET51464.2021.9456431.

Lawhern, V., David Hairston, W., McDowell, K., Westerfield, M., Robbins, K., 2012. Detection and classification of subject-generated artifacts in EEG signals using autoregressive models. J. Neurosci. Methods 208 (2), 181–189. https://doi.org/10.1016/j.jneumeth.2012.05.017.

Lum, W.Y., Lau, F.C.M., 2002. A context-aware decision engine for content adaptation. IEEE Pervasive Comput. 1 (3), 41–49. https://doi.org/10.1109/MPRV.2002.1037721.

Peksa, J., Mamchur, D., 2023. State-of-the-art on brain-computer interface technology. Sensors 23 (13), 6001. https://doi.org/10.3390/s23136001.

Popoola, O., Rodrigues, M., Marchang, J., Shenfield, A., Ikpehai, A., Popoola, J., 2024. A critical literature review of security and privacy in smart home healthcare schemes adopting IoT & blockchain: problems, challenges and solutions. Blockchain Res. Appl. 5 (2), 100178. https://doi.org/10.1016/j.bcra.2023.100178.

Rudroff, T., 2025. Decoding thoughts, encoding ethics: a narrative review of the BCI-AI revolution. Brain Res. 1850, 149423. https://doi.org/10.1016/j.brainres.2024.149423.

Seena, V., Yomas, J., 2014. A review on feature extraction and denoising of ECG signal using wavelet transform. In: 2nd International Conference on Devices, Circuits and Systems (ICDCS). Coimbatore, India, pp. 1–6. https://doi.org/10.1109/ICDCSyst.2014.6926190.

Sun, Y., Chen, X., Liu, B., Liang, L., Wang, Y., Gao, S., Gao, X., 2025. Signal acquisition of brain–computer interfaces: a medical-engineering crossover perspective review. Fundam. Res. 5 (1), 3–16. https://doi.org/10.1016/j.fmre.2024.04.011.

Wu, H., Wang, P., 2021. Fast-convergent federated learning with adaptive weighting. IEEE Trans. Cogn. Commun. Netw. 7 (4), 1078–1088. https://doi.org/10.1109/TCCN.2021.3084406.

## Further reading

Javed, H., Eid, F., El-Sappagh, S., et al., 2025. Sustainable energy management in the AI era: a comprehensive analysis of ML and DL approaches. Computing 107, 132. https://doi.org/10.1007/s00607-025-01485-0.

Ninno Muniz, R., Frizzo Stefenon, S., Gouvêa Buratto, W., Nied, A., Meyer, L.H., Finardi, E.C., Marino Kühl, R., Silva de Sá, J.A., Ramati Pereira da Rocha, B., 2020. Tools for measuring energy sustainability: a comparative review. Energies 13 (9), 2366. https://doi.org/10.3390/en13092366.

Palaniappan, K., Lin, E.Y.T., Vogel, S., 2024. Global regulatory frameworks for the use of artificial intelligence (AI) in the healthcare services sector. Healthcare 12 (5), 562. https://doi.org/10.3390/healthcare12050562.

Sarkar, M., Lee, T.-H., Sahoo, P.K., 2024. Smart healthcare: exploring the internet of medical things with ambient intelligence. Electronics 13 (12), 2309. https://doi.org/10.3390/electronics13122309.

Saxena, V., Wu, X., Srivastava, I., Zhu, K., 2018. Towards neuromorphic learning machines using emerging memory devices with brain-like energy efficiency. J. Low Power Electron. Appl. 8 (4), 34. https://doi.org/10.3390/jlpea8040034.

# Index

*'Note:* Page numbers followed by "f" indicate figures and "t" indicate tables.'

## F

## G



## H



## I

## S

9780443415944